Michael Farry

B.C.L., Dip. Ed. A., M.Litt., Ph.D.
of King's Inns, Barrister-at-Law,
Lecturer in Law, Regional College, Carlow

CASES

ON

CONTRACT

PHOENIX PRESS

DUBLIN

Published by Phoenix Press
160 Georgian Village, Dublin 15.

© Michael Farry 1995

BRITISH LIBRARY CATALOGUING IN PUBLICATION DATA
Farry, M.J.
Cases on Contract
1. Contracts—Ireland
1. Title

ISBN 0-9524741-07

The author and publisher accept no
responsibilty for loss occasioned to
any person acting or refraining from acting
as a result of the material in this publication.

Printed in Ireland by
Betaprint, Dublin

Preface

While it has been stated by Hughes J. in *Furlong v. Burns & Co. Ltd.* [1964] 2 D.R. at p.13 that cases which have similar facts seldom prove to be satisfactory authorities, the use of cases to illustrate the formulation and application of legal principles and the reason for decisions, has long been a feature of law teaching. In my own time as a student this meant English cases.

When I began to lecture I started to give handouts on Irish cases as they occurred and was gradually drawn to research Irish cases on specific aspects of the Law of Contract.

I was amazed at the range and number of such cases and at the paucity of citation, a factor I attributed to the lack of a book on Irish Contract Law. Few people knew of, or had access to, F.E. Dowrick's seminal Irish supplement to the third edition of Cheshire and Fifefoot in 1954.

The late Mr. Justice Niall McCarthy in a foreword to *The Irish Legal System*, R. Byrne & P. McCutcheon, Professional Books, 1986 attributed this lack of citation to what he termed 'forensic forelock tipping' a part of the cultural cringe that has beset our country. Be that as it may, the welcome advent of Robert Clarke's book on Contract led to the emergence of indiginous cases from the shadows.

While verbose and rambling judgments are the bane of practitioner and student alike, the combination of anecdote and principle in an easily assimilated form demonstrates the relevance of the law in a vivid way. No synopsis of cases however meticulous, can be regarded as satisfactory and reference must be made to the full reports or judgments for a full exposition of each case and the reasoning and law involved.

I have sought to provide a summary of cases which might prove useful to the man on the DART or the Cabra bus. The selection of cases is arbitrary, likewise the selection of passages quoted and like other writers I must caution readers that they must take this book with no express or implied condition or warranty as to fitness for purpose. Highlights have been inserted by the author in both text and judgments for emphasis.

I must express my gratitude to my staunch friend and colleague Martin Nevin for his unfailing help and encouragement, to colleagues Maebh Maher, Austin Kinsella, Michael O'Grady and Liz Hutton. My thanks also to Margaret Byrne Librarian and Mary Gaynor, Assistant Librarian of the Incorporated Law

Society, Jonathan Armstrong, Librarian, Kings Inns, Charles Corcoran B.L.

Although this publication falls between two stools and is neither a text book or a case book in the proper sense, it is my hope that it will prove sufficient for some and a useful source of reference for others.

I wish to thank the following for permission to reproduce and adapt material from their reports:

The Incorporated Council of Law Reporting for Ireland for extracts from the Irish Reports.

The Incorporated Council of Law Reporting for England and Wales for extracts from the Weekly Law Reports, Queen's Bench, King's Bench and Appeal Courts.

The Incorporated Council of Law Reporting for Northern Ireland for extracts from the Northern Law Reports.

Butterworth Law Publishers (UK) Ltd. for extracts from the All England Law Reports.

The Round Hall Press for extracts from the Irish Law Reports Monthly and the Irish Law Times.

SLS Legal Publications (NI) for extracts from the Bulletin of Northern Ireland cases.

The Irish Times for extracts from the Irish Times Law Reports.

The Chief Justice, the Judges and the Department of Justice: unreported judgments.

The Jurist Publishing Company from the Irish Jurist Reports

Michael J. Farry
3 February 1995
Feast of St Blaise

Abbreviations

A.C.	Appeal Cases
All E.R.	All England Reports
Beav.	Beavan's Rolls Court Reports
BNIL.	Bulletin of Northern Ireland Law
C.A.	Court of Appeal
Ch.D.	Chancery Division
Cir.Ct.	Circuit Court
Ch.	Chancery
C.J.	Chief Justice
C.L.	Common Law
C.P.D.	Law Reports, Common Pleas Division
EAT/UD	Employment Appeals Tribunal
Eq.	Equity
Exch. Rep.	Excheqour Reports
H.C.	High Court
I.L.R.M.	Irish Law Reports Monthly
I.L.T.	Irish Law Times
I.L.T.R.	Irish Law Times Report
ITLR	Irish Times Law Report
I.R.	Irish Reports
I.R.C.L.	Irish Reports Common Law
I.R.Eq.	Irish Reports Equity
Ir. Ch. Rep.	Irish Chancery Reports
Ir. Jur. Rep.	Irish Jurist Reports
J./JJ.	Mr Justice, Miss Justice
L.C.	Lord Chancellor
L.J.	Ir. Law Journal Ireland
L.R.Ir	Law Reports Ireland
L.T.	Law Times Reports
M.R.	Master of the Rolls
M&W.	Meeson & Welsby's Exchequer Reports
N.I.	Northern Ireland Reports
NILR	Northern Ireland Law Reports
Q.B.D.	Queens Bench Division
S.C.	Supreme Court
W.L.R.	Weekly Law Reports

Contents

Preface

Abbreviations

Chapter 1. Agreement

Concensus ad idem
    MEGAW v. MOLLOY 2

Necessity of consensus ad idem
    MESPIL LTD. v. CAPALDI 2

Unauthorised communication
    WILSON v. BELFAST CORPORATION 3

An offer to a specific person
    BOULTON v. JONES 4

An offer to the world at large
    CARLILL v. CARBOLIC SMOKE BALL CO. 5

Notice as an offer
    BILLINGS v. ARNOTT & CO. LTD. 6

Government scheme an offer
    KYLEMORE BAKERY LTD. v. THE MINISTER FOR TRADE
        COMMERCE & TOURISM 7

Conditions of Sale an Offer
    TULLY v. IRISH LAND COMMISSION AND DRADDY 8

Display in shop window not an offer
    MIN. FOR INDUSTRY & COMMERCE v. PIM BROS. LTD. 9

Quotation not an offer
    BOYERS & CO. LTD. v. DUKE 9

A statement of price is not an offer
    HARVEY v. FACEY 10

Sweepstake ticket not an offer
      APICELLA AND CONSTANTINO v. SCALA AND ORS.   11

An advertisement is not an offer
      HARRIS v. NICKERSON   12

Statement of Intention not an offer
      MACKEY v. JONES   12

Revocation of an offer
      WALKER v. GLASS   13

Indirect communication of revocation
      DICKINSON v. DODDS   14

A counter-offer operates as a rejection
      HYDE v. WRENCH   15

Acceptance must be unequivocal
      CENTRAL MEAT PRODUCTS CO. LTD. v. CARNEY   16
      GRADWELL v. MAGUIRE   17

Acceptance must be unconditional
      SWAN v. MILLER   17

Acceptance cannot be imposed
      RUSSELL & BAIRD v. HOBAN   17

Acceptance must be communicated
      GUARDIANS OF NAVAN UNION v. M'LOUGHLIN   18

Performance constituted acceptance
      KENNEDY v. THE LONDON EXPRESS (1).   18

Silence accompanied by conduct may amount to acceptance
      ROYAL AVENUE HOTEL LTD. v. RICHARD SHOPS   19

Acceptance takes place when letter is posted
      SANDERSON v. CUNNINGHAM   20

Acceptance by post
      ADAMS v. LINDSELL   20

Contract made where acceptance takes place
      DOOLEY v. EGAN   21

Condition precedent to agreement
      KELLY v. IRISH NURSERY & LANDSCSAPE CO.LTD.   21

Oral agreement-no condition precedent
      PERNOD RICARD & COMRIE PLC. v. F.I.I. FYFFES PLC.   22

Conditional Agreement
     LOWIS v. WILSON   23

Incomplete Agreement
     BOYLE v. LEE AND GOYNS   23

Chapter 2. Intention to create legal relations

Mother and son
     SMITH v. ROGERS   26

Sister and Brother
     MACKEY v. JONES   27

Husband and Wife seperating
     COURTNEY v. COURTNEY   27

Aunt and Niece
     SAUNDERS v. CRAMER   28

Non-family
     THE McGILLYCUDDY OF THE REEKS v. JOY AND JOY   29

Collective Agreements
     O'ROURKE & ORS. v. TALBOT (IRELAND) LTD.   30

Contract binding on Union but not on members
     GOULDING CHEMICALS LTD. v. BOLGER & ORS.   31

Chapter 3. Consideration

Consideration not needed for contract under seal
     DRIMMIE v. DAVIES   33

Performance of public duty owed by law
     COLLINS v. GODEFROY   34
     GLASBROOK BROS v. GLAMORGAN CO. CO.   35

Performance of legal duty owed by statute
     WARD v. BYHAM   36

Duty imposed by a contract with the promisor
     STILK v. MYRICK   36

More than contractual duty to promisor
     HARTLEY v. PONSONBY   37

Promise to perform pre-existing contractual duty to third party
     PAU ON v. LAU YIU LONG   38

Performance of existing duty
    WILLIAMS v. WILLIAMS   39

Performance of pre-existing contractual duty to third party
    THE EURYMEDON   40

Performance of pre-existing legal duty is not consideration
    PMPA v. KEENAN AND ORS.   41

The rule in
    PINNELS' CASE   42
    FOAKES v. BEER   42

Consideration must move from the promisee
    M'COUBRAY v. THOMSON   44

Consideration need not be adequate
    IN RE METRO INVESTMENT TRUST LTD.   44

Consideration must be real or genuine
    WHITE v. BLUETT   45

Consideration must be sufficient
    O'NEILL v. MURPHY   46

Forbearance can constitute consideration
    BARRY v. BARRY (1)   46

Consideration must not be past
    PROVINCIAL BANK OF IRELAND v. DONNELL   47

Consideration must be certain or capable of being made certain
    CARR v. PHELAN   47

Chapter 4. Estoppel & Legitimate Expectation

Estoppel at Common Law and Equitable Estoppel
    MORROW v. CARTHY   49

Estoppel where there is a liability to pay money
    REVENUE COMMISSIONERS v. MORONEY   50

A Contract by Estoppel
    CLAYTON LOVE v. B & I.   50

The rule in
    HUGHES v. METROPOLITAN RWY. Co.   51

Promissory estoppel — quasi-estoppel
    CENTRAL LONDON PROPERTY TRUST LTD. v. HIGH TREES   52

Estoppel as a shield not as a sword
  CULLEN v. CULLEN   52

Legitimate Expectation
  WEBB v. IRELAND   53

Chapter 5. Form

Contract required to be under seal
  ATHY GUARDIANS v. MURPHY   56

Promise to answer for the debt of another — Guarantee
  FENNELL v. MULCAHY   56

Promise to answer for the debt of another — Indemnity
  DUNVILLE & Co. LTD. v. QUINN   57

Sale of Land
  LORD BELLEW'S ESTATE   58

Agreement not to be performed within a year
  NAUGHTON v. LIMESTONE LAND CO. LTD. 58
  FARRINGTON v. DONOHUE   58

Sufficiency of Memorandum
  BARRETT v. COSTELLO   59

Description of parties
  BACON & CO. v. KAVANAGH   59

Joinder of documents
  CRANE v. NAUGHTEN (1)   60
  McQUAID v. LYNAM   61

Sufficiency of Memorandum
  DAVIS v. GALLAGHER   62

Signature
  HALLEY v. O'BRIEN   63

Statute of Frauds and Part Performance
  LOWRY v. REID (1)   64

'Subject to contract'
  THOMPSON & SON LTD. v. THE KING 66

All terms not agreed
  CARTHY v. O'NEILL   66

Note or memo must acknowledge a contract
      TIVERTON ESTATES LTD. v. WEARWELL LTD.   67

'Subject to contract' inconsistent with contract
      MULHALL v. HAREN   68

Memo must contain terms and acknowledge existence of contract
      BOYLE AND BOYLE v. LEE AND GOYNS   69

Agreement subject to the preparation of a formal contract
      LOWIS v. WILSON   70

Chapter 6. Terms

Terms must be certain
      PLUNKETT v. DEASE   73

Knowledge of terms
      SIEBEL & SEUM v. KENT (See Chapter 8, p. 79)   74

Terms contrary to Public Policy
      DALTON v. DALTON   74
      ORMSBY v. ORMSBY   74

Implied terms
      WARD & FEGAN v. SPIVACK   74
      TRADEX (IRELAND) LTD. v. IRISH GRAIN BOARD LTD.   75

Reasonable Care and Skill
      DUNDALK SHOPPING CENTRE LTD. v. ROOF SPRAY LTD.   76

Terms implied by custom
      O'CONAILL v. THE GAELIC ECHO   76

Warranty Common Law definition
      CHANTER v. HOPKINS   77

Condition Common Law definition
      BEHN v. BURNESS   77

Conditions
      POUSSARD v. SPIERS   78

Warranty
      BETTINI v. GYE   79

Chapter 7. Interpretation of Contract

Generalia Specialibus non derogant
    WELCH v. BOWMAKER (IRELAND) LTD.   81

Contra Proferentem
    IN RE SWEENEY AND KENNEDY ARBITRATION   81

Ejusdem Generis
    BRADY v. IRISH NATIONAL INSURANCE CO. LTD.   82

Expressio Unius Est Exclusio Alterius
    HARE v. HORTON   83

The Parol Evidence Rule.-Extrinsic evidence excluded
    FALLON v. ROBBINS   84

Parol evidence admitted to explain the circumstances
    See REVENUE COMMRS v. MORONEY (Ch. 4 Estoppel)   85

Extrinsic evidence admitted to establish subject matter
    CHAMBERS v. KELLY   85

Parol evidence admitted to identify a party
    BACON & CO. LTD. v. KAVANAGH (See Ch. 5 Form)   86

Parol evidence to establish the terms
    CLAYTON LOVE v. B & I (See Ch. 4 Estoppel)   86

Parol evidence admitted to explain customs
    O'CONAILL v. THE GAELIC ECHO (See Ch. 6 Terms)   86

Parol evidence to explain a mistake for rectification
    MONAGHAN CO. CO. v. VAUGHAN (See Ch. 10 Mistake)   86

Parol evidence as to price
    NOLAN v. GRAVES   86

Parol evidence that written agreement subject to a condition
    PYM v. CAMPBELL   87

Chapter 8. Exemption Clauses

Signed agreement
    L'ESTRANGE v. GRAUCOB LTD   91

Exemption Clause — Signed Contract
    KNOX v. GREAT NORTHERN RLYW. CO.   93

Document signed during performance of contract
SLATTERY v. C.I.E.   93

Signed contract — knowledge of terms
SIEBEL AND SEUM v. KENT   94

Unsigned document — Degree of Notice of Exemption Clause
PARKER v. STH. EASTERN RAILWAY CO.   94

Notice of exemption clause
WESTERN MEATS v. NATIONAL ICE & COLD STORAGE
CO. LTD.   96

Unsigned document-notice of exemption clauses
EARLY v. G.S.R. CO.   96

Notice from course of dealing
MILEY v. McKECHNIE LTD.   97

Previous knowledge of terms — carriage of goods
McCUTCHEON v. MACBRAYNE LTD.   98

Notice must be before or contemporaneaously
OLLEY v. MARLBOROUGH COURT LTD.   99

Nature of Document
CHAPLETON v. BARRY U.D.C.   100

Notices must be conspiciously displayed
HENNIGAN v. BALLYBUNNION PICTURE HOUSE LTD.   100

Strict interpretation — implied-express terms
ANDREW BROS (Bmth) LTD. v. SINGER & CO. LTD.   101

Strict interpretation — conditions — waranties
BALDRY v. MARSHALL   102

Clear words needed to exempt from serious breach
O'CONNOR v. McCOWEN & SONS LTD.   102

Clear words neeeeded to exempt from Negligence
ALEXANDER v. IRISH NATIONAL STUD   103

Strict liability
WHITE v. JOHN WARRICK & CO. LTD   103

Words not construed to defeat main object
GLYNN v. MARGETSON & CO.   104

Cannot exempt from own fraud
PEARSON & SON LTD. v. DUBLIN CORP.   105

Misrepresentation as to extent of exemption clause

        CURTIS v. CHEMICAL CLEANING & DYING CO. LTD.   106

Contra Proferentem

        LEE & SON (GRANTHAM) LTD v. RAILWAY EXECUTIVE   107

Exemption Clause and Breach of a Fundamental Term

        CLAYTON LOVE v. B & I   108

Fundamental Breach

        SUISSE ATLANTIQUE   109

        PHOTOPRODUCTIONS LTD. v. SECURICOR TRANSPORT LTD   111 .

Third parties

        ADLER v. DICKSON   112

Limitation Clauses

        AILSA CRAIG FISHING CO. LTD. v. MALVERN FISHING CO.   113

Chapter 9. Insurance Contracts

Truth and Accuracy

        FARRELL v. S. E. LANCASHIRE INS. CO. LTD .   115

Non Disclosure

        CHARIOT INNS LTD. v. ASSICURAZIONI GENERAL S.P.A.   116

        KEATING v. NEW IRELAND ASSURANCE CO. PLC .   118

        KELLEHER v. IRISH LIFE ASSURANCE CO. LTD.   118

Over the counter insurance

        ARO ROAD & LAND VEHICLES v. I.C.I.   120

Insurable interest

        O'LEARY v. IRISH NATIONAL INS. CO. LTD.   120

Indemnity

        St. ALBANS INVESTMENT CO. LTD. v. SUN ALLIANCE INS.

          CO.   121

Contribution

        ZURICH INSURANCE CO.LTD. v. SHIELD INS. CO. LTD.   122

Subrogation

        IN RE KELLY'S CARPETDROME   123

Insurance Agents — Note on

        TAYLOR v. YORKSHIRE INS. CO.   124

Chapter 10. Mistake

Operative Mistake must be fundamental
     BELL v. LEVER BROS.   127

Non-operative mistake of public law
     O'LOUGHLEN v. O'CALLAGHAN   128

Common Mistake / Mistake of Law
     COOPER v. PHIBBS   129

Mistake about the existence of a person
     SCOTT v. COULSON   130

Mistake about being married
     GALLOWAY v. GALLOWAY   131

Mistake as to existence of subject matter
     COUTURIER v. HASTIE   132

Terms must be construed objectively
     O'NEILL v. RYAN   132

Mistake at equity
     GUNN v. M'CARTHY   134

Equity will set aside
     SOLLE v. BUTCHER   135

Rectification
     MONAGHAN CO. CO. v. VAUGHAN   136

Intention of the parties not relevant
     LUCEY v. LAUREL CONSTRUCTION CO. LTD.   136

Refusal of Specific Performance
     GRIST v. BAILEY   137

Mistake as to terms — unilateral mistake
     HARTOG v. COLIN & SHIELDS   138

Mistake about terms which negates consent
     WOOD v. SCARTH   139

Mistake as to subject matter
     MEGAW v. MOLLOY   140

Mistake as to the identity of the person contracted with by letter
     CUNDY v. LINDSAY   141

Mistake as to identity
    J. L. SMALLMAN LTD. v. O'MOORE AND NEWMAN   142

Mistake as to identity — face to face
    PHILLIPS v. BROOKS LTD.   143

Mutual mistake as to the true nature of an agreement
    MESPIL v. CAPALDI   1444

Non est factum — Document not fundamentally different
    SAUNDERS v. ANGLIA BUILDING SOCIETY   145

Document fundamentally different
    BANK OF IRELAND v. McMANAMY   147

Chapter 11. Misrepresentation

Silence equivalent to a representation
    POWER v. BARRETT   151

Silence and a change between negotiation and contracting
    WITH v. O'FLANAGAN   152

A half-truth can amount to a misrepresentation
    NOTTS PATENT BRICK AND TILE CO. v. BUTLER   153

Misstatement of fact
    EDGINGTON v. FITZMAURICE   154

Statement of opinion
    SMYTH v. LYNN   155

Made to contracting party
    SECURITIES TRUST LTD. v. HUGH MOORE & ALEXANDER
    LTD.   157

Non reliance on misrep. — representee could see for himself
    GRAFTON COURT v. WADSON SALES   157

Non-reliance on a representation — experts called in
    ATTWOOD v. SMALL   158

Not aware of representation
    HORSFALL v. THOMAS   159

Disclaimer and Misrepresentation
    PEARSON v. DUBLIN CORPORATION   160

Qualification / Disclaimer
    JOHN SISK AND SON LTD. v. FLINN AND ORS.   161

Fraudulent Misrepresentation

     SARGENT v. IRISH MULTIWHEEL LTD.   162

     FENTON & ANOR. v. SCHOFIELD & ORS.   162

     CARBIN v. SOMMERVILLE   163

Innocent misrepresentation

     DERRY v. PEEK   164

Negligent misrepresentation

     ESSO PETROLEUM CO. LTD. v. MARDON   165

     BROGAN v. BENNETT   167

Negligent misstatement

     MACKEN v. MUNSTER AND LEINSTER BANK & ANOTHER   167

     HEDLEY BYRNE & CO. LTD. v. HELLER & PARTNERS LTD.   168

     CARELESS STATEMENTS AND SPECIAL RELATIONSHIPS   169

Innocent misrepresentation treated as breech of warranty

     BANK OF IRELAND v. SMITH AND ORS.   170

Rescission of Sale by Auction for Misrepresentation

     AIRLIE & KEENAN v. FALLON   171

Chapter 12. Duress and Equitable Relief

Duress

Duress — Threat to life

     BARTON v. ARMSTRONG   174

Duress — personal suffering — threat of loss of liberty

     CUMMING v. INCE AND HOOPER   174

Matrimonial Duress

     GRIFFITH v. GRIFFITH   175

Strain-lack of ability for normal thought

     W. v. C.   175

Matrimonial duress — Irish concept of

     N. v. K.   176

Economic Duress

     PAO ON v. LAU YIU LONG   177

     UNDUE INFLUENCE   179

Child/Parent

     GREGG v. KIDD AND KIDD   181

Spiritual Advisor
     O'NEILL v. MURPHY AND ORS.   181

Undue influence / spiritual terror of vows
     McCARTHY v. McCARTHY   182
     ALLCARD v. SKINNER   182

Friend
     O'FLANAGAN v. RAY-GER LIMITED.   183

Solicitor/Client obligation   184

'Without Prejudice'   185

Inequality of bargaining power
     SLATOR v. NOLAN   187

Improvident disposition
     GREALISH v. MURPHY   188

Unconscionable Bargain
     LYDON v. COYNE   189

Advice
     KELLY v. MORRISROE   189

Improvident disposition
     McCORMACK v. BENNETT   190

Chapter 13. Illegal Contracts

Illegality — Burden of proof
     WHITECROSS POTATOES v. COYLE   192

Contract to defraud the Revenue
     LEWIS v. SQUASH IRELAND LTD.   193

Contracts illegal by Statute
     CONWAY v. SMITH   193
     O'SHAUGHNESSY v. LYONS   194

Puffer at an Auction
     AIRLIE & KEENAN v. FALLON   194

Gaming
     ANTHONY v. SHEA   195

Agreement against public policy
     CORPORATION OF DUBLIN v. HAYES   195

Public Policy and the Constitution — Illegal
    DALTON v. DALTON   195

Public Policy and the Constitution — Not illegal
    ORMSBY v. ORMSBY   196

Chapter 14. Contracts in Restraint Of Trade

Restraint of trade / Contract for the sale of a business
    JOHN ORR LTD. AND VESCOM B.V. v. JOHN ORR   198

Restraint of Trade /Associations
    McELLISTRIM v. BALLYMACELLIGOTT CO. OP.   200

Area of restraint
    TIPPERARY CO-OP. v. HANLEY   200

Association
    MACKEN v. O'REILLY AND ORS.   200

Duration — reasonableness
    ESSO PETROLEUM v. HARPERS GARAGE (LTD.)   201

Duration Five Years reasonable
    CONTINENTAL OIL CO. OF IRELAND LTD. v. MOYNIHAN   202

Duration — Twenty Years excessive
    McMULLAN BROS. LTD. v. CONDELL   203

Restraints in cintract of employment
    DOSSOR v. MONAGHAN AND ORS.   204

Area of restraint
    MULLIGAN v. CORR   204
    SKERRY, WYNNE v. MOLES   204

Duration of restraint
    ARCLEX OPTICAL CORP., LTD. v. McMURRAY   205

Activity covered by restraint
    OATES v. ROMANO   206

Chapter 15. Capacity

Infants   207

Necessaries
    SKRINE v. GORDON   207

Infant not liable for non-necessaries
    GRIFFITH v. DELANEY   208

Liability of infant for possesion and occupation of land
    BLAKE v. CONCANNON   208

Repudiation within a reasonable time — There had not been a
    total failure of consideration
    STAPLETON v. PRUDENTIAL INSURANCE CO. LTD.   209

Repudiation must be in a way the other party can dispute
    SLATOR v. BRADY   210

Contract for infants benefit
    KEAYS v. GREAT SOUTHERN RLYW. CO.   210

Apprenticeship
    BUTLER, (AN INFANT) v. DILLON   211

Lunatic and Drunken Persons   212

Insane persons
    HASSARD v. SMITH   212

Lunetic obliged to pay for necessaries
    IN RE BYRNE   213

Drunkness
    WHITE v. McCOOEY   214

Ratification
    MATTHEWS v. BAXTER   215

Ward of Court not competent to contract
    IN RE R.   215

Corporations   216

Ultra Vires
    ASHBURY RAILWAY CARRIAGE CO. LTD. v. RICHE   216

Ultra vires — Corporations and Associations
    MARTIN v. IRISH INDUSTRIAL BUILDING SOCIETY   217

Knowledge that act ultra vires
   IN RE CUMMINS; BARTON v. BANK Of IRELAND   217

Actual Notice within s. 8(1) Companys Act, 1963
   NORTHERN BANK FINANCE CORPORATION LTD. v. QUINN   218

Foreign States   219

Foreign State not impleaded merely because its agent is sued
   SAORSTAT & CONTINENTAL S.S. Co. LTD. v.
   DE LAS MORENAS   219

Application of restrictive immunity
   GOVERNMENT OF CANADA v. THE E.A.T.   220

Chapter 16. Privity of Contract

Privity of contract
   MURPHY v. BOWER   223
   CLITHEROE v. SIMPSON   223
   MACKEY v. JONES   224

Statutory Exception
   BELLEW v. ZURICH G.A. & LIABILITY INS. CO. LTD.   224

Constructive Trust Exception
   KELLY v. LARKIN & CARTER (1)   225
   DRIMMIE v. DAVIES   225

Intention to create trust must be proved
   VANDEPITTE v. PREFERRED ACCIDENT INS. CORP.   226

Assignment
   PRICE v. EASTON   227

Implied contract
   MAUNSELL v. THE MINISTER FOR EDUCATION AND BREEN   227

Chapter 17. Collateral Warranties & Contracts

Consideration — the making of the main contract
   WEBSTER v. HIGGIN   231

Parol Evidence — additional oral terms
   J. EVANS & SON (PORTSMOUTH) LTD. v. MERZARIO   231

Representation a Warranty
   SCHAWEL v. READE   233

Innocent Misrepresentation not a warranty
    HEILBUT, SYMONS & CO. v. BUCKLETON   233

Warranty and Exemption Clause
    COUCHMAN v. HILL   234

Main contract illegal and void
    STRONGMAN (1945) LTD., v. SINCOCK   2357

Difficulty of proving a contractual relationship
    CLARKE v. DUNRAVEN   236

Defective memorandum
    GODLEY v. POWER   237

Difficulty proving consideration
    SHANKLIN PIER LTD. v. DETEL PRODUCTS LTD.   238

Chapter 18. Discharge of Contract

Performance   240

Entire Contract
    CREAGH v. SHEEDY   243

Complete Performance
    COUGHLAN v. MOLONEY   244

Substantial performance
    KINCORA BUILDERS v. CRONIN   245

Breach   246

Explicit Repudiation
    HOCHESTER v. DE LA TOUR   246

Anticipatory breach
    FROST v. KNIGHT   246

Anticipatory Breach
    LEESON v. NORTH BRITISH OIL & GAS CO.   247

Repudiation and Breach of an intermediate term
    HONG KONG FIR SHIPPING CO. LTD. v.
    KAWASAKI KISEN KAISHA LTD.   247
    FRUSTRATION   249

Contract discharged by Frustration

      KEARNEY v. SAORSTAT & CONTINENTAL SHIPPING CO.
      LTD.   249

      HERMAN & ORS. v. THE OWNERS OF THE S.S. VICIA   249

      BROWN v. MULLIGAN & ORS.   250

Subject matter ceasing to exist

      CUMMINGS v. STEWART (No. 2)   250

Contract not Frustrated by becoming more onerous

      DAVIS CONTRACTORS LTD. v. FAREHAM U.D.C.   251

Impossible of performance by Act of God

      THE EARL OF LEITRIM v. STEWART   252

Liability of party in default.

      M'CONNELL v. KILGALLEN   252

Principles to be applied

      McGUILL v. AER LINGUS TEO & U.A.   253

Discharge by change of law

      O'CROWLEY v. MIN. FOR FINANCE   253

Chapter 19. Remedies for Breach of Contract

DAMAGES   255

The Rule

      HADLEY v. BAXENDALE   257

Measure of Damages

      PARKER v. DICKIE   258

Liquidated Damages

      TOOMEY v. MURPHY   259

Penalty or Damages

      SCHIESSER INTER. (IRELAND) LTD. v. GALLAGHER   259

Penalty

      LOMBANK LTD. v. KENNEDY & WHITELAW   260

      LOMBANK LTD. v. CROSSAN   260

Remoteness of Damage

      LEE & DONOGHUE v. ROWAN   261

Contingency not too remote

      HAWKINS v. ROGERS   262

Duty to mitigate damages
    MALONE v. MALONE   263

Quantum of damages
    JOHNSON v. LONGLEAT PROPERTIES (DUBLIN) LTD.   263

Damages for physical inconvenience and discomfort
    SINEY v. CORPORATION OF DUBLIN   264

Inflation and tax
    HICKEY & COMPANY v. ROCHES STORES (DUBLIN) NO. 2   265

Damages in contracts for the sale of real estate

The Rule in
    BAIN v. FOTHERGILL   267

Damages plus specific performance
    MURPHY v. QUALITY HOMES   267

Damages for pre-contractual expenditure
    ANGLIA TELEVISION v. REED   268

QUANTUM MERUIT   269
    O'CONNELL v. LISTOWEL U.D.C.   269

RESTITUTION AND QUASI CONTRACT   269

Unjust enrichment
    HICKEY & CO. v. ROCHES STORES (DUBLIN) LTD.   270

Money paid under a mistake of fact
    KELLY v. SOLARI   272

Money paid under Mistake of law- not in pari delicto
    KIRIRI COTTON CO. LTD. v. DEWANI   272

Money paid for a consideration which has totally failed
    FIBROSA v. FAIRBAIRN LTD.   273

Money paid where no total failure of consideration
    STAPLETON v. PRUDENTIAL ASSURANCE
      (See Ch. 15 Capacity)   275

Money paid under a conditional contract
    LOWIS v. WILSON (See Ch. 1 Agreement)   275

Restitution of money obtained wrongfully
    G.S. & W. RLW. v. ROBERTSON   275

Money paid under an illegal contract
      PARKINSON v. COLLEGE OF AMBULANCE LTD.   276

Recovery — Non-reliance on illegal contract
      SINGH v. KULUBYA   276

Money paid under a void contract
      STRICTLAND v. TURNER   277

QUASI CONTRACT
      FOLENS & CO. LTD. v. MIN. FOR EDUCATION   278

SPECIFIC PERFORMANCE   279

Time of Hardship
      ROBERTS v. O'NEILL   279

Specific Performance — grounds for refusal
      BUCKLEY v. IRWIN   281

Specific Performance and Mistake
      SMELTER CORP. OF IRELAND v. O'DRISCOLL   282

Specific Performance and Deceit
      BASCOMB v. BECKWITH   283

INJUNCTION   284

Injunction and Penalty or Liquidated damages
      FRENCH v. MACALE   284

Interlocutory injunction/criteria for granting
      CAMPUS OIL LTD. v. MIN. FOR INDUSTRY AND ORS.
      (NO. 2)   285

Injunction — Trade secrets
      MEADOX MEDICALS INC. v. V.P.I. LTD. AND ORS.   286

MAREVA INJUNCTION
      MAREVA — SA v. INTERNATIONAL BULKCARRIERS SA.   287

Ex Parte — Order to permit entry
      ANTON PILLER KG v. MANUFACTURING PROCESSES LTD.   289

RESCISSION

Rescission and Mistake
      GUNN v. McCARTHY   291

Rescission on Terms
      SOLLE v. BUTCHER   291

Remedies for breach of Contract
    GRIST v. BAILEY   291

Rescission and misrepresentation
    CARBIN v. SOMMERVILLE   291

Rescission and Duress
    BARTON v. ARMSTRONG   291

Rescission refused
    STAPLETON v. PRUDENTIAL INSURANCE CO.   291

Index   293

CHAPTER 1

Agreement

The first essential for a valid contract is that of consensus or agreement between the parties. This agreement is usually expressed in terms of offer and acceptance and the test of offer and acceptance has long been used by the courts as the principal method to determine if an agreement has been made or can be deemed to have been made by the parties. There cannot be an agreement in the absence of a *consensus ad idem*, and this fact is illustrated by the cases of *Megaw v. Molloy and Mespil Ltd. v. Capaldi*.

On occasion other criteria have also been used and it has been suggested that offer and acceptance may be merely a convenient rule of thumb for calculating when and where a contract is formed, but are not of themselves essential to the existence of a contract. That the notion of offer and acceptance in bilateral contracts is to establish the finis negotiorum for the parties and where and precisely when the contract is made, i.e. the point when the agreement was made.

Some support for this theory is engendered by the fact that not all contracts are amenable to the test of offer and acceptance, particularly implied contracts and unilateral contracts.[1] Lord Denning M.R., in *Gibson v. Manchester City Council* [1978] 1 W.L.R. 520 C.A. stated that it was a mistake to think that all contracts could be analysed into the form of offer and acceptance. "I know in some of the text books it has been the custom to do so; but, as I understand the law, there is no need to look for a strict offer and acceptance. You should look at the correspondence as a whole and at the conduct of the parties and see therefrom whether the parties have come to an agreement on everything that was material. If by their correspondence and their conduct you can see an agreement on all material terms — which was intended thenceforth to be binding — then there is a binding contract in law even though all the formalities have not been gone through; see *Brogden v. Metropolitan Railway Co.* (1877) 2 App. Cas. 666."

In *Boyle v. Lee and Goyns* all material terms had not been agreed, further negotiation would have been necessary to determine the amount and date of payment of the deposit.

---

1. See Jeremy Phillips, Offer and Acceptance from Felthouse to Council House: DULJ (1978) 36-43.

Agreement of itself is not, however, sufficient to establish the existence of a simple contract, there must also be an intention to create legal relations and consideration.

CONSENSUS AD IDEM
Megaw v. Molloy (1) L.R.1. Vol. 11 (1878) 530 (C.A.)

The plaintiff employed a broker to sell maize for him. The maize he intended to sell had been imported in a ship called the "Emma Peasant". The plaintiff also had other maize imported in a ship called the "Jessie Parker". Both cargoes were stored in the same building but the maize from the "Jessie Parker" was superior to that from the "Emma Peasant".

By accident a sample was taken from the "Jessie Parker" cargo and exhibited at the auction, the auctioneer believing it to be from the "Emma Peasant".

The defendant was the highest bidder for 200 quarters of the sample grain and he refused to accept delivery of the inferior grain from the "Emma Peasant".

Held: (*inter alia*) on Appeal, that as the plaintiff intended to sell one bulk and the defendant to buy another, there was no contract between them. A dealing, where the parties are not intending the same subject matter, evidently, cannot be an agreement.

NECESSITY OF CONSENSUS AD IDEM
Mespil Ltd. v. Capaldi [1986] I.L.R.M. 373 (S.C.)

The plaintiff claimed possession of premises from the defendants, their tenants, together with arrears of rent. The actions were listed for hearing in the High court.

On the morning of the hearing, a settlement was agreed between counsel for both parties, reduced to writing and authenticated by the signatures of counsel. Subsequently the parties failed to agree on the scope of the settlement. The High Court ordered that its terms be enforced and the defendants appealed to the Supreme Court.

Held: Allowing the appeal and ordering that the actions proceed to trial.

(1) the settlement, reached in limited time that did not allow the reduction of its terms to unambiguous written expression, rested on a mutual mistake, for which no blame attached to the counsel involved.

(2) the general rule is that a person who enters into an agreement, giving the other person the impression that he understands the nature and effect of the agreement, will not afterwards be allowed to say that he should not be bound

by it because he did not at the time understand its import, but the agreement in the present case was surrounded by circumstances of latent ambiguity and mutual misunderstanding such as indicated that there was no *consensus ad idem*, and the seeming agreement was a nullity.

"It is of the essence of an enforceable simple contract that there be a *consensus ad idem*, expressed in an offer and an acceptance. Such a consensus cannot be said to exist unless there is a correspondence between the offer and the acceptance. If the offer made is accepted by the other person in a fundamentally different sense from that in which it was tendered by the offeror, and the circumstances are objectively such as to justify such an acceptance, there cannot be said to be the meeting of minds which is essential for an enforceable contract.— Henchy J.

OFFER

An offer is an expression of a willingness to enter into a contract on stated terms. It is therefore crucial to determine if in fact a communication between the parties amounts to an offer because some forms of communication merely provide information or are in the nature of invitations to treat or bargain. Case law has established that certain actions do not constitute an offer viz. the display of goods in a shop window, *Minister for Industry and Commerce v. Pim*. A quotation may, *Dooley v. Egan*, or may not, be an offer *Boyer & Co. v. Duke*. A notice may be an offer *Billings v. Arnott & Co. Ltd.*, or it may not be an offer *Wilson v. Belfast Corporation*. The fact that an offer may be revoked at any time before it is accepted is illustrated by *Walker v. Glass*, while a counter offer operates as a rejection of an original offer is demonstrated by *Hyde v. Wrench*.

UNAUTHORISED COMMUNICATION
Wilson v. Belfast Corporation (1921) 55 I.L.T.R 205 (C.A.S.I.)

Belfast City Council passed a resolution that they would pay half-wages to any of their employees who joined the British armed forces. This was reported in the press without the Council's authority. One month later the Council passed a second resolution limiting the offer to persons who were in their employment on 5th August, 1914.

Wilson, an employee who joined the Council workforce after the date specified in the second resolution (of which he was unaware) claimed entitlement to the payment. He was killed in action and the claim was continued by his widow.

Held: There was no contract, the council's resolution was not intended as an offer. The unauthorised publication in the press did not constitute communication and furthermore, any offer there might have been, had been revoked by the subsequent resolution of the council on 1st October.

Note: It would have been possible to find that the second resolution limited the offer to qualified persons and that the plaintiff was not one. See also *Powell v. Lee* (1908) 99 L.T. 284. In the *Carbolic Smoke Ball* case the defendants paid to have the communication made, and it was their wish and will. In this case the reporter could not be excluded from the meeting, nor could the corporation control what the newspaper published. Wilson had no right to assume that the resolution was unalterable. No contract existed.

AN OFFER TO A SPECIFIC PERSON
Boulton v. Jones (1857) 2 H&N 564

The plaintiff had been foreman and manager of Brocklehurst's hose manufacturing business, with which the defendants were in the habit of dealing, and with which they had a running account. On the 13th January, 1857, the plaintiff bought the business from Brocklehurst and in the afternoon of the same day, the defendants sent a written order addressed to Brocklehurst, which the plaintiff supplied without telling the defendant that the goods were not being supplied by Brocklehurst. Later, when an invoice was sent by the plaintiff to the defendants they said that they knew nothing of him and refused to pay.

Held: The plaintiff could not maintain an action for the price of the goods against the defendant. There was no contract between the parties. The defendant intended to contract with Brocklehurst.

Pollock C.B.:

> "The point raised is, whether the facts proved did not show an intention on the part of the defendants to deal with Brocklehurst . . . It is a rule of law, that if a person intends to contract with A., B. cannot give himself any right under it. Here the order in writing was given to Brocklehurst. Possibly Brocklehurst might have adopted the act of the plaintiff in supplying the goods, and maintained an action for the price. But since the plaintiff has chosen to sue, the only course the defendants could take was to plead that there was no contract with them."

Chamsell B.:

> "In order to entitle the plaintiff to recover he must show that there was a contract with himself."

Bramwell B.:

> "When a contract is made, in which the personality of the contracting party is or may be of importance, as a contract with a man to write a book, or the like, or where there might be a set-off, no other person can interpose and adopt the contract. . . . I decide the case on the ground that the defendants did not know that the plaintiff was the person who supplied the goods, and that allowing the plaintiff to treat the contract as made with him would be a prejudice to the defendants."

AN OFFER TO THE WORLD AT LARGE

Carlill v. Carbolic Smoke Ball Co. [1893] 1. Q.B. 256 (C.A.)

The defendants manufactured a medical preparation called "The Carbolic Smoke Ball" and to promote its sale published an advertisement in the Pall Mall Gazette of November 13, 1891, which offered a reward of £100 to any person who contracted a cold or influenza after having used the smoke ball as directed. The advert stated "£1,000 is deposited with the Alliance Bank, Regent Street, shewing our sincerity in the matter."

On the faith of the advertisement the plaintiff bought one of the balls, used it as directed but nevertheless contracted influenza.

It was argued for the defence that there was no contract, that the words expressed an intention, but did not amount to a promise. It was stated that the case was similar to *Harris v. Nickerson* and that the advert was too vague to be the basis of a contract. It was also claimed that there was no consideration moving from the plaintiff and that there had been no communication by the plaintiff of intention to accept the offer. It was held at first instance that the plaintiff was entitled to recover the £100 and the defendants appealed.

Held: that the facts established a contract by the defendants to pay the plaintiff £100 in the event which had happened, and the plaintiff was entitled to recover.

(1) The advertisement was an offer to anyone who performed the conditions in it.

(2) Performance constituted acceptance.

(3) The deposit of the £1,000 showed an intention to be bound by the promise.

Lindley L.J.:

> "We are dealing with an express promise to pay £100 in certain events . . . was it a mere puff ? My answer to that question is No, and I base my answer upon this passage: "£1,000 is deposited in the Alliance Bank, shewing our sincerity in the matter." Now, for what was the money

deposited or that statement made except to negative suggestions that this was a mere puff and meant nothing at all . . . . we are not inferring a promise; there is the promise, as plain as words can make it."

In relation to the contention that if there was a promise it was not binding. Lindley L.J. stated:

"In the first place it is said that it was not made with anybody in particular. Now that point is common to the words of this advertisement and to the words of all other advertisements offering rewards. They are offers to anybody who performs the conditions named in the advertisement, and anybody who does perform the condition accepts the offer. **In point of law this advertisement is an offer to pay £100 to anybody who will perform these conditions, and the performance of the conditions is the acceptance of the offer.** . . . Unquestionably, as a general proposition, when an offer is made, it is necessary in order to make a binding contract, not only that it should be accepted, but that the acceptance should be notified. But is that so in cases of this kind? I apprehend that they are an exception to that rule, or, if not an exception, they are open to the observation that the notification of the acceptance need not precede the performance. This offer is a continuing offer . . . if notice of acceptance is required, the person who makes the offer gets the notice of acceptance contemporaneously with his notice of the performance of the contract. If he gets notice of the acceptance before his offer is revoked, that in principle is all you want."

In relation to consideration his lordship continued:

"It is quite obvious that in the view of the advertisers a use by the public of their remedy, if they can only get the public to have confidence enough to use it, will react and produce a sale which is directly beneficial to them. Therefore, the advertisers get out of the use an advantage which is enough to constitute a consideration. . . . Does not the person who acts upon this advertisement and accepts the offer put himself to some inconvenience at the request of the defendants? Is it nothing to use this ball three times daily for two weeks according to the directions, at the request of the advertiser? Is that to go for nothing? It appears to me that there is a distinct inconvenience, not to say a detriment, to any person who so uses the smoke ball. I am of opinion, therefore, that there is ample consideration for the promise."

NOTICE AS AN OFFER

Billings v. Arnott & Co. Ltd. [1945] 80 I.L.T. 50 (H.C.)

The defendant company put up a notice on a notice board in their premises offering to pay half salary to employees who joined the Defence Forces during the emergency.

The plaintiff informed the company of his intention to avail of the offer but was told that he could not be spared. He nevertheless joined the Defence Forces but the company refused to pay him half salary.

Held: The company's notice was unconditional. It was not a mere declaration of intent it was an offer. Acceptance was completed when the plaintiff joined the Defence Force. The company were obliged to pay. There was an inducement to the employees to join the Defence Forces.

Maguire J.:

> "The notice I find is unconditional with no reservation to allow a refusal to release an employee. I can not take the view that it was a mere declaration of intention. It is a clear expression of what the company would do. Acceptance was then completed when the plaintiff joined the defence forces and intimated his intention of so doing. . . . On that view a contract was completed under which the defendants undertook to pay the plaintiff the allowance."

Note: The digest of the case states that the plaintiff was entitled to succeed as the defendants could not properly plead revocation once the plaintiff had acted on their offer. Maguire J's statement that acceptance was completed when the plaintiff joined the Defence Forces and intimated his intention of so doing must be open to question. The company obviously intended performance (i.e. joining the defence forces) to constitute acceptance.

GOVERNMENT SCHEME AN OFFER

Kylemore Bakery Ltd. v. Min. for Trade, Commerce and Tourism & Ors.
[1986] ILRM 529 (H.C.) Costello J.

The terms and conditions for the operation of a bread subsidy scheme were sent out by the Minister to all bakeries including the Plaintiff together with application forms for the payment of the subsidy. The Plaintiffs plant was inspected and they were informed that certain of their products were eligible for payment of the subsidy. They submitted application forms and some subsidies were paid. Later payments were withheld and the company instituted proceedings against the Minister.

Held: By indicating that certain products were eligible provided certain conditions were complied with, the Minister was in effect making an offer from which he could not subsequently resile once it was accepted.

CONDITIONS OF SALE AN OFFER

Tully v. Irish Land Commission and Draddy
(1961) 97 I.L.T.R. 174 (H.C.) Kenny J.

The Land Commission wished to sell part of the lands at Kilkee Demesne, near Athy, Co. Kildare and a public auction was advertised to take place on 31 August, 1961. The conditions of sale were read out before the bidding began. Clause 2 stated:

> "the highest bidder shall be the purchaser and if a dispute arises as to the bidding, the property shall again be put up for sale at the last undisputed bidding. There will be a reserve price and the I.L.C., the vendors or their agents shall be at liberty to bid. The amount of the advance of each bidding shall be regulated by the auctioneer and no bidding shall be retracted."

Clause 3 provided that the purchaser should immediately pay 25% of the purchase price plus the auctioneer's fee and sign an agreement to complete the purchase.

An agent bid for the plaintiff. A bid of £8,200 was made. The auctioneer believed that it was made by a solicitor acting for a Mr. Draddy and knocked the property down to him. The solicitor then signed the memorandum attached to the conditions of sale. The plaintiff then went to the auctioneer and claimed that the highest bid of £8,200 had been made by his agent. He then required the auctioneer (in accordance with clause 2 of the Conditions) to put the property up for sale again. The auctioneer refused. The plaintiff then sought an injunction to prevent the Land Commission from vesting the lands in the defendant.

Held: in a sale by public auction the contract is concluded when the property is knocked down either by rising the traditional hammer or by giving some indication to the public that the property has been sold.

Kenny J.:

> "I am therefore, of opinion that clauses 2 and 3 of the Conditions of Sale were an offer which could be accepted so as to create a contractual relationship between the Irish Land Commission and the highest bidder at the auction. the contract being that the highest bidder should be the purchaser and that if any dispute arose as to any bidding, the property would be put up for sale at the last undisputed bidding."

Note: The Conditions of Sale showed that a sale did take place when the property was knocked down by the auctioneer. Clause 3 referred to what was done immediately after the sale therefore the sale must have taken place before any of the things mentioned in clause three were done. The contract which came into existence when the property was knocked down might not be enforceable because of the absence of a memorandum in writing as required by the Statute of Frauds but this did not prevent a valid contract coming into existence. *Philips v. Butler* (1945) Ch. 358.

A DISPLAY OF GOODS IN A SHOP WINDOW IS NOT AN OFFER
Minister for Industry and Commerce v. Pim Brothers Ltd.
[1966] I.R. 154 (H.C.) Davitt P.

Pim Brothers Ltd., displayed a notice attached to a coat in their shop window which stated that the cash price of the coat was 24 guineas and that weekly payments were 5s.10d.

They were charged with displaying an advertisement (in a shop window) for goods for sale on Hire-Purchase which did not comply with the Hire-Purchase, Credit Sale (Advertising) Order, 1961 in that it failed to state the Hire-Purchase Price, the deposit and the total number of payments.

Held: A notice by way of advertisement placed on an article displayed in the premises of a retailer indicating that the cash price of the article was 24 guineas and that the weekly payment was 5s.10d. is not an offer for sale but is an offer to treat for the sale of the article with an indication that credit facilities, not specified, would be available.

Held also: That if the notice was an advertisement relating to goods available for sale, whether by way of Hire-Purchase or Credit Sale agreement, it complied with the requirements of Article 6(1) of the Credit-Sales (Advertising) Order, 1961.

Note: See *Fisher v. Bell* [1961] 1 Q.B. 394. A display of goods on the shelves of a self service store is not an offer but merely an invitation to treat. Also *Pharmaceutical Society of Great Britain v. Boots Cash Chemists Ltd.* [1952] 2 Q.B. 795.

A QUOTATION IS NOT AN OFFER
Boyers & Co. Ltd. v. Duke [1905] 2 I.R. 617 (K.B.D.)

The plaintiff company wrote to the defendant asking for their lowest quotation to supply 3,000 yards of canvas. The defendant replied stating that their lowest price was 4 5/8d.per yard. The plaintiff then wrote "please get made for us 3,000 yards as per your quotation at 4&5/8d. per yard." The defendant then replied that they had made a clerical error and that the price should have been 6&5/8d. per yard. The plaintiff replied that they had acted in reliance on the first quote and sold 3,000 yards at a small profit and under the circumstances would have to hold the defendants to their contract.

Held: The defendant's letter was merely a quotation and not an offer. The plaintiff's letter in reply was an offer of an order, and not an acceptance. There was no completed contract between the parties.

Madden J.:

> "Business could not be carried on if each recipient of a priced catalogue offering a desirable article — say a rare book — at an attractive price, were in a position to create a contract of sale by writing that he would buy at the price mentioned. The catalogue has probably reached many collectors. The order of one only can be honoured the writer knew well that he was giving an order, not accepting an offer for sale."

A STATEMENT OF PRICE IS NOT AN OFFER
Harvey v. Facey [1893] A.C. 552 (Privy Council)

The appellant sought an order of specific performance of an agreement allegedly made with the Respondent Facey for the sale of a property named Bumper Hall Pen, in Kingston Jamaica. Three telegraphs were exchanged by the parties, on the same day, as follows.
  H. to F.:

> "Will you sell us Bumper Hall Pen? Telegraph lowest cash price."

F. to H.:

> "Lowest price for Bumper Hall Pen £900."

H. to F.:

> "We agree to buy Bumper Hall Pen for the sum of £900 asked by you. Please send us your title deed in order that we may get early possession."

Held: There was no contract between the parties. Specific performance refused. The final telegraph was not the acceptance of an offer to sell, for none had been made. The statement of price in Facey's telegram was not an offer.

Lord Morris:

> "The first telegram asks two questions. The first question is as to the willingness of L.M Facey to sell to the appellants; the second question asks the lowest price, and the word "Telegraph" is in its collocation addressed to the second question only. L.M. Facey replied to the second question only and gives his lowest price. The third telegram from the appellants treats the answer of L.M. Facey stating his lowest price as an unconditional offer to sell to them at the price named.
>   Their Lordships cannot hold the telegram from L.M. Facey as binding

him in any respect except to the extent it does by its terms, viz., the lowest price. Everything else is left open and the reply telegram from the appellants cannot be treated as an acceptance of an offer to sell to them; it is an offer that requires to be accepted by L.M. Facey The contract could only be completed if L.M. Facey had accepted the appellant's last telegram . . . L.M. Facey's telegram gives a precise answer to a precise question, viz., the price. The contract must appear by the telegrams, whereas the appellants are obliged to contend that an acceptance of the first question is to be implied.

Their Lordships are of opinion that the mere statement of the lowest price at which the vendor would sell contains no implied contract to sell at that price to the person making the inquiry."

A SWEEPSTAKE TICKET IS NOT AN OFFER

Apicella and Constantino v. Scala and Ors.
(1931) 66 I.L.T.R. 33 (H.C.) Meredith J.

Apicella, Constantino and Scala, who lived in England, agreed to combine for the purchase of tickets in the Irish Hospitals Sweepstakes. They purchased a number of books of tickets and entered into a written agreement with regard to them. They decided to acquire more tickets and S, wrote for two more books. He then told A and C that he wished to sell some of these tickets to his friends and relatives. A and C objected and said if he wanted to do this he should procure another book.

S wrote for two more books and in February, 1931 a written agreement was entered into which comprised the last two books. Unknown to A and C, S retained the previous two books for his own use. One of the tickets in the retained books drew the first prize in the Sweepstake and A and C sued to recover two thirds of the share accruing to S.

Held: The purchase of a ticket in such a sweepstake and the sending in of the money and counterfoil was an offer and not an acceptance of an offer.

Deciding on the number of books to send for was not evidence of an intention to contract. If the arrangement to purchase two books was a contract for some two books, such contract was discharged by the joint purchase of the two later books, as there was no appropriation of the first two to the contract.

Note: Robert Clark, *Contract*, 3rd ed., p. 19, cites this case and states that the the postal rule regarding acceptance will not be allowed to operate so as to breach principles of international law.

AN ADVERTISEMENT IS NOT AN OFFER

Harris v. Nickerson [1873] L.R. 8 Q.B. 286

The defendant an auctioneer, advertised in the London newspapers that a sale by auction of brewing materials, plant and office furniture would be held by him at Bury St. Edmunds, on Monday, 12th August, 1872 and on the two following days.

The plaintiff, a commission broker in London, having a commission to buy the office furniture, went down to the sale; but on the third day (without any previous notice) all the lots of office furniture were withdrawn from the auction.

The plaintiff brought an action to recover for his loss of time and expenses. He claimed that the advertisement amounted to a contract with anybody who should act upon it, that all the things advertised would be actually put up for sale, and that he would have an opportunity of bidding and buying them.

Held: the advertisement was a mere declaration of intention and did not amount to a contract with anyone who might act upon it nor to a warranty that all the articles advertised would be put up for sale. The plaintiff could not maintain an action.

Archbold J.:

"... to say that a mere advertisement that certain articles will be sold by auction amounts to a contract to indemnify all who attend, if the sale of any part of the articles does not take place is a proposition without authority or ground supporting it."

Note: Compare and contrast with *Carlill v. The Carbolic Smoke Ball Co.*

A STATEMENT OF INTENTION IS NOT AN OFFER

Mackey v. Jones (1958) 93 I.L.T.R. 177 (Cir. Ct.)

In March 1943 the plaintiff, then aged about 14, went to live with his childless grand-uncle (Richard Jones) and his wife on a farm at Donard, Co. Wicklow and he lived and worked on the farm for a period of fourteen years without remuneration.

The plaintiff claimed that his uncle had verbally agreed with the plaintiffs mother to make a will leaving the farm to the plaintiff and that he had stated "he (the plaintiff) could have the place when he (the deceased) was done with it" and on another occasion "You need not give him pocket-money. I will give him anything he wants. He can have the place when I am done with it."

Subsequently the uncle left the farm by will to a cousin and the plaintiff sued for specific performance of the alleged contract.

Held: There was no binding contract to leave the farm to the plaintiff but only a statement of intention which did not amount to a contract.

Deale J.:

> "Even if the words did amount to a promise and if the whole conversation could bind the deceased in a contractual manner, there was a further difficulty in that the plaintiff was not a party to the proposal. He was not consulted about it, and in no way considered the matter; he was simply told by his mother to go to his uncle's farm and he obeyed . . . he did not accept the offer, if offer it was; he obeyed his mother's orders and that was not enough to create the relationship of contracting parties between the deceased and himself."

Note: A statement of intention is usually associated with cases like *Harris v. Nickerson* (1873) L.R. 8 Q.B. 286 where an advertisement that a sale of office furniture would take place was held to be a mere statement of intent, and the auctioneer was not liable for breach of contract when the office furniture was not auctioned. Robert Clark, *Contract, Irish Law Texts*, Sweet & Maxwell, 2nd. ed. 1986 at page 41 states that the *Mackey v. Jones* case can only be explained as one where the court refused to find that the promissor intended his promise to be binding. Remember that there is a presumption that domestic or family arrangements are not intended to create legal relations.

REVOCATION OF AN OFFER
Walker v. Glass [1979] N.I. 129 (N.I.H.C.) (Ch. D.)

Glass signed a form of offer prepared by his solicitor offering to sell his farm to Walker. A clause in the document stated that the offer was to remain open until 13 March and that acceptance should be on a form annexed to the offer, which had to be completed by the purchaser and lodged, with a deposit of £40,000 with the vendor's solicitor before 5 o'clock on the 13 March. If these stipulations were not complied with the offer was to be deemed withdrawn, and in this respect time was to be of the essence. Walker signed the acceptance on 1 March and telephoned the defendant's solicitor and told him that he had done so.

On 2 March the defendant's solicitor told Walker that the offer was withdrawn and that he had sent telegrams and letters withdrawing the offer. On 12 March Walker left the signed acceptance and a cheque for £40,000 with the vendor's solicitor who returned it the following day.

Held: There was no binding contract.

Lord Lowry:

> "I start with the following propositions:
>
> 1. An offer may be withdrawn at any time before it has been accepted.

This is so, even where the offer is expressed to be kept open for a specified period, provided no consideration has been given by the offeree. (*Dickinson v. Dodds* (1876) 2 Ch. D. 463).

2. If an offeror prescribes a particular mode of acceptance, no contract is created unless the offer is accepted in that mode or in a way which is as beneficial to the offeror. (*Manchester Diocesan Council v. Commercial and General Investments Ltd.* [1969] 3 All E.R.1593).

3. Revocation of an offer is not effective on the posting of a letter of revocation or the dispatch of a telegram but only when the offeree receives notice of the revocation.(*Henthorn v. Fraser* (1892) 2 Ch. 27).

. . . An oral communication to the vendor by a purchaser saying that the latter has signed does not put the vendor in as good a position as if the signed acceptance had been delivered to his solicitor. And in the second place, signature of acceptance by the purchaser unaccompanied by payment of the deposit is not a complete performance of the prescribed mode of acceptance and does not put the vendor in as good a position as he demanded. If the purchaser does not go through with the contract a vendor who has not received a deposit is obviously in a worse position than a vendor who has received one. . . ."

INDIRECT COMMUNICATION OF REVOCATION
Dickinson v. Dodds [1876] 2 Ch. D. 463

On Wednesday the 10th of June, 1874 the defendant signed and delivered to the plaintiff, a memorandum stating:

"I hereby agree to sell to Mr. George Dickinson the whole of the dwelling house, garden ground, stabling and outbuildings, thereto belonging, situated at Croft, belonging to me, for the sum of £800. Signed John Dodds. P.S. This offer to be left over until Friday, 9 o'clock, a.m. J.D."

During the afternoon of the Thursday the plaintiff was informed by a third party that Dodds had been offering or agreeing to sell the property to Thomas Allen. Thereupon, the plaintiff , at about half past seven in the evening, went to where Dodds was staying and left a formal acceptance in writing of the offer to sell the property.

On the following (Friday) morning at about 7 o'clock the plaintiffs agent found Dodds at Darlington Railway Station and handed him a duplicate acceptance. Dodds replied that it was too late, as he had sold the property. It appeared that on Thursday the 11th., of June Dodds had signed a formal contract for the sale of the property to Allen for £800 and received a deposit of £40 from him.

Held: An offer to sell may be withdrawn before acceptance without any formal notice to the person to whom the offer is made. It is sufficient if that person has actual knowledge that the person who made the offer has done some act inconsistent with the continuance of the offer, such as selling to a third person.

The document of the 10th of June amounted only to an offer, which might be withdrawn at any time before acceptance and that a sale to a third person which came to the knowledge of the person to whom the offer was made was an effectual withdrawal of the offer.

James L.J.:

"There is neither principle nor authority for the proposition that there must be an express and actual withdrawal of the offer, or what is called a retraction."

A COUNTER-OFFER OPERATES AS A REJECTION OF THE ORIGINAL OFFER

Hyde v. Wrench [1840] 3 Beav. 334

On the 6th June, 1840 Wrench offered to sell his farm at Luddenham to Hyde for £1,000. Hyde offered £950 which Wrench considered but declined to accept in a letter on the 27th June.

On the 29th June, Hyde wrote "I beg to acknowledge the receipt of your letter of the 27th instant, informing me that you are not disposed to accept the sum of £950 for your farm at Luddenham. This being the case, I at once agree to the terms on which you offered the farm, viz. £1,000. . . ." Hyde claimed that while Wrench had not accented to his counter offer of £950 he had not withdrawn the first offer and was contractually bound when he (Hyde) accepted it by agreeing to pay the £1,000.

Held: There was no valid binding contract between the parties. The counter-offer of £950 operated as a rejection of the original offer which could not afterwards be revived by tendering an acceptance of it.

Lord Langdale, M.R.:

"The defendant offered to sell it for £1,000, and if that had been at once unconditionally accepted, there would undoubtedly have been a perfect binding contract; instead of that, the plaintiff made an offer of his own to purchase the property for £950 and he thereby rejected the offer previously made by the defendant.

I think that it was not afterwards competent for him to revive the proposal of the defendant, by tendering an acceptance of it; and that, therefore, there exists no obligation of any sort between the parties."

ACCEPTANCE

There cannot be an agreement unless the offer that has been made is accepted and except in cases where performance constitutes acceptance as in *Kennedy v. The London Express Newspapers Ltd.*, the offeror must know that his offer has been accepted. This type of contract where one party promises a sum of money (*Carlill v. Carbolic Smoke Ball Co.* (1893) 1 Q.B. 256) or a benefit to another party for doing or abstaining from doing some act, e.g. as in reward cases like *Williams v. Carwardine* (1833) 4 B& Ad. 621 is known as a unilateral contract. Such contracts are called unilateral or one sided because only the promissor makes a promise the promisee does not make a counter promise to the promissor. Reward cases fall into this category. In general there is no contract until the required act or forebearance has been carried out.

Such acceptance cannot be imposed — *Russell & Baird v. Hoban*. The acceptance must be unequivocal. *Central Meat Products v. Carney: Gradwell v. Maguire* and it must be unconditional *Swan v. Miller* otherwise it will be considered to be a counter-offer, as in *Dooley v. Egan*.

In *Guardians of the Navan Union v. M'Loughlin* it was decided that mental acceptance is not sufficient, long before *Felthouse v. Bindley* the traditional authority for the proposition that acceptance must be communicated. That such communication can be non-verbal is illustrated by the decision of the Northern Ireland Court of Appeal in *Royal Avenue Hotel Ltd. v. Richard Shops Properties Ltd., & Another* wherein it was held that silence plus relevant conduct constituted acceptance. See also *Brogden v. Metropolitan Railway Co.* (1877) 2 App. Cas. 666 1.

Sanderson v. Cunningham the Irish equivalent of *Household Fire Insurance Company v. Grant* illustrates the principle that acceptance by letter is effective when the letter is posted (provided it is correctly addressed and properly stamped) unless a specified mode of acceptance has been prescribed by the offeror as in *Walker v. Glass* or that it is obvious from the circumstances that the post was not the mode intended by the offeror.

ACCEPTANCE MUST BE UNEQUIVOCAL

Central Meat Products Co. Ltd. v. Carney
[1944] Ir. Jur. Rep. 34 (H.C.) Overend J.

The defendant was a director of a limited company Dublin Boned Meat Limited. This company wrote to CMP proposing to supply cattle to them for canning purposes for 3 or 6 months subject to alteration in prices to be mutually arranged and also an alteration in an insurance scheme.

Held: The letter was merely an outline of a proposition and not an offer. No number of cattle were stated and the parties had still to agree an alteration in price and in the insurance scheme.

A letter written by CMP which stated "Our Directors are prepared to accept your terms in principle subject to suitable arrangements regarding offal" was tantamount to a refusal to accept the proposition and hardly even a counter-offer.

Note: See *Irish Mainport Holdings v. Crosshaven Sailing Centre*, High Court, unreported, 14 October, 1980 re "agreement in principle".

EQUIVOCAL WORDS
Gradwell v. Maguire [1872] 6 Ir.R. Eq. 477 (Ch. App.)

Colonel Maguire offered to sell lands at Ballinacrad, Co. Meath to Richard Gradwell for £5,000. When they met in a solicitors office Gradwell said that he (Maguire) was asking too much, that he would give £4,800 and no more. Maguire replied "all right, there is an end to the matter". Gradwell then said "You are very hard on me, but I suppose I must give what you ask". Maguire refused to accept the offer and complete the transaction.

Held: There was not a completed contract. The words of Gradwell taken by themselves were equivocal words. It was not clear that they would bind Gradwell as he would have been bound if he had said "I will give you what you ask."

Note: This case also illustrates the notion that a counter offer operates as a rejection. (See also *Hyde v. Wrench ante*).

ACCEPTANCE MUST BE UNCONDITIONAL
Swan v. Miller [1919] I.R. 151 (C.A.)

Miller engaged an agent to sell premises in Maxwell Street, Belfast for the sum of £4,750 plus £50 per annum ground rent. An agent acting for Swan telegraphed offering £4,750 for the premises, but making no reference to the £50 ground rent. Miller's agent wrote in reply that Miller had accepted the offer plus £50 annual ground rent. Swan claimed specific performance.

Held: The letter from Miller's agent was not an unconditional acceptance of the offer because it contained a new term, namely the payment of £50 ground rent. The plaintiff was not entitled to a decree for specific performance.

ACCEPTANCE CANNOT BE IMPOSED
Russell & Baird v. Hoban [1922] 2 I.R. 159 (C.A.S.I.)

H asked R if they could supply 224 bags of oatmeal. R replied that they could and stated "If this sale note be retained beyond 3 days after this date, it will be held to have been accepted by the buyer". Some months later H wrote "kindly cancel my order for oatmeal which was without signing contract note". R refused to cancel the order and forwarded an invoice for 224 bags which they subsequently delivered. H refused delivery and returned the invoice.

Held: There was no contract between the parties. H was not obliged to accept and pay for the oatmeal. "No man can impose such conditions upon another.": *per* Ronan L.J.

ACCEPTANCE MUST BE COMMUNICATION
Guardians of Navan Union v. M'Loughlin
[1855] 4 I.C.L.R 451 (Common Pleas)

The Guardians advertised requesting tenders for the supply of articles. The defendant submitted a tender which was approved of at a meeting of the board and the word "approved " written across it by the Chairman.

Before acceptance was communicated to M'Loughlin he wrote to the Guardians stating that unless they paid him monthly he could not undertake the contract. The Guardians insisted that his tender had been accepted prior to his letter.

Held: The tender was only a proposal for a contract. Where there are written communications between the parties, it is not enough for one of them to accept the other's proposal in his mind or in his own office. He must by some act, binding on himself, communicate his acceptance to the other party.

Note: Felthouse v. Bindley (1863) 11 C.B. (N.S.) 869 was decided some eight years after the above case.

PERFORMANCE CONSTITUTED ACCEPTANCE — UNILATERAL CONTRACT
Kennedy v. The London Express Newspapers Ltd. [1931] I.R. 532 (S.C.)

The defendant published an advertisement of a free insurance scheme for the benefit of "registered readers" of "The Daily Express". The scheme provided that a sum of £100 (death benefit) would be paid to the personal representatives of a "registered reader" . . . killed by accidental impact with a moving vehicle. . . ." To become a "registered reader" a person had to forward a signed registration coupon to the Daily Express and give a newsagent a signed order for the newspaper and be receiving it daily. Disputes were to be referred to arbitration "in accordance with the statutory provisions for the time being in force applicable thereto," and the obtaining of any (sic) award was a condition precedent to liability.

The following year the free insurance scheme was renewed by another advertisement which provided that registered readers did not have to re register and that arbitrations were to be held in London. In 1929, the plaintiff's wife was registered as a reader and in August, 1930 she was accidentally killed by a bus at Arran Quay, in Dublin. The plaintiff claimed the £100 payable under the scheme.

The defendants admitted that the plaintiff's wife was a registered reader but denied that she was in receipt of the paper daily, as required by the conditions. They therefore contended that a dispute had arisen which must be referred to arbitration in London. The plaintiff contended that a contract was made in the Irish Free State and that arbitration should take place there with a member of the Irish Bar as arbitrator.

Held: There had been two different contracts. The first contract was constituted by the offer made by the advertisement in "The Daily Express" of 1st January, 1929, accepted by the posting of the coupon registration form to the company and the placing of the order for the delivery of the paper with the local newsagent.

The second contract was constituted by the offer made in the advertisement of "The Daily Express" of 1st January, 1930 and the continuance of the order with the newsagent for the delivery of the newspaper. The arbitration in London condition, in the 1930 advertisement was a term of the 1930 contract and the arbitration must take place in London as agreed.

Note: This case also illustrates the notion of an advertisement being an offer. See *Carlill v. The Carbolic Smoke Ball Co.* (1891-94) All E.R. 127 and of a unilateral contract. In general there is no contract until the required act or forbearance required by the offeror has been carried out and communication of acceptance is usually not necessary because performance constitutes acceptance There are circumstances, however, where part-performance of a unilateral contract amounts to an acceptance but the offeror is not bound if the performance is not completed. See *Errington v. Errington* [1952] 1 K.B. 290.

SILENCE ACCOMPANIED BY RELEVANT CONDUCT MAY AMOUNT TO ACCEPTANCE
Royal Avenue Hotel Ltd. v. Richard Shops Properties Ltd.
[1986] 4 BNIL No. 10 (C.A.)

An offer by the plaintiff to purchase premises in Royal Avenue, Belfast, was accepted by the first defendant. Three days later the solicitor for the defendant wrote to the plaintiff proposing to amend clause 11 of the Conditions of Sale by making the purchaser liable for interest on outstanding purchase money after the completion date. The purchaser refused to accept this amendment or to pay interest demanded and nothing more was said. Later the vendor refused to complete, claiming that no contract had been concluded.

Held: Acceptance could be shown by silence accompanied by relevant conduct. The correspondence pointed overwhelmingly to a completed and agreed contract. Decree of specific performance granted.

Note: See also *Brogden v. Metropolitan Railway* (1877) 2 App. Cas. 666 where a contract was created through acceptance by conduct.

ACCEPTANCE TAKES PLACE WHEN LETTER IS POSTED
Sanderson v. Cunningham [1919] 2 I.R. 234 (C.A.)

An insurance policy issued by the defendants contained a number of conditions which were not in the proposal, and of which the plaintiff had no knowledge until he received the policy from his insurance broker. The policy contained a clause that the assured should read it and if incorrect return it to the agents at once. The plaintiff claimed that the contract was not completed until he had signified acquiescence by accepting it.

Held: The contract was completed by the signing and posting of the policy in London.

Adams v. Lindsell 1 B & Ald. 681 (1818)

The defendants, who were wool-dealers at St. Ives, Huntingdon, wrote the following letter to the plaintiffs, woolen manufacturers in Worcestershire, on Tuesday the 2nd of September, 1817.

> "We now offer you eight hundred tods of wether fleeces, of a good fair quality of our country wool at 35s. 6d per tod . . . receiving your answer in course of post."

The letter was misdirected by the defendants to Bromsgrove, Leicestershire and it was not received by the plaintiffs in Worcestershire until 7 p.m. on Friday September 5th. On that evening the plaintiffs wrote, agreeing to accept the wool on the terms proposed. This acceptance was not received by the defendants until Tuesday, September 9th. On Monday, September 8th, the defendants not having, as they expected, received an answer on Sunday, September 7th, (which would have been in the usual course of the post) sold the wool to another person.

Held: that there was a contract binding the parties from the moment the offer was accepted, and that Adams was entitled to recover against Lindsell in an action for not completing his contract.

Note: It was contended that there could be no binding contract until the plaintiff's acceptance was actually received and that before that, the defendants had retracted their offer, by selling the wool to other persons. The court said "if the defendants were not bound by their offer when accepted by the plaintiff until the answer was received, then the plaintiff ought not to be bound till after they had received the notification that the defendants had received their answer and assented to it. And so it might go on *ad infinitum*. The defendants must be considered in law as making, during every instant of the time their letter was travelling, the same identical offer to the plaintiffs; and then the contract is completed by the acceptance of it by the letter.

As to the delay in notifying the acceptance, that arose entirely from the mistake of the defendants, and it therefore must be taken that the plaintiffs' answer was received in course of post." See also *The Household Fire Insurance Co. Ltd. v. Grant* (1879) L.R. 4 Ex. 216 where the postal rule was also applied to an acceptance.

CONTRACT MADE WHERE ACCEPTANCE TAKES PLACE
Dooley v. Egan (1938) 72 I.L.T. 155 (H.C.) Meredith J.

D in Dublin, sent a written quotation to supply one instrument cabinet to E "for immediate acceptance only. . . ." E in Cork replied "We enclose herewith order for 2 cabinets". D replied ". . . thank you for your valued order for 2 cabinets. We are placing the work in hands immediately and shall let you have delivery as soon as possible".

Held: The order for the 2 cabinets was not an unqualified acceptance, but another offer. D's subsequent letter was an acceptance of the counter-offer and the contract was made where the acceptance took place *viz.* in Dublin.

CONDITION PRECEDENT TO AGREEMENT
Kelly v. Irish Nursery & Landscape Co. Ltd. [1983] I.R. 221 (S.C.)

The defendants solicitor sent two copies of a proposed contract of sale, of land in county Wicklow, to the plaintiffs solicitor. In their accompanying letter, the defendants solicitor stated "it must be understood that no agreement enforceable at law is created or intended to be created until exchange of contracts has taken place." The plaintiffs solicitor accepted that condition and returned the duplicate contracts signed by the plaintiff.

When a deposit was later sent to the defendants solicitor, it was returned with a statement that the defendant had decided not to proceed with the sale. The plaintiff claimed specific performance.

Held: There was no enforceable contract for the sale of the defendant's lands as no exchange of contracts had taken place.

"The plaintiffs claim must fail for the simple reason that he contracted out of such right as he might have had to enforce the contract since he agreed to have the enforceability dependant upon an exchange of contracts. As no such exchange took place, the contract cannot be enforced." *per* Walsh J.

"Subject to any special stipulation agreed between the parties, the general law in Ireland as to the necessity of exchanging contracts is that it is not necessary for the vendor and purchaser to exchange contracts to make the agreement enforceable at law: See pp.. 20, 49 and 337-380 of Wylie's *Irish Conveyancing Law.* In England, however, it is settled by the decision of the Court of Appeal in *Eccles v. Bryant & Pollack* [1948] Ch. 93 that, when there is an agreement for the sale of land "subject to contract", a binding contract comes into existence only when there is a mutual exchange of contracts: see also *Winn v. Bull* (1877) 7 Ch.D. 29 and *Chillingworth v. Esche* [1924)] 1 Ch. 97-" Kenny J.

ORAL AGREEMENT — NO CONDITION PRECEDENT
Pernod Ricard & Comrie plc v. F.I.I. Fyffes plc
High Court, unreported, 21 October, 1988, Costello J.
Supreme Court, unreported, 11 November, 1988

The board of Irish Distillers sought the assistance of Pernod Ricard to ward off a takeover bid from G.C. & C. and Pernod entered into negotiations to acquire the defendants 20% holding in Irish Distillers. Originally it was agreed that the defendants would sell their holding when the plaintiffs made a general offer to the shareholders of Distillers, and it would be conditional upon the plaintiffs procuring an opinion from an inspector of taxes that the transaction would qualify for relief provided by paragraph 4 of the Second Schedule of The Capital Gains Tax Act, 1975.

Pernod claimed that at meetings between the 2nd and 4th September, the original agreement was varied by allowing the defendants to give an irrevocable undertaking to sell their holding, instead of the conditional agreement. This oral agreement was reached with the defendant, to acquire twenty per cent of the shares in Irish Distillers owned by them for 450p a share. There was a spontaneous shaking of hands and arrangements were made to complete the formalities by signing a written agreement.

G.C.& C. announced a further offer of 522p per share and when Pernod representatives went to a meeting to complete the share transaction FII/Fyffes referred to the increased G.C.& C. offer, claimed that a new situation had been created and that they would have to consider it. Pernod claimed that nothing had changed, that they had an agreement, and sought specific performance of the oral agreement. FII/Fyffes claimed that there was no agreement, that there had been a number of conditions precedent, (including one about relief on capital gains) which had not been complied with.

Held:

(1) An oral contract had been concluded between the parties. The defendant could not legally resile from the verbal contract it entered into and the plaintiff was entitled to have it specifically enforced.

(2) It was not dependant on a written contract being executed by the defendant.

(3) It was not subject to a condition precedent that the defendants worries about tax clearance should be removed.

Per Costello J. in the High Court:

> ". . . What happened was what frequently occurs in all sorts of negotiations-namely a point was reached when the parties had made a bargain and agreed that a written document should be executed. When a dispute subsequently arises, what the court has to decide is whether the preparation of a further document is a condition precedent to the creation of a contract or merely an incident in the performance of an already binding obligation. I have no doubt that the negotiations had in this case ripened into an agreement, that an obligation had been imposed on FII to sell its shares to Pernod Ricard if certain conditions were fulfilled by it, and that the preparation and execution of a written contract was merely an incident in the performance of the obligations the parties had undertaken to one another."

Held by the Supreme Court, Finlay C.J. (Griffin J. and Hederman J. in agreement) the Appeal must be dismissed.

CONDITIONAL AGREEMENT
Lowis v. Wilson [1949] I.R. 347 (H.C.) Dixon J.

The plaintiff agreed to purchase land from the defendant "subject to the preparation of a formal contract, to be prepared" by the vendor's, (defendant's) solicitor. A formal contract was prepared but the purchaser refused to sign it or to proceed with the sale and claimed the return of the deposit he had paid.

Held: The agreement was conditional upon the full agreement of the parties being embodied in a formal contract and accordingly was not enforceable. The deposit which was paid could be recovered.

INCOMPLETE AGREEMENT
Boyle v. Lee and Goyns [1992] I.L.R.M. 65 (S.C.)

Following negotiations with an estate agent, the plaintiffs agreed to purchase a dwelling house and premises situated at Elgin Road, Dublin for £90,000. The question of a deposit was discussed but no sum was agreed upon. The estate agent wrote to (his client's) the vendors solicitor confirming that his company had received instructions to accept the offer of £90,000 made by the plaintiff 'subject to contract' and setting out that the letter itself was for information purposes only and 'did not by itself constitute part of a binding contract'. Later the plaintiffs sought specific performance of the agreement which they claimed had been concluded for the sale of the premises.

Held:

(1) There was no complete and binding oral agreement entered into by the parties for the sale of the property. The failure to make provision regarding the details of the deposit to be paid by the purchaser and the fact that all the essential terms of the contract had not been finalised led inevitably to this conclusion.

(2) The estate agent's letter did not constitute a note or memorandum of an oral agreement capable of satisfying the requirements of s.2 of the Statute of Frauds (Ireland) Act, 1695.

Per Finlay C.J. with Hederman J. concurring:

A note or memorandum of a contract made orally is not sufficient to satisfy the Statute of Frauds unless it directly or by very necessary implication recognises, not only the terms to be enforced, but also the existence of a concluded contract between the parties. A note of memorandum which contains a term or expression such as 'subject to contract', even if it can be established by oral evidence that such a term or expression did not form part of the original agreement, is insufficient for this purpose.

CHAPTER 2

Intention to create Legal Relations

An intention to create legal relations is not universally accepted as a requirement for the existence of a valid contract, some commentators consider it sufficient if offer and acceptance is accompanied by consideration; in essence that a bargain has been struck. (See J. O'Reilly, *Intention to create Legal Relations*, 6 Ir. Jur (1971) 323-4).

It is suggested that an intention to create legal relations is an inherent constituent of an offer. Without such intent a statement may only be an invitation to treat, or a statement of price. Clearly if the parties do not intend to create legal relations they do not intend to contract. The existence of this legal intent is an essential requirement of a contract. If the parties express their intent, that an agreement shall or shall not give rise to legal relations, this resolves the matter but where necessary a court can infer intention from the conduct of the parties. The courts deduce what a reasonable man would deduce the intention to be, from the circumstances — not what the parties privately intended. Evidence of the parties intentions during negotiations is not admissible. *Prenn v. Simmonds* [1971] 3 All E.R. 237.

Where there is a possibility of ambiguity an indication of intention is the determining factor to a court. In the absence of expressed intent the courts may have to infer intent from the conduct of the parties. Normally the circumstances and environment in which the transaction took place are either conclusive or presumptive evidence. An indication of evidence of intention was found by the court in *Carlill v. Carbolic Smoke Ball Co.*, to lie in the fact that money had been lodged by the company in anticipation of having to pay claims, otherwise the advertisement like that in *Harris v. Nickerson* would have been held to be a mere statement of intent, or an invitation to treat.

The presumption is that social or domestic agreements are not intended to be legally binding while business or commercial agreements are intended to be so. The presumption in each instance may be rebutted by evidence. The fact that discussion has taken place in a family environment with a consequent lack of precision or formality has undoubtedly led to questionable judgments in individual cases but decisions based on the balance of probability are inherently so. The requirement of clear evidence of intention in domestic situations is illustrated by *Smith v. Rogers* and *Saunders v. Cramer*.

The practicality of the laws approach is however, very apparent in the implication of different intent to domestic arrangements between parties who are married and living together in amity, *Balfour v. Balfour* [1919] 2 K.B. 571 than that implied to parties not living together or about to separate, *Merritt v. Merritt* [1970] 2 All E. R. 760, *Courtney v. Courtney.*

Collective agreements are neither domestic or commercial. There is therefore no presumption possible. The intention of the parties is paramount. Some commentators take the view that because the principle of voluntarism underlies our system of collective bargaining there is an implication that collective agreements are not legally enforceable. The Irish Courts examine a collective agreement very closely. In *O'Rourke and Ors. v. Talbot Ireland* [1984] ILRM the court was satisfied that the workers intended to enter into a legally binding agreement, the 'objective test' of the intention of the parties as set out in *Edwards v. Skyways Ltd.*, had been satisfied. The agreement was one which could be enforced by law and the plaintiffs were entitled to relief.

In *Goulding Chemicals Ltd. v. Bolger & Ors.* [1977] I.R. 211 although the agreement between the plaintiffs and the trade unions appeared to be an enforceable contract the defendant workers were not bound by it. It had not been incorporated into their contracts of employment. *Riordan v. Butler* [1940] I.R. 347 is authority for the proposition that breach of a "no strike" clause in a collective agreement is a breach of contract.

FAMILY ARRANGEMENT — MOTHER AND SON
Smith v. Rogers, unreported, 16 July 1970 (S.C.)

Smith claimed £1,467.19s against his mother's estate on foot of an agreement between himself and his mother. She had stated ". . . any money I owe you. When I am dead and gone you will probably take it from the estate . . . when I am dead and gone you will be able to claim anything you have spent on me." Payments had been made by Smith to his mother during his father's lifetime and it was his father's intention that he should continue to look after his mother when he took over the father's business. He gave evidence that he would have continued to support his mother even had she not made any promises regarding repayment.

Held: The mother's statements were made in the course of conversations relating to family affairs. The payments were made as part of the family arrangements and not as a result of any contractual agreement.

> ". . . it must be shown that it can be inferred from the evidence that what was said viewed in the light of the surrounding circumstances, amounted to offer and acceptance . . . there is also in my view, no sufficient evidence of the intention of the parties to enter into a contract having legal consequences." *per* Budd J.

See *Saunders v. Cramer* (1843) 5 I. Eq. R. 12 (Ch)

BROTHER AND SISTER — MERE STATEMENT OF INTENT
Mackey v. Jones (1958) 93 I.L.T.R. 177 (Cir. Ct.)

In March 1943 the plaintiff, then aged about 14 went to live with his childless grand-uncle (Richard Jones) and his wife, on a farm at Donard, Co. Wicklow. He lived and worked on the farm for a period of fourteen years without remuneration.

The plaintiff claimed that his uncle had verbally agreed with the plaintiffs mother to make a will leaving the farm to the plaintiff and that he had stated "he (the plaintiff) could have the place when he (the deceased uncle) was done with it" and on another occasion that the uncle had stated to his mother "You need not give him pocket-money. I will give him anything he wants. He can have the place when I am done with it." Subsequently the uncle left the farm by will to a cousin and the plaintiff sued for specific performance of the alleged contract.

Held: (*inter alia*) by Deale J. There was no binding contract to leave the farm to the plaintiff but only a statement of intention which did not amount to a contract.

Note: A statement of intention is usually associated with cases like *Harris v. Nickerson* (1873) L.R. 8 Q.B. 286 where an advertisement by an auctioneer that a sale of office furniture would take place was held to be a mere statement of intent and not an offer, and that the auctioneer was not liable when the office furniture was withdrawn from the auction. Robert Clark, *Contract, Irish Law Texts*, Sweet & Maxwell, 1992 at page 69 states that the Mackey v. Jones case can only be explained as one where the court refused to find that the promissor intended his promise to be binding. See also Chapter 16 Privity of Contract.

HUSBAND AND WIFE
Courtney v. Courtney [1923] 2 I.R. 31 (C.A. I.F.S.)

In May 1921, the parties agreed in the presence of a priest, to separate and not to molest each other. The husband also agreed to pay £150 to the wife, who agreed in turn to return a watch and ring to the husband. The £150 was given to the wife and she signed a receipt for it "in full discharge of all claims of every nature and kind by me against the said Michael Courtney." The husband contended that because the agreement was a legally binding contract the wife was estopped from taking divorce proceedings by virtue of its terms. There was no express provision not to sue and in May 1922, the wife filed a petition for a divorce *a mensa et thoro*.

Held: A contract between spouses to live separate and apart is one which may be upheld and enforced. Such a contract need not be in any particular form provided there is evidence of an agreement made for valuable consideration; nor is it necessary that it should contain an express covenant not to sue, to be a bar to subsequent proceedings for divorce, if that can be shown to have been the real character of the agreement entered into by the parties.

The decision to grant the decree *a mensa et thoro* should be reversed. The agreement was a legally binding contract and its terms precluded further action. The consideration from the wife was that if the husband agreed the terms she would abstain from bringing proceedings for separation or alimony. The allowance in the form of a lump sum, agreed by the parties threw light on their intention.

> "Was this merely an agreement between spouses such as Lord Justice Atkin referred to, or was it intended to be a bargain . . . when this contract was entered into the wife was in a position in which she could have sued her husband. What relief could she get in a suit? A separation from bed and board, and an allowance from the court from the husbands means for alimony. The allowance would have been in the usual practice granted as an annual payment; that it was arranged for between the parties to be granted at once as a lump sum in this case throws light on the intention of the parties. It was to be given once and for all — no further dealings." *per* Dodd J.

Note: The intention of the parties was vital because in *Balfour v. Balfour* [1919] 2 K.B. 571 at p. 578 Lord Justice Atkin had stated "It constantly happens that such arrangements made between husband and wife are arrangements in which there are mutual promises, or in which there is consideration in form . . . nevertheless they are not contracts because the parties do not intend that they should be attended by legal consequences."

AUNT AND NIECE

Saunders v. Cramer [1843] 5 I. Eq. R. 12 (Ch.)

In 1839, Lady Caldwell signed a memorandum she had dictated to her agent Mr. Cramer to the effect that she intended to leave a sum of £2,000 on her death to her niece Elizabeth Pratt in consideration of the niece's intended marriage to Robert Saunders. The gift was to be secured by a bond. On the same day Cramer on Lady Caldwell's direction wrote to Saunders, the future groom, informing him of her intention to give Elizabeth Pratt £2,000 on her death and also a house at Cheltenham called 'Loretto".

The marriage took place in February, 1840. Lady Caldwell died in March, 1840 without executing either a bond or a conveyance, her state of health preventing her from attending to business. In her will the undisposed property at Cheltenham was left to her agent Cramer and the niece and her husband

Saunders sought a declaration that Cramer was bound to convey the house at Cheltenham.

Held: The letters amounted to an offer. The marriage was an acceptance of that offer by the intended husband. There was a sufficient memorandum to satisfy the Statute of Frauds.

The Lord Chancellor:

> "I consider her evidence as showing that nothing could be more deliberate upon the part of Lady Caldwell than the offer which she made, and she intended to be bound by it.
>
> The reference to a bond and a conveyance shows, that it was not intended to be a mere offer which was not to be binding . . . it was intended to be secured legally, and that would leave no option to Lady Caldwell, whether she would perform it or no, and therefore she was bound by it so as that she could not retire from it at any event. The consideration is apparent upon the face of this offer; the terms of it are free from doubt, and I should have no difficulty in saying that it constitutes a binding contract, if it has been accepted by the other party . . . No more solemn acceptance of an offer can possibly be than the act of marriage and upon that acceptance the offer became binding upon the party who made it."

Note: This case is sometimes used to illustrate:

(1) An agreement made in consideration of marriage. (Section 2 St. of Frauds)

(2) A Note or memorandum in writing signed by a lawfully authorised person.

(3) Intention to create legal relations.

NEIGHBOURS

The McGillycuddy of the Reeks v. Joy [1959] I.R. 189 (H.C.) Budd J.

The plaintiff and the defendants verbally agreed that they would join in the purchase of lands known as "Breen's Farm." The plaintiff to contribute one third and to be entitled to have for himself a portion of "Breen's Farm" known as "The Inches", together with the fishing rights in the River Laune. The defendants were to pay the other two thirds and to have for themselves the balance of the lands comprised in "Breen's farm" with the fishing rights thereto belonging.

It was agreed that David Joy and a solicitor, nominated by both parties would negotiate the sale and that the contract for purchase would be signed by David Joy alone and that the plaintiff would not enter into the negotiations for the purchase or make any bid or offer for the property on his own behalf. David

Joy purchased 'Breen's farm" for £5,000, the plaintiff paid his one-third part of the purchase price and Auctioneer's fee to the solicitor, but the defendant David Joy later repudiated the contract and claimed to be entitled to the land and fisheries to the exclusion of the plaintiff.

Held: There was no uncertainty as to the areas of the said farm "The Inches", intended to become the property of the plaintiff. Both parties knew exactly what was involved.

The plaintiff's agreement to refrain from making an offer or bid or to negotiate for the purchase of "Breen's farm" on his own behalf constituted consideration for the said agreement. "In refraining from making an offer or bid the plaintiff allowed the defendant's to negotiate their own terms, permitting them, as they thought, the advantage of buying at a cheaper price than if he came into the market, all believing that his presence at the negotiations would increase the price."

In entering into the agreement the parties had intended to create legal relations between themselves. "it was no mere social arrangement, it was a business compact, over a business matter, intended very clearly to be carried out in a legal way with the intervention of a solicitor." *Devine v. Fields* 54 ILTR 101 *considered and applied.*

INTENTION AND COLLECTIVE AGREEMENTS
O'Rourke & Ors. v. Talbot (Ireland) Ltd.
[1984] I.L.R.M. 587 (H.C.) Barrington J.

The plaintiffs who were employed as foremen by the defendant, apart from their trade union representatives, elected a committee of three men which negotiated on their behalf with the management.

In 1979 when the defendant company were experiencing difficulties because of rising costs and falling production and sales, they were anxious to secure an agreement that foremen who had left car assembly or were being redeployed would not be replaced. The management met with the foremen's representatives on a number of occasions and ultimately reached agreement. A draft of a written assurance that there would be no compulsory redundancy of foremen was signed on behalf of the management but rejected by the foremen who wanted something that would bind the company legally. They asked that the word "guarantee" be substituted for "assurance". They considered it a better word from the legal point of view, being familiar with the term in the sense of a legally binding warranty in the motor trade. The management created no difficulty in giving the guarantee. Draft minutes of the meeting with the foremen's representatives, and agreed by them stated: "The company gave a guarantee of no compulsory redundancy prior to 1984 and that surplus supervisors would be redeployed." In 1980 the company made the foremen redundant and they instituted proceedings against the company for breach of the agreement.

Held: The company was in breach of the agreement with the plaintiffs. While the company may not have intended by the agreement to create legal relations, they had not made this known to the plaintiffs who were seeking a legally binding agreement. The company knew this; and in the circumstances there was a presumption, based on an objective legal test, that the parties intended to create legal relations; and the company had failed to discharge the heavy onus on them to rebut that presumption. *Edwards v. Skyways Ltd.* [1964] 1 WLR 349 *approved. Ford Motor Co. Ltd. v. Amalgamated Union of Engineers and Foundry Workers* [1969] 2 Q.B. 303 *considered.*

CONTRACT BINDING ON UNION BUT NOT ON MEMBERS
Goulding Chemicals Ltd. v. Bolger & Ors. [1977] I.R. 211 (S.C.)

The plaintiffs, manufacturers of fertilizers, decided to close their Dublin plant and reached agreement with trade unions about the manner of the closure and redundancy payments to employees.

A majority of the members of each union accepted the proposals and the plaintiff terminated the contracts of all the staff in accordance with the agreement and closed the Dublin plant. The defendants had always objected to the closure, refused to accept the redundancy payments offered to them, and picketed the plant without the authority of their trade union. The plaintiffs sought a High Court injunction restraining the defendants from picketing the premises.

Held: (*inter alia*) That the defendants were not bound by the terms of the agreement between the plaintiff and the trade unions.

Held: (On appeal to the Supreme Court): Although the agreement between the plaintiffs and the trade unions appeared to have been an enforceable contract which prevented officials of the unions from picketing the plaintiffs property, the plaintiffs had not produced either law or evidence to support their contention that the defendants were bound by the agreement, and that accordingly, the defendants were not so bound. *Edwards v. Skyways Ltd.* [1964] 1 WLR 349 *considered.*

CHAPTER 3

Consideration

Consideration has been described by Sir Frederick Pollock (1) as the price that one party pays for the other party's promise. In *Currie v. Misa* (18750 L.R. 10 Ex. 153, 162 valuable consideration was defined as consisting "either of some *right, interest, profit or benefit* accruing to the one party, or some *forbearance, detriment, loss or responsibility*, given suffered or undertaken by the other."

A contract is a bargain and the notion of bargain has within it the idea of *quid pro quo* as distinct from an agreement or a bare promise (*nudum pactum*). An agreement may or may not contain the element of reciprocity and it is this entitlement to have an agreement not under seal enforced, that the Courts look for, when a party seeks its assistance in relation to a simple contract.

A simple contract must be supported by consideration if it is sought to enforce it. In *Rann v. Hughes* (1778) 4 Bro. Part Cas. 27 (H.L.), 53 R.R. 262, 263 it was stated "... the law of this country supplies no means, nor affords any remedy, to compel the performance of an agreement made without sufficient consideration; such agreement is *nudum pactum ex quo non oritur actio*; ... All contracts are, by the laws of England, distinguished into agreements by specialty, and agreements by parol.... If they be merely written and not specialties, they are parol, and a consideration must be proved." Consideration is not needed in a contract under seal. See *Drimmie v. Davies.*

The consideration given for the other party's promise must be something extra or something different from that which the party is already legally or morally obliged to do, and except in the case of a contract under seal the presence or absence of consideration will determine whether a promise is legally binding or not.

What constitutes sufficient consideration has been explored in the following cases in relation to duties imposed by law. Performance of a public duty imposed by law in *Collins v. Godefroy*, performance of more than a public duty owed by law in *Glasbrook Bros. v. Glamorgan County Council*, performance of a duty imposed by statute in *Ward v. Byham.*

The tests of consideration in the contractual arena may be divided into performance of a contractual duty owed to the promissor *Stilk v. Myrick* the doing or promising to do more than a contractual duty owed to the promissor *Hartley v. Ponsonby*, promising to perform a duty owed to a third party *Pau On v. Lau Yiu Long* and *Williams v. Williams* and actually performing a duty owed to a third party. "The Eurymedon."

The cardinal rule that consideration must not be past is illustrated by *Provincial Bank of Ireland Ltd. v. Donnell*. Some writers claim that an exception to this rule exists where services are rendered at the request of the promissor, and it is understood that payment will be made for such service, the payment for the service is then legally recoverable, as in *Lampleigh v. Braithwait* (1615) Hob. 105 and *Re. Casey's Patents* [1892] 1 Ch. 104. The rationale of the contra argument that these cases are not true exceptions to the rule is that there was always an implied promise to pay, and that a subsequent express promise merely particularises the previous implied one.

Tritel, *Law of Contract*, 7th ed., London, 1987, p. 62, takes the line that apart from the subsequent promise, the promisee is entitled to a *quantum meruit* for his services and any subsequent promise can be regarded as fixing the amount of the *quantum meruit* or as consideration for the promisee releasing his *quantum meruit* claim. The Privy Council has held in *Pao On v. Lau Yiu Long* [1980] A.C. 614 that consideration for a promise can consist of an earlier promise provided it is given at the promissors request and on the understanding that some form of compensation will be forthcoming.

Consideration must be certain or capable of being made certain. In the case of *Carr v. Phelan* the consideration could not be ascertained and therefore the assistance of the court was not forthcoming. Another rule relating to consideration is that while consideration need not be adequate it must be sufficient i.e. acceptable in the eyes of the law.

In *Re Metro Investment Trust Ltd.*, forbearance in the form of a stay of execution to enable a debtor to pay by instalments was held to be sufficient whereas in 1963 the Court of Appeal in *O'Neill v. Murphy and Others* held that a promise to say prayers did not amount in law to good and valuable consideration. However the Supreme Court decision in *PMPA v. Keenan* affords some evidence that the Irish Courts may have regard to the adequacy of consideration in collective agreements where a floor of rights have been established by statute.

The essential difference between consideration and estoppel is that consideration enables a contract to be enforced while estoppel prevents a contract being enforced. (See Chapter 4.) Consideration and the part payment of a debt is illustrated by the rule in *Pinnel's* case and the exceptions to it at common law and equity.

CONSIDERATION NOT NEEDED FOR CONTRACT UNDER SEAL

Drimmie v. Davies [1899] 1 I.R. 176 (Ch., C.A.)

The facts of this case are set out in Chapter 16 Privity of Contract at page 189.

It was submitted that the executors had no interest entitling them to sue. That there was no consideration for the defendant's agreement.

Fitzgibbon L.J. stated:

> "The agreement of June 25, 1895, was made between father and son; being under seal it did not require valuable consideration to support it, but even if it did, there was, in my opinion, valuable consideration for it in the fact that the defendant got a share in the business during his father's life, and the right of succession to it on his father's death. *Facio ut facias* is just as good consideration as *do ut des*; the deed of partnership contained covenants binding upon both father and son, and it was a contract for valuable consideration on both sides. That being so the parties to it could enforce it."

DUTY IMPOSED BY LAW

(1) A promise in return for performing or promising to perform a public duty imposed by law will will not be enforced if it would be contrary to public policy to do so. The performance of the public duty not being consideration.

Collins v. Godefroy (1883) 1 B&Ad. 950 (K.B.)

Godefroy brought an action against an attorney, for negligence and un-skilfulness in the conduct of an action and he caused Collins to be subpoenaed to attend court as a witness. Collins attended in court for a period of six days but was not called to give evidence. Later he demanded that Godefroy pay him six guineas as his fee for attending and Godefroy said that he thought that it had been paid by his then attorney.

Held: Lord Tenterden, Ch. J.:

> "If it be a duty imposed by law upon a party regularly subpoenaed to attend from time to time to give his evidence, then a promise to give him any remuneration for loss of time incurred in such attendance is a promise without consideration. We think that such a duty is imposed by law. On principle an action does not lie for compensation to a witness for loss of time in attending under a subpoena."

Note: "Where no such grounds of public policy exist, a promise given in consideration of the performance of a public duty can be enforced", Treitel p. 73.

(2) Promising to do or doing more than a duty imposed by law, can amount to consideration

Glasbrook Bros. v. Glamorgan County Council [1925] A.C. 270 (H.L.)

On the occasion of a strike, a colliery manager applied for police protection for his colliery in Glamorganshire and insisted that it could only be efficiently protected by billeting a police force on the premises. The police Superintendent demurred saying that he was able to protect the colliery without installing a police garrison and that in the event of a large body of miners appearing, a mobile force of police could be sent at once.

The colliery manager insisted on a garrison. The Superintendent said that as it would be 'special duty' a requisition must be signed containing a promise to pay. The colliery manager, who had been previously authorised by his directors to sign, assented and signed.

When the strike ended the colliery owners refused to pay, claiming that there was no consideration for the agreement in the requisition, that the police were only carrying out the legal duties and obligations of the county council, and that such an agreement was against public policy. The police authority, Glamorgan County Council instituted proceedings for payment and the company counterclaimed for the expense of housing and maintaining the police at the colliery.

Held: The agreement was not void for want of consideration and it was not contrary to public policy. The garrison formed an additional and not a substituted or alternative means of protection. The police had done more than their legal duty.

> "If in the judgement of the police authority, formed reasonably and in good faith, the garrison was necessary for the protection of life and property they were not entitled to make a charge for it, for that would be to extract a payment for the performance of a duty which they clearly owed to the appellants and their servants; but if they thought the garrison a superfluity and only acceded to Mr. Jones request with a view to meeting his wishes, then in my opinion they were entitled to treat the garrison duty as 'special duty' and to charge for it." — Viscount Cave L.C. at page 282.

DUTY IMPOSED BY STATUTE

It appears that the performance of a legal duty imposed by statute will constitute sufficient consideration for a promise.

Ward v. Byham [1956] 1 W.L.R. 496 (C. A.)

The father of an illegitimate child agreed to pay an allowance of £1 per week to the mother provided the child was well looked after and happy. Later the mother married and the father discontinued the payments. The mother sued to enforce continuance of the payment.

Held: Even though the mother was bound by the provisions of section 42 of the National Assistance Act, 1948 to maintain the child, there was good consideration for the father's promise. *Hicks v. Gregory* (1849) 8 C.B. 378 *followed.*

Denning L.J.:

> "I approach the case, therefore, on the footing that the mother, in looking after the child, is only doing what she is legally bound to do. Even so, I think that there was sufficient consideration to support the promise.
>
> I have always thought that a promise to perform an existing duty, or the performance of it, should be regarded as good consideration, because it is a benefit to the person to whom it is given. Take this very case. It is as much a benefit to the father to have the child looked after by the mother as by a neighbour. If he gets the benefit for which he stipulated, he ought to honour his promise; and he ought not to avoid it by saying that the mother was herself under a duty to maintain the child. I regard the father's promise in this case as what is sometimes called a unilateral contract, a promise in return for an act, a promise by the father to pay £1 a week in return for the mother's looking after the child. Once the mother embarked on the task of looking after the child, there was a binding contract. So long as she looked after the child, she would be entitled to £1 a week. The case seems to me to be within the decision of *Hicks v Gregory*, on which the judge relied. I would dismiss the appeal."

DUTY IMPOSED BY A CONTRACT WTIH THE PROMISSOR

(1) A promise to perform or performance of, a pre-existing contractual duty owed to a promissor, is not consideration for a new promise.

Stilk v. Myrick (1809) 2 Camp. 317 11 R.R. 717

In the course of a voyage from London to the Baltic and back two seamen deserted a ship. The Captain was unable to recruit other seamen to take their places and he entered into an agreement in the port at Cronstadt that if he could not procure replacements for the deserters their wages would be divided equally among the rest of the crew. The ship was worked back to London without the deserters being replaced and the defendant refused to divide the wages as promised. He claimed that crews were often thinned by death and desertion, and that exorbitant claims would be set up on such occasions if the action succeeded.

Held: by Lord Ellenborough:

"There was no consideration for the ulterior pay promised to the mariners who remained with the ship.
Before they sailed from London they had undertaken to do all they could under all emergencies of the voyage. They had sold all their services till the voyage should be completed. The desertion of a part of the crew is to be considered an emergency of the voyage as much as their deaths and those who remained are bound by the terms of their original contract to exert themselves to the utmost to bring the ship in safety to the destined port."

(2) A promise made in return for doing or promising to do, more than one is contractually bound to do for the promissor, will be sufficient consideration.

Hartley v. Ponsonby (1857) 7 E & B. 872, (Q.B.)

The plaintiff, a mariner, agreed by articles to serve on board a ship, the Mobile, on a voyage from Liverpool to Port Philip, Australia and from there to India or China and back to England.
The proper complement of men for the ship was thirty six. While in Port Philip, seventeen of the crew refused to work, and were sent to prison and there were only four or five able seamen among the remaining nineteen crew.
The Master promised, in writing, to pay some of the remaining crew extra money in addition to their wages to sail the ship shorthanded to Bombay, which they did.
On arrival back in England the owner and the Master refused to make this payment.

Held: The jury found that it was unreasonable for a vessel of that size to proceed on the voyage to India with only nineteen hands.

On this finding there was consideration for the contract, which the captain had made without coercion. It was dangerous to life for the ship to go to sea with so few hands. The seamen were not bound by their original contracts to proceed with the diminished number of hands and their undertaking to do so was therefore a good consideration for the Master's promise. The plaintiff was entitled to the extra payment.

DUTY IMPOSED BY A CONTRACT WITH A THIRD PARTY

"A promise to perform, or the performance of a pre-existing contractual obligation to a third party can be valid consideration." *Pao On v. Lau Yiu Long* [1980] A.C. 614, 632.

PROMISE TO PERFORM PRE-EXISTING CONTRACTUAL DUTY

Pau On v. Lau Yiu Long [1980] A.C. 614, (Privy Council)

The plaintiffs agreed in writing with the defendant company (the main agreement) to sell their shares in a private company whose principal asset was a building under construction. No money was to pass, the consideration being the issue of shares in the public company to the plaintiffs.

To protect the plaintiffs against any loss from a possible fall in the value of the shares between the date of acquisition and date on which the could be disposed of (30 April, 1974). the plaintiffs made a subsidiary agreement to sell and the defendant's to buy 60 per cent of the allotted shares which formed the consideration in the main agreement on or before the 30 April, 1974, at $2.50 a share.

When the plaintiffs realised that in protecting themselves from a fall in the share price they had in effect also agreed to forgo any profit from a possible rise they refused to complete the main agreement unless the defendants agreed to cancel the subsidiary agreement and replace it with a guarantee by way of indemnity.

The defendants, fearing a public loss of confidence in their company, signed a written contract of guarantee. The contract of guarantee stated that in consideration of the plaintiffs having agreed to sell their shares in the private company the defendant's agreed to indemnify the plaintiffs for any loss in respect of their 60 per cent share-holding if the price fell below $2.50 a share.

The sale under the main agreement took place but the share price dropped before 30 April and the defendants refused to honour the contract of indemnity. The plaintiffs appealed to the Privy Council on the questions whether there was consideration for the contract of indemnity and whether the defendant's consent was vitiated by duress.

Held:

(1) An act done before the giving of a promise could be valid consideration for that promise if the act had been done at the promissor's request, the parties understood that the act was to be remunerated either by payment or conferment of a benefit and the payment or conferment of a benefit would have been enforceable had it been promised in advance.

The defendant's promise of an indemnity was not independent of the plaintiff's antecedent promise made at the defendants request and therefore **since the guarantee fixed the benefit on the faith of which the plaintiff's antecedent promise had been given**, it **stated a valid consideration for the promise of indemnity**. *In re Casey's Patents* (1892) 1 Ch. 104, C.A. applied.

(2) **Extrinsic evidence was admissible to show** that **the real consideration** for the promise of indemnity was the plaintiffs promise to the defendants to perform their contractual obligations under the main agreement. Since the plaintiffs obligation to the defendants to perform their contract with a third party could be sufficient consideration for the promise of indemnity, the defendants were bound by the contract of guarantee unless there were grounds for avoiding the contract. *New Zealand Shipping Co. Ltd. v. A.M. Satterthwaite & Co. Ltd.* [1975] A.C. 154, P.C. applied.

(3) (See Chapter 12 on Economic Duress) That, although the defendants had been subjected to commercial pressure, the facts disclosed that they had not been coerced into the contract of guarantee and, therefore, the contract was not voidable on the ground of duress; that in the absence of duress, public policy did not require a contract negotiated at arm's length to be invalidated because a party had either threatened to repudiate an existing contractual obligation or had unfairly used his dominant bargaining position in negotiating the agreement and that therefore, the defendants, having failed to show that the contract of guarantee was either invalid or voidable, were bound by its terms.

Note: The artificiality of the distinction in treatment between performance of a contractual duty owed to the promissor and one owed to a third party cannot be justified according to A.G. Guest, *Anson's Law of Contract*, 26th. ed. at p. 96 "by any exercise of legal logic, but only by the policy considerations involved."

Denning L.J. in *Williams v. Williams* [1957] 1 W.L.R. 148 150 stated "a promise to perform an existing duty, is I think, sufficient consideration to support a promise, so long as there is nothing in the transaction which is contrary to the public interest."

PERFORMANCE OF EXISTING DUTY
Williams v. Williams [1957] 1 W.L.R. 148 (C.A.)

The plaintiff wife claimed payments due to her under a maintenance agreement entered into after she had deserted the defendant husband. The agreement provided that the husband would pay a weekly sum during the joint lives of the parties so long as the wife "shall lead a chaste life" and that she would support and maintain herself and indemnify the husband against debts incurred by her and not pledge his credit.

Held: There was consideration, as the wife by her desertion had not forfeited but merely suspended her right to be maintained by her husband, such right would revive if she made a genuine offer to return, in which case the wife's promise would be of no value to the husband. *Goodison v. Goodison* [1954] 2 All E.R. 225 applied.

Per Denning L.J.:

> "There was also consideration in that a promise to perform an existing duty was a sufficient consideration and the wife's promise afforded to the husband an additional and simplified defence to claims which might be made against him by the National Assistance Board or unpaid creditors of the wife.
>
> Now I agree that, in promising to maintain herself whilst she was in desertion, the wife was only promising to do that which she was already bound to do. Nevertheless, a promise to perform an existing duty is, I think, sufficient consideration to support a promise, so long as there is nothing in the transaction which is contrary to the public interest."

PERFORMANCE OF PRE-EXISTING CONTRACTUAL DUTY TO THIRD PARTY

The Eurymedon [1975] A.C. 154 (Privy Council)

A bill of lading for the shipment of a drilling machine from Liverpool to New Zealand discharged the carrier from all liability for loss or damage unless suit was brought within one year. The bill of lading further stipulated that the same immunity was extended to the carrier's servants or agents, including independent contractors.

The carrier was a wholly owned subsidiary company of the stevedore, who acted as the carrier's agent in New Zealand and the carrier had authority to enter into the contract on behalf of the stevedore. As a result of the stevedore's negligence the drill was damaged in unloading and the consignee brought an action, after one year had elapsed, against the stevedore.

Held:

The bill of lading brought into existence a bargain, initially unilateral but capable of becoming mutual, between the shipper and the stevedore made through the carrier as agent.

It became a full contract when the stevedore performed services by unloading goods and the performance of these services for the benefit of the shipper was consideration for the agreement by the shipper that the stevedore should have the benefit of the exemptions in the bill of lading.

PERFORMANCE OF A PRE-EXISTING STATUTORY DUTY IS NOT SUFFICIENT

PRE-CONTRACTRUAL LEGAL OBLIGATION

PMPA v. Keenan & Ors. [1983] I.R. 330 (S.C.)

A trade union acting on behalf of the respondents concluded an agreement with the PMPA compromising their claim for arrears of equal pay. The agreement was "in full and final settlement of all claims". The respondents claimed a further two years entitlement in accordance with the provisions of section 2 of the Anti-Discrimination (Pay) Act, 1974. The appellant claimed that the respondents had waived their claim to past claims in the agreement and were estopped from pursuing the claim further.

Held: (High Court) There had not been a valid waiver of past claims, since the employer would have done nothing that he was not obliged to do by law, therefore there would have been no consideration given to support the waiver. That accordingly the defendants were not estopped from making their claim.

Held:by the Supreme Court in disallowing the appeal:
(1) That the reference in the agreement to the settlement of "all claims" must be construed in the light of the salary claims made in the course of negotiations leading to that agreement.
(2) That, as there was no evidence that the defendants claim constituted an element in those negotiations, the words "all claims" did not preclude the defendants from making their present claim.

Henchy J.:

"Any compromise of the female employees present claim for less that the entitlement under the Act of 1974 would be unlawful."

Note: See also *Collins v. Godefroy* (1831) 1 B & Ad 950. As to performance of pre-existing contractual duty see *Stilk v. Myrick* (1809) 2 Camp. 317 and *Hartley v. Ponsonby* (1857) 7 E. & B. 872.

THE RULE IN PINNEL'S CASE

When payment of a debt has fallen due a part payment (i.e. payment of a lesser sum that the amount of the debt) does not discharge the debt. However, part payment at the creditor's request when accompanied by additional consideration, will give a good discharge of a larger debt. At equity despite the absence of consideration, if a promise by a creditor to accept a smaller sum in satisfaction of a larger debt, is acted on by the debtor the creditor will be bound by the promise.

PART PAYMENT OF A DEBT AND THE RULE IN PINNEL'S CASE

Pinnel's Case (1602) 5 Co. Rep. 117

Pinnel brought an action against Cole for payment of a debt of £8.10s. due on the 11th November 1600. The defendant pleaded that at the first instance of the plaintiff he had paid the sum of £5.2s.2d. on the 1st October and that the plaintiff had accepted it in full satisfaction of the debt.

Held: Judgment for the plaintiff. The defendant had not pleaded that he had paid the £5.2.2d. in full satisfaction (as by law he ought).

It was resolved by the Court of Common Pleas:

> "that payment of a lesser sum on the day in satisfaction of a greater, cannot be any satisfaction for the whole . . . But the gift of a horse, hawk or robe, etc. in satisfaction is good . . . For it shall be intended that a horse, hawk or robe, etc. might be more beneficial to the plaintiff than the money in respect of some circumstances . . . ."

Note: But for the defect in pleading, the payment and acceptance of the lesser amount before the due date would have constituted sufficient consideration to discharge the debt and resulted in judgment for the defendant.

This rule in Pinnel's case (1602) was approved by the House of Lords in *Foakes v. Beer* (1884) 9 App. Cas. 605 over two hundred and eighty years later.

Foakes v. Beer (1884) 9 App. Cas. 605

Foakes a judgment debtor and Beer, his creditor signed an agreement in 1876, that in consideration of his paying the debt and costs by instalments, the creditor (Beer) could not take any proceedings. In 1882 when the debt and costs had been paid Julia Beer issued proceedings claiming payment of interest on the debt. Cave J. was of opinion that whether the judgment was satisfied or not, by reason of the agreement, not entitled to issue execution for any sum on the judgment. Cave J. was of opinion that whether the judgment was satisfied or not, the respondent was, by reason of the agreement, not entitled to issue execution for any sum on the judgment. The Court of Appeal gave judgment for the respondent and the debtor appealed.

Held: The agreement was a *nudum pactum*, being without consideration, and ddi not prevent the creditor from proceedings to enforce payment of the interest after the whole debt and costs had been paid. *Pinnel's* case (5 Co. Rep. 117) and *Cumber v. Wane* (1 Str. 426) followed.

Earl of Shelbourne L.C.:

> "No doubt if the appellant had been under no antecedent obligation to pay the whole debt, his fulfilment of the condition might have imported some consideration on his part for the promise. But he was under that antecedent obligation; and payment at those deferred dates, by the forbearance and indulgence of the creditor, of the residue of the principle debt and costs, could not (in my opinion) be a consideration for the relinquishment of interest and discharge of the judgment . . ."

The common law exceptions to the rule are:

(1) Payment of a smaller sum than the amount of the debt, if made **at the creditor's request, before the day payent falls due** is sufficient consideration.

(2) Payment of a smaller sum than the amount of the debt, at **different place, at the creditor's request** is sufficient consideration.

(3) Payment of a smaller sum than the amount of the debt, **with the addition of delivery of a chattel at the creditor's request** is sufficient consideration.

(4) The rule does not apply **where the creditor's claim is disputed.**

(5) The rule does not apply where the amount is an **unliquidated one.**

(6) A creditor who receives a smaller payment than his debt as a result of a **composition agreement** will not be entitled to the balance.

(7) If **the creditor accepts partial payment of the debt from a third party** in full settlement, the debt is discharged and he cannot later succeed against the original debtor for the balance. *Welby v. Drake* (1925) 1 C&P 557.

EXCEPTION TO THE RULE AT EQUITY

Under the doctrine of promissory estoppel (see Chapter 4) where a creditor by his words or actions leads a debtor to believe that he will not enforce his strict legal rights regarding payments due under a contract and the debtor acts in reliance on this promise. (See *Central London Property Trust Ltd. v. High Trees House Ltd.*) the creditor will be prevented or stopped from going back on his promise where it would be equitable for him to do so.

Note: As to whehter the effect of the promise is suspensive or extinctive contrast *Central London Property Trust Ltd. v. High Trees Ltd.* (1947) K.B. 130, *Hughes v. Metropolitan Railway Co.* (1877) 2 App. Cas. 439 with *Jorden v. Money* (1854) 5 H.L. Cas. 185. See A.G. Guest, *Ansons, Law of Contract*, 26th ed., page 104. The exact intention of the parties, the nature of the transaction and the particular facts of the case undoubtedly influence a court in this regard. When a debt is an ongoing or rolling one, like payments under a lease it appears that the effect of a promise to forego part payment is suspensive rather than extinctive. But if the promise indicates an unequivocal intention to renounce or waive all right to payment of a sum due it may be extinctive. See *Brikom Investments Ltd. v. Carr* (1979) Q.B. 467, 484-485.

RULES OF CONSIDERATION

CONSIDERATION MUST MOVE FROM THE PROMISEE
M'Coubray v. Thomson [1868] 2 I.R. C.L. 226 (Q.B.)

A Mr. Galway agreed with M'Coubray and Thomson that in consideration of him handing over and transferring possession of his farm and chattels valued at £196 to Thomson, Thomson would pay £98 to M'Coubray. When the farm was handed over Thomson did not pay the £98 and was sued by M'Coubray.

Held: The promise of Thomson was made to Galway from whom the consideration moved. No person can maintain an action on a parol contract unless consideration moves from him. *Price v. Easton* (1833) 4 B & Ad, 433 applied.

Note: See also *Tweedle v. Atkinson* (1861) 1 B&S 393.

CONSIDERATION NEED NOT BE ADEQUATE
In re Metro Investment Trust Ltd.
unreported, 26 May 1977 (H.C.) McWilliam J.

S brought proceedings against I. These proceedings were compromised on terms whereby S got judgment with a stay of execution to enable I to pay by instalments. In consideration of this forbearance Metro Investment Trust Ltd., a sister company gave a joint and several promissory note to pay the debt.

The liquidator of Metro opposed the claim on the ground that it was *ultra vires* and void, there being no benefit to Metro from the transaction.

Held: However trifling the detriment to S of the forbearance it exercised it was entitled to have the debt admitted. S was not claiming a gratuitous payment, although the assistance given by Metro to Invest appeared to have been gratuitous. To this extent *Charterbridge Corp. v. Lloyds Bank* [1969] 3 W L.R. 122 (Ch.D.) most resembled the present case.

McWilliam J.:

> "The Court found that such a transaction could, under the circumstances have been of benefit to the company giving it and a third party who enters into a transaction involving a company which has power to enter into that transaction is not concerned to investigate the possibility of the transaction not being for the benefit of the company."

CONSIDERATION MUST BE REAL OR GENUINE
White v. Bluett (1853) 23 L.J. Ex. 36, 98 R.R. 492

When the defendant was sued upon a promissory note which he had given to his deceased father, he claimed that his father had agreed to discharge him from all liability for the debt in consideration for him ceasing to complain that he had not received as much money or advantages as the other children. His father also agreed to discharge him from the debt to do justice to him and because of the father's natural love and affection.

Held: The plea must fail. The defendant had not given any consideration for the promise by his father. The son had no right to complain for the father could make any distribution of his property he liked, and the son's abstaining from doing what he had no right to do could be no consideration.

Pollock C.B.:

> "It is said, the son had a right to an equal distribution of his father's property, and did complain to his father because he had not an equal share, and said to him, I will cease to complain if you will not sue upon this note. Whereupon the father said, if you will promise not to complain I will give up the note. If such a plea as this could be supported, the following would be a binding promise. A man might complain that another person used the highway more than he ought to do, and that other might say, 'Do not complain, and I will give you five pounds.' It is ridiculous to suppose that such promises could be binding.
>
> So if the holder of a bill of exchange were suing the acceptor, and the acceptor were to complain that the holder had treated him hardly, or that the bill ought never to have been circulated, and the holder were to say, 'Now, if you will not make any more complaints I will not sue you.' Such a promise would be like that now set up."

Alderson B.:

> "If the agreement were good, there could be no such thing as a nudum pactum."

Note: Study the distinction between *Ward v. Byham* and *White v. Bluett*. Treitel, *The Law of Contract*, 7th ed.p.74 states "But if a son's promise not to bore his father is not good consideration, it is hard to see why a mother's promise to make her child happy should stand on a different footing The better explanation of the case therefore seems to be that given by Lord Denning L.J. viz., that the mother provided consideration by merely performing her legal duty to support the child."

Could the answer be that one case involved the discharge of a statutory duty while the other involved the discharge of a contractual duty?

CONSIDERATION MUST BE SUFFICIENT
O'Neill v. Murphy [1936] N.I. 16 (N.I.C.A.)

The plaintiff sued for payment for architectural services and claimed inter alia that there was no consideration for an agreement by him not to insist on payment of his fee. The defendant claimed that daily prayers offered in every house of the Cross and Passion Order for the plaintiff's intentions was the consideration given for his agreement.

Held: A mere promise by one person to say prayers or to cause prayers to be said for another does not amount in law to a good and valuable consideration. There was no sufficient consideration in law for the agreement: Andrews L.J.

FORBEARANCE CAN CONSTITUTE CONSIDERATION
Barry v. Barry (1) (1891) L.R. Ir. Vol. 28 45 (Q.B.D.)

The plaintiff Edward Barry and the defendant, his elder brother, John, were sons of John Barry, senior. Upon the marriage of his eldest son, John the father assigned part of his farm held under a yearly tenancy, in trust for John on the 8th February 1877. but continued to reside on and manage the farm until his death, John and the other members of his family residing with him.

On 13th December, 1885 John Barry senior, taking no notice of the previous settlement made and executed a will, bequeathing the whole of the lands at Lyredane to the same son, the defendant. subject to certain legacies and *inter alia* a legacy of £20 to the plaintiff. After the testators death, his executors, in the presence of the plaintiff Edward, asked John, (the eldest son) would he "possess" and pay the legacies and the defendant said that he would.

He did not pay the £20 legacy to the plaintiff who sued for payment plus interest.

Held: The statement that he would "possess" the lands meant that the elder brother elected to take under the will. There was sufficient consideration for his promise to pay the legacy of £20. The consideration was in the nature of forbearance.

The plaintiff exercised forbearance, he might have taken steps to enforce payment of his legacy, by means of proceedings against the land or assets, but he entered into an agreement by which he agreed to give up his right to go against the property, and to permit the defendant to hold it, and the defendant undertook personally to pay the sum of £20.

The defendant got an advantage to which he was not entitled: the plaintiff could have objected.

Note: See also *Blanford & Houdret Ltd. v. Bray Travel (Holdings) Ltd. & Anor.*

unreported, High Court, 11 November, 1983 where it was held that the consideration given by the plaintiff for obtaining the contract by Bray Travel Ltd., to discharge its indebtedness and by Bray Travel (Holdings) Ltd., to guarantee these payments, was the forbearance of Blanford and Houdret to insist upon withdrawing the flights because of the non clarification of the accounts.

CONSIDERATION MUST NOT BE PAST
Provincial Bank of Ireland v. Donnell [1934] N.I. 33 (N.I.C.A.)

Mrs Donnell signed a guarantee in favour of the bank "in consideration of advances, heretofore made or that may hereafter be made . . .". The bank sued on the guarantee.

Held: There was not sufficient consideration to support the guarantee because:
    (1) as regards past advances, the agreement was not forbearance to sue and
    (2) as regards future advances that might be made, there was no agreement binding the bank to make any advance and none had in fact been made. The guarantee was conditional. The defendant would be bound if the condition were fulfilled, but not otherwise.

CONSIDERATION MUST BE CERTAIN
Carr v. Phelan unreported, 18 June 1976 (H.C.) Hamilton J.

C leased premises at Market Street, Bagenalstown, Co. Carlow from P. A clause in the lease gave an option to purchase the fee simple. The consideration payable was to be the number of years purchase "as shall be ascertained under the provisions of the Landlord and Tenant (Ground Rent) Act, 1967 as if the rent was a ground rent." (i. e. determined by the County Registrar.)
    The Carlow County Registrar refused to determine the purchase price for the fee simple because the provisions of the Landlord and Tenant (Ground Rents) Act, 1967 did not apply to the premises. C applied for a mandatory injunction to compel P to convey the fee simple.

Held: The agreed mode of ascertaining the price having failed a decree for specific performance could not be granted. There was no contract between the parties until the consideration had been ascertained, price being of the essence of a contract for sale.

See *Scammell v. Ouston* [1941] A.C.

CHAPTER 4

Estoppel and Legitimate Expectation

Estoppel is a rule of law by which a party is prevented from denying the truth of facts he has stated previously, from reneging on a promise or from insisting on his strict legal rights. It was described by Blackstone (Com. (1794) Bk. 3. 307-8) in the following terms "An estoppel is likewise a special plea in bar which happens where a man hath done some act, or executed some deed, which estops or precludes him from averring anything to the contrary." In *Cave v. Mills* (1862) 7 H & N 913 at 927-928 Wilde B. stated "A man shall not be allowed to blow hot and cold, to affirm at one time and deny at another, making a claim on those whom he has deluded to their disadvantage, and founding that claim on the very matters of the delusion. Such a principle has its basis in common sense and common justice."

"There is said to be an estoppel where a party is not allowed to say that a certain statement of fact is untrue, whether in reality it is true or not. Estoppel, or "conclusion" as it was frequently called by the older authorities may therefore be defined as a disability whereby a party is precluded from alleging or proving in legal proceedings that a fact is otherwise than it had been made to appear by the matter giving rise to that disability." (See *Halsbury's Laws of England*, 4td ed., para. 1501).

Denning M.R. explained:

> "For the word 'estoppel' only means stopped. . . . Someone is stopped from saying something or other, or doing something or other, or contesting something or other. (*Mcilkenny v. West Midlands Police Force* [1980] 2 All ER 227 at 235) The doctrine of estoppel is one of the most flexible and useful in the armoury of the law. . . . It has evolved during the last 150 years in a sequence of separate developments: proprietary estoppel, estoppel by representation of fact, estoppel by acquiescence and promissory estoppel." (*Amalgamated Investment & Property Co. Ltd. v. Texas Commerce International Bank Ltd.* [1981] 3 All ER 577 at 584.

At common law and equity this doctrine was confined to statements of existing fact and did not apply to promises. See *Morrow v. Carthy*. In the case of *Central London Property Trust Ltd. v. High Trees House Ltd.* [1947] K.B. 130. The reliance interest was developed to cover promises on the basis that it would be unconscionable in circumstances where a party has made a promise which he intends should be relied upon and which is relied upon by another who alters his situation to his detriment to allow the promissor to deny his promise **even though it was not given in return for some consideration**. This is known as promissory estoppel or quasi estoppel. Promissory estoppel was referred to by Roskill L.J. in *Brikom Investments Ltd. v. Carr* (1979) Q.B. 467 as a "somewhat uncertain doctrine". The doctrine of "legitimate expectation" is another aspect of the equitable concept of promissory estoppel first dealt with under this nomenclature by the Supreme Court in *Webb v. Ireland* (1988) I.R. 353.

Estoppel has been described as a rule of evidence: because you cannot found an action upon an estoppel: (*Low v Bouverie* (1891) 3 Ch. 882 at 105) This means that it may only be used as a defence i.e. as a shield. It may not be used as a cause of action i.e. as a sword,.per Denning M.R. in *Combe v. Combe* [1951] 2 K.B. 215, but where only a declaration is sought by a plaintiff it may be possible to invoke the the doctrine.

Proprietary estoppel relates to land or goods and is an application of the equitable doctrine of acquiescence whereby a party who leads another to expend money on property in reliance on a promise to transfer title to it is estopped from asserting ownership. Estoppel by acquiescence is an example of estoppel by words or conduct whereby a person who stands idly by (in such a way as to indicate assent) while another commits an act infringing a right, cannot afterwards disavow the act.

ESTOPPEL AT COMMON LAW AND EQUITABLE ESTOPPEL
Morrow v. Carthy [1957] N.I. 174 (Ch. D.)

The plaintiff was the successful bidder for a bungalow at a public auction. It was a condition of sale that the deposit should be paid in cash immediately after the sale. He signed the purchase agreement but was unable to pay the deposit and was allowed one hour to produce it. He failed to return within that time and the bungalow was resold to another person.

The plaintiff arrived later and tendered a cheque in payment of the deposit. This was refused and he was told that the bungalow had been resold. He now claimed specific performance of the original contract or alternatively of the contract as "rectified" in relation to the condition regarding payment of the deposit.

Held: The deposit was required to be paid in cash. The plaintiff had not shown that he was ready and willing to perform his obligation. Specific performance must be refused.

Held further: There was no estoppel at common law since there was no representation of existing fact. Equitable estoppel did not apply since the statement did not cause him to alter his position to his detriment.

ESTOPPEL WHERE THERE IS A LIABILITY TO PAY MONEY
Revenue Commissioners v. Moroney [1972] I.R. 372 (S.C.)

The father of the defendants executed a deed assigning a licensed premises at Pearse Street, Dublin to himself and to the two defendants in consideration of £16,000, the receipt of which was acknowledged in the deed. It was a paper transaction and the £16,000 was never paid or intended to be paid.

When the father died the Revenue Commissioners claimed that two thirds of the £16,000 was a debt due to the fathers estate and that estate duty was chargeable on it.

Held: (Kenny J. High Court) The representations of the deceased before the execution of the deed brought the doctrine of promissory estoppel into effect and would have prevented him from enforcing any right to payment of the purchase money. There was no debt due to the father's estate and the plaintiffs' claim failed.

Held: (Supreme Court) The doctrine of promissory estoppel arose in a case such as the present one only when there was a liability in law to pay the money. There was never any indebtedness and therefore the question of the deceased's representation causing the defendants to enter into such a liability did not exist. It was unnecessary to express any view of the application of promissory estoppel to a case such as this.

The fact that there was no consideration, could be established in evidence notwithstanding a statement to the contrary in the deed.

Note: Parol evidence could be admitted as an exception to the parol evidence rule.

A CONTRACT BY ESTOPPEL
Clayton Love v. B & I [1970] I.L.T.R.157 (S.C.)

The plaintiff claimed that they contracted for the shipment of scampi from Dublin to Liverpool, on the basis that it would be loaded into a ships hold which was already refrigerated and at a temperature of 28 to 20 degrees Fahrenheit. The defendant claimed that they contracted on the basis that the scampi would be loaded at atmospheric temperature. The parties were not *ad idem* because of mutual mistake.

Held: Even where the parties were not *ad idem* there can nevertheless be a contract by estoppel. (*Freeman v. Cooke*, 2 Ex. 654.) The terms proposed by the plaintiff and accepted by the defendant were that the scampi was to be carried as a refrigerated cargo and loaded into a hold which was refrigerated at the time.

Estoppel entered in only in determining whether there was a contract and what were its terms. The rights the plaintiff sought to enforce flowed from that contract that had been established by the application of the doctrine of estoppel. The defendants did not have a valid objection that estoppel is a weapon of defence and could not afford the plaintiffs a cause of action.

REPRESENTATION OF INTENTION
The rule in **Hughes v. Metropolitan Railway Co.**
(1877) 2 App. Cas. 439 (H.L.) (E.)

On the 22 October 1874 the respondents M were given a notice to repair houses at Euston Road which they leased from the appellant within six months. On the 28 November agents for the respondents wrote to solicitors of the applicant freeholder asking if he desired to buy out their leasehold interest and that they intended to defer commencing repairs until they got a reply. Inconclusive negotiations took place and on the 19 April the respondents stated they would commence the repairs. The six months notice to repair expired on 22 April and on the 28 April an ejectment notice was served on M for breach of the covenant to repair within the six months.

Held: that the company was entitled in Equity to be relieved against forfeiture, for the letters had the effect of suspending the notice. The appeal must be dismissed.

Lord Cairns L.C.:

> ". . . it is the first principle upon which all courts of Equity proceed, that if parties who have entered into definite and distinct terms involving certain legal results — certain penalties or legal forfeiture — afterwards by their own act or with their own consent enter upon a course of negotiation which has the effect of leading one of the parties to suppose that the strict rights arising under the contract will not be enforced, or will be kept in suspense, or held in abeyance, the person who otherwise might have enforced those rights will not be allowed to enforce them where it would be inequitable having regard to the dealings which have thus taken place between the parties."

Note: Treitel, *The Law of Contract*, 7th ed. London, 1987 states at pages 86, 92 and 93 that this doctrine is often (misleadingly) referred to as equitable or promissory estoppel. While the doctrine has certain features in common with estoppel by representation It is closer to the common law rules of waiver. The doctrine in Hughes is a representation of intention or a promise; whereas estoppel by representation can only be based on a representation of existing fact. (*Jorden v. Money* (1854) 5 HLC 185)

PROMISSORY ESTOPPEL — QUASI-ESTOPPEL

Central London Property Trust Ltd. v. High Trees House Ltd.
[1947] 1 K.B. 1130 (K.B.D.)

The plaintiff company let a block of flats to the defendant company by a lease under seal in September 1937, at a rent of £2,500 a year. Early in 1940, owing to war conditions prevailing only a few of the flats were let and following discussion the plaintiff company agreed by letter to reduce the rent to £1,250. In September 1945 (when all the flats were let) the plaintiffs wrote to the defendants claiming that rent was payable at £2,500 a year. The defendants pleaded that the agreement to reduce the rent operated for the whole term of the lease and that the plaintiffs were estopped from demanding the higher rent.

Held: that when parties enter into an arrangement which is intended to create legal relations between them, and in pursuance of such an arrangement one party makes a promise to the other which he knows will be acted on and which is in fact acted on by the promisee, the court will treat the promise as binding on the promissor to the extent that it will not allow him to act inconsistent with it.

This is so **even though the promise may not be supported by consideration in the strict sense** and the effect off the arrangement made is to vary the terms of a contract under seal by one of less value.

The agreement fell within this category, and was binding on the plaintiff, but it only remained operative so long as the conditions giving rise to it continued to exist. From the evidence it was a temporary expedient.

Note: Denning J. stated that with regard to estoppel the representation was not one of existing fact but that the law had not stood still since *Jorden v. Money* and in a series of cases had stated that a promise must be honoured. These were not cases of estoppel in the strict sense. They were really promises intended to be binding, intended to be acted on, and in fact acted on. The courts had not gone so far as to give a cause of action in damages for the breach of such a promise but they had refused to allow the party making it to act inconsistently with it.

ESTOPPEL AS A SHIELD NOT AS A SWORD

Cullen v. Cullen [1962] I.R. 268 (H. C.) Kenny J.

The plaintiff carried on a business of a licensed grocer and merchant at Adamstown, Co. Wexford. There was also a small farm attached to the business.

In 1959 the plaintiff was examined by a mental specialist at his wife's request, and diagnosed as having a paranoid illness. An attempt was made to move him to a mental hospital but he escaped to Dublin. While in Dublin, he sent a message to his wife that he was transferring the property at Adamstown to her, and that she should carry on the business in her own name. In return he required a signed statement from his wife and sons that he was sane and the withdrawal of any order of arrest to commit him to a mental hospital.

The wife won a portable house in a competition and she gave it to her son M. She sought her husband's permission to have the house erected on the lands at Adamstown. The husband replied that he was making the place over to her and she could erect the house where she liked.

Some time later the plaintiff took an action *inter alia* for an injunction to exclude M from the house and lands at Adamstown and M counterclaimed that he was entitled to the house he had built and the site on which it stood and that the plaintiff be made convey it to him.

Held: An injunction would not be granted to the plaintiff. M could not require the plaintiff to convey the site of the house, but the plaintiff was estopped by his conduct from asserting his title to it.

Semble (It appears): After twelve years M. could bring a successful application under s.52 of The Registration of Title Act, 1891, to be registered as owner.

Note: R. Byrne and W. Binchy in the *Annual Review of Irish Law*, 1991, The Round Hall Press, suggest that in *Sun Fat Chan v. Osseous Ltd.* [1991] 30 July, Supreme Court, the plaintiff was arguably not automatically debarred from High Trees. In that case the plaintiff was seeking a declaration that a contract was a valid and subsisting one. The authors state "Whilst a declaration can have a remedial dimension, it should surely be categorised jurisprudentially in neutral terms, a declaration may be invoked by a prospective defendant in hypothetically or actually forthcoming judicials just as much as by a prospective plaintiff." The son, while seeking the declaration was the one against whom the putative legal rights had been asserted.

LEGITIMATE EXPECTATION
Webb v. Ireland [1988] I.R. 353 (S.C.)

The plaintiffs claimed enforcement by the court of a right of reward in respect of so much of the Derrynaflan hoard as constituted "Treasure Trove" which they found by using metal detectors on an island owned by other persons. They claimed that they had a legitimate expectation to a reward based on the practices of the British Treasury prior to 1922 and of the National Museum since that time in paying rewards in respect of findings of antique objects and of the general approach to such rewards. In particular they relied on a statement made by the Director of the National Museum that they would be treated honourably.

Held: The unqualified assurance given to the first plaintiff by the Director of the National Museum that he would be treated honourably was an integral part of the transaction under which the hoard was deposited in the Museum and accepted on behalf of the State, and the State could not now, go back on that assurance.

It must be given effect to, in the form of a monetary award of an amount which was reasonable in the light of all relevant circumstances.

Finlay C.J.:

> "It would appear that the doctrine of 'legitimate expectation' sometimes described as 'reasonable expectation', has not in those terms been the subject matter of any decision of our courts. However, the doctrine connoted by such expressions is but an aspect of the well recognised equitable concept of promissory estoppel (which has been frequently applied in our courts), whereby a promise or representation as to intention may in certain circumstances be held binding on the representor or promissor.
>
> The nature and extent of that doctrine in circumstances such as those of this case has been expressed as follows by Lord Denning M.R. in *Amalgamated Property Co. Texas Bank* [1982] Q.B. 84, 122:
>
> 'When the parties to a transaction proceed on the basis of an underlying assumption — either of fact or of law — whether due to misrepresentation or mistake makes no difference — on which they have conducted the dealings between them — neither of them will be allowed to go back on that assumption when it would be unfair or unjust to allow him to do so. If one of them does seek to go back on it, the courts will give the other such remedy as the equity of the case demands'. . . ."

CHAPTER 5

Form

Certain contracts will not be enforced by the courts unless they are in the form prescribed by law. Some contracts must be by deed, some contracts must be in writing, and some contracts are required to be evidenced in writing.

Contracts required to be **by deed** are; a conveyance of title to land, a lease of land for more than a year, a legal mortgage of land, and a contract not supported by consideration. NOTE; that there is a difference between a conveyance of land which must be by deed, and a contract for the sale of land which must be evidenced in writing under the Statute of Frauds (Ireland) Act, 1695.

Contracts which **must be in writing** are those required to be in writing by specific Acts of the Oireachtas e. g. Hire Purchase contracts by virtue of the Hire Purchase Acts 1946-1960.

Contracts which must be **evidenced in writing** are those prescribed by Section 2 Statute of Frauds 1695 as follows:

> "And be it further enacted by the authority aforesaid that **no action shall be brought** whereby to charge any executor or administrator **upon any special promise**, to answer damages out of his own estate or whereby to charge the defendant upon any special promise, **to answer for the debt, default, or miscarriage of another person**, or **to charge any person upon any agreement made upon consideration of marriage**, or **upon any contract or sale of lands, tenements, or hereditaments, or any interest in or concerning them, or upon any agreement that is not to be performed within the space of one year from the making thereof, unless the agreement** upon which such action shall be brought, **or some memorandum or note thereof, shall be in writing, and signed by the party to be charged therewith, or some other person thereunto by him lawfully authorised.**"

The matters which should be included in the note or memorandum in order to satisfy section 2 of the Statute of Frauds have been established by case law and some relevant Irish cases on description of the parties, *Bacon & Co. v. Kavanagh* and on sufficiency of the memorandum, *Barrett v. Costello* and *Davis v. Gallagher* are included.

If one document on its own is insufficient to satisfy the requirements of s.2 of the Statute of Frauds joinder of documents is sometimes possible *Crane v. Naughton*, and was in fact possible in *McQuaid v. Lynam*.

In the past courts frequently had to consider whether a note or memorandum in writing which contained the words "subject to contract" was sufficient to satisfy the requirements of the statute and to support a decree for specific performance. In some cases the courts first establish if there has been an oral agreement between the parties on all the material terms of the contract, (See *Boyle v. Lee and Goyns* (S.C.) [1992] ILRM 65 Ch 1. ante) or if something fundamental still remains to be agreed. If there has been agreement on all material terms, the courts then address the problem of the sufficiency of the note or memorandum.

CONTRACT REQUIRED TO BE UNDER SEAL

Athy Guardians v. Murphy [1896] 1 I.R. 65 (Ch.D.)

The defendant signed an agreement at a meeting of the Castledermot Dispensary Committee agreeing to sell a plot of land in Main Street, Castledermot for a sum of £60 as a site for a dispensary and doctor's residence. The committee purported to act as agents for the Athy Guardians and the agreement was signed on their behalf by the Chairman.

The defendant subsequently withdrew his offer, and refused to carry out the agreement. The dispensary committee did not have the authority of the Athy Guardians to contract to purchase of land but their actions were ratified by the Guardians who then sought specific performance.

Section 201 of the Public Health (Ireland) Act, 1878 provided (1) Every contract made by a sanitary authority whereof the value or amount exceeds fifty pounds shall be in writing and sealed with the common seal of such authority.

Held: There being nothing under the seal of the Guardians to give effect to the agreement in the only way in which they could bind themselves — there was not any contract which could be ratified by them. The Guardians were not entitled to enforce the agreement.

Note: The agents had no authority under seal either original or retrospective. The ratification was by a resolution passed at a meeting of the Guardians, entered in the minutes and marked approved. There was no ratification under seal which was also a fatal objection.

PROMISE TO ANSWER FOR THE DEBT OF ANOTHER

GUARANTEE

Fennell v. Mulcahy (1845) 8 I.L.R. 434 (Exch.)

An agent of the plaintiff seized stock belonging to a tenant of the plaintiffs as distress for £104 arrears of rent outstanding. The agent was later approached by the tenant accompanied by the defendant Mulcahy who requested that the distress be withdrawn on his undertaking to pay the arrears due, within a reasonable time.

In reliance on this promised the plaintiff withdrew the distress and returned the goods to the tenant, but the defendant did not pay. The plaintiff sued the defendant on foot of his promise, claiming that the promise was a valid contract, did not come within the provisions of the Statute of Frauds, and did not have to be evidenced in writing.

Held: This was a collateral undertaking to pay the debt of another (i.e. a guarantee), and not being reduced to writing, was void under the Statute of Frauds.

Note: The requirements of the Statute of Frauds only apply to a promise "**to answer for the debt, default, or miscarriage of another person**" i.e. to a promise which is a guarantee, they do not apply to an indemnity. The main distinction is that under a contract of guarantee the guarantor only has secondary liability. The debtor has primary liability. The promise of the guarantor is a collateral promise. Under a contract of indemnity the indemnifier undertakes primary liability and his promise is an original, not a collateral one. No note or memorandum is necessary to enforce a contract of indemnity.

INDEMNITY

Dunville & Co. Ltd. v. Quinn [1908] 42 I.L.T.R. 49 (Cir. App.) (C.A.)

The defendant, a solicitor was acting for the vendor and also the purchaser of a hotel. At the request of the vendor he wrote to the plaintiffs who were threatening legal action stating "I will pay you the amount of your account out of the proceeds of the sale . . . your account will certainly be paid in full." The purchase money was subsequently paid directly to the vendor, who paid off other creditors to the exclusion of the plaintiff. The plaintiff issued a writ against the defendant solicitor for the amount of their account.

Held: The defendant was liable on his undertaking to pay the account as it amounted to a promise to see that the plaintiffs were paid out of the proceeds and it was not conditional on the proceeds of the sale coming into his hands.

CONTRACT FOR SALE OF LANDS

May not be void for all purposes although there is no note or memorandum as required by the Statute of Frauds.

Lord Bellew's Estate [1921] 1 I.R. 174 (Ch. D.)

For the purpose of aiding the sale of estates under the Irish Land Act, 1903, the Land Commission could pay the vendor of each estate sold, a sum calculated at the rate of twelve per cent on the amount of the purchase money advanced under the Land Purchase Acts. If the purchase agreement was entered into after the 24th November, 1908 the percentage payable was on a sliding scale instead of the twelve per cent.

The negotiations for the sale of the Chatsworth Estate, near Kilkenny, began on the 1st October, 1908 and concluded on the 7th. October, but it was not until after the 24th November that the agreements were actually reduced to writing and signed. The Land Commission certified for payment on the sliding scale and the plaintiff claimed entitlement to payment at the twelve per cent rate.

Held: Section 2 of the Irish Statute of Frauds did not say that the agreement is void for all purposes if it is not reduced to writing, it did not affect the validity of the contract. It followed that a concluded agreement although not in writing, cannot be ignored or treated as void. A valid agreement for the purchase of the two estates was entered into before the 24th November, 1908 and the vendor was entitled to a percentage at the rate of twelve per cent.

AGREEMENT NOT TO BE PERFORMED WITHIN ONE YEAR

Naughton v. Limestone Land Co. Ltd.
[1952] Ir. Jur. Rep. 18 (H.C.) Dixon J.

The plaintiff was employed by the defendants as a farm labourer. He claimed that in the month of November, 1946 the defendants through their agent entered into a verbal contract with him whereby they agreed that in consideration of his going to England for a period of three months, to study and learn under-draining, they would have work available for him on his return for a period of four years at the same wages as those paid in England.

He went to England for the three months, learned the under-draining and returned to work for the defendant who failed to pay him at the English rate of wage.

Held: The agreement was to be performed in four years and three months and could not be regarded otherwise than as a contract not to be performed within a year. The Statute of Frauds had to be applied and the absence of any note or memorandum in writing signed by the defendants meant that the agreement was unenforceable.

Farrington v. Donohue [1866] I.R. I.C.L. 675 (C.P.)

The plaintiff was the mother of an illegitimate child, alleged to be the daughter of the defendants brother, who died in 1859.

The plaintiff claimed that during his life the deceased had paid her £44 a year for the support of the child, and that after his death, the defendant, his brother, paid her £5, and promised orally to pay her £20 a year for the support of the child "until she was able to support herself." Payment of the allowance stopped after July, 1862 and the plaintiff sued, the child being six years of age at the time.

Held: A parol agreement to maintain a child, known to be about five years old, until she was able to 'do for herself', is "an agreement not to be performed within a year" within the meaning of the Statute of Frauds, and required to be in writing if it was to be enforceable.

It was an agreement not to be performed within a year even though it could have been ended within the year by the death of the child (a collateral event).

Note: See also *In the Goods of Good, decd.*, High Court, unreported, Hamilton P., 14 July 1986.

SALE OF LAND — SUFFICIENCY OF MEMORANDUM
Barrett v. Costelloe, 107 I.L.T.S.J. 239 (H.C.) Kenny J.

The only written evidence of the contract did not contain a date for granting possession, a figure for a deposit or any reference to title.

Held: The only terms which must appear in the written contract are those regarded by the parties as material provisions stipulated in the prior oral agreement.

On the evidence the matters omitted from the correspondence and relied on as constituting a sufficient memorandum to satisfy the Statute of Frauds, were not, in the circumstances of the case, of importance to the parties. A valid contract adequately evidenced existed.

DESCRIPTION OF THE PARTIES
Bacon & Co. Ltd. v. Kavanagh, 42 I.L.T. 120 (K.B.D.)

The plaintiffs required a traveller employed by them to obtain a guarantee against any loss which they might sustain by continuing to employ him. The defendant gave a written guarantee as follows.

Carnew,
August 30th, 1904

I hereby guarantee you against loss of any money by Mr. Hayes while in your employment to the amount of 40 pounds (40).

Kate Kavanagh.
Commercial Hotel, Carnew

The traveller Hayes, became indebted to the firm for £25 odd which he failed to pay and the firm sought to recover this amount from Miss Kavanagh the guarantor.

It was submitted for the defence that the document was not a sufficient memorandum within the Statute of Frauds because the plaintiffs were not named in it, and the word "**you**" was the only description of the person intended to benefit from the guarantee.

Held: On the uncontradicted evidence given in court it was clear that the plaintiffs were the persons referred to by the words "**you**" and "**your employment**".

The words formed a sufficient description and the document was a sufficient note within the Statute of Frauds. *Williams v. Byrnes* 1 Moore P.C. (n.s.) 154 and *Rossiter v. Miller* 3 App. Cas. 1140 clearly established the principle that it is not necessary that the actual names of the parties should appear in the memorandum, but if the parties are sufficiently described or indicated or referred to, so that there is no real doubt as to their identity the statute is satisfied.

JOINDER OF DOCUMENTS

Crane v. Naughten (1) [1912] 2 I.R. 318 (K.B.D.)

The plaintiff instructed an auctioneer to let grazing rights of land at Cloonakillia, near Athlone, Co. Westmeath for a period of six months, by public auction. The auctioneer published a poster:

WINTER GRAZING

Subscriber is instructed by Miss Crane to let by auction on the lands, on Monday next, October 9th, about 30 acres of the lands of Cloonakillia, within 3 miles of Athlone, for grazing purposes, from date of letting to 1st. April, 1912.
There is a heavy crop of grass on the farm, as it has not been stocked since 1st. May.
Terms at letting, at 12 o'clock.

Robert English
AUCTIONEER
Athlone.

A man named McManus attended the sale and offered £13 10s., which the auctioneer accepted, stating that "any bid should be submitted to Miss Crane". McManus then disclosed that he had bid on behalf of Naughten and the auctioneer entered in his book "Miss Crane's meadows: Bernard Naughten, £13.10s."

Some days later he added to this entry so as to make it read "Miss Crane's meadows — from letting to 1st April — Bernard Naughten 13.10s. Sent herd to ask if Miss Crane was satisfied. October 14, told Bernard Naughten Miss Crane objected." The defendant insisted on putting cattle on the lands and the plaintiff claimed damages for wrongful entry, and an injunction to restrain the defendant putting cattle on them.

The plaintiff claimed that there was no contract, because of the absence of a note or memorandum sufficient to satisfy the Statute of Frauds.

Held: The contract was one in respect of lands whereby the relation of landlord and tenant was intended to be created for a definite period of time "less than a year" within section 4 of Deasy's Act, 1860 and therefore it was not required to be in writing.

Gibson. J.:

"There is nothing else remaining except the purely theoretical question under the Statute of Frauds, which does not apply as the case falls within Deasy's Act. The Statute of Frauds requires a memorandum in writing of the true contract. I have stated what this contract was. Is it evidenced in writing? It emphatically is not.

The original limit of six months is not to be found in the memorandum written by the auctioneer; that part of the entry was made afterwards. You cannot get at the six months without reading the green poster. We may believe that the green poster was part of the agreement. But the defect is that the auctioneer did not profess to sell under the green poster,and if he had, he must incorporate it in his book. If an auctioneer sells on his catalogue, he must refer to it in his auction-book: *Pierce v. Corf* L.R. 9 Q.B. 210 is an authority for that proposition. In *Boydell v. Drummond* 11 East. 142, which is still law, it was held that documents relied on as constituting the contract must refer to each other in such a way as dispense with parol evidence of connection."

JOINDER OF DOCUMENTS
McQuaid v. Lynam [1965] I.R. 564 (H.C.)

In September, 1963 the defendants told the plaintiff that a house at No. 1, Kinvara Road, Dublin was for sale for £2,800. On the 4th September, 1963 the plaintiff paid a deposit of £800 for which he received a receipt which stated" Received from Mr. Michael McQuaid the sum of £800 being deposit on No. 1 Kinvara Road." The Name E. & J. Lynam was put on the receipt with a rubber stamp and underneath this it was signed by the J.J. Lynam. At the same time a building society, Loan Application form was partly filled in, and the defendants' names inserted as builders. The form was completed and the defendant signed it on the 27th September, 1963.

On the 4th November, 1963 the plaintiff was told by one of the defendants that the house would not be sold as freehold, but would be leased at a price reduced by £100, he then paid the defendants an additional £500 by way of deposit and received a receipt. Later the defendants informed him that the sale could not proceed because of an undertaking given to Dublin Corporation. The plaintiff sought damages.

Held: by Kenny J. That the loan application to the building society did not constitute a note or memorandum sufficient to satisfy the Statute of Frauds as it was signed by the plaintiff only but the receipt of the 4th September, 1963, and the loan application to the building society could be read together and, when thus read, constituted a sufficient note or memorandum.

That the parties agreement was varied by consent on 4th November and being a variation of an oral contract evidenced by note, a note of the variation would not be necessary; but the variation was from a freehold to a leasehold sale, and, applying *Kerns v. Manning* (1935) I.R. 869 since the variation of the lease and the rent had not been agreed there was never a valid contract for sale.

Semble (It appears), that on the authority of Bain v. Fothergill L.R. 7 H.L. 158 (See Chapter 19 post), *Kelly v. Duffy* [1922] 1 L.R. 62 and *McDonnell v. McGuinness* [1939] I.R. 223, even had the plaintiff established that there was a valid contract, the only damages to which he would have been entitled by reason of the defendants' inability to make good title would be £3. 3s. 0d., the amount of the surveyor's fee.

SUFFICIENCY OF MEMORANDUM
Davis v. Gallagher [1933] L.J.Ir. 26 (H. C.) Sullivan P.

In 1928 the plaintiff instructed an auctioneer to sell land by public auction. Although a poster had been printed and widely distributed the auction was abortive.

Three years later the defendant agreed to buy the land. The conditions of sale were left blank but the memorandum at the foot was filled in and signed. A few days later the conditions were filled in by the plaintiffs solicitor in the absence of both plaintiff and defendant.

The memorandum was worded: ". . . the purchaser hereby agrees to purchase, subject to the foregoing conditions, the premises referred to in the advertisement and conditions. . . ." The plaintiff sued for specific performance and the poster used three years previously, which described the land was put in evidence. The question at issue was, whether the reference to the advertisement in the signed memo, could be held, by necessary implication, to refer to the poster.

Held: To the knowledge of all the parties, and by necessary implication the advertisement referred to in the memo was the poster, and it was sufficient to identify the lands. That poster was to the knowledge of all parties incorporated with the memorandum.

On appeal to the High Court the court pointed out that the difficulty as to whether there was sufficient memorandum to satisfy the Statute of Frauds was that the agreement did not set out what the property was, it merely referred to the advertisement. The court would not vary the finding of the Circuit Court that the memorandum was sufficient to satisfy the Statute of Frauds.

SIGNATURE
Halley v. O'Brien [1920] 1 I.R. 149 & 330 (C.A.)

The defendants were executors who sold part of an estate to the plaintiff by public auction without obtaining the sanction of the court which had made an order for the administration of the estate. They later refused to complete on the ground that they could not exercise their power of sale without court sanction. On their instructions their solicitor had drawn up a typewritten memorandum which stated "*I, John Halley, of Marlfield, do hereby acknowledge myself the purchaser from Thomas O'Brien and Francis Woods, the vendors of the property described in Lot 1. . . .*" It was signed by the purchaser but not by the vendors (the executors) or by the auctioneer.

When the plaintiff sought specific performance the executors pleaded that there was not a sufficient memorandum to satisfy section 2 of the Statute of Frauds as they had not signed the memorandum.

Held: The document constituted a sufficient compliance with section 2 of the Statute of Frauds. The words Thomas O'Brien and Francis Woods in the typewritten memorandum, were a sufficient signature.

O'Connor L.J in the Court of Appeal

> ". . . one has first to rid one's mind of certain wrong and confused impressions that leap to it. When we speak of 'signing' or 'signature' we usually think of the person's name, signed by himself in the form he generally uses, as a clue to or mark of his identity. That is the meaning of the term when we ask, 'Is that Mr. H's signature?'"

Further, we usually associate "signed" and "signature" with a name subscribed or put at the end of a document. But these are not the sole meaning of "signature" at all. One of the meanings, and for the purpose of this case, the appropriate meaning, is 'the name of a person, or something used as representing his name, affixed or appended to a writing or the like, either by himself or his deputy as a verification, authentication, or assent': Century Dictionary.

Accordingly the signature may — as has been decided in many cases under this statute — take any one of a great variety of forms. It may be **typewritten; . . . lithographed or printed . . . Initials will do**: *Phillimore v. Barry*, 1 Ca. 513, Sweet v. Lee 3 M & G. 452 . So also the signature may consist of **the name in the third person**; "Mr.John Jones accepts the offer" is quite as effectual as "I, John Jones, accept the offer," or "I accept the offer, John Jones": see *Ogilvie v. Foljambe*, 3 Mer. 62. And, as a memorandum or instrument may be signed in a variety of forms, so also it can be placed in any position, provided that, on the fair and true reading of the instrument, it authenticates the instrument and every part of it: . . . the statute does not require the signature to be in the contract itself; it is sufficient if there is a signed note or memorandum of the contract.

On this point the following decisions may be noted: The signature may be contained in a memorandum to a third person: *Leroux v. Brown 12 C.B. 818* or to the party's own agent: *Clerk v. Wright*, 1 Atk. 12. And where an agreement, complete in all its terms, was reduced to writing, and the contents of the writing were known to the defendant, it was held that the signature to it by the defendant signing as a witness was sufficient. *Welford v. Beazely*, 3 Atk. 504. Any document signed by the party, and containing the terms of the contract, is sufficient: per Bowen L.J. in *Re Hoyle* (1893) 1 Ch., at p. 99."

> . . . reliance was placed upon certain cases in which draft or agreements containing names of the parties were held to be not sufficiently signed memoranda to satisfy the statute, even though the name of the party sought to be charged was put in the draft or engrossment by the agent of such party: . . . I think these cases are explained by this: that there was no complete agreement at all; that there was according to the intention of the parties, *a locus poenitentiae* unless and until both parties signed; in truth there was a memorandum of an offer, and not a memorandum of a contract."

STATUTE OF FRAUDS AND THE DOCTRINE OF PART PERFORMANCE
Lowry v. Reid (1) [1927] N.I. 142 (N.I.C.A.)

Mary Lowry wanted her son William and his wife to come and live with her at Drumhirk, Co. Down. On her suggestion, a verbal agreement was entered into by her with her sons, Andrew and William, by which she agreed that she would give her two farms at Drumhirk, to William on her death (subject to certain conditions), in consideration of William giving his farm of 48 acres in Ballykeyle to Andrew and also paying him £200.

In 1916 Mary Lowry made a will giving effect to this verbal agreement,

William conveyed his farm to Andrew, paid him the £200, and brought his wife to live with his mother at Drumhirk.

Seven years later Mary Lowry made a new will, revoking all previous wills and codicils, and in it left William a mere life interest in the two farms. William sought a decree of specific performance.

At first hearing the action was dismissed on the grounds that there was no sufficient note or memorandum as required by the Statute of Frauds and there had not been any sufficient part performance by Mary Lowry to take the contract out of the provisions of that statute. William appealed to the Court of Appeal.

It was submitted on his behalf that Fry on Specific Performance 6th edition, page 276, par. 578 correctly stated "The part performance of a contract by one of the parties to it, may, in the contemplation of equity, preclude the other party from setting up the Statute of Frauds." *Caton v. Caton* L.R. 1 Ch. 137 expressly recognized the principle. The plaintiff also relied on *M'Manus v. Cooke* 35 Ch.D. 681.

Held: The acts of part performance by William were sufficient to take the case out of the operation of the Statute of Frauds.

Having given up his own property to his detriment, on the faith of his mother's representations, he was entitled in equity to a decree to carry those representations into execution. Decree for specific performance granted.

Andrews L.J. stated that under the doctrine of part performance the equity must be possessed, not by the party to be charged, but by the plaintiff — the person who seeks relief. See also *Crowley v. Sullivan* [1900] 2 I.R. 478.

SUBJECT TO CONTRACT

The phrase "subject to contract" has had a rather chequered history both in England and Ireland. The traditional and orthodox view was that the use of the term "subject to contract" in contracts relating to the transfer of land or buildings meant that there was no enforceable contract between the parties, who were thus free to change their minds.

To meet perceived inequities the Irish High court applied tests:

(a) as to whether there was a complete agreement concluded between the parties at all. (See *Carthy v. O'Neill* (S.C.), unreported, 30 January, 1981) and

(b) as to whether the words "subject to contract" were used by the contracting parties or added later. (*Kelly v. Park Hall School* [1979] I.R. 340).

Following *Boyle v. Lee and Goyns* it is no longer important that the **expression did not form part of the original oral agreement. If the words are contained in the written note of the oral agreement they will prevent that document acknowledging the existence of a contract and satisfying the requirements of the Statute of Frauds.** In order to satisfy the statute it is essential that the note or memo must acknowledge the existence of a contract. (*Tiverton Estates Ltd. v. Wearwell Ltd., Mulhall v. Haren*).

"SUBJECT TO CONTRACT"

Thompson & Son Ltd. v. The King [1920] 2 I.R. 365 (K.B.D.)

Thompson & Son Ltd., a Carlow engineering company claimed a sum of £4,000 damages for breach of a contract by the English Minister for Munitions to sell them the munition factory and stores at Waterford for £24,2000.

In a letter to T on 26 April the Minister stated that the highest offer above £20,000 would be accepted, subject to it being in a form which was satisfactory.

On 24 May, 1919 the Minister had telegraphed T "Will accept subject contract £24,2000 for Waterford factory including stores subject your acceptance and confirmation by noon Tuesday 27 instant." On the 27th., T telegraphed in reply "We accept your offer . . . kindly forward draft contract to Carlow."

Held: The expression "subject to contract" deferred contractual obligation until a formal contract was settled, accepted and executed.

When an offer and acceptance are made (a) subject to a subsequent formal contract, if such contract is a condition or term which until performed, keeps the agreement in suspense, the offer and acceptance have no contractual force. On the other hand, if all the terms are agreed on, and (b) a formal contract is only contemplated as putting the terms in legal shape, the agreement is effected before and irrespective of such formal contract.

The present agreement came within (a) and therefore was not enforceable.

The Court of Appeal dismissed an appeal (See [1921] I.R. 2. 438) holding:

" . . . if the documents or letters relied on as constituting a contract, contemplate the execution of a further contract between the parties, it is a question of construction whether the execution of the further contract is a condition or a term of the bargain, or whether it is a mere expression of the desire of the parties as to the manner in which the transaction already agreed to, will in fact go through.

In the former case there is no enforceable contract, either because the condition is unfulfilled, or because the law does not recognise a contract to enter into a contract. In the latter case, there is a binding contract and the reference to the more formal contract may be ignored."

ALL TERMS NOT AGREED

Carthy v. O'Neill (S.C.) Unreported, 30 January, 1981

An estate agent agreed to sell The Silver Tassie Restaurant and public house to the plaintiff on behalf of the defendant for £190,000, "subject to contract". When the defendant executed a contract to sell the same premises to another purchaser for £2000,000, the plaintiff claimed specific performance.

Held: The agreement with the estate agent made "subject to contract" was no empty formula as was the case in *Kelly v. Park Hall School*, where all the terms of a completed contract had been agreed on. In the instance case, essential parts, the date of completion, the title on offer, the price to be paid for stock etc., remained to be negotiated. Consequently the words "subject to contract" meant what they normally meant; that what had been agreed was subject to a full contract being agreed.

Note: The decision in *Mulhall v. Haren* was not opened to the Supreme Court in this case.

NOTE OR MEMO MUST ACKNOWLEDGE A CONTRACT
Tiverton Estates Ltd. v. Wearwell Ltd. [1975] 1 Ch. (C.A.)

A director of the plaintiff company orally agreed with a director of the defendant company to sell a property to them. On the same day the defendants' solicitor wrote to the plaintiffs solicitor regarding the sale of the property "subject to contract." The plaintiffs solicitor sent a letter and a draft contract for approval but later the plaintiffs decided not to go ahead with the sale. The defendants lodged a caution against the property in the Land Registry and the plaintiff issued proceedings claiming that there was no valid and enforceable contract between them. The defendants claimed that that there was a concluded oral contract which together with the letter and draft was a sufficient note or memorandum of the oral contract.

Held: that the letter and draft contract were not a sufficient note or memorandum. Such note or memorandum had no only to state the terms of the contract but also had to contain an acknowledgment or recognition by the signatory to the document that a contract had been entered into. *Buxton v. Rust* (1872) L.R. 7 Exch 279 and *Thirkell v. Cambi* [1919] 2. K.B. 590, C.A. *followed. Law v. Jones* [1974] Ch. 112, C.A. *not followed.*

Held: also, that since the words 'subject to contract' in the letter of the defendants' solicitor showed that the signatory did not acknowledge a contract, there was no sufficient memorandum. The entry of the caution must be vacated.

"SUBJECT TO CONTRACT" — INCONSISTENT WITH THE EXISTENCE OF A CONCLUDED CONTRACT

Mulhall v. Haren [1981] I.R. 364 (H.C.) Keane J.

The plaintiffs claimed specific performance of an oral agreement for the sale to them of a house at Kilmacud Road, Stillorgan Co. Dublin. They claimed that the agreement was evidenced in writing(as required by the Statute of Frauds) by a memorandum in a letter dated 20th July and in five subsequent letters, in a receipt, and in a draft contract executed by Mrs. Mulhall.

Held: Prior to the letter of 29 July the parties had concluded an oral agreement for the sale of the house. The statement in the initial letter of that date that the sale was "subject to contract" was inconsistent with a recognition of the existence of a concluded agreement between the parties and prevented the letter and the subsequent connected documents from being accepted as a sufficient memorandum or note in accordance with the provisions of the s. 2 of the Statute of Frauds. *Tiverton Ltd. v. Wearwell Ltd.* [1975] Ch. 146 **applied**; *Kelly v. Park Hall School* [1979] I.R. 340 and *Casey v. Irish Intercontinental Bank* [1979] I.R. 364 **distinguished.**

Keane J. stated:

> "I think that the Park Hall, case should properly be regarded as a special one decided on particular facts which do not arise in the present case and, as such, to be more akin to the St. Saviour's case. While the decision in the Park Hall school case might on first reading appear to lend support to the proposition that the words "subject to contract" are not inconsistent with the existence of a concluded contract . . . if that were the effect of the decision, it would mean that the Supreme Court by necessary implication, was overruling or disapproving of the long line of authority on the "subject to contract" topic. I doubt very much if it was their intention to disapprove of Tiverton or to disturb the authorities and if it were this would have been made clear in the judgment of Henchy J."

Keane J. concluded:

1. A memorandum or note cannot **satisfy the Statute of Frauds** if, when it is read alone or with other documents which can properly be read with it, **it does not contain a recognition, express or implied, of the existence of the oral contract** sought to be enforced.

2. A letter, which expressly states that a transaction is "subject to contract" cannot be a sufficient note or memorandum since **the use of those words is normally inconsistent with the existence of a concluded contract**.

It is **only in certain rare and exceptional circumstances** such as arose in *Kelly v. Park Hall School and Michael Richards Properties v. St. Saviour's*

Parish **that the words** "subject to contract" **can be treated as being of no effect** (i,e, that they were not a condition precedent and did not prevent a concluded contract coming into existence) (*Note:* This part of the judgment has been rejected by the Supreme Court in *Boyle v. Lee and Goyns.*)

3. In applying the foregoing principles it is immaterial whether the writing relied on itself contains the words "subject to contract" or is part of a chain of correspondence initiated by a letter which makes it clear that any oral agreement already arrived at is "subject to contract".

Note: There were 39 cases mentioned in this case which ranks as one of the most important and cogent decisions of the Irish High Court and is deserving of more detailed study by reading the Irish Reports, nonetheless, it must be remembered that this decision was unfortunately not considered by the Supreme Court, the appeal not being prosecuted. However in *Boyle v. Lee & Goyns post* the Supreme Court cited and endorsed Keane J's finding that the use of the words "subject to contract" was inconsistent with the existence of a concluded agreement save in the most exceptional circumstances.

MEMO MUST CONTAIN TERMS AND ACKNOWLEDGE EXISTENCE OF CONTRACT

Boyle and Boyle v. Lee and Goyns [1992] ITLR 10 February. (S.C.)

The plaintiffs claimed specific performance of an agreement purportedly concluded with the defendants for the sale of premises at Elgin Road, Dublin. Auctioneers for the defendants (vendors) wrote to their solicitor-and sent a copy to the vendors themselves-confirming that his company were instructed to accept the plaintiffs offer of £90,000 "subject to contract" and stating that the letter itself was for information purposes only and did not "by itself constitute part of a binding contract." The High court held that the parties had reached an oral agreement and that there was a sufficient note or memorandum to satisfy the Statute of Frauds (Ireland) Act, 1695. The defendants appealed on the grounds that there had been no agreement concerning the deposit to be paid or the proposed closing date, and no identification of the house-contents included in the sale or the notice, or duration of tenancies in the premises.

Held:

(1) There was no complete and binding oral agreement. The failure to agree details of the deposit to be paid was too important a part of a contract for the sale of land in the amount of £90,000 to be omitted.

(2) The auctioneers letter of 8 July did not constitute a sufficient note or memorandum of an oral agreement to satisfy section 2 of the Statute of Frauds (Ireland) Act 1695.

Finlay C.J. (Hederman J. in agreement) stated that the true test as to the sufficiency of the auctioneer's letter as a note or memorandum under the Statute of Frauds was to be found in the judgment of Mr. Justice Keane in *Mulhall v. Haren* (1981) I.R. 364 where the latter had commented that **the use of the words "subject to contract" was inconsistent with the existence of a concluded agreement** save in the most exceptional cases. (Note that the underlined portion was rejected.)

A note or memorandum of a contract made orally is not sufficient to satisfy the Statute of Frauds unless it directly or by very necessary implication recognises, not only the terms to be enforced, but also the existence of a concluded contract between the parties.

A note or memorandum which contains a term such as "subject to contract" is insufficient to satisfy the Statute of Frauds even if it can be established by oral evidence that such term or expression did not form part of the original orally concluded contract. *Kelly v. Park Hall School* [1979] I.R. 340 *not followed. Casey v. Irish Intercontinental Bank* [1979] I.R. 364 doubted. *Mulhall v. Haren followed* with the exception of dicta of Keane J. regarding exceptional cases which was *not followed.*

Finlay C.J. pointed out that the Statute of Frauds was intended to avoid the mischief of amending by deletion or ignoring of its terms, the note or memorandum relied upon by the plaintiff and signed by the defendant, such amendment or deletion depending on the finding by the court on oral evidence as to what was the agreement between the parties. "Such a principle clearly puts the oral evidence as superseding the only written evidence that is available. In broad terms, **it is the clearest possible purpose of the Statute of Frauds, 1695, to put the written evidence as dominant and superseding any oral evidence.**"

Note: Dr. Eamonn G. Hall writing in Lawbrief, ILSI Gazette states "the difficult question of what the 'essential' terms are, which must be recited in the note or memorandum still survives."

AGREEMENT SUBJECT TO THE PREPARATION OF A FORMAL CONTRACT

Lowis v. Wilson [1949] I.R. 347 (H.C.) Dixon J.

L signed a document agreeing to purchase 76 acres of land, at Girley, Kells, Co. Meath from W for £6,000 plus 5% auction fees. She paid the 5% fee plus a deposit of £1,500 and the balance was payable on the 1 December, 1948. The document which she signed contained a clause "this agreement is subject to the preparation of a formal contract to be prepared by W.O. Armstrong, solicitor for the vendor."

A formal contract of sale was drafted and submitted to the plaintiff who refused to sign it or proceed with the sale and sought the return of the monies paid, claiming that she had not entered into a binding contract.

It was argued for the defence that the preparation of a formal contract was a condition subsequent satisfied by the mere preparation of the document whether it was executed by the purchaser or not.

Held: The agreement was a contract to enter into a contract. It was conditional upon the full agreement of the parties being embodied in a formal contract and accordingly was not enforceable.

Held further: The deposit having been paid without consideration, was recoverable.

Dixon J. thought that the condition contemplated the completion of a contract between the parties. The use of the word "contract" was important. The Vendor's solicitor could prepare a draft of a proposed contract, but he could not prepare a contract as that would depend on the agreement of the parties evidenced by their signing or sealing the document. In view of the whole context of the agreement, it was impossible to give it such a strict literal meaning as contended.

CHAPTER 6

Terms

Although freedom of contract may in some instances be restricted by statute, in general the parties themselves decide the terms. No one else can do that for them, even a court of law. If the terms are not certain a court cannot make them so. In *Plunkett v. Dease* (1846) 120 Ir. Eq. R. 124 where an agreement was *"subject to any clauses I choose to insert"* it was held to be too uncertain to be enforced where the defendant had not named those terms he choose to insert.

Uncertainty as to the consideration for the purchase of stock in *Godley v. Power* [1961] 95 I.L.T.R. 135 did not prevent the Supreme Court from granting a decree of specific performance for the sale of as licensed premises. The stratagem of holding that there were two contracts, one for the premises, and another collateral contract relating to the stock, enabled the court to enforce the sale. See Chapter 17, page 199.

Traditionally it has been the custom to classify terms as either conditions or warranties and this distinction was based on the intention of the parties at the time of entering into the contract. A term will only be a condition if it has been designated as such by statute, by judicial decision, or expressly or impliedly by the parties.

In the *Hong Kong Fir* case (1962) Diplock L.J. commented that many contractual undertakings cannot be categorized as being 'conditions' or 'warranties' and that the legal consequences of the breach unless expressly provided for, depend on the nature of the event to which the breach gives rise, and do not follow automatically from prior classification.

This has led to a third class of term described as innominate (or intermediate) terms the breach of which may be minor, leading to an award of damages, or fundamental leading to discharge of the contract.

The common law definitions of a condition and a warranty stated in the cases cited were established prior to the Sale of Goods Act 1893. Section 62 of this Act does define a warranty for the purposes of the sale of goods but the term condition is not expressly defined in the Act. Section 11(1)(b) has implicitly defined a condition in terms of the remedy available for breach of such a term.

The legal principle that a person of full capacity who signs a contract, is thus accepting the offer, and is bound by that contract, in the absence of misrepresentation or fraud, even though he has not read the document, was established in *L'Estrange v. Graucob Ltd.* [1934] 2 K.B. 394. This principle was examined by Finlay P. (as he then was) in *Siebel and Seum v. Kent*, High Court, unreported, 1 June 1976. In this case he extended the principle of notice which applies in relation to incorporation of exemption clauses, to a forfeiture clause. He also laid down two tests to be required to base the application of the L'Estrange principle.

In addition to restrictions imposed by Statute, terms of a contract may not be upheld on the grounds of public policy as in *Dalton v. Dalton* [1982] I.L.R.M. 418 where the court refused to uphold an agreement containing a clause providing that the parties would obtain a divorce a vinculo. Such divorce being contrary to public policy as expressed in the Constitution.

Terms may be implied into a contract in a number of ways. By Statute e.g. The Sale of Goods Acts and employment legislation, by custom *O'Conaill v. Gaelic Echo*, by the Constitution e. g. a right of disassociation, a right to fair procedures.

Terms may also be implied by the courts. A court cannot imply terms in order to find that a contract has come into existence, it can only imply terms if it has first concluded that there is a contract. It cannot substitute its own ideas for those of the parties.

In the *Moorcock* case the court implied a term to give the contract **business efficacy**, founded on the presumed intention of the parties. In *Shirlaw v. Southern Foundries* [1926] Ltd. [1939] 2. K.B. 206 MacKinnon L.J. introduced the "**officious bystander**" test. In *Ward v. Spivack Ltd.* and *Fagan v. Spivack Ltd.* [1957] I.R. Chief Justice Maguire adopted **the clear intention of both contracting parties** as the criteria. (See *Gardner v. Coutts & Co.* [1968] 1 W.L.R. 173) The note on *Liverpool City Council v. Irwin* [1977] A.C. is included as a practical application of a term implied in order to give business efficacy.

TERMS MUST BE CERTAIN
Plunkett v. Dease [1846] 10 Ir. Eq. R. 124 (Ch.)

The plaintiff sued for specific performance of an agreement by the defendant to lease him lands at Drumhillagh, *"from the 1 May, 1825, subject to any clauses I choose to insert"*.

Held: The contract could not be enforced. Dease had never specified what covenants he required. There was no writing specifying what they were to be; and therefore the contract was uncertain in a very important part of it.

Note: Where a contract is that a lease shall contain the usual covenants a court will execute it, but the Plunkett case was different because it was clearly intended that the intending lessor would have the power to select the covenants. As to knowledge of terms, see *Siebel & Seum v. Kent*, Chapter 8, p. 79.

KNOWLEDGE OF TERMS

Siebel and Seum v. Kent Finlay P., High Court, unreported, 1 June, 1976

For the facts of this case see Chapter 8, p. 94 *post*.

Held: In the absence of evidence that the plaintiffs understood that the general conditions of sale formed part of the contract which they were witnessing or signing, they were not bound by the printed conditions.

TERMS CONTRARY TO PUBLIC POLICY

Dalton v. Dalton [1982] I.L.R.M. 418 (H.C.) O'Hanlon J.

The plaintiff applied to have a separation agreement made a rule of court. The agreement contained a clause that the husband and wife agreed to obtain a divorce *a vinculo* and that the husband agreed not to contest any divorce proceedings. The parties were domiciled in Ireland.

Held: To ask the court to make the agreement a rule of court, was to ask the court to lend its support to a course of conduct which was contrary to public policy within this jurisdiction. For this reason the application must be refused.

Note: Kingsmill Moore J. in *Mayo-Perrott v. Mayo-Perrott* [1958] I.R. 336. was cited as stating, "It cannot be doubted that the public policy of this country as reflected in the Constitution does not favour divorce *a vinculo*."

Ormsby v. Ormsby [1945] I.L.T. 97 (S.C.)

A deed of separation was executed by both parties. In it the defendant agreed to make a weekly payment. When he ceased to make the payment the plaintiff sued. The defendant claimed that the deed was not binding and that it was invalid and contrary to public policy.

Held: The State does not regard, under Article 41 of the Constitution that separation deeds are an attack on the institution of marriage. The deed was not contrary to public policy.

IMPLIED TERMS

Ward & Fegan v. Spivack [1957] I.R. 40 (S.C.)

Ward was appointed sole agent for the defendant's products in the city and county of Dublin. Fegan was appointed sole agent for the other twenty five counties. When the agencies were terminated by the company each of the plaintiffs claimed that a term should be implied into their contracts that they should continue to be paid commission on all orders from customers introduced by them.

Held: To read such a term into the contract would not be to make clear the intention of the parties, unexpressed at the time the contract was made, but would be to make a new contract.

The test applied by the Court to imply a term into a contract must be something approaching certainty or as put by Jenkins L.J. in *Sethia [1944] Ltd. v. Partabmull Rameshwar* [1950] 1 All E.R. 51 it must be "clear beyond a peradventure that both parties intended a given term to operate although they did not include it in so many words."

Tradex (Ireland) Ltd. v. Irish Grain Board Ltd. [1984] I.R. 1 (S.C.)

The defendant agreed to sell 25,000 metric tonnes of feed barley to the plaintiffs who were to pay by a letter of credit "maturing on the 1st May, 1978." The defendants made deliveries of grain until the 21st April, 1978 and then refused to make further deliveries because they claimed that the plaintiff was in breach of contract by failing to furnish a letter of credit. By a letter of the 21st April, 1978 the defendants referred to the terms of the sale and repudiated the contract.

On the 24th April the plaintiffs bank issued two letters of credit which would have enabled the defendants to obtain payment on 1st May, 1978.

When the plaintiff claimed damages for the defendants breach of contract the defendants submitted that there should be implied in the contract a term requiring the plaintiffs to furnish letters of credit before the start of the shipment of the goods.

Held: As the parties had expressly agreed upon the date and method of payment of the contract price, the implied term sought by the defendants was not required in order to implement the intention of the parties. No such term would be implied.

The provisions of s. 4 of the Sale of Goods Act, 1893 were satisfied by the defendants letter dated 21st April, 1978:

> "It goes without question that, in any class of contract, the Courts may imply a term in order to repair an intrinsic failure of expression. This is done to give *business efficacy*, as it is said, to a contract which would otherwise lack it. The existence of this power was asserted in the well known case of The Moorcock. . . . However, this power must be exercised with care. The Courts have no role in acting as contract makers, or as counsellors, to advise or direct what agreement ought to have been made by two people, whether businessmen or not, who choose to enter into contractual relations with each other." — O'Higgins C.J. (As to knowledge of terms see *Siebel and Seum v. Kent post.*)

IMPLIED TERM

Dundalk Shopping Centre Ltd. v. Roof Spray Ltd.
High Court, unreported, 21 March 1979 Finlay P.

The plaintiffs claimed damages for the breach by the defendants of a contract to supply and execute insulation and finish on a shopping centre in Dundalk.

They claimed that the work was not carried out in a proper workman-like manner, was not of merchantable quality and was carried out in a negligent and defective manner using defective equipment and materials.

The defendants were completely absent from the site between 2 October and 18 October, 1974 and they contended that during that period work which they had already carried out was extensively damaged and that damage continued until they left the site on the repudiation of the contract by the plaintiff.

Held: There was a term implied into the contract that the defendant would use reasonable care and skill in carrying out their work. They had a duty to provide for and insist upon any special precautions which were required. There was no evidence that they had done so. The repudiation was justified the defendants had failed in a fundamental term of the contract, namely to provide an effective waterproofing of the roof within a reasonable time.

TERMS IMPLIED BY CUSTOM

O'Conaill v. The Gaelic Echo (1954) Ltd.
[1958] 92 I.L.T.R. 156 (D.C) Hannan D.J.

The plaintiff was employed on the editorial staff of the defendant from January 2nd, 1957. On June 1st, 1957, his employment was terminated by one week's notice. The plaintiff claimed that he was entitled to one month's notice and holiday pay.

The honorary secretary of the National Union of Journalists gave evidence that the customary period of notice, in the absence of express agreement, to terminate the employment of journalists in the Dublin City area was one month in the case of reporters, three months in the case of sub-editors, and six months in the case of a chief sub-editor.

Held: The plaintiff was entitled to at least one months notice and was awarded damages for wrongful dismissal measured at three week's wages, having already received one week's wage for the period of the notice actually given. He was entitled to a further one and a half weeks' wages in respect of his claim for holiday pay.

WARRANTY
Chanter v. Hopkins (1838) 4 M. & W. 399 (Ex.)

The defendant sent a written order to the plaintiff asking him to supply a hopper and furnace which he had patented.

The plaintiff supplied and installed the furnace but it was found not to be of any use for the purposes of the defendants brewery, and he returned it to the plaintiff. The plaintiff sought payment and the defendant refused, claiming that there was an implied warranty that the furnace should be fit for the purposes of a brewery.

Held: There was no such implied warranty. The defendant having defined by his order the particular machine to be supplied, the plaintiff performed his part of the contract by supplying the machine, and was entitled to recover the whole price. The object for which the defendant wanted the furnace was immaterial; that was his own affair, the article was accurately defined independently of that object.

"A **warranty** is an express or implied statement of something which the party undertakes shall be part of a contract; and though part of the contract, yet collateral to the express object of it." — *per* Lord Abinger, C.B.

Note: In addition to defining a warranty Parke B. cited the parol evidence rule "The rule of law is clear, that you cannot add to or diminish a written contract by anything parol which may have occurred between the parties".

CONDITION
Behn v. Burness (1862) 1 B&S 877

The defendant agreed by a contract in writing dated the 19 October, 1860 to charter the plaintiff's ship "MARTABAN" **"now in the port of Amsterdam"** to proceed with all possible dispatch to Newport, Monmouthshire, to load a cargo of coal within ten days, and to carry it to Hong Kong. The ship was not in Amsterdam at the time of contracting, and it did not arrive there until the 23 October. When the ship reached Newport on the 5 December the defendant refused to load the coal and the plaintiff sued for damages for not doing so.

Held:
(1) The words "now in the port of Amsterdam" amounted to a condition that the ship was there at the time of making the contract.
(2) At the time of making the contract, time and the situation of the ship were material and essential parts of the contract.

The defendant was entitled to repudiate the contract and be relieved from performing his part of it.

Condition

"But with respect to statements in a contract descriptive of the subject matter, or of some material incident thereof, the true doctrine established by principle as well as authority appears to be, generally speaking, that if such statement was intended to be a substantive part of the contract, it is to be regarded as a warranty (term), that is to say **a condition** on the failure or non performance of which the other party might, if he was so minded, repudiate the contract *in toto*, and be relieved from performing his part of it, provided it has not been partially executed in his favour." –Williams J.

Williams J. also referred to the meaning of the term warranty when not used in its general sense to denote a term of a contract as: "A **warranty** in the narrower sense of the word-viz, a stipulation by way of agreement for the breach of which a compensation must be sought in damages."

He also referred to **ex post facto warranties** as follows:

"If, indeed, he has received the whole or any substantial part of the consideration for the promise on his part, the warranty looses the character of a condition, or to speak perhaps more properly, ceases to be available as a condition, and becomes a warranty in the narrower sense of the word, viz., a stipulation by way of agreement, for the breach of which a compensation must be sought in damages."

CONDITION

Poussard v. Spiers and Pond (1876) 1 Q.B.D. 410

Madame Poussard, agreed in writing with the defendants to sing and play the main female role in a new opera about to be staged at the Criterion Theatre, owned by the defendants. She was taken ill and was unable to attend the first four days performance.

Another artiste, a Miss Lewis, had been engaged to take the part and when Madame Poussard recovered and tendered her services on the fifth day, the defendants refused to accept or allow her perform. Madame Poussard brought an action for wrongful dismissal.

Held: The plaintiffs inability to perform on the opening and early performances went to the root of the matter. There had been a breach of condition and the defendants were justified in rescinding the contract.

WARRANTY
Bettini v. Gye (1876) 1 Q.B.D. 183

The plaintiff, a professional singer and dramatic artist, entered into a written agreement with the defendant, the director of the Royal Italian Opera, London, to fill the part of first tenor, in operas and concerts in Britain and Ireland. The performances were to commence on the 30th March. A term of the contract provided that Bettini would be in London, without fail, for the purpose of rehearsals at least six days before the commencement of performances.

Bettini suffered a temporary illness and did not arrive in London until the 28 March, which was less than six days before the 30th. The defendant repudiated the contract and refused to proceed with it. Bettini instituted proceedings.

Held: The stipulation as to rehearsals was not a condition, it did not go to the root of the matter. The defendant was not entitled to repudiate the contract but only to claim damages.

Note: In *Liverpool City Council v. Irwin* [1977] A.C. 239 when the tenants on the 9th and 10th floors of a 15 storey tower block withheld rent as a protest against conditions in the building, it was held that there had to be implied an easement for the tenants and their licensees to use the stairs, a right in the nature of an easement to use the lifts and an easement to use the rubbish chutes.

CHAPTER 7

Interpretation of Contract

The terms of a contract may be express or implied. The courts apply a number of rules in interpreting a contract. Apart from the rules that words are to be given their plain ordinary meaning and in the case of two meanings the one which will make the contract valid or effective and carry out the intention of the parties, there are a number of other rules known by latin phrases detailed below.

Express terms are normally straightforward but may nonetheless complicate matters where it appears that two express terms contradict each other. The rule of interpretation of terms **generalia specialibus non derogant** was applied in *Welch v. Bowmaker (Ir.) Ltd.* [1980] I.R. 251 S.C. and it was held that general words will not, in the absence of an indication of a definite intention to do so, undermine the effect of special words.

The **contra proferentum** rule is another rule of construction used by the courts where a contracting party seeks to rely on ambiguous words which he himself has introduced into the contract. The courts construe such words against the party who proffers them by adopting the meaning which is least favourable to him. This rule has particular relevance in the areas of exemption clauses and insurance contracts.

The **ejusdem generis** (of the same kind or genre) rule encompassed by the maxim is used by the courts to restrict the meaning of general words which follow particular words, to matters or things of the same kind referred to by the earlier particular words.

The **expressio unius est exclusio alterius** rule is that where one thing has been expressly stated other things of a similar nature are excluded. In the case of *Hare v. Horton* the fixtures in two dwelling-houses were specifically mentioned and this meant that the fixtures in the iron-foundry were excluded.

The courts regard the written form of contract as sacrosanct, and there is a general rule that parol(extrinsic) evidence cannot be admitted to contradict, vary, add to, or subtract from, the terms of a written contract. (*Fallon v. Robbins: Henderson v. Arthur* [1907] C.A.). This rule is referred to as **the parol evidence rule**. There are of course exceptions to it, some of which are cited post. F.R. Davies, *Contract*, 5th ed., London, 1986, states that if the rule were applied over a broad front, it would lead to injustice in many cases and that the number of exceptions has now limited its scope.

GENERALIA SPECIALIBUS NON DEROGANT

Welch v. Bowmaker (Ir.) Ltd. [1980] I.R. 251 (S.C.)

A debenture was issued by a company in favour of the defendant. Clause 3 of the debenture charged the company's "undertaking and all its property and assets present and future including its uncalled capital." The first condition in the debenture stated that the charge "is to be, as regards the company's lands and premises for the time being and all its uncalled capital, a specific charge. . . ." It also provided that the company was not to be at liberty to create any mortgage or charge on its property in priority to the debenture.

The company owned another property which was not described in the schedule and a month later created an equitable mortgage by deposit of title deeds to secure sums due to the bank.

The bank were unaware of the restriction on the creation of further mortgages in the debenture. The company became insolvent and Bowmaker claimed that the specific charge in the first condition in the debenture covered the premises over which the bank had an equitable mortgage.

Held: The qualifying provision was in conflict with the charging provision. The relevant rule of interpretation was that encapsulated in the maxim *generalia specialibus non derogant*. The general words will not, in the absence of an indication of a definite intention to do so, be held to undermine or abrogate the effect of the special words which were used to deal with the particular situation.

The special words show that the primary and transcendent intention was that the property not included in the schedule was not to be subject to a special charge. The claim of the Bank of Ireland prevailed.

Note: In *Tokn Glass Products v. Sexton & Co.*, High Court, unreported, 3 October 1983 where terms were written in manuscript on the obverse and printed standard conditions were on the reverse of each page, it was held that the printed conditions applied except where in conflict with the manuscript.

CONTRA PROFERENTEM

Re Sweeney and Kennedy Arbitration [1950] I.R. 85 (H.C.)

Sweeney signed a proposal form for insurance. The form contained a number of questions, one of which asked "Are any of your drivers under 21 years of age or with less than twelve months driving experience?" Sweeney answered "No." The last paragraph of the proposal form stated "I declare that the above statements and particulars are true, that the vehicles described are my property and in good condition, and I hereby agree that this declaration shall be held to be **promissory**, and so form the basis of contract. . . ."

Sweeney's son Thomas, who was under 21 was driving one of the vehicles when a fatal accident occurred. The insurance company refused to accept liability and when the dispute was referred to arbitration the arbitrator found the company liable but on request sought the opinion of the High Court. In the High Court the insurance company contended that the word "promise" and its cognate words must always refer to a future time.

Held:

(1) That the expression "this declaration shall be held to be promissory" was referable to the facts existing at the time the proposal form was completed and did not refer to any time thereafter.

(2) That the proposer's answer to question 9 did not amount to a warranty as to the age of any drivers which might be employed by him subsequent to the completion of the proposal form.

(3) Where an insurer uses ambiguous language in a proposal form or insurance policy such language will be strictly construed against him by the Court. Accordingly the insurers were liable to indemnify S in respect of his liability (if any) in respect of the said fatal accident. *Woolfall & Rimmer Ltd. v. Moyle* [1942] 1 K.B. 66 *approved. Glicksman v. Lancashire and General Assurance Co.* [1927] A.C. 139 and *Provincial Insurance Co. v. Morgan* [1933] A.C. 240 *adopted.*

> "The wording of the proposal form and the policy was chosen by the underwriters. . . . If then, they choose to adopt ambiguous words it seems to me good sense, as well as established law, that those words should be interpreted in the sense which is adverse to the persons who chose and introduced them; *Anderson v. Fitzgerald*, 4 H.L. Cas 484, per Lord St. Leonards, at p. 507; *Fowkes v. Manchester and London Life Assurance and Loan Association*, 3 B. & S. 917 per Cockburn C.J. at p. 925, and Blackburn J. at p. 929; *Fitton v. Accidental Death Ins. Co.*, 17 C.B. (N.S.) 122 per Willes J. at p. 135." — per Kingsmill Moore J.

EJUSDEM GENERIS

Brady v. Irish National Insurance Co. Ltd. [1986] ILRM. 669. (S.C.)

The plaintiff's boat was damaged while laid up for the winter, when a friend unwittingly released gas from the supply to the cooker. The defendant refused to indemnify the plaintiff claiming that he had shown a "want of due diligence" within the meaning of the policy and that he was in breach of a special warranty.

The special warranty stated "The insured hereby warrants that at the commencement of the period of indemnity and at all times during the period of indemnity, the insured vessel is and shall be:

1. Seaworthy or otherwise fit for the purpose and use intended, tight, staunch, strong, sound and in good condition.

2. During the laid up-period, laid up in a place of safety, dismantled, not fitted out or available for immediate use and not used for any purpose whatsoever other than dismantling, fitting out or customary overhauling.

Section 33 (3) of the Marine Insurance Act, 1906 provides that a warranty in a contract of marine insurance is to be treated as a condition, breach of which, discharges the insurer from liability.

Held: Declaration granted that the plaintiff was entitled to be indemnified by the defendant against any loss or damage arising to the said motor cruiser or its equipment and to be indemnified for any claims for personsl injuries brought by all persons who were lawfully on the said cruiser and who were injured in an accident on board on or about the 8 March, 1983.

Finlay C.J.:

> "I, therefore, conclude that on the true construction of Special warranty number 2. having regard to the findings of the learned trial judge, the use of the galley was part of the customary overhaul and ancillary to it and not a failure exactly to comply with this special warranty ... as to whether Special Warranty Number 1 was applicable to this boat while it was laid up afloat. ... The terms of this warranty must be construed in accordance with the *ejusdem generis* rule. ... Applying, therefore, the *ejusdem generis* rule to the terms of Special Warranty Number 1, I am satisfied that the proper interpretation would be that it is applicable only to periods when the boat is in commission rather than laid up. ... If both these warranties apply during the laid up period, then the obligation on the insured, or boat owner, would be, on the one hand to have the boat fit for the purpose and use intended, and on the other hand to have the boat **not** fitted out or available for immediate use. ... I am therefore satisfied that the terms of Special Warranty Number 1 do not apply during the laid up period and that no question of a breach of them, therefore arises in this action."

Note: Ejusdem generis (of the same kind or nature). If particular words are followed by general words, the general words are limited to the same kind or nature as the particular.

EXPRESSIO UNIUS EST EXCLUSIO ALTERIUS
Hare v. Horton (1833) 5 B& Ad. 715 (K.B.)

A sold an iron-foundry and two dwelling-houses to B. There were fixtures and fittings in the foundry valued at £600. The conveyance referred to "the said iron-foundry together with the said dwelling-houses, warehouses, shops, yards, gardens ... together with all grates boilers, bells and other fixtures in and about the said two dwelling-houses. . . ." A dispute arose as to whether the fixtures etc., in the foundry were included.

Held: the specification of the grates and other fixtures in and about the dwelling-houses, showed that those in the foundry were not intended to pass, though they would have passed if the others had not been mentioned.

Taunton J.

> "I think the mention of these fixtures (in the dwelling-houses) excludes those in the foundry on the principle *expressio unius est exclusio alterius*. Why, it may be asked, were these particular ones mentioned if the whole were intended to pass?"

THE PAROL EVIDENCE RULE

The general rules of the Common Law provided that if a contract had been reduced into writing, verbal evidence would not be allowed to be given of what the parties said either before or during the making of the written instrument to vary, add to, or contradict it, in any way. (*Fallon v. Robbins*)

A number of exceptions to the rule have developed and parol evidence is now admitted inter alia, to explain the circumstances (*Revenue Commissioners v. Moroney*), to explain the subject matter (*Chambers v. Kelly*), to identify a party *Bacon & Co. Ltd. v. Kavanagh*, to determine the price (*Nolan v. Graves*); (*Jeffcott v. North British Oil Co.* (1873) I.R. 8 C.L. 17 Exch), to establish the terms, (*Clayton Love v. B & I*); (*De Lassalle v. Guildford* (1901) 22 K.B. 215), to explain customs (*O'Conaill v. Gaelic Echo*), to explain a mistake for purposes of rectification (*Monaghan Co. Co. v. Vaughan*), to provide evidence of an agreement to rescind a written contract (*Morris v. Baron & Co.* (1918) A.C. 1.) and to show that a written agreement was made subject to a condition *Pym v. Campbell* (1856) E.& B. 370.

EXTRINSIC EVIDENCE EXCLUDED
Fallon v. Robbins (1865) Vol. 16 Ir. Ch. Rep. 422 (Ch.)

The petitioner, a surgeon and apothecary in the town of Athlone made a verbal agreement in 1861, to rent premises at Church Street, from the respondent for thirty one years, at a rent of £30 a year. The petitioner to be at liberty to make certain alterations to the premises.

A solicitor was employed by the respondent to reduce the agreement to writing and he asked the petitioner whether he would wish to have a surrender clause. He replied that he would and such a clause was included providing for surrender at the end of each third year on six months notice.

The petitioner took possession and made improvements and alterations but was served with a notice to quit on 29 February, 1864. The respondent claimed that the agreement was subject to a provision that either party, might determine it at the end of any third year. The petitioner denied this.

The clause actually stated "And it is further agreed that the said premises are to be held for a term of thirty one years, from 1 September next, with liberty, however, to have same determined at the end of the third, sixth etc. should it be so desired."

Held: The respondent had no right under the clause to determine the tenancy. The case was to be decided by reference to the agreement itself without reference to the conflicting affidavits of the petitioner and the respondent. The claim that either party might determine the agreement was a miss-statement. There was no such provision in the agreement.

Cusack Smith M.R.:

> "A deed which agrees with the intention of one of the parties, although under a mistake as to the other, cannot be rectified. . . . By the general rules of the Common Law, if there be a contract which has been reduced into writing, **verbal evidence is not allowed** to be given of what passed between the parties, either before the instrument was made, or during the time it was in a state of preparation, so as **to add to or subtract from, or in any manner to vary or qualify**, the written contract. *Goss v. Lord Nugent*, 5 B. & Ad. 58.
>
> A court of Equity may, under particular circumstances admit such evidence, but a Court of Equity should not act upon doubtful evidence, either in a suit to reform the deed, or in defence to a suit for specific performance. . . ."

PAROL EVIDENCE ADMITTED TO EXPLAIN THE CIRCUMSTANCES

See **Revenue Commissioner v. Moroney** (Ch. 4 Estoppel)

EXTRINSIC EVIDENCE ADMITTED TO ESTABLISH SUBJECT MATTER

Chambers v. Kelly (1873) 7 I.R. C.L. 231 (Exch.)

The plaintiff agreed in writing to sell larch trees growing on lands at Greenmount, near Enniscorthy to the defendant and three days later they talked about a sale of additional timber and a further written agreement was made on the 10 April.

The agreement referred to the purchase of oaks "together with all other trees growing through the oak plantations, **and mixed with the oak.**" The plaintiff claimed that he had walked through the oak wood with the defendant and pointed out the fence round the oak wood.

The defendant cut timber not only in the oak wood but in plantations in which oak was found alleging that such timber was **mixed with oak** within the meaning of the agreement.

Held: It was necessary to go outside the written agreement to ascertain the subject matter, that is to say, "oak plantations." The evidence of conversations between the parties in reference to the sale, prior to the agreement, was properly received in order to identify the subject matter of the contract.

PAROL EVIDENCE ADMITTED TO IDENTIFY A PARTY
Bacon & Co. Ltd. v. Kavanagh (See Ch. 5 Form)

PAROL EVIDENCE ADMITTED TO ESTABLISH THE TERMS WHERE A WRITTEN DOCUMENT IS NOT THE ENTIRE CONTRACT
Clayton Love v. B & I (See Ch. 4 Estoppel and Ch. 8 Exemption Clauses)

PAROL EVIDENCE ADMITTED TO EXPLAIN CUSTOMS
O'Conaill v. The Gaelic Echo (See Ch. 6 Terms)

PAROL EVIDENCE ADMITTED TO EXPLAIN A MISTAKE FOR PURPOSES OF RECTIFICATION
Monaghan County Council v. Vaughan (See Ch. 10 Mistake)

PAROL EVIDENCE AS TO PRICE
Nolan v. Graves [1946] I.R. 376 (H.C.) Haugh J.

The plaintiff purchased premises in Churchtown, Co. Dublin at a public auction. The vendor contended that the premises were knocked down at £5,550, but the plaintiff contended that the price was £4,550. In the memorandum of the contract attached to the conditions of sale, the price was stated to be £4,550, and the deposit and auctioneers fees were calculated accordingly.

The vendor refused to complete the sale at the lower price or return the deposit and fees. The plaintiff sued for damages for breach of agreement and for return of the deposit and fees. The vendor sought rectification of the memorandum and specific performance at the higher figure. Parol evidence was tendered by the defendants to show that the price at which the premises were knocked down was £5,500 but the plaintiff argued that such evidence should not be admitted, that the written contract only should be considered.

Held: Parol evidence should be admitted, that it was relevant, and solely relevant, to the one issue to be tried. "I am bound in fact to listen to it." Haugh J.

Note: See also *Pau On v. Yiu Long* [1980] A.C. 614 in Chapter 3 where parol evidence was admitted to show consideration.

WRITTEN AGREEMENT WAS MADE SUBJECT TO A CONDITION
Pym v. Campbell (1856) 6 E & B. 370 (Q.B.)

The plaintiff invented a machine and negotiated with the defendant for the sale of an interest in it. The defendant claimed that they agreed on a price and it was arranged that they should draw up and sign a memorandum of agreement of sale. Before they signed it, the defendant orally made it clear to the plaintiff that it would not constitute a bargain until an engineer, Abernethie, inspected the invention and approved of it. Abernethie did not approve the invention when he saw it; and the defendants contended that there was no bargain.

Held: The written memorandum was executed subject to a condition. The condition had not been fulfilled and there was no contract. Parol evidence was admitted to prove that there was no contract not to add to, or vary an existing contract.

Lord Campbell C.J.:

> "No addition to or variation from the terms of a written contract can be made by parol; but in this case the defense was that there never was any agreement entered into. Evidence to that effect was admissible; and the evidence given in this case was overwhelming. It was proved in the most satisfactory manner that before the paper was signed it was explained to the plaintiff that the defendants did not intend the paper to be an agreement till Abernethie had been consulted, and found to approve of the invention; and that paper was signed before he was seen only because it was not convenient to the defendants to remain. The plaintiff assented to this, and received the writing on those terms. That being proved, there was no agreement." — *Davis v. Jones* 104 R.R. 819 *referred to.*

CHAPTER 8

Exemption and Limitation Clauses

An exemption clause is a term of a contract which purports to exempt one of the parties from liability which otherwise might accrue to him. A limitation clause is a term which purports to limit the extent of the liability of one of the parties in the event of liability arising. Such clauses are used to exempt or limit liability arising out of negligence as well as out of contract.

In *Photo Productions v. Securicor Transport* (1978) 1 W.L.R. 856 Lord Diplock defined an exclusion clause as "one which excludes or modifies an obligation, whether primary, general secondary or anticipatory secondary."

INCORPORATION TEST

In dealing with exemption clauses the courts apply two tests a) the incorporation test and b) the construction test. The incorporation test is applied to establish if an exemption clause is part of the particular contract at all. This will depend on whether (1) the exemption clause is contained in a contractual document signed by the offeree, *L'Estrange v. Graucob Ltd.* or (2) whether it is contained in a document which is not signed. In the case of an unsigned contractual document an exemption clause will only be effective if the offeree knows of its existence or reasonable steps have been taken to bring it to his notice. The nature of the document, the degree of notice given and the time of notice are relevant considerations.

The requirement to establish if the clause is incorporated in the particular contract, causes the question of notice of the existence of the clause being given to the other party to become central.

UNSIGNED DOCUMENTS

In *Western Meats v. National Ice and Cold Storage Co. Ltd. and Anor.*, Barrington J. held that the defendants had not given the plaintiffs reasonable notice of the contents of their standard conditions. These standard conditions would have been a complete answer to the plaintiffs claim had they been part of the contract.

In *Early v. Great Southern Railway*, the plaintiff claimed that he had not got reasonable notice of the conditions on which his ticket was issued but

Sullivan C.J. cited Lord Hanworth in *Thompson v. L.M.S. Railway.*, that "it has not ever been held that mere circuitry which has to be followed to find the actual conditions prevents the passenger having notice that there was a condition."

The defendants were not liable in *Knox v. Great Northern Railway Co.*, where the contract was not signed until after the contract had begun. The general rule is that notice given after the contract has been made is ineffective, (*Olley v. Marlborough Court*) but it should be noted that the contract in Knox protected from all past negligence.

The Court of Appeal held in *O'Keefe v. London and Edinburgh Insurance Co. Ltd.* (1) [1927] A.C. 85 that knowledge acquired by a defendants agent prior to his appointment as agent could not be imputed to the defendants. This is totally different to Sanderson v. Cunningham Ch. 1 where the knowledge of the agent was imputed to the principal.

In *Johnson v. Great Southern & Western Railway* (1874) I.R. 9. C.L. 108 Chief Baron Palles in what Robert Clark described as a 'particularly savage example of the doctrine of constructive notice, held that an exemption clause of which the plaintiff was unaware applied, because he was taken as knowing that which he had the possible means of knowing.

CONSTRUCTION TEST

Judges have displayed outright hostility toward exemption clauses, in particular when one of the parties is a consumer. Lord Denning in *Levison & Anor. v. Patent Steam Carpet Cleaning Co. Ltd.* [1977] 3 All E.R. 499 C.A. very candidly referred to "other means which have been used by the courts to get around the injustice of these exemption and limitation clauses, . . . one means is by construing the clauses strictly, so as to cut it down to reasonable proportions."

As part of the construction test a strict interpretation may be applied to the words used. *Andrew Bros v. Singer* and *Baldry v. Marshall*. Clear words are needed to exempt from a serious breach — *O'Connor v. McCowen* or from negligence — *Alexander v. Irish National Stud*. Words will not be construed to defeat the main object or main purpose — *Glynn v. Margetson but may be construed contra proferentem — Lee v. Railway Executive. See In re Sweeney and Kennedy Arbitration* [1950] I.R. 85 Chapter 7 *ante*.

As to interpretation in cases of fundamental breach see *Clayton Love v. B & I* (Irish position) and *Photo Production Ltd. v. Securicor* (English position). Construction to exempt from strict liability is instanced by *White v. John Warrick*, while the non applicability of exemption clauses to third parties is illustrated by *Adler v. Dickson*.

NEGLIGENCE

An exemption clause which exempts from liability in the event of injury but does not expressly refer to injury caused by negligence will not be effective to exclude injury so caused. The proper test is to consider what the ordinary sensible customer would understand by the words — *per* McMahon J. in *Alexander v. Irish National Stud*. An accident might occur without negligence and an offeree would not read these words as a warning that he could not hold the offeror responsible if injury was suffered as a result of his negligence.

UNREASONABLENESS

Another means of curtailing such clauses suggested by Lord Denning in *Gillespie Bros. & Co. Ltd. v. Roy Bowles Transport Ltd.* [1973] 1 All E.R. 193 at 210 was that an exemption or limitation clause should not be given effect if it was unreasonable, or if it would be unreasonable to apply it in the circumstances of the case. (Section 55 Sale of Goods Act, 1893 introduced in a new form by Section 22 of the Sale of Goods and Supply of Services Act, 1980 provides that in any case where the buyer does not deal as a consumer any term purporting to exempt from implied terms (other than title) shall not be enforceable except to such extent as it is shown to be fair and reasonable.) See also Section 3(2) of the English Unfair Contract Terms Act 1977.

FUNDAMENTAL BREACH

A further strategem used by the courts to get around exemption clauses was a principle of construction later elevated into a doctrine of fundamental breach. This doctrine was applied by the Irish Supreme Court in *Clayton Love v. B & I* in 1970. This decision was totally apposite to that of the English House of Lords in the *Suisse Atlantique* case, the previous day, that as a rule of law the doctrine was unsound.

Lord Denning made a number of unsuccessful attempts to re-establish the doctrine and in *Levinson* held that the doctrine of fundamental breach still applied in standard form contracts, where there was inequality of bargaining power. The decision of the House of Lords, the following year in *Photo Production Ltd. v. Securicor* put the position beyond doubt in England.

The Irish judgment in *Clayton Love* has never been over-ruled and is technically still the law but significantly Barrington J. in *Western Meats v. National Ice and Cold Storage Co. Ltd.*, has indicated that the relevant principles which the Irish courts would follow, would appear to be those in the *Photo Production Ltd.* case. Many commentators have expressed the view that the Irish Supreme Court would reverse or distinguish *Clayton Love* should a suitable case arise and thus bring Irish case law into line with that in Britain. The absence of an Irish equivalent to the British Unfair Contract Terms Act,

1977 could severely disadvantage Irish litigants were this to happen.

There can be little doubt that the lack of statutory protection has been a factor which has influenced judicial interpretation of exemption clauses. The more amenable approach of the courts to limitation clauses illustrated in *Ailsa Craig Fishing Co. Ltd v. Malvern Fishing Co Ltd. & Anor.* tends to make them attractive as an alternative to exemption clauses.

At one time it was thought that a person who exempted himself from liability for not performing the fundamental obligation under the contract must have lacked contractual *animus* at the time the contract was made. The fallacy of this logic became apparent and it now appears that we have entered an era of unilateral contractual obligations, where one side only may be liable in the event of non performance, the other side having protected himself by the use of exemption and limitation clauses.

INCORPORATION

SIGNED AGREEMENT
L'Estrange v. Graucob Ltd. [1934] 2. K.B. 394

The plaintiff Miss L'Estrange was the owner of premises in Llandudno where she carried on the business of a cafe. She decided to buy an automatic cigarette machine from the defendant company and she signed a document headed "Sales Agreement" in which she agreed to pay a deposit of £8 and 18 instalments of £3. odd. One clause in the agreement stated "**This agreement contains all the terms and conditions under which I agree to purchase the machine specified above, and any express or implied condition, statement or warranty, statutory or otherwise not stated herein is hereby excluded.**" The machine, delivered on the 28 March, 1933 did not work satisfactorily, and after a few days it became jammed and unworkable. During the month of April it was repaired a number of times and on May 8, her patience exhausted, the plaintiff wrote to the defendants stating that she had decided to forfeit her deposit, and requested that the machine be removed. When the defendants declined to terminate the transaction the plaintiff brought an action for money had and received by the defendant for a consideration which had wholly failed and she also claimed damages for breach of an implied warranty that the machine was fit for the purpose for which it was sold.

The plaintiff contended (1) that she was induced to sign the document under the impression that it was an order form; and (2) that at the time when she signed it she knew nothing of the conditions on which the defendants relied. She had not read the document and the defendants had not read it to her, or told her to read it, that she never read the words in small type and did not remember that the defendants agents had ever called her attention to them. She also claimed that although she signed the document intentionally she had no clear idea of what she was signing. She thought that the document was an order form or a form consenting to the purchase.

The company pleaded that the signed contract expressly provided for the exclusion of all implied warranties, denied that the machine delivered was in a condition unfit for the purpose intended, and counterclaimed for payment of the balance of the purchase price. Evidence was given on behalf of the defendants that they met her for two hours, that the whole of the document, including the small print was read to her, that she asked no questions and signed the document.

Held: that as the plaintiff buyer had signed the written contract, and had not been induced to do so by an misrepresentation, she was bound by its terms, and that it was wholly immaterial that she had not read it and did not know its contents. The action failed and the sellers were entitled to judgment. *Parker v. South Eastern Railway* (1877) 2 C.P.D. 416, 421 observations *approved and applied. Richardson, Spence & Co. v. Rowntree* (1894) A.C. and other railway ticket cases, distinguished.

Scrutton L.J.:

"In *Parker v. South Eastern Railway*, Mellish L.J. laid down in a few sentences the law which is applicable to this case. He there said 'In an ordinary case, where an action is brought on a written agreement which is signed by the defendants, the agreement is proved by proving his signature, and, in the absence of fraud, it is wholly immaterial that he has not read the agreement and did not know its contents.' Having said that, he goes on to deal with the ticket cases, where there is no signature to the contractual document, the document being simply handed by one party to the other: 'The parties may, however, reduce their agreement into writing, so that **the writing constitutes the sole evidence of the agreement, without signing it; but in that case there must be evidence independently of the agreement itself to prove that the defendant has assented to it**. In that case, also, if it is proved that the defendant has assented to the writing constituting the agreement between the parties, it is, in the absence of fraud, immaterial that the defendant had not read the agreement, and did not know its contents.

In cases in which the contract is contained in a railway ticket or other unsigned document it is necessary to prove that an alleged party was aware, or ought to have been aware, of its terms and conditions. These cases have no application when the document has been signed. **When a document containing contractual terms is signed, then, in the absence of fraud, or, I will add, misrepresentation, the party signing it is bound, and it is wholly immaterial whether he has read the document or not.** . . .

Moreover, whether the plaintiff was or was not told that the document was an order form, it was in fact an order form, and **an order form is a contractual document. It may be either an acceptance or a proposal which may be accepted**, but it always contains some contractual terms . . . the plaintiff has signed a document headed 'Sales Agreement', which she admits had to do with an intended purchase, and which contained a clause excluding all conditions and warranties . . . having put her signature to the document, and not being induced to do so by fraud or **misrepresentation**, cannot be heard to say she is not bound by the terms of the document because she has not read them."

Note: The statement of Scrutton L.J. about the non applicability of an exemption clause because of misrepresentation was followed by the judgment in *Curtis v. Chemical Cleaning Co. Ltd.* some seventeen years later.

EXEMPTION CLAUSE — SIGNED CONTRACT
Knox v. Great Northern Railway Co. [1896] 2 I.R.632 (C.A.)

The plaintiff's horse was taken by a groom to Armagh station to be sent to Dublin by train. The horse received serious injuries while being loaded by a GNR porter. The groom later purchased a ticket which he signed. It contained a condition that the carriage was at the owner's risk, and that the company was exempt from all liability not occasioned by the wilful misconduct of their servants.

Held: The negligence did not amount to wilful misconduct. The defendants were not liable. If the groom had taken the horse away after the injury and declined to book him, the plaintiff might have sued successfully, but he did not do so.

Note: See *L'Estrange v. Graucob (F.) Ltd.* [1934] 2 K.B. 394 and *Slattery v. CIE* 106 I.L.T.R. 71 H.C. where a consignment note "On owner's risk" terms was signed after the completion of carriage but before completion of the contract. Holmes J. stated "it is neither illegal, unreasonable, nor unusual for the terms of a contract to be reduced to writing after the performance of the services contracted for has begun."

DOCUMENT SIGNED DURING PERFORMANCE OF CONTRACT
Slattery v CIE (1968) 106 I.L.T.R. 71 (H.C.) Teevan J.

The plaintiff arranged for the defendant to transport three thoroughbred horses by road to the bloodstock sales at Ballsbridge. No terms of contract were arranged and nothing was said about rates, charges or conditions of carriage.

One horse was injured while being loaded by the defendants driver, had to be withdrawn from the sale and later sold for less than it would have fetched.

On reaching Ballsbridge the driver presented a consignment note; containing the terms and conditions of carriage which the plaintiff signed. These conditions exempted the defendants from liability for injury except on proof of wilful misconduct.

Held: The defendant's driver had been negligent and this was the cause of the injury. The consignment note as signed, contained the terms of the contract. It was not totally performed when signed; the plaintiff had not carried out his part of it, namely to pay the carriage charge. Although signed on delivery it was binding on the parties.

SIGNED CONTRACT — KNOWLEDGE OF TERMS
Siebel and Seum v. Kent, unreported, 1 June 1986 (H.C.) Finlay P.

Two Germans paid a deposit of £18,000 and signed a contract to buy land near Nenagh, Co. Tipperary. The conditions attached to the contract contained a forfeiture clause. The memorandum or contract of sale was on a separate sheet, whereas the general conditions and the forfeiture clause were on separate sheets bound in with the memorandum. There was no evidence that the plaintiffs were aware at the time they signed the memorandum that the pages of printed conditions were incorporated in the terms of it.

Held: In the absence of evidence that the plaintiffs understood that the conditions of sale formed part of the contract, they were not bound by them.

Before the principle that a person who signs a contract is bound can be applied, (*L'Estrange v. Graucob (F.) Ltd.* [1934] 2 K.B. 394) the contracting party must understand:

(a) that what he is signing is a contract, final in its form containing conditions and clauses, and

(b) that the particular written or printed conditions are incorporated with whatever document he signs and form part of the contract: — per Finlay P.

UNSIGNED DOCUMENTS

DEGREE OF NOTICE OF EXEMPTION CLAUSE
Parker v. South Eastern Railway Co. (1877) C. P. D. 416

Parker deposited a bag in the cloakroom of the defendant's railway station, paid a clerk 2d, and received a ticket. On one side of the ticket was printed the words "**see back**". On the other side were printed several clauses including "The company will not be responsible for any package exceeding the value of £10." Later that same day the bag could not be found. Parker claimed £24.10 as the value of it. The company pleaded the exemption clause on the back of the ticket.

Held: There ought to be a new trial. The second question left to the jury ought to be whether the company did that which was reasonably sufficient to give the plaintiff notice of the condition. The proper direction to be given to the jury was:

(1) that if the person receiving the ticket did not see or know that there was any writing on the ticket, he is not bound by the conditions,

(2) that if he knew that there was writing and knew or believed that the writing contained conditions, then he is bound by the conditions,

(3) that if he knew that there was writing on the ticket, but did not know or believe that it contained conditions, he would be bound by the delivery of the ticket in a manner that he could see that there was writing on it, was, in the opinion of the jury, reasonable notice that the writing contained conditions.

Mellish L.J. stated:

"... in an ordinary case, where an action is brought on a written agreement which is signed by the defendant, the agreement is proved by proving his signature, and, in the absence of fraud, it is wholly immaterial that he has not read the agreement and does not know its contents."

Note: Fifty seven years later these observations were approved and applied in *L'Estrange v. Graucob Ltd.* [1934] 2 K.B. 394, the absence of misrepresentation being added to that of fraud.

In relation to ticket cases, the three tests laid down in *Parker v. South Eastern Railway* and approved in *Burnett v. Westminster Bank* are still valid. *Hollingworth v. Southern Ferries Ltd.* [1977] 2 Lloyds Rep. 70 has been construed by some commentators as eroding or revising these tests but it is suggested that Hollingworth is a questionable authority. Deputy Judge Ogden Q.C. held that the contract had been concluded before the ticket was delivered, therefore it was not a contractual document. This would be in accord with the dictum of Mellish J. in *Parker v. South Eastern Railway* (See *Chapleton v. Barry U.D.C.* [1940] 1 K.B. 532) but holding that a brochure containing terms although read by the plaintiff's agent was not a contractual document as a way of disposing of the issue of notice of terms, is more difficult to accept.

NOTICE OF EXEMPTION CLAUSE

Western Meats v. National Ice & Cold Storage Co. Ltd.
High Court, unreported, 2 June 1981, Barrington J.

The plaintiffs were approached by the defendants and offered the facilities of the defendants cold storage plant. The parties entered into a contract under which the plaintiff stored pig meat with the defendants but when they wished to withdraw the meat for the Christmas market they were unable to do so because the defendants could not locate it.

The defendants relied on their standard conditions of trade. Clause 1 provided that all goods were stored at the owner's risk and clause 2 provided that the company would not be answerable for any delay, loss or damage arising (*inter alia*) from negligence, thefts, including theft by the company's servants or any other cause whatsoever.

The plaintiffs claimed that they were not aware of these clauses and there was no evidence that they were ever expressly brought to their attention. The only evidence was a photostat copy of the original letter between the parties. Certain terms were set out in the letter but there was no reference to the conditions in the text of the letter itself nor did they appear on the back of the copy although they might have been on the back of the original.

Held: The defendants were guilty of negligence and breach of contract. The defendants did not give the plaintiffs reasonable notice of the contents of the standard conditions:

> ". . . it appears to me also that a business man offering a specialist service, but accepting no responsibility for it must bring home clearly to the party dealing with him that he accepts no such responsibility." — *per* Barrington J.

Note: It also appeared to Barrington J. that the conditions if part of the contract, were a complete answer to the plaintiffs claim, that the relevant principles appeared to be those laid down in *Photo Production Ltd. Ltd. v. Securicor Transport Ltd.* [1980] All E.R. 556. But the primary question was whether the plaintiffs were given reasonable notice of these conditions.

NOTICE OF EXEMPTION CLAUSES

Early v. G.S.R. Co. [1940] I.R. 409 (S.C.)

The plaintiff purchased a return ticket at Fanagh for an excursion to Mohill by rail. A poster displayed at Fenagh stated that excursion tickets were issued at less than ordinary and subject to the notices and conditions shown in the company's time tables. The ticket bore on its face the words; "Special train . . . see back." On the back was printed "Issued subject to the conditions and regulations in the Company's time tables, books, bills and notices."

One of those conditions was that the holder of a ticket issued at less than ordinary fare should not have any right of action against the company in respect of injury, fatal or otherwise. No document containing these conditions was available for inspection at Fenagh. The plaintiff, however, had not enquired about them.

Held: The defendants had taken reasonable steps to bring to the plaintiff's notice the conditions upon which he was accepted as a passenger and the plaintiff was bound by those conditions so long as he continued to be a passenger in the train.

Note: The judgment cites Lord Hanworth in *Thompson v. L.M.S. Railway Co.* [1930] 1 K.B. 41 ". . . it has **not ever been held that** the **mere circuitry** which has to be followed **to find the actual conditions prevents the passenger having notice** that there was a condition." See also *Devlin v. Great Northern Railway Co. (Ir)* [1936] Ir.Jur. 55 decided two years earlier.

NOTICE FROM COURSE OF DEALING
Miley v. McKechnie Ltd. (1949) 84 I.L.T.R. 89 (Cir. Ct.) Shannon J.

The plaintiff left in a costume for cleaning at the defendant's depot and was given a receipt bearing on its face in capital letters the words "ALL ORDERS ACCEPTED WITHOUT GUARANTEE," followed in smaller letters "**please read conditions overleaf.**" The conditions overleaf stated that the defendants did not accept liability for loss, damage, or shrinkages, however caused. There were notices to similar effect in the defendants depot, one at the back of the counter and one facing the customer as he or she would leave. The plaintiff said that she had never seen these. When the costume was returned there was a hole in the jacket and the plaintiff sought damages. Her action was dismissed in the District Court and she appealed to the Circuit Court.

Held: The acceptance by the plaintiff of the receipt and of similar receipts previously relieved the defendants of liability.

Note: It was only after the contract had been made that the ticket was received but the plaintiff was in the habit of receiving such tickets. It would be a different matter if a customer were to send a small boy with the article. By the time he would have given the ticket to the customer the article might be on its way to Cork to be cleaned at the defendants works.

If the notices in the shop were the only documents the defendant relied on, his Lordship thought they would not be sufficient. (See *Hennigan v. Ballybunnion Picture House Ltd. post.*) A document, however, was invariably handed to the customer, it was marked IMPORTANT and if a customer saw this and did not care to read it, he could not complain at the loss ensuing to him.

Section 39 of the Sale of Goods and Supply of Services Act, 1980 provides that where the supplier is acting in the course of a business there are implied terms that he has the necessary skill to render the service, that he will supply the service with due skill, care and diligence and that materials used are sound and reasonably fit for the purpose. Section 40 states that any of the terms implied by section 39 may be negatived by an express term of the contract or by the course of dealing between the parties or by usage except that where the recipient **deals as a consumer**. It must be shown that the express term is fair and reasonable and has been specifically brought to his attention.

PREVIOUS KNOWLEDGE OF TERMS

CARRIAGE OF GOODS

McCutcheon v. MacBrayne Ltd. [1964] 1 W.L.R. 125 (H.L.)

The owner sought to recover the replacement value of a car lost when a ship sank through the negligence of the company's servants on a voyage from the Hebrides to the mainland. The conditions of carriage displayed in the company's office exempted the company from liability for negligence and the receipt stated "Passengers, passengers luggage and livestock are carried **subject to the conditions specified in the company's sailing bills, notices and announcements**."

The normal practice of the company was to give the consignor a "risk note" containing the conditions for signature. On previous occasions the car owner had sometimes signed a risk note but on the present occasion none was issued or signed. The car owner knew that certain conditions of carriage were normally imposed, but did not know specifically what they were.

Held: that this was an oral contract and the conditions relied on were not imported into it so as to exempt the company from liability for negligence. In the absence of any contractual document a consignor of goods cannot, by a course of previous dealing, be bound by conditions of which he is generally aware but the specific terms of which he has no knowledge.

Per Lord Reid and Lord Pearce:

> "If there was bad faith on the part of a consignor who knew that an omission to proffer for his signature a document which was always required, was due to mere forgetfulness, he might not be able to take advantage of that error".

Per Lord Devlin:

"Previous dealings are relevant only if they prove knowledge of the terms, actual and not constructive, and assent to them. If a term is not expressed in a contract, there is only one other way in which it can come into it and that is by implication. No implication can be made against a party of a term which was unknown to him. . . . The respondents in the present case have failed to prove that the appellant made himself acquainted with the conditions they had introduced into previous dealings. He was not estopped from saying that, for good reasons or bad, he signed the previous contracts without knowing what was in them . . . either he does not make the contract at all because the parties are not *ad idem* or he makes the contract without conditions"

Observations of Bagallay L.J. in *Parker v. S. E. Railway* (1877) 2 C.P.D. 416, 425 C.A. distinguished.

TIME OF NOTICE MUST BE BEFORE OR CONTEMPORANEOUSLY WITH MAKING OF CONTRACT

Olley v. Marlborough Court Ltd. [1949] 1 K.B. 532 (C.A.)

The plaintiff and her husband booked into the defendants hotel and paid for a week in advance. They then went upstairs to the bedroom allotted to them, where a notice behind a door stated "The proprietors will not hold themselves responsible for articles lost or stolen, unless handed to the manageress for safe custody. Valuables should be deposited for safe custody in a sealed package and a receipt obtained."

The plaintiff left her room, closed the self-locking door and hung the key of the room on the hook on the Reception Office keyboard provided for that purpose. When she returned the key was missing from the keyboard and furs, clothing and jewellery worth £50 was missing from the room. The plaintiff claimed that the defendants were negligent and breach of an implied term in the contract to take proper care for the safety of her property. The defendants denied negligence and relied on the terms of the notice in the room.

Held: that the terms of the notice in the bedroom formed no part of the contract. The contract had been made before the guests could see the notice. The hotel were negligent.

Denning L.J.:

"The first question is whether the notice formed part of the contract. In my opinion, notices put up in bedrooms do not of themselves make a contract. As a rule the guest does not see them until after he has been accepted as a guest. The hotel company, no doubt hope that then guest will be bound by them, but the hope is in vain unless they can clearly show that he agreed to be bound by them, which is rarely the case."

NATURE OF DOCUMENT
Chapleton v. Barry U.D.C. [1940] 1 K.B. 532

The plaintiff, while on a beach approached a stack of deck-chairs belonging to the defendant and obtained two chairs from an attendant for which he paid 4d and received two tickets. There was a notice beside the stack of chairs:

"BARRY UDC,
Hire of chairs 2d per session of 3 Hours."

There was no exemption clause on the notice. The plaintiff glanced at the tickets and slipped them into his pocket having no idea that they contained conditions. One side of the tickets contained the words "Barry UDC Chair Ticket 2d. not transferable." On the other side was a clause "**The Council will not be liable for any accident or damage arising from the hire of chair**."

The plaintiff was injured when a chair gave way and he sued the defendants who claimed that the clause on the ticket exempted them.The plaintiff replied that there was nothing on the face of the tickets to call attention to the fact that there were conditions printed on the back of it.

Held: that the ticket was a mere voucher or receipt for the money paid for the hire of the chair, and the conditions were those on the notice near the chairs. There was no clause in the notice limiting liability and the defendant authority were liable to the plaintiff.

Slesser L.J.:

"In my opinion, this ticket is no more than a receipt, and is quite different from a railway ticket which contains upon it the terms upon which a railway company agrees to carry the passenger."

MacKinnon L.J.:

"He (the plaintiff) cannot be deemed to have entered into a contract in the terms of the words that his creditor has chosen to print on the back of the receipt, unless, of course, the creditor has taken reasonable steps to bring the terms of the proposed contract to the mind of the man."

NOTICES MUST BE CONSPICUOUSLY DISPLAYED
Hennigan v. Ballybunion Picture House Ltd.
[1944] Ir. Jur. Rep. 62 (Cir. Ct.) O'Briain J.

During a dance held in the defendant's hall, the plaintiff deposited his overcoat in a room attached to the hall, marked "Cloakroom". There was no separate charge for the use of the cloakroom and there was no attendant. Several copies of a notice were displayed in the hall and cloakroom stating:

> **"The management will not accept responsibility for loss or damage to property of patrons left in this hall**."

There was evidence that the plaintiff did not see any of the notices. His coat was missing and could not be found, so he claimed £10 for its value.

Held: The defendants were not liable, the notices were displayed in a reasonably conspicuous manner. *Hegarty v. Robert Roberts & Co. (Ireland) Ltd.*, 64 1 I.L.T.R. 215 applied:

> "The fact that the plaintiff did not see the notices was irrelevant, if, in fact, the defendants displayed the notices in a reasonably conspicuous place as they had done." — O Briain J.

INTERPRETATION

STRICT INTERPRETATION — IMPLIED-EXPRESS TERMS
Andrew Bros (Bournemouth) Ltd. v. Singer Co. Ltd. [1934] 1 K.B. 17

The plaintiff dealer, ordered a "new Singer car" from the defendant under an agreement which contained a guarantee to repair or replace faults disclosed due to defective material or workmanship within twelve months and which excluded "all conditions, warranties and liabilities **implied** by statute, common law or otherwise." The car provided had a speedometer reading 550 odd miles, and a parking ticket issued at Leicester. In had in fact, been driven to Darlington to show to a prospective customer who did not buy it.

The plaintiff claimed breach of contract, that the car was not a new car. The defendants pleaded that the plaintiffs took delivery and paid for the car as new and that they were exempt from liability by virtue of the exemption clause.

Held: that the term "new Singer car" was an **express** and not an implied term of the contract, and that as a "new Singer car" had not been delivered the defendants were liable. The exemption clause related to **implied** conditions and warranties.

Scrutton L.J.:

> "In my view there has been in this case a breach of an express term in the contract. If a vendor desires to protect himself from liability in such a case he must do so by much clearer language than this, which in my opinion, does not exempt the defendant from liability where they have failed to comply with the express terms of the contract."

CONDITIONS — WARRANTIES

Baldry v. Marshall [1925] 1 K.B. 260 (C.A.)

The plaintiff who knew nothing about Bugatti cars told the defendant car dealer that he wanted "a comfortable car suitable for touring purposes." The defendant (a Bugatti dealer) said that a Bugatti would satisfy those requirements and showed him a specimen. The plaintiff then signed an order form on the terms that the defendants would guarantee the car for 12 months against defects of manufacture. The form provided that the guarantee if accepted, "expressly excludes any other guarantee or **warranty,** statutory or otherwise." The car delivered was uncomfortable and unsuited for touring purposes and the plaintiff sought to reject it and sued to recover back the purchase price he had paid.

Held:

(1) That the requirement that the car should be comfortable and suitable for touring purposes was **a condition** and not a warranty and the implication of that condition was not excluded by the terms of the contract.

(2) If the buyer, while asking to be supplied with a car of a named make, indicates to the seller that he relies on his skill and judgment for it being fit for a particular named purpose, he does not buy it "under its trade name" within s. 14, s.s. 1 Sale of Goods Act 1893. The implied condition as to fitness for particular purpose applied.

CLEAR WORDS NEEDED TO EXEMPT FROM SERIOUS BREACH

O'Connor v. McCowen & Sons Ltd.
[1943] 77 I.L.T.R. 64 (H.C.) Overend J.

The plaintiff (through his son) purchased Swede Turnip seeds from the defendants shop in Tralee. The transaction was a sale by description the purchaser had no opportunity of examining the seed and if he had it would have been no use to him. It was stated on the sale docket that **while the defendants selected their seeds with the greatest care, no warranty of any seeds was given by the seller either expressly or by implication as to description, quality, productiveness or any other matter**. Before O'Connor signed the sale docket he was told that McCowens had not got the seed from their usual supplier and could not guarantee them. When the seed was sown it produced a crop which was not turnips and which was useless to the plaintiff. A decree was given against the defendants in Tralee Circuit Court and they appealed.

Held: the words used at the time of the sale were not sufficient to warn the buyer that the seeds might not be turnip seeds at all and that the conditions on the sale docket were not applicable in the circumstances as the defendants had not selected their goods with the greatest care but had taken what they were able to get.

Overend J. referring to the statement that McCowens had not got the seed from their usual supplier and could not guarantee them said "these words were not sufficient. . . . **If purchasers were to be precluded, when they purchased articles by description and got different goods, then the very clearest words must be used by the seller**, such as; "You may be purchasing seeds that are not turnip seeds at all."

CLEAR WORDS NEEDED TO EXEMPT FROM NEGLIGENCE
Alexander & Another v. Irish National Stud
(H.C.) Unreported, 10/6/77, McMahon J.

The plaintiff sent a mare "Chips" to the stud to be covered by the stallion "Sallust". In the covering yard the mare broke loose before hobbles could be released and was killed by crashing into a wall. A clause in the contract provided "The Irish National Stud will not be responsible to any owner of any mare or foal in the event of accident occurring to that mare or foal. . . ."

Held: The contract terms are to be construed in the sense which an ordinary sensible person would understand them. A breeder would read these words as a warning that the stud would not be liable for an accident which might befall a mare without negligence on the part of anyone, he would not understand the words to mean that if his mare was injured in an accident caused by the negligence of the employees of the stud he could not hold the stud responsible.

Human failure in operating the procedures amounted to negligence and the defendants were not exempted from liability by the condition in question.

STRICT LIABILITY
White v. John Warrick & Co. Ltd. [1953] 1 W.L.R. 1285 (C.A.)

The plaintiff a newsagent hired a cycle with a large carrier in front of it for use in delivering newspapers. The contract of hire was on a printed form used by the defendant company which contained one clause that the defendant company agreed to maintain the machine in working order and condition, without any additional charge and another clause (clause 11) which stated:

> "Nothing in this agreement shall render the owners liable for any personal injuries to the riders of the machines hired, nor for any third party claims, nor loss of any goods belonging to the hirer of the machines."

When the plaintiff was riding a cycle hired from the defendant, the saddle went forward and he was thrown off onto the ground causing serious injury to his knee and right leg. As a result he was hospitalized and unable to work. When the bicycle was examined it was found that the saddle was quite loose. The plaintiff claimed damages for breach of warranty to supply a cycle which was reasonably fit for the purpose required and in the alternative claimed that the accident was due to the negligence and/or breach of contract of the defendants their servants or agents.

For the plaintiff it was conceded that clause 11 would prevent the plaintiff from succeeding on a claim based on breach of contract but it was submitted that the clause did not protect the defendant from an action for damages for negligence. For the defendant it was contended that the negligence alleged was a breach of contract not an independent tort and that the plaintiff should not succeed by framing his action in tort instead of contract.

Held: that, although clause 11 excepted the defendants (even if they were negligent) from their liability in contract, which was more strict than their liability in tort, it did not exempt them from liability in negligence. *Rutter v. Palmer* [1922] 2 K.B. 87 *applied.*

Lord Denning L.J.:

"In the present case there are two possible heads of liability on the defendants, one for negligence, the other for breach of contract. The liability for breach of contract is more strict than the liability for negligence. The defendants may be liable in contract for supplying a defective machine, even though they were not negligent. (See *Hyman v. Nye* (1861) 6 Q.B. 685) In those circumstances, the exemption clause must, I think, be construed as exempting the defendants only from their liability in contract and not from their liability for negligence."

Singleton L.J.:

". . . the primary object of the clause . . . is to relieve the defendants from liability for breach of contract or for breach of warranty. Unless, then, there be clear words which would also exempt from liability for negligence, the clause ought not to be construed as giving absolution to the defendants if negligence is proved against them."

Note: In *Alderslade v. Hendon Laundry* the exemption clause did apply because negligence liability was the only liability it could apply to.

WORDS NOT CONSTRUED TO DEFEAT MAIN OBJECT
Glynn v. Margetson & Co. [1893] A.C. 351 (H.L.)

G contracted to ship oranges on M's ship under a bill of lading which stated that it was the "lying in the port of Malaga, and bound for Liverpool, with liberty to proceed to and stay at any port or ports in any station in the Mediterranean,

Levant, Black Sea or Adriatic, or on the coasts of Africa, Spain, Portugal, France, Great Britain and Ireland." the bill also contained a clause whereby the shipper expressly agreed to all its stipulations whether written or printed. The deviation clause was printed with the name of the port of shipment left blank and filled up in writing.

The ship left Malaga for a port on the east coast of Spain and out of her course for Liverpool, then returned and made for Liverpool where the oranges were delivered in a damaged condition owing to the delay. The shipper took an action against the shipowner for damages for breach of contract.

Held: that the printed clauses must not be be construed so as to defeat the main object of the contract, which was to carry oranges from Malaga to Liverpool; that the liberty must be restricted to ports which were in the course of the voyage; that the deviation in question was therefore not justified; and that the shipowner was liable.

CANNOT EXEMPT FROM OWN FRAUD

Pearson & Co. Ltd. v. Dublin Corporation [1907] A.C. 351 (H.L.)

A clause in the contract stipulated that the contractor should satisfy himself as to the dimensions, levels and the nature of all existing works and that the Corporation did not hold itself responsible for the accuracy of the information as to sections or foundations of existing walls and works. The contract also provided that no charges for extra work or otherwise would be allowed in consequence of incorrect information or inaccuracies in the drawings or specifications.

The appellants performed the contract and brought an action of deceit against the corporation, claiming damages for false representations as to the position, dimensions and foundation of the wall which make the work more costly. Corporation engineers admitted that they had purposely set out to provide inaccurate information in order to get a cheap price from the contractor.

Held: That the contract, truly construed, contemplated honesty on both sides, and protected only against honest mistakes. The decision of the Kings Bench in entering judgment for the appellants must be restored upon the ground that there was a question of fact for the jury upon the allegation of fraud.

Lord Loreburn:

> "Now it seems clear that no one can escape liability for his own fraudulent statements by inserting in a contract a clause that the other party shall not rely on them."

Lord Ashbourne:

"Such a clause (as used) may be appropriate and fairly apply to errors, inaccuracies and mistakes, but not to cases like the present."

Lord James of Hereford:

"Such a clause would be good protection against any mistake or miscalculation but fraud vitiates every contract and every clause in it. As a general principle I incline to the view that an express term that fraud shall not vitiate a contract would be bad in law, but it is unnecessary in this case to determine whether special circumstances may not create an exception to that rule." See also chapter 11.

MISREPRESENTATION AS TO EXTENT OF EXEMPTION CLAUSE

Curtis v. Chemical Cleaning & Dyeing Co. Ltd. [1951] 1 K.B. 805

The plaintiff, Mrs. Curtis, took a white satin wedding dress to the shop of the defendant Chemical Cleaning and Dying Company for cleaning. She was given a paper headed "Receipt" and asked by a shop assistant to sign it. She inquired why her signature was required and was told that it was because the defendant company would not accept liability for certain specified risks including the risk of damage by or to the beads and sequins with which the dress was trimmed. The plaintiff then signed the "Receipt"; which in fact contained the following condition.

"This or these articles is accepted on condition that the company is not liable for any damage howsoever arising or delay."

When the dress was returned it was found to be stained and the plaintiff was awarded damages by the County Court judge, who held that the defendants had been negligent and were not protected by their exemption clause by reason of the misrepresentation as to its character by the assistant. The company appealed.

Held: that the defendants could not rely on the exemption clause because their assistant by an innocent misrepresentation had created a false impression in the mind of the plaintiff as to the extent of the exemption and thereby induced her to sign the "receipt".

Denning L.J.:

"In my opinion, any behaviour by words or conduct, is sufficient to be a misrepresentation if it is such as to mislead the other party about the existence or extent of the exemption. If it conveys a false impression, that is enough. **If the false impression is created knowingly**, it **is a fraudu-**

lent **misrepresentation**; if it is **created unwittingly**, it **is an innocent misrepresentation**; but **either** is **sufficient to dissentitle** the creator of it to the benefit of the exemption.

When one party puts forward a printed form for signature, failure by him to draw attention to the existence or extent of the exemption clause may in some circumstances convey the impression that there is no exemption at all, or at any rate not so wide an exemption as that contained in the document. The present case is a good illustration . . . by failing to draw attention to the width of the exemption clause, the assistant created the false impression, that the exemption only related to the beads and sequins and that it did not extend to the material of which the dress was made. It was done perfectly innocently but nevertheless a false impression was created. It was a sufficient misrepresentation to dissentitle the cleaners from relying on the exemption, except as regards beads and sequins."

CONTRA PROFERENTEM

Lee & Son (Grantham) Ltd. v. Railway Executive
[1949] 2 All E.R. 581 (C.A.)

Goods stored in a railway warehouse let to a tenant, were damaged by fire and the tenant brought an action against the Railway Executive alleging that the accident was due to their negligence because a spark or other combustible material ejected from their railway engine had caused the fire.

The Railway Executive relied on a clause in their tenancy agreement which provided:

"The Tenant shall be responsible for and shall release and indemnify the company and their servants and agents from and against all liability for personal injury (whether fatal or otherwise) loss of or damage to property and any other loss, damage, costs and expenses, however caused or incurred (whether by the act or neglect of the company or their servants or agents or not) **which but for the tenancy hereby created** or anything done pursuant to the provisions hereof **would not have arisen**."

Held: the words "which but for the tenancy hereby created . . . would not have arisen" were confined to liabilities which arose by reason of the relationship of landlord and tenant; the fact that the tenant occupied the warehouse under an agreement from the Railway Executive was immaterial to the allegation in the present case of negligence; and the tenant, therefore, could not be called on to release or indemnify the Railway Executive in the event of negligence being established.

Sir Raymond Evershed, M.R. referred to a steam engine emitting sparks which set fire to property in the warehouse and continued:

"Although it may have been the defendants intention to protect themselves from possible claims of that character, the difficulty I have found in considering this clause is that the parties, not being willing to be explicit in their language or to confine themselves to damage of this kind, have evolved a form of words . . . which seems to me to have most remarkable, if not extravagant results.

Counsel for the plaintiffs has taken the example of a customer of the first plaintiffs who sets forth from London for the express purpose of visiting the first plaintiffs at their warehouse, and owing to the negligence of the defendants the customer is injured in an accident between Kings Cross and Grantham, Is such a case covered? Counsel for the defendants may say;' Everything is covered assuming such a case can be proved." But — if it is covered — and I would agree with the argument that reading "but for the tenancy hereby created" as equivalent to: "but for the existence of the tenancy," it would be covered — then the clause has a scope which I regard as too vague and too extravagant to be supported if a narrower construction presents itself and can be adopted with equal justice to the language. . . .

There is an **alternative construction** equally available on the language, namely that the words "**which but for the tenancy hereby created** or anything done pursuant to the provisions hereof **would not have arisen**." mean, and are confined to liabilities which only arise by reason of the relationship of landlord and tenant which this document creates, . . . we are presented with **two alternative readings of this document** and the reading which one should adopt is to be determined, among other things, by a consideration of the fact that the defendants put forward the document. They have put forward a clause which is by no means free from obscurity and have contended that, on the view for which they argue, it has a remarkable, if not an extravagantly wide scope, and I think that the rule *contra proferentem* should be applied and that the result is that the present claim is not one which obliges the first plaintiffs to give to the defendants a release and an indemnity."

EXEMPTION CLAUSE AND BREACH OF A FUNDAMENTAL TERM

Clayton Love v. B. & I. (1970) 104 I.L.T.R. 157 (S.C.)

The plaintiff's agent signed the defendant's consignment note for the transportation of a consignment of scampi from Dublin to Liverpool. The note contained the company's standard conditions. Clause 3 exempted the company from liability for damage, loss, detention, deterioration, delay, misdelivery or non delivery even though due to the wrongful act neglect or default of the company, its servants or agents. Clause 16 required that any claim be made in writing within three days of arrival; otherwise it would be absolutely barred.

The plaintiff claimed that they contracted on the basis that the scampi would be loaded and shipped under refrigerated conditions whereas the defendants claimed that they contracted on the basis that it would be loaded at atmospheric conditions. (See contract by estoppel *ante*.) When the High Court held that there had been a fundamental breach and that the defendants could not rely on the exemption provisions in clause 3 but that they could rely upon clause 16 the plaintiffs appealed to the Supreme Court.

Held: The basis on which the doctrine of fundamental breach rests requires that a party, who like the defendants, has been held to be in breach of a fundamental obligation cannot rely on a time bar in the contract to defeat a claim for damages. Equally with other exempting provisions, such a time clause cannot be prayed in aid. The plaintiffs appeal must be allowed.

Note: The Supreme Court judgment was mainly concerned with whether there was a contract at all between the parties and a much smaller part of the judgment deals with exemption clauses and breach of a fundamental term. It ignored the opinion of Davitt P. in the High Court and did not take account of the House of Lords judgment, the previous day, in the *Suisse Atlantique* case [1967] 1 A.C. 361 which reverted to the view that the rule was one of construction only.

Davitt P. in the High Court seemed to anticipate *Suisse Atlantique* and *Photo Production Ltd. Ltd. v. Securicor* when he stated (*obiter*):

". . . there is nothing to prevent parties who wish to do so from entering into a contract containing exemption clauses which will exempt one or other or both from liability even in the case of a breach of a fundamental term. If that is done clearly and unequivocally I see no reason why such a provision should not be effective."

Note: See Lord Upjohn's definition of a "**fundamental term**" in Suisse Atlantique *post*.

FUNDAMENTAL BREACH

Suisse Atlantique Societe S.A. v. N.V. Rotterdamsche Kolem Centrale
[1967] A.C. 361 (H.L.)

In December 1956 the respondents chartered a ship the m.v. Silvretta from the appellants for the carriage of coal from the USA to Europe. A clause in the charter specified that cargo was to be loaded at an average of 1,500 tons a day. If the respondents took longer demurrage (a fine) of $1,000 U.S was payable per day by the charterer. Similar demurrage was payable for delay in unloading. Between October 16 1957 and the end of the charter period the vessel made eight round voyages whereas the appellants alleged that a further six voyages could have been made if the loading and unloading had been completed within the times scheduled.

Held:

(1) that no contractual right that not less than a certain number of voyages should be accomplished was to be implied either on the construction of the contract or by operation of law.

(2) that where delay was due to retention of the vessel and demurrage provisions applied the damages obtainable were limited to the demurrage payments.

(3) that the question **whether an exceptions clause was applicable where there was a fundamental breach** of contract **was one of the true construction** of the contract.

Per Lord Upjohn:

"There is no magic in the words "**fundamental breach**"; this expression is no more than a convenient shorthand expression for saying that a particular breach or breaches of contract by one party is or are such as to go to the root of the contract which entitled the other party to treat such breach or breaches as a **repudiation of the whole contract**. Whether **such breach** or breaches do constitute a fundamental breach depends on the construction of the contract and on all the facts and circumstances of the case.

The innocent party may accept breach or those breaches as a repudiation and treat the contract as at an end and sue for damages generally or he may at his option prefer to affirm the contract and treat it as continuing on foot in which case he can only sue for damages for breach or breaches of the particular stipulation or stipulations in the contract which has or have been broken.

But the expression "**fundamental term**" has a different meaning. A fundamental term of a contract is a stipulation which the parties have agreed either expressly or by necessary implication, or which the general law regards as a condition which goes to the root of the contract so that **any breach of that term** may at once and without further reference to the facts and circumstances be regarded by the innocent party as a fundamental breach and thus is conferred on him the alternative remedies at his option that I have just mentioned."

Lord Upjohn referred to the fact that exclusion clauses are strictly construed and to the doctrine of *contra proferentes* and stated:

"But where there is a breach of a fundamental term the law has taken an even firmer line for there is a strong, though rebuttable, presumption that in inserting a clause of exclusion or limitation in their contract the parties are not contemplating breaches of fundamental terms, and such clauses do not apply to relieve a party from the consequences of such a breach even where the contract continues in force. This result has been achieved by a robust use of a well known canon of construction, that wide words which taken in isolation would bear one meaning must be so construed as to give business efficacy to the contract and the presumed intention of the parties, upon the footing that both parties are intending to carry out the contract fundamentally."

Photo Production Ltd. v. Securitor Tranport Ltd. [1980] A.C. 827 (H.L.)

The plaintiffs were the owners of a factory premises at Gillingham in Kent where they produced greeting cards and Christmas cards. They contracted with the defendant, on a printed standard form contract, for the provision of a night patrol service visiting the factory 4 times most nights. The defendants patrolman, aged 23, deliberately started a fire by lighting a match and throwing it into a cardboard box or other material. The fire spread and a large part of the factory was destroyed. The patrolman subsequently pleaded guilty to the offence of maliciously damaging the building, stock and machinery and was sentenced to three year's imprisonment. The plaintiff claimed damages of £648,000 for breach of contract and/or negligence.

The contract contained clauses as follows:

(1) Under no circumstances shall the company be responsible for any injurious act or default by any employee of the company unless such act or default could have been foreseen and avoided by the exercise of due diligence on the part of the company as his employer; nor in any event, shall the company be held responsible for:

(a) any loss suffered by the customer through . . . fire or any other cause except insofar as such loss is solely attributable to the negligence of the company's employees acting within the ordinary course of their employment.

Clause 2 limited the liability of the company to specific amounts if notwithstanding clause 1 any liability arose on the part of the company.

Held: (1) That the doctrine of fundamental breach by virtue of which the termination of a contract brought it, and, with it, any exclusion clause to an end was not good law; that the question **whether and to what extent an exclusion clause was to be applied to any breach of contract was a matter of construction of the contract** and normally when the parties were bargaining on equal terms they should be free to apportion the risks as they though fit, making provision for their respective risks according to the terms they chose to agree. *Suisse Atlantique Societe d'Armement Maritime S.A. v. N.V. Rotterdanscha Kalen Centrale* [1967] 1 A.C. 361 HL(E) explained.

(2) That the words of the exclusion clause were clear and on their true construction covered deliberate acts as well as negligence so as to relieve the

defendants from responsibility for their breach of the implied duty to operate with due regard to the safety of the premises.

THIRD PARTIES
Adler v. Dickson [1955] 1 Q.B. 158 (C.A.)

Mrs. Adler, a widow, booked a first class ticket for a Mediterranean cruise on a P&O steamship the "Himalaya". The sailing ticket contained conditions as follows:

> "Passengers and their baggage are carried at passengers entire risk and the company will not be responsible for and shall be exempt from all liability in respect of any damage or injury whatsoever of or to the person of any passenger, whether the same shall arise from or be occasioned by the negligence of the company's servants in the discharge of their duties, or whether by the negligence of other persons directly or indirectly in the employment or service of the company."

Mrs. Adler went ashore at Trieste and on her return was walking up the gangway from the quay to the ship, when it fell, throwing her 16 feet to the wharf below. She sustained a broken leg, a broken pelvis and broken ribs and claimed damages against the Master and the Boatswain of the ship.

Held: the clauses protected the company but not the defendants and the plaintiff was entitled to sue them in tort. *Cosgrove v. Horsfall* [1945] 62 T.L.R. 140 *applied; Elder, Dempster & Co v. Paterson Zochonis & Co. Ltd.* [1924] A.C. 522 *distinguished.*

Note: There is a degree of uncertainty as to whether a properly drafted exemption clause can exempt servants or agents who are not parties to the contract. The "obiter" remarks of the three judges reveal the following. Jenkins L.J.and Morris L.J. considered that since the company's servants were not parties to the contract they could not claim immunity under it unless the company contracts as agent for its servants. Denning L.J. took the view that the law permits a carrier to stipulate for the exemption of those he engages to carry out the contract, even though they are not parties to it, provided the injured party assents expressly or by necessary implication to the exemption.

Privity of contract was fatal to the defendants relying on a limitation clause in *Scruttons Ltd., v. Midland Silicones Ltd.* [1962] A.C. 446.

LIMITATION CLAUSES

Ailsa Craig Fishing Co. Ltd. v. Malvern Fishing Co. Ltd.
[1983] 1 All E.R. 101 (H. L.)

A motor trawler belonging to the appellants sank while berthed in Aberdeen Harbour where the respondents were to provide a security service. The damage suffered was assessed at £55,000 but the respondents relied on a clause in the contract which limited their liability to £1,000. The appellants appealed against this.

Held: The appeal must be dismissed.

Lord Wilberforce:

> "Clauses of limitation are not regarded by the courts with the same hostility as clauses of exclusion." Lord Fraser referred to *Canada Steamship Lines Ltd. v. R.* [1952] 1 All E.R. 305 where Lord Morton stated "these principles are not applicable in their full rigour when considering the effect of conditions merely limiting liability . . . there is no reason why they should be judged by the specially exacting standards which apply to exclusion clauses."

Note: The approach of the courts as outlined in the above case must serve to make limitation clauses more attractive to a lawyer as a means of safeguarding clients interests than exemption clauses. It remains to be seen whether this in fact proves to be the case.

CHAPTER 9

Insurance Contracts

Insurance contracts come within the special category of contracts, contracts *uberrimae fidei*, i.e. of the utmost good faith. The principle of good faith involves disclosing all material facts which might influence a prudent insurer as to whether he will take the risk and the premium he will charge. In the *Chariot Inns* case non-disclosure enabled the insurer to avoid liability for a claim of over a million pounds.

The assured need not disclose facts which the insurer already knows, nor facts which lessen the risk. The *Keating* case illustrates that insurers cannot avoid liability for non disclosure of facts which were unknown to the insured at the time when he entered into the contract. Non-disclosure in over the counter insurance is illustrated by the *Aro Road Transport* case where the insurance company could be said to have waived disclosure. *Kelleher v. Irish Life Assurance Co. Ltd.* (High Court, unreported, 16 December, 1988) indicates that if the need to produce medical evidence has been waived by the insurer the obligation to make full disclosure may still exist.

In addition to the duty of disclosure insurance companies often add additional protection for themselves by inserting a clause that the truth and accuracy of the answers given to the questions in the proposal form will be the basis of the contract.

Insurance is provision in respect of an event which may happen i.e. a fire or an accident and is an indemnity contract. Assurance is provision in respect of an event which will happen i.e. death and is a non indemnity contract.

An insurance contract is illegal and void unless the insured has an insurable interest. (*O'Leary v. Irish National Insurance Co. Ltd.*) A person has an insurable interest if he will suffer a loss if the event insured against happens. If an insured does not have an insurable interest the transaction is in the nature of a wager or bet.

An indemnity is an undertaking to make good a loss suffered by one person as a result of an act or default of another. (*Rohan Construction v. I.C.I.* [1986] I.L.R.M. 419.[1987] S.C.) It gives the person indemnified a right to recover the amount of the loss suffered 'no more, and no less'. Therefore an insured under an indemnity policy, cannot make a profit or be better off than he was before the event. A contract of insurance against fire is only a contract of indemnity *per* O'Connor M.R. in *Driscoll v. Driscoll* [1918] I.R. 152. It may or may not, cover the reinstatement of a building. *St. Albans Investment Co. Ltd. v. Sun Alliance Insurance Co. & Provincial Insurance Co.* [1984] I.L.R.M. 501.

Contribution is a right which one insurer has to payment of a proportionate share of a liability borne by him, from another insurer. This was explained by McCarthy J. when *Zurich Insurance Co. Ltd. v. Shield Insurance Co. Ltd.* [1988] I.R. 182 was appealed to the Supreme Court.

Subrogation is a right to substitute for another. In insurance, the insurer can by subrogation take over the rights of the insured to maintain an action against a third party; generally the party who caused the loss or damage suffered by the insured. (*Driscoll v. Driscoll* [1918] I.R. 152. In the Kelly's Carpetdrome case, High Court, unreported, 14 April, 1985 subrogation was not a right to withhold payment merely a right to take over and enforce rights in anothers name. The claim to a 50% contribution lay against the other insurance company not against the insured.

BASIS OF CONTRACT CLAUSE

TRUTH AND ACCURACY

Farrell v. S.E. Lancashire Insurance Co. Ltd. [1933] I.R. 36 (S.C.)

The plaintiff signed a proposal form filled in by a brokers clerk, to the effect that the actual cash price that he paid for a bus was £800. It had in fact cost him a total of £205.

A clause in the proposal form provided "I/We warrant the truth of the foregoing and declare that I/We have not concealed any circumstances affecting the risks to be insured against." Other clauses provided that the proposal should be the basis of the contract and that the truth of the statements and answers in the proposal should be conditions precedent to any liability of the insurance company.

The bus was destroyed by fire and the insurance company refused to pay.

Held: The warranty of price was untrue to the knowledge of the plaintiff. He had entrusted the clerk with writing in the particulars, adopted the proposal form answers as his own and signed it vouching the truth of the matters stated.

The truth of the facts having been agreed to be the basis of the contract, the question of materiality did not enter into the issue. The contract failed.

NON-DISCLOSURE

Chariot Inns Ltd. v. Assicurazioni General Spa & Ord.
[1981] I.R. 199 (S.C.)

The plaintiff claimed that an Insurance policy issued to them by the defendant was valid and that they were entitled to indemnity against losses caused by a fire at the insured premises The Chariot Inn, Ranelagh, Dublin.

The defendants alleged that material facts were not disclosed in the proposal form signed by a director of the plaintiff company and on the basis of which a policy of insurance was issued by them. They regarded the policy as void ab initio and repudiated all liability.

Held: (S.C.) The plaintiff owed the defendant a duty to disclose every material circumstance which would influence the judgment of a prudent insurer and their failure to inform the insurance company, via the proposal form, that in 1976 goods belonging to another company owned by the same directors, had been damaged by fire, and that a sum of money had been paid out by the insurers, was a breach of the duty to disclose, and enabled the defendant company to avoid liability under its policy.

The plaintiff was entitled to judgment against the broker for such damages as they sustained by the brokers' breach of contract or negligence.

In the Supreme Court Mr. Justice Kenny (with the majority of the court in agreement) accepted that the onus of establishing that the matter not disclosed was material to the risk undertaken, lay on the defendant insurers and continued:

"A contract of insurance requires the highest standard of accuracy, good faith, candour and disclosure by the insured when making a proposal for insurance to an insurance company. It has become usual for an insurance company to whom a proposal for insurance is made to ask the proposed insured to answer a number of questions. Any misstatement in the answers given when they relate to a material matter affecting the insurance, entitles the insurance company to avoid the policy and to repudiate liability if the event insured against happens. But the correct answering of the questions asked is not the entire obligation of the person seeking insurance, he is bound in addition, to disclose to the insurance company every matter which is material to the risk against which he is seeking indemnity.

What is to be regarded as material to the risk against which the insurance is sought? It is not what the person seeking insurance regards as material, nor is it what the insurance company regards as material. It is a matter or circumstance which would reasonably influence the judgment of a prudent insurer in deciding whether he would take the risk, and if so, in determining the premium which he would demand.

The standard by which materiality is to be determined is objective and not subjective. In the last resort the matter has to be determined by the court; the parties to the litigation may call experts in insurance matters as witnesses to give evidence of what they would have regarded as material, but the question of materiality is not to be determined by such witnesses.

The test of materiality which is generally accepted in all forms of insurance against risks where property of any kind is involved is stated in s. 18, sub-s.2, of the Marine Insurance Act, 1906: "**Every circumstance is material which would influence the judgment of a prudent insurer in fixing the premium, or determining whether he will take the risk.**"

Although the test is stated in an Act which deals with marine insurance, it has been accepted as a correct guide to the law relating to insurance against damage to property or goods of all types.

The rule to determine the materiality of a fact which has not been disclosed to an insurer was expressed by MacKinnon L.J. with his customary pungency in *Zurich General Accident and Liability Insurance v. Morrison* at page 60 of the report: "Under the general law of insurance an insurer can avoid a policy if he proves that there has been misrepresentation or concealment of a material fact by the assured. What is material, is that which would influence the mind of a prudent insurer in deciding whether to accept the risk or fix the premium, and if this be proved it is not necessary further to prove that the mind of the actual insurer was so affected. In other words, the assured could not rebut the claim to avoid the policy because of a material misrepresentation by a plea that the particular insurer concerned was so stupid, ignorant, or reckless, that he could not exercise the judgment of a prudent insurer and was in fact unaffected by anything the assured had represented or concealed."

The statement of Samuels J. in *Mayne Nickless Ltd. v. Pegler* on the law relating to the materiality of facts not disclosed to insurers was approved and followed by the Judicial Committee of the Privy Council in *Marene v. Greater Pacific Insurance*. Samuels J. said:

"Accordingly, I do not think that it is generally open to examine what the insurer would in fact have done had he had the information not disclosed. The question is whether that information would have been relevant to the exercise of the insurer's option to accept or reject the insurance proposed. It seems to me that the test of materiality is this: a fact is material if it would have reasonably affected the mind of a prudent insurer in determining whether he will accept the insurance, and if so, at what premium and on what conditions."

Note: The plaintiffs insurance broker was held to be in breach of contractual duty to exercise the skill and knowledge which he professed to have, for the benefit of the plaintiff and the plaintiff was entitled to recover damages from the broker.

NON-DISCLOSURE OF UNKNOWN FACTS

Keating v. New Ireland Assurance Co. plc
ITLR 17 April, 1989 (H.C.) Egan J,
unreported, 6 December, 1989, Supreme Court

The plaintiff and her husband James entered into a life insurance policy with
the defendant which provided that the survivor would be entitled to £35,000 or
the encashed value of the policy on the death of either party. On the death of
James Keating, the defendant repudiated liability to pay on the ground that the
policy was conditional upon full and true disclosure in the proposal and medical
statement, of all material facts of which the company ought to have been
informed.

   The deceased had given the name and address of his medical doctor, and
stated that in April 1985 he had spent two days undergoing heart tests in Baggot
Street Hospital, Dublin, that nothing abnormal had been discovered and he had
no affliction of his heart. The hospital tests had in fact revealed a considerable
narrowing in some of Mr. Keating's arteries and a condition of angina. On an
objective test within the meaning of the Supreme court judgment in *Chariot
Inns Ltd. v. Assicurazioni Generali* this would have constituted a material matter
entitling the defendant to repudiate. The deceased, however, had not been told
the full extent of his condition by his doctors.

Held: The deceased did not know of his condition at the time of the execution
of the policy. A person can not be obliged to disclose some fact which he knows
nothing about. Non-disclosure can only be relevant to some fact of which the
person had knowledge at the relevant time. The insurance policy was not
invalidated.

Held: (Supreme Court). The appeal must be dismissed and order of the High
Court affirmed.

   On appeal to the Supreme Court, 6 December 1989, McCarthy J. stated that
while the insurer might contend that the deceased ought to have known that
there was some problem arising with his heart, the onus of proving that he did
know lay on the insurer. "One cannot disclose what one does not know, albeit
that this puts a premium on ignorance." The insurer had failed to establish either
material non-disclosure or a breach of warranty.

Kelleher v. Irish Life Assurance Co. Ltd.
High Court, unreported, 16 December, 1988, Costello J.

The plaintiff entered into a contract of insurance with the defendant under which
the life of the plaintiff's husband was insured for £80,000.

   Her husband died not long after the insurance was effected and when she
claimed on foot of the policy the company sought to avoid liability.

The policy stated that the contract of assurance would consist of the policy and the proposal i.e. the general application form. Page 2 of the general application form contained a series of questions which were required to be answered by a person using the form in the normal course of events, but these were explicitly excluded and crossed out. The end of the form contained a declaration of disclosure and a statement that the application form was the basis of the contract. Both the plaintiff and her husband signed the declaration and statement.

This policy was under a special scheme and a special form which obviated the necessity for members of the IMA to produce medical evidence, before a contract of insurance was entered into was used. Dr. Kelleher had suffered from cancer of the prostate gland in 1981 and received treatment which stopped the cancer but caused radiation damage.

The defendant claimed that both matters were material facts which had not been disclosed, and that the non-disclosure entitled them to repudiate the policy.

Held: The fact that the insured had suffered from cancer and radiation damage were material facts and would have effected the mind of a prudent insurer.

> "The declaration at the end of the application form was I think, made part of the contract between the parties and the statement "I/We understand that failure to disclose a material fact . . . may constitute grounds for rejection of the claim" means that there was because of the view I have taken of these two facts, a breach of the obligation contained in the declaration to disclose material facts. . . . The special promotional offer was obviating the necessity of producing medical evidence but it did not obviate the obligation to make full disclosure and this was, in fact, underlined in the other document which was sent to persons availing of the special scheme.
>
> Finally it has been suggested that the effect of the Supreme court decision in *Aro Road & Land Vehicles v. I.C.I.* is that in this case full disclosure was not necessary. For the purpose of considering this submission I will assume that this decision covers life assurance cases and I will assume that it covers cases in which there have been proposals signed by the insured. But if the test is, as suggested on the plaintiffs behalf, that facts which are material and which must be disclosed are only those facts which an insured person himself would consider to be reasonable to disclose, then I must hold that Dr. Kelleher failed to pass the test as did the plaintiff. . . . There was a contractual duty to disclose which was stated in clear terms. In my view the breach of that contractual duty entitled the defendants to repudiate liability." — Costello J.

OVER THE COUNTER INSURANCE

Aro Road & Land Vehicles v. I.C.I. (1986) I.R. 403

The plaintiff insured a consignment of goods with the defendant by means of "over the counter" insurance issued by the carrier C.I.E.

No proposal form was completed and the only question asked was the value of the consignment.

One load was destroyed by fire but the insurance company refused to meet the claim on the ground of non-disclosure that the Managing Director of the plaintiff company had been convicted of an offence some twenty years previously.

Held: In the case of "over the counter" insurance, if no questions are asked of the insured, then, in the absence of fraud, the insurer is not entitled to repudiate liability on the grounds of non-disclosure.

INSURABLE INTEREST

O'Leary v. Irish National Insurance Co. Ltd.
(1958) Ir. Jur. Rep. 1 (H.C.) Budd J.

On 13 September, 1955, Stephen Murphy signed a proposal form for a third party motor insurance policy in respect of the driving of a Skoda motor car. In the proposal form he described himself as the owner of the vehicle in question, and stated that it was registered in his name. Subsequently a policy was issued to him by the defendant company.

Stephen Murphy was not the owner of the car in question, nor was it registered in his name. The car was at all material times owned by his son Andrew.

The plaintiff instituted proceedings claiming damages for personal injuries. She was unable to serve Andrew Murphy with the civil bill and was permitted by the court to add The Irish National Insurance Company Ltd., as a defendant in lieu of him. (See Privity of contract) The Insurance company denied liability *inter alia* on grounds that they were not the insurers of Andrew Murphy.

The policy covered 1) the insured; 2) any person who was driving on the insured's order, or with his consent. The action was dismissed in the Circuit Court and the plaintiff appealed to the High Court. She claimed that a valid policy was issued to Stephen Murphy and that under its terms the driving of Andrew Murphy was covered as a person driving with the insured persons consent, that the indemnity and cover was of a person driving with the "insured's" consent and not with the "owner's" consent.

Held (*inter alia*): There never was any valid contract of insurance between Stephen Murphy and the defendant insurance company. It followed that the extension clause relied on never came into operation. Accordingly the plaintiff failed in her claim and the proceedings must be dismissed.

Where a person purports to take out a policy of insurance in respect of a motor vehicle, of which he is not the owner, it being represented or understood that he is the owner, no valid contract of insurance ever comes into operation for want of subject matter and lack of insurable interest and no extension clause can ever come into valid operation.

INDEMNITY
St. Alban's Investment Co. Ltd. v. Sun Alliance Insurance Co.
[1984] I.L.R.M. 501 (S.C.)

The plaintiff company entered into contracts of insurance with the defendants in respect of property at Maxwell Street, Glasgow. The property was purchased in May 1977, with another adjoining property for £25,000 and of this price the sum of £15,000 approximately was apportioned on the property concerned.

The plaintiff's director and chief shareholder gave evidence that he sought £300,000 worth of fire cover insurance to ensure full re-instatement of the property in the event of its destruction. (£250,000 with Sun Alliance and £50,000 with Provincial).

The policies which had been issues were in the standard form of an indemnity contract only the insurance company undertook to pay the market value of destroyed property, the amount of damage, or, at its option, to reinstate or replace damaged property.

Held in the High Court by McWilliam J. that there had been no re-instatement contract, that the plaintiff did not intend to rebuild and should be awarded a sum of £54,000 to represent the market value of the property at the time of the fire less the value of the site. The plaintiff appealed to the Supreme Court.

Held by the Supreme Court dismissing the appeal:
  (1) The evidence did not support the existence of a re- instatement contract.
  (2) That the plaintiff did not intend to rebuild and that the extent of its entitlement was the market value at the time of the fire, an amount increased to £64,000 by consent.

O'Higgins C.J. quoted Pennefether B. in *Vance v. Foster & Ors.* (1841) I.R. Cir. Rep. 47 at p. 50:

"It has been truly stated that a policy of insurance is a contract of indemnity, and that while the insured may name any sum he likes as the sum for which he will pay a premium, he does not, by so proposing that sum, nor does the company by accepting the risk, conclude themselves as to the amount which the plaintiff is to recover beyond the sum insured upon each particular item of insurance, he cannot recover even that sum unless he proves that he has sustained damage, and then he will recover a sum commensurate to the loss which he has sustained.' and he added "Where, however there has been total destruction of the property the average clause does not apply and the amount recoverable depends on what is established as a full indemnity."

CONTRIBUTION

Zurich Insurance Co. Ltd. v. Shield Insurance Co. Ltd.
[1992] I.R. 182 (S.C.)

The plaintiff was liable, under a motor insurance policy, to indemnify Quinnsworth Ltd., against liability for damages suffered by a Quinnsworth employee Martin Sinnott. Mr. Sinnott was a passenger in a car driven by another Quinnsworth employee, in the course of their business, which was involved in a collision with a bus. He was awarded damages of £569,640.

The plaintiff, on behalf of Quinnsworth, paid the full amount of the award and claimed a contribution of 50% from Shield on the grounds that Quinnsworth, had enjoyed a double indemnity against its liability to Mr. Sinnott. The plaintiff had provided indemnity under a policy of motor insurance. The defendant undertook to provide indemnity under an employers liability policy against liability for injury sustained by any employee out of, or in the course of, his employment by the insured.

Held by Gannon J. in the High Court in dismissing the plaintiffs claim and affirmed by the Supreme Court:

(1) that the nature and purpose of the equitable relief of contribution was to give equality of remedy, to two insurers where the rights of both were equal.

(2) that the right of contribution only arose where the interest of the insured and the risk assumed by the insurers were the same under both policies.

(3) that the only liability of Quinnsworth covered by the motor policy, was its vicarious liability as owner of the motor car, in respect of the breach by the driver of a duty owed to the public in general. That policy did not cover any breach of duty owed by Quinnsworth to Mr. Sinnott as his employer.

(4) that the liability covered by the employers' liability policy, which might be direct as well as vicarious was the liability of Quinnsworth for breach of its duty to take care for the safety of Mr. Sinnott in the performance of the duties imposed on him by his employment.

(5) that while liability to afford indemnities under each of the policies could arise on the happening of the same event, neither the interests of the insured under those policies nor the risks assumed by the plaintiff and defendant respectively, was the same.

(6) that, moreover, since Quinnsworth was entitled to a full indemnity from D, the defendant would be entitled to recover by subrogation from D — and from the plaintiff as his insurer — the full amount of any sum it might pay on behalf of Quinnsworth, whether directly to Mr. Sinnott, or by way of contribution to the plaintiff and would accordingly defeat the purpose of the plaintiffs claim.

> "Where there is double indemnity and one insurer pays the full amount, ordinarily, he is entitled to recover contribution from the other insurer; where there are but two, then fifty per cent. The locus classicus of this part of insurance law is *North British and Mercantile Insurance Co. v. London, Liverpool and Global Insurance Co.* (1877) 5 Ch.D. 569. In my view, the right of contribution does not apply where different persons are insured in respect of different interests. . . ." — McCarthy J. Supreme Court.

SUBROGATION

In re Kelly's Carpetdrome Ltd.
High Court, unreported, 14 April, 1985 Barrington J.

A member of the accountancy firm of Coopers and Lybrand was appointed liquidator of Kelly's Carpetdrome Ltd. on the 28 July 1981. On his appointment he became the beneficiary of an insolvency insurance policy which provided automatic cover to members of the firm appointed as liquidators or receivers of companies.

Premises owned by the business were destroyed by fire on the 14 June, 1982 and the agreed damages amounted to £585,000. Kelly's Carpet Drive-In who leased the premises had taken out fire insurance of the premises with Lloyds and when the Liquidator claimed under this policy Lloyds repudiated liability. The liquidator then claimed under the insolvency policy of his own firm and the Insurers claimed that their liability was limited to 50% of the damage.

Held The relevant principle in the present case was not that of double insurance but of subrogation.

The respondent insurance company were obliged to discharge the fire loss in full but upon indemnifying the liquidator were entitled by subrogation, to any rights which the liquidator may have had against the tenant or its insurers.

Note: The case was on all fours with *Andrews v. The Patriotic Assurance Co. of Ireland. Messrs Monk Properties Ltd. and Messrs Kelly's Carpetdrome Drive-in Ltd.*, had interests in the same property but their interests were quite different. The landlord was entitled to receive his rent and his interest consisted of the revisee or expectant on the determination of the tenancy. The tenant was entitled to the enjoyment and occupation of the premises subject to the terms and conditions of the tenancy agreement.

INSURANCE AGENT

In *Taylor v. Yorkshire Insurance Co. Ltd. (No. 1)* [1913] 2 I.R. 1 Palles C.B. in the High Court stated: "I hold with Mr. Justice Wright, that, although "He may have been an agent to put the answers in the form," the agent of an insurance company cannot be treated as their agent to invent the answers to the questions in the proposal form: and that, if he is allowed by the proposer to invent the answers, and to send them as the answers of the proposer, the agent is, to that extent, the agent, not of the insurance company, but of the proposer. In arriving at this conclusion, I have not overlooked the fact that both in *Biggar v. The Rock Company* [1902] 1 K.B. 516 and *Levy's Case*, 17 Times L.R. 229 there was a provision in the proposal that verbal statements to the agent should not be imputed to the company; but, in relation to the question of authority, as distinct from that of imputations of notice, this is immaterial."

As to Motor Insurance see *Bellew* and *Vandepitte* cases in Chapter 16, Privity.

CHAPTER 10

Mistake

Mistake is one of the matters which can interfere with the genuine consent necessary for a valid contract. Mistake is said to be operative when it is recognised by the courts as effecting an agreement to the extent of rendering a contract void at common law or voidable at equity. Operative mistake is illustrated by *Monaghan County Council v. Vaughan*, non operative mistake by *O'Loghlen v. O'Callaghan*.

Mistake may be unilateral i.e. made by one party, (Nolan v. Graves and Hamilton) mutual i. e. different mistakes made by each party, (*Gun v. McCarthy*) or common i. e. the same mistake made by both parties. (*Couturier v. Hastie*).

In order to be operative the mistake must be one of fact not of law. The *maxim ignorantia legis non excusat* applies. This rule was qualified in *Cooper v. Phibbs* in relation to a mistake of private law.

MISTAKE OF LAW

There is a distinction between a mistake of public law and a mistake of private law.

(a) Mistake of Public Law. Because all persons are presumed to know the law ignorance of the law or the contents of Public Acts of parliament is not a mistake which will effect a contract. *O'Loughlen v. O'Callaghan*.

(b) Mistake of Private Law. A mistake of private law or of private rights enshrined in a private Act of Parliament, or in agreements or wills, will constitute an operative mistake because of the decision in *Cooper v. Phibbs*. This decision is sometimes cited as authority for the proposition that a mistake of private law is treated as a mistake of fact.

MISTAKE OF FACT

A mistake of fact can be a mistake involving both parties or a mistake involving only one party. Mistake involving both parties can be either common mistake or mutual mistake.

(a) Where an agreement reached between the parties is void because both parties have made a common (the same) mistake, **consent is nullified by the mistake** or

(b) Where the mistake prevented any agreement being concluded, **consent is negatived by the mistake**.

(A) Mistake which nullifies consent after agreement

In relation to A) to be operative at common law the common mistake must be fundamental (*Bell v. Lever Bros*) and go to the root of the contract. This has been interpreted by Cheshire Fifoot and Furmston, op. cit., at page 219 as meaning that **a common mistake appears to have no effect at common law unless it empties the agreement of all content.** This may be because the subject matter has ceased to exist at the time of the agreement (*Scott v. Coulson* and *Couturier v. Hastie*) in which cases "**the ground of nullity is not mistake but the absence of a res**" or persona. The very existence of a general doctrine of common mistake is now highly questionable despite the reference to "fundamental" in *Bell v. Lever Bros*.

The following mistakes of fact have been held operative at common law, mistake about an insured person being alive, (mistake about the existence of a person) *Scott v. Coulson* [1903] 2 Ch. 249, a mistake by both parties believing that they were married, *Galloway v. Galloway* [1914] TLR 531 and mistake as to the existence of the subject matter. (*Couturier v. Hastie* (1856) 6 H. L.C. 673.

EQUITY

Because of the common law restriction on the doctrine of common mistake affecting the foundation of a contract, equity may provide relief where the common mistake is not fundamental enough to render a contract void at common law. The equitable measures available are; setting the contract aside on terms (*Solle v. Butcher*), a grant of rescission, (*Grist v. Bailey* [1967] Ch 532) rectification, (*Monaghan County Council v. Vaughan*) and refusal of specific performance. (*Grist v. Bailey*).

Rectification was granted in *Monaghan County Council v. Vaughan* where the common intention of the parties in an antecedent agreement had, by mistake, been incorrectly expressed in a subsequent written document. An offeror is estopped from adducing evidence of intention or relying on his own error if detriment would result to the other party.

(B) Mistake which negatives consent and prevents agreement

This occurs when the mistake prevents any agreement being concluded. One party is mistaken about the other party's intentions although neither appreciates that he is misunderstood. The mistake negatives consent. The following mistakes not shared by the parties have been held to render contracts void; a) mistake as to the terms of a contract, *Hartog v. Colin & Shields*, (b) mistake as to the subject matter, *Megaw v. Molloy, Raffles v. Wichelhous* and (c) mistake as to the identity of the other party, *Cundy v. Lindsay, Smallman v. O'Moore and Newman*, (d) mutual mistake as to the true nature of an agreement in *Mespil v. Capaldi* meant that there was no *consensus ad idem* and no agreement.

(C) Mistake about a document signed and non est factum

Under the principle established in *Graucob v. L'Estrange* a person who signs a document, is as a rule, bound by it, even if he has not read it or cannot read it.

An exception to this principle may be a plea of non est factum (not my deed) which can enable a court to set aside a document signed under a fundamental mistake. The basis of the plea is the requirement of a consensus ad idem for a valid contract. In order for this plea to succeed a party must show that the document signed was totally, fundamentally or radically different from the document which the person signing, on some grounds, believed it to be. This defence relates to a mistake about the nature or class of document but not to a mistake about the contents of a document.

OPERATIVE MISTAKE MUST BE FUNDAMENTAL
Bell v. Level Bros. [1932] A.C. 161 (H. L.)

Bell entered into a contract of employment to work for Lever Bros for five years, (subsequently extended for a further five,) to act as Chairman of a subsidiary company and to look after their interests in West Africa. The subsidiary company was amalgamated with another company and Bell agreed and accepted £30,000 compensation for ending the contract and giving up his position.

Had they been aware of it, the company would have been justified in terminating his contract of service and dismissing him without compensation, because he had entered on his own account into secret speculations in cocoa, a commodity in which the company dealt.

Later when the company was informed of the secret transactions by Bell on his own account, they claimed rescission of the compensation agreement and repayment of the money on the ground (*inter alia*) of mistake.

Held: by the House of Lords:

The action must fail; as to mutual mistake, on the ground that the mutual mistake related not to the subject-matter, but to the quality of the service contract; it was **not fundamental**, as to unilateral mistake the action failed on the ground that the defendant under his contract of service owed no duty to L to disclose the impugned transactions. *Kennedy v. Panama, New Zealand and Australian Royal Mail* (1867) L.R. 2 Q.B. 580 followed. Dictum of Avory J. in

Healey v. Societe Anonyme Francaise Rubastic [1917] 1 K.B. 946, 947
approved.

Note: Robert Clark, *Contract*, 3rd ed., Irish Law Texts, 1992 opines at page 208
"the Irish ancestry of the leading case of *Cooper v. Phibbs* suggests that the Irish
Courts would decline to follow the narrower doctrine of mistake, as espoused
in *Bell v. Lever Bros.*, preferring instead the *Solle v. Butcher* line of authority."

Cheshire Fifoot and Furmston's, *Law of Contract*, 11th ed., London, 1986,
page 225 states that the decision in *Bell v. Lever Bros* is not authority for any
general doctrine of common mistake and that the preferred interpretation of the
judgments in this case is "that **the only fatal assumption sufficiently fundamental to rank as operative mistake is the assumption that the very subject
matter of the contract is in existence.**"

A.G. Guest, *Anson's Law of Contract*, 26th ed., Oxford, 1984 p. 255 refers
to the claim that *Bell v. Lever Bros* establishes that there is no such doctrine of
mistake, rendering the contract void ab initio and he refers to Lord Denning's
judgment. (See extract later.) He points out that Lord Atkin and other members
of the House of Lords assume throughout that certain types of mistake will avoid
a contract although they differ as to the circumstances in which it will do so.
He then states "the effect of the decision in *Bell v. Lever Bros* is **to confine the
doctrine of mutual mistake within the most narrow limits;** it is only in the
most extreme cases that the Court will intervene."

See judgment of Costello J. in *O'Neill v. Ryan post.*

NON-OPERATIVE MISTAKE OF PUBLIC LAW
O'Loughlen v. O'Callaghan (1884) I.R. 8 C.L. 116 (Q.B.)

The plaintiff held lands at Ballycon, and Ballynaboy, County Clare as a tenant
in fee farm. The defendant was a tenant of the plaintiff and had let all the lands
to sub-tenants. The defendant had been in the habit, for the previous eleven
years, of deducting one half of the poundage poor rate on every £1 of rent paid
and the plaintiff made a similar deduction from the head rent paid by him.

The plaintiff claimed payment of the deductions of poor rent made by the
defendant and erroneously allowed by the plaintiff for the previous twenty
years. It was admitted that the deductions for poor rate should have been made
under section 75 of 1&2 Vict. c.56 instead of under s.74

Held: The money was paid, not under a mistake of fact but under a mistake of
law. It was the business of the gentlemen who settled their accounts to make
themselves acquainted with that law and to act accordingly. The deductions
having been made and allowed under a mistake of law and with the knowledge
of the facts could not be recovered back by legal process.

Note: The inaccuracy of the aphorism that money paid under a mistake of fact may be recovered but that money paid under a mistake of law cannot, was referred to by Kenny J. in *Rogers v. Louth County Council* [1981] I.L.R.M. 144 when the Supreme Court adopted the principle applied by the Judicial Committee of the Privy Council in *Kiriri Cotton Co. Ltd., v. Dewani* [1960] 2 W.L.R. 127 to the effect that a plaintiff may recover money paid on a mistake of law provided that he is not in *pari delicto* with the defendant in mistaking the law. See also *Lord Mayor of Dublin v. Provost of TCD* [1982] H.C.

MISTAKE OF PRIVATE LAW
Cooper v. Phibbs (1867) I.R. 2 H.L. 149

Edward Cooper of Markee Castle, County Sligo entered into an agreement to lease a fishery, with a fishing house and grounds at Ballysadere from Mr. William Phibbs, for a term of three years, from 1 November 1863. Phibbs was acting as administrator of Edward Joshua Cooper the plaintiff's deceased father. Cooper claimed that at the time the agreement was executed he had never read a copy of the Act of Parliament relating to the fishery and that it was only some time later that he purchased a copy of the Act to see what his rights were. He discovered that the deceased Edward Joshua Cooper had only been a tenant for life and that the fishery was the freehold property of himself for life with remainder to his children.

In ignorance of his own claim, he had taken a lease of his own property. He immediately asked the administrator Phibbs to cancel the lease but he refused to do so and he sought relief through the courts.

At first hearing it was held that it would be very unconscientious to set aside the agreement and that the petition must be dismissed, without prejudice, as between the parties to their ultimate rights to the fishery.

Held: (On appeal to the House of Lords) That the agreement having been made in mutual mistake, the Plaintiff although there was no fraud, was entitled to have it set aside. The present appeal should be set aside.

The Lord Chancellor:

> ". . . a mistake in point of law may be corrected both in this Court and in a Court of Law. . . . I apprehend it is now settled that, when money has been paid or a conveyance executed in ignorance of a point of law, relief may be granted, but it appears also to be well settled, that neither in a Court of Law nor in this Court will relief be given when it is against good conscience that the party who made the mistake should be free from the consequences of his error . . . there must be something unconscientious on either one side or the other in order that the aid of this Court should be called for."

Lord Westbury:

> "In the maxim '*Ignorantia juris haud excusat*,' the word '*jus*' has the sense of general law or of private right according to circumstances . . . in that maxim the word '*jus*' is used in the sense of denoting general law, the ordinary law of the country. But when the word '*jus*' is used in the sense of denoting a private right, the maxim has no application. Private right of ownership is a matter of fact; it may be the result also of matter of law; but if parties contract under a mutual mistake and misapprehension as to their relative rights the result is, that the agreement is liable to be set aside as having proceeded upon a common mistake."

Note: In *Cooper v. Phibbs* illustrates that rescission may be granted even after execution and part performance of a tenancy agreement. The court adopted this tactic of distinguishing a mistake of private rights under a private act of Parliament to avoid the absurdity of making Cooper pay for a lease of property which he himself owned. It has been claimed that the principles of equity dictated this approach.

MISTAKE WHICH NULLIFIES CONSENT AFTER AGREEMENT

MISTAKE ABOUT THE EXISTENCE OF A PERSON
Scott v. Coulson [1903] 2 Ch. 249

Both parties entered into a contract for the sale of a life assurance policy, in the belief that the assured, a man named A.T. Death was alive, and the contract was completed by assignment. In fact Mr. Death was dead at the time of the agreement and of the deed.

The plaintiff claimed that it was an implied term and condition of the agreement and deed of assignment that the assured was alive at the dates thereof, and that in the circumstances both instruments were void. In the alternative they claimed that the agreement and deed were entered into and executed by both parties in ignorance of the fact that Death was dead, and that the agreement and deed should be set aside, the policy returned and money lodged in court be repaid to the plaintiffs. The defendants admitted the allegation in the alternative plea.

It was also argued that the moment a contract is completed by conveyance it cannot be rescinded through innocent misrepresentation, the rights of the parties having become fixed by the conveyance.

Held: The plaintiff was entitled to have the transaction set aside notwithstanding that it had been completed by assignment. At the date of the contract there had been a common mistake, both parties believing that the assured was alive.

Vaughan Williams L.J.:

"If we are to take it that it was common ground that, at the date of the contract for the sale of this policy, both the parties to the contract supposed the assured to be alive, it is true that both parties entered into this contract upon the basis of a common affirmative belief that the assured was alive; but as it turned out that this was a common mistake, the contract was one which cannot be enforced.

This is so in law; and the plaintiffs do not require to have recourse to equity to rescind the contract, if the basis which both parties recognised as the basis is not true. . . . All I say with regard to the matter is that the material date all through is the date of the contract. If at that date a good contract was entered into, I cannot conceive that it could be rescinded. But it turns out that it was as contract entered into under a common mistake existing at the date of it, and therefore it follows that an assignment executed in pursuance of such a contract cannot be supported." — *Taylor v. Caldwell* (1863) 3B.&S. 826 *referred to.*

MISTAKE ABOUT BEING MARRIED

Galloway v. Galloway [1914] 30 T.L.R. 531 (K.B.D.)

On the 6th of November, 1898, the defendant was married to Olive Mabel Smith. In April, 1903 she left him. The defendant made enquiries but could learn nothing of her, and assuming that she was dead, he married the plaintiff Elizabeth Ellen Crandwell on the 22nd of December, 1907. He was described in the marriage certificate as a widower.

On the 6th October, 1913 the defendant and the plaintiff (Elizabeth) entered into a deed of separation under which the defendant agreed to pay £1 a week to the plaintiff to support their children. Subsequently the defendants first wife Olive was discovered and the defendant fell into arrears with payments under the deed. The plaintiff then took an action for payment of the arrears and the defendant counter-claimed for rescission of the deed on the ground of a mutual mistake of fact as to the relationship between himself and the plaintiff.

Held: The agreement (deed) between the parties was void. There was a mutual mistake of fact which was material to the existence of the agreement. Looking at the terms of the deed of separation its basis was the belief of both parties that they were respectively husband and wife. As that was in fact, not the case the deed of separation was void.

MISTAKE AS TO EXISTENCE OF SUBJECT MATTER
Couturier v. Hastie (No. 1) (1852) 8 Ex 40 (H.L.)

H a factor sold a cargo of corn which was en-route by sea from Salonica to London. The contract was entered into in ignorance of the fact that, a short time before the date of the contract the corn had been sold at Tunis "in consequence of getting so heated that it was impossible to bring it to England." The purchaser repudiated the contract and took an action against H to recover the price.

Held: The contract contemplated that there was in existence something to be sold and bought and capable of transfer, which, not being the case at the time of sale. H was not liable.

Note: Later cases show that such mistake will only nullify a contract in very limited circumstances. The common law hostility towards mistake rendering a contract void arises to some extent from the notion that the parties could have provided against such an eventuality in their agreement. Their failure to do so is their affair (*caveat emptor*). Needless to say common mistake is not operative if a provision in an agreement does cover the eventuality or if one of the parties has undertaken or assumed the risk of such mistake.

TERMS NOT BE CONSTRUED OBJECTIVELY
O'Neill v. Ryan (No. 2) [1992] I.R. Costello J. (H.C.)

The plaintiff instituted proceedings as a petitioner under section 205 of the Companies Act, 1963, claiming oppression as a minority shareholder in Ryanair Ltd. In addition he instituted proceedings against a number of defendants (including the first defendant) claiming, *inter alia*, damages for wrongful dismissal, innocent misrepresentation and conspiracy.

The defendants solicitor by letter dated 24 May, 1990 offered to buy his shares in Ryanair Ltd., and to pay his costs in the proceedings. The plaintiff accepted this offer by letter of 30th May, 1990.

The defendants claimed that their letter of 24th offering to buy the shares was made on the basis that both sets of proceedings would be terminated other than his claim for wrongful dismissal against Ryanair Ltd. The plaintiff sought specific performance of the offer in the terms that he understood and accepted it.

The defendants claimed that since the plaintiff had purported to accept the offer on a different basis (to settle the s. 205 proceedings only) to what they intended, there was no consensus, the parties were not *ad idem*, there was no contract capable of being specifically enforced.

Held: There was a valid contract and specific performance would be granted.

While the authors of the letter of 24 May intended the offer to settle both proceedings under s.205 and the plenary action against the first defendant, they failed to convey this in the letter.

Where each party to a contract is mistaken as to the other party's intention, although neither appreciates that he is misunderstood, such as where one party makes an offer which the other party accepts in a fundamentally different sense from that intended by the offeror, **the terms of the contract must be construed objectively in the sense in which they would reasonably be understood**.

The words used by the defendants solicitors in their letter of 24 May would be reasonably understood as constituting an offer to settle the s. 205 proceedings only and it was in that sense that the letter of acceptance of 30 May, 1990, was sent by the plaintiffs solicitor.

Costello J.:

"There is a category of cases in which it is accepted that there was an offer and acceptance and agreement reached between the parties but in which it is claimed that the parties shared a common mistake which has resulted in the agreement being void for example where both parties agree on the purchase and sale of a painting believing it to be a Gainsborough and it is subsequently established that this is not so, or where both parties agree on the sale of a tenanted property and both believe that the tenant is protected by the Rent Restriction Acts and subsequently ascertain that this is not so, the existence of a valid offer and acceptance is not in doubt and what is in issue is the effect on the parties' contract on what I will call a shared common mistake.

There is another category of cases (in which the present case falls) in which it is alleged that the effect of the mistake was that there was no concluded agreement. Before referring to this category it will help if I first briefly refer to the principles applicable to that of the first category.

There were a number of **earlier cases** in which a shared common mistake as to the existence of the subject matter of the contract, enabled the court to declare the contract to be void. Thus an assignment of a life assurance policy was held to be void where it was shown that at its date the person whose life was assured was wrongly assumed by both parties to have been alive, (*Scott v. Coulson* [1903] 2 Ch. 249), and a separation deed was declared a nullity because it was made by the common and shared mistake that the parties were married to each other (*Galloway v. Galloway* [1914] 30 TLR 531). But **later cases have shown that the circumstances in which a shared common mistake will nullify a contract are extremely limited**.

Solle v. Butcher [1950] 1 K.B. 671 was a case of a shared common mistake, both parties believing that a flat had been so extensively recon-structed that it was no longer controlled by the Rent Restrictions Acts as a result of which a rent was agreed that was higher than that which would have been payable had the true position been known. But the tenant failed in his claim to recover the rent he had paid over on the ground of the common mistake. The law on the subject was stated by Denning L.J., in terms which were approved in a later case as follows at p. 691.

... Once a contract has been made, that is to say, **once the parties**, whatever their innermost states of mind, **have to all outward appearances agreed with sufficient certainty in the same terms on the same subject matter, then the contract is good** unless and until it is set aside for failure of some condition on which the existence of the contract depends, or for fraud, or on some equitable ground. Neither party can rely on his own mistake to say it was a nullity from the beginning, no matter that it was a mistake which to his mind was fundamental, and no matter that the other party knew that he was under a mistake. *A fortiori*, if the other party did not know of the mistake, but shared it."

Note: See *Mespil v. Capaldi* post where the Supreme Court held that mutual mistake as to the true nature of an agreement where the circumstances were objectively such as to justify an acceptance of an offer in a fundamentally different sense from that in which it was tendered by the offeror, meant that there was no true consensus and no agreement.

MISTAKE AT EQUITY
Gunn v. McCarthy (1884) 13 L.R. Ir. 304 (Ch.)

G intended to lease premises at the Mall, Tralee to M. R acting on behalf of G wrote to M offering a lease at a rent of £33.10 yearly, which was immediately accepted in writing and a lease executed.

G brought an action to have the agreement and lease rectified by inserting £53.10 as the yearly rent, or to have the lease cancelled. The County Court granted a decree for rectification and the defendant appealed.

Held: When he accepted the offer the defendant knew perfectly well that R had inserted £33.10 by mistake, that the evidence clearly showed that £53.10 was the rent which the plaintiff intended. Where there is a clear mistake by one party in reference to a material term and the other party seeks to avail himself of that and to bind the other to the mistake the court will not allow such a contract to be binding on the parties. The lease and the agreement must be cancelled.

EQUITY WILL SET ASIDE
Solle v. Butcher [1950] 1 K.B. 671 (C.A.)

The plaintiff leased a flat and a garage from the defendant for a term of 7 years at an annual rent of £250, both parties being satisfied that the Rent Restriction Acts did not apply, because of alterations done to the flat and the inclusion of the garage in the lease.

Later the plaintiff sued the defendant alleging that the standard rent of the flat was £140 a year, under the Rent Restriction Acts and claiming the re-payment of the excess rent which he had paid.

The defendant claimed that he had relied on the plaintiff's oral assurance that the rent was not controlled and pleaded *inter alia* common mistake. He also claimed rescission of the lease.

Held: The rent was controlled under the Rent Restriction Acts, and by reason of the common mistake of fact, the lease must be set aside on terms such as would enable the plaintiff to stay on at the proper rent or to leave. *Garrard v. Frankel* (1862) 30 Beav 445 and *Paget v. Marshall* (1884) 28 Ch. D. 255 *followed.*

Denning L.J.:

"In order to see whether the lease can be avoided for mistake it is necessary to remember that mistake is of two kinds; first, mistake which renders the contract void, that is, a nullity from the beginning, which is the kind of mistake which was dealt with by the courts of common law; and secondly, mistake which renders the contract not void, but voidable, that is, liable to be set aside on such terms as the court thinks fit, which is the kind of mistake which was dealt with by the courts of equity.

Much of the difficulty which has attended this subject has arisen because, before the fusion of law and equity, the courts of common law, in order to do justice in the case in hand, extended this doctrine of mistake beyond its proper limits and held contracts to be void which were really only voidable... Since the fusion of law and equity, there is no reason to continue this process, and it will be found that only those contracts are now held void in which the mistake was such as to prevent the formation of any contract at all.

Let me first consider **mistakes which render a contract a nullity**. All previous decisions on this subject must now be read in the light of *Bell v. Lever Bros Ltd*. The correct interpretation of that case, to my mind, is that, once a contract has been made, that is to say, once the parties, whatever their inmost states of mind, have **to all outward appearances agreed with sufficient certainty in the same terms on the same subject matter, then the contract is good** unless and until it is set aside for failure of some condition on which the existence of the contract depends, or for fraud, or on some equitable ground."

Note: Because the normal rules of equity apply to the grant of this remedy, rescission was refused in *Stapleton v. Prudential Insurance Co.* (Delay defeats Equity)

RECTIFICATION
Monaghan County Council v. Vaughan [1948] I.R. 306 (H.C.)

The plaintiffs advertised inviting tenders for the demolition of the workhouse buildings at Clones, Co. Monaghan.

The defendant tendered a price of £1,200 and a formal contract provided that £1,200 should be paid by the County Council to the Defendant. The County Council had intended that he should pay them £1,200 and they sought to have the written contract rectified on the ground of mistake.

Held: by Dixon J. that the written contract must be rectified . . . both parties were agreed upon certain matters and the completed contract did not correctly represent the substance of their agreement. This was a case of mutual mistake.

MISTAKE

RECTIFICATION AND INTENTION OF THE PARTIES
Lucey v. Laurel Construction Co. Ltd.
High Court, unreported, 18 December 1970, Kenny J.

The plaintiff selected a site for a house in the defendant's development at Blanchardstown, Co. Dublin. He signed his name on a site plan which showed the site as being 170 feet long and entered into an agreement for a lease of the ground. A director of the defendant company decided that he would fit two more houses into the development if he reduced Lucey's site. He did not have the development plan changed or any alteration made in the agreement for the lease.

When Lucey measured his site and found that it was short he knocked down the back wall, extended his garden to 170 feet and sought a perpetual injunction to restrain the defendant from interfering with the site. The defendant claimed that their director intended the site to be 120 feet long and that the agreement for the lease should be rectified.

Held: The plaintiff was entitled to a perpetual injunction restraining the defendants from entering on or doing any work on the plot of ground.

Note: Kenny J. following *Rose v. Pim* [1953] 2 Q.B. 451 held that a concluded contract must exist between the parties before rectification will be granted. Rectification according to Denning M.R in *Rose and Pim* [1953] 2 All E. R. 739 at 747 is concerned with contracts and documents, not with intentions. Kenny J. refused to grant rectification holding that it is granted only where something different was agreed not where something different was intended. This should be contrasted with *Joscelyn v. Nissen* [1970] 2 Q.B. 86 where the English Court of Appeal held that a party seeking rectification must show "a continuing common intention" to contract on particular terms.

Kenny J. in *Lucey v. Laurel Construction* referred to a passage in *Crane v. Hengeman Harris Co. Inc.* [1939] 1 All E.R. 664 which suggested that a continuing intention alone would suffice and stated:

> ". . . I am clearly of opinion that **a continuing intention is not** sufficient **unless it has found expression in outward agreement.**" Robert Clark points out Contract 2nd Ed. p. 136 that the site map was the only objective manifestation of the other party's intentions.

REFUSAL OF SPECIFIC PERFORMANCE
Grist v. Bailey [1967] Ch. 532

The plaintiff sought an order of specific performance by the defendant of a contract for the sale of a house at a price of £850 "subject to the existing tenancy thereof." At the time of contracting the defendant believed that the house was occupied by a statutory tenant under the Rent Restriction Acts and that as a consequence the market value was £850.

In fact, unknown to the defendant owner, the protected statutory tenant had died and her son, who had no tenancy, was in occupation and paying the rent. There was therefore no protected tenancy in existence at the time of the contract. The market value of the house with vacant possession was £2,250 and the defendant counterclaimed for rescission.

Held:

(1) There was a common mistake as to the nature of the tenancy.

(2) While at common law the mistake was not such as would avoid the contract, in equity the mistake was fundamental in that there was not in fact an existing tenancy' and neither party knowing the state of affairs would have negotiated for so small a price.

(3) Specific performance must be refused. Rescission granted on terms that the defendant enter into a fresh contract at a proper vacant possession price. Dicta of Denning L.J. in *Solle v. Butcher* [1950] 1 K.B. 671, 693 *applied. Bell v. Lever Bros Ltd.* [1932] A.C. 161 (H.L.) *considered.*

MISTAKE WHICH NEGATIVES CONSENT AND PREVENTS AGREEMENT

MISTAKE AS TO TERMS — UNILATERAL MISTAKE

Hartog v. Colin & Shields [1939] 3 All E.R. 566 (K.B.)

The defendants agreed to sell 30,000 Argentine hare skins to the plaintiff. In the verbal negotiations which took place the price had been discussed per piece (i..e. per skin) and similarly in correspondence. On 3 November the defendant's quoted a price of 10.75d per piece for winter skins. On 23 November the defendants quoted a price of 10.25d per lb. (a price corresponding roughly, to 3.75d per piece.) Expert evidence was given that Argentine hare skins were generally sold at prices per piece.

On receipt of the quote of 10.25d per lb., the plaintiff at once entered into a contract to purchase 30,000 skins. The defendants claimed that their offer had been wrongly expressed by mistake, that they intended to offer the skins at prices per piece and not at prices per pound and they refused to deliver the skins.

The plaintiff claimed damages for breach of contract and the defendants claimed that the plaintiff was well aware of the mistake on their part in relation to the price, that he fraudulently accepted an offer which he knew the defendant never intended to make and they denied that there was any binding contract.

Held: There was no binding contract, The offer did not express the real intention of the persons making it. It was a mistake which caused the offer to be expressed in the way it was. The plaintiff did in fact know that such a mistake had occurred and did not by his acceptance make a binding contract.

Singleton J. (Kings Bench Division):

> "I am satisfied, however, from the evidence given to me, that the plaintiff must have realised, and did in fact know, that a mistake had occurred . . . it was a mistake on the part of the defendants or their servants which caused the offer to go forward in that way, and I am satisfied that anyone with any knowledge of the trade must have realised that there was a mistake . . . the offer was wrongly expressed and the defendants by their evidence, and by the correspondence, have satisfied me that the plaintiff could not reasonably have supposed that that offer contained the offeror's real intention."

Note: An editorial note to this case states that an intending purchaser is not permitted to "snap up" an offer which he knows to have been made under a mistake. See *Tamplin v. James* (1880) 15 Ch.D. 215; 35 Digest 101.

MISTAKE ABOUT TERMS WHICH NEGATES CONSENT
Wood v. Scarth (1858) 1F&F 293

The defendant Scarth, being the owner of a newly erected building at Putney, intended for a public house wrote to the plaintiffs a firm of brewers offering them a lease for 25 years at a rent of £63. He asked to be informed at their earliest convenience, if the offer suited them "as I am giving all the brewers who have left cards the offer in rotation."

Subsequently Wood sent a clerk to view the premises, to discuss the terms and to report to him. He then wrote agreeing to lease the premises. Two months later W received a draft agreement from the defendant's solicitor containing a clause that a premium of £500 was to be paid to the defendant within two months of a licence being obtained. W refused to pay the £500 and sought specific performance of the agreement as contained in the letters. Scarth's defence was that he had always intended to lease on the terms in the solicitor's draft agreement and that if the £500 was not mentioned in his letter, it was omitted by mistake. Evidence was given that it was the custom to require a premium for similar leases.

Held:

(1) the letters constituted a valid agreement for a lease.

(2) that *prima facie*, the terms on which the lease was to be granted must be taken to be those expressed in the first letter.

(3) that the defendant was at liberty to resist a suit for specific performance, by proving that he had made a mistake in stating the terms for the lease in the first letter.

(4) that the mistake was well proved in this case, by showing that the defendant had, previously to writing the letter to the plaintiff offered the premises to other brewers upon terms which included the stipulation which he stated had been omitted in the letter by mistake, and because the previous offer must be taken to be "the offer" which he stated in his letter that he was giving to the applicants in rotation.

Vice-Chancellor Sir W. Page Wood:

"... I would not allow the defendant to escape merely because he himself swears that he always intended to insert the term of the £500 premium in his letter, or because of the oath of his agent, to the effect that the defendant had given him accordingly instructions as to the terms of letting the house. But I find something written, which coupled with overt acts proved by the evidence of disinterested witnesses, seems to bring the case up to the numerous authorities in which mistake has been permitted as a defence to a suit for specific performance. The fact which the defendant mentions in his first letter is, that he is giving to all brewers in rotation the offer ..."

the offer mentioned in the letter must be the identical offer which he thereby intended to make to the plaintiff. I think, therefore that the defendants first letter was founded entirely upon mistake; and that it was the offer adverted to and accepted in the plaintiff's subsequent letter."

MISTAKE AS TO SUBJECT MATTER

Megaw v. Molloy (1) L.R. Ir. Vol 11 (1878) 530 (C.A.)

The plaintiff employed a broker to auction a cargo of maize for him at Corn Exchange, Dublin. The maize he intended to be sold had been imported in a ship called the "Emma Peasant" and small bags labelled "ex Emma Peasant" containing samples of sound maize, were exhibited at the auction. The plaintiff also had other maize imported in a ship called the "Jessie Parker". Both cargoes were stored in the same building but the maize from the "Jessie Parker" was superior to that from the "Emma Peasant".

The defendant who had not inspected the bulk, bid on the basis of the sample and became the purchaser. Subsequently the defendant refused to accept delivery of the maize which was of inferior quality, on the ground that it was not of the same quality as the sample. The plaintiff re-sold the maize and sued the defendant for about £60 loss on the re-sale.

The jury found that the sample shown at the auction had been taken by accident from the cargo of another ship the "Jessie Parker" a superior cargo. The auctioneer believed the sample to be from the "Emma Peasant".

Held (*inter alia*): on Appeal, that as the plaintiff intended to sell one bulk and the defendant to buy another, there was no contract between them.

A dealing, where the parties are not intending the same subject matter, evidently, cannot be an agreement.

The Lord Chancellor The Right Hon. John Thomas Ball:

> "What did the purchaser buy? Something of which the sample had been part — he bought the bulk out of which the sample had been taken — he knew of nothing else. What did the vendor intend to sell? Not that bulk out of which the sample had been taken, but a wholly different commodity which had come by the "Emma Peasant". The vendor and purchaser were therefore not dealing for the same subject matter. . . . A dealing where the parties are not intending the same subject matter, evidently cannot be an agreement. . . . On the true nature of the transaction as it existed . . . it appears to me that there was no contract."

Per Christian L.J. If there was a contract "it was a contract as to the bulk of which a sample had been exhibited at the auction; the exhibiting of the sample amounted to a representation by the sellers that it was taken from the bulk which was about to be sold."

Note: In *Scott v. Littledale* (1858) E & B 815 where the sample shown was of a lower quality than the bulk the contract was not held void. See also *Raffles v. Wichelhaus* (1864) 2 H & C 906.

MISTAKE AS TO THE IDENTITY OF THE PERSON CONTRACTED WITH BY LETTER

Cundy v. Lindsay (1878) 3 A.C. 459 (H.L.)

Alfred Blenkarn who occupied a room in a house (not on) but overlooking Wood Street, Cheapside, London, wrote to Lindsay & Co., linen manufacturers in Belfast proposing to purchase a supply of goods made by them. (chiefly cambric handkerchiefs) His letter was written as being sent from "37 Wood Street, Cheapside and was signed as to appear Blenkiron & Co. There was a highly respectable firm of W. Blenkiron & Son carrying on business at 123, Wood Street.

Messrs Lindsay, who knew of Blenkiron & Son, but not the number of their premises in Wood Street, answered the letter and sent goods addressed to Messrs Blenkiron & Co., 37, Wood Street. Blenkarn accepted them and sold them to different people including Messrs Cundy, who were a *bona fide* purchaser and who re-sold them in the ordinary way of trade. Blenkarn's fraud was discovered and he was prosecuted, convicted and sentenced. Messrs Lindsay then brought an action against Messrs Cundy for unlawful conversion of their goods.

The question was whether the property in the goods passed from Lindsay to Blenkarn? Was there a contract between the original owner and the intermediate person (Blenkarn) such as to enable him to pass a title to the goods?

Held: There was no contract made with Blenkarn, he never had a title which he could transfer to the defendants, who were consequently liable to the plaintiffs for the value of the goods. Though purchased *bona fide*, the title obtained was not good against the real owner.

The contract was void and C must return the goods.

The Lord Chancellor Lord Cairns:

> "Was there any contract which, with regard to the goods in question in this case, had passed the property in the goods from Messrs Lindsay to Alfred Blenkarn? If there was any contract passing that property, even although . . . that contract might afterwards be open to a process of reduction, upon the ground of fraud, still in the meantime, Blenkarn might have conveyed a good title for valuable consideration to the present appellants . . . if the property in the goods in question passed, it could have only pass by way of contract. . . . Blenkarn . . . was acting here just in the same way as if he had forged the signature of Blenkiron & Co., the respectable firm, to the applications for goods, and as if, when in return

the goods were forwarded and letters sent accompanying them, he had intercepted the goods and intercepted the letters, and taken possession of the goods and of the letters which were addressed to and intended for, not himself but the firm of Blenkiron & Co.

... how is it possible to imagine that in the state of things any contract could have arisen between the Respondents and Blenkarn, the dishonest man? Of him they knew nothing, and of him they never thought. With him they never intended to deal. Their minds never, even for an instant of time, rested upon him, and as between him and them there was no consensus of mind which could lead to any agreement of any contract whatever."

Lord Hartley:

"... there was no real contract whatever with Alfred Belnkarn; no goods had been delivered to anyone except for the purpose of transferring the property to Blenkiron & Co (not Blenkarn) ... no contract was made with Blenkarn, nor any contract was made with Blenkiron & Co., because they knew nothing at all about it, and therefore there could be no delivery of the goods with the intent to pass the property. . . . Blenkarn cannot, by so obtaining the goods have by possibility made a good title to a purchaser, as against the owner of the goods who had never in any shape or way parted with the property nor with anything more than possession of it."

MISTAKE AS TO IDENTITY

J.L. Smallman Ltd. v. O'Moore and Newman
[1959] I.R. 220 (H.C.) Davitt P.

The defendants were partners in a firm of building contractors which carried on business under the name of O'Moore and Newman. The plaintiff company dealt with them, selling them goods on credit and keeping a running account for them. In September, 1954, the defendants decided to carry on the business from then on, as a limited company. All suppliers, including the plaintiff were notified by circular and notice of the formation of the company was published in Stubbs' Gazette and in the Merchant's Gazette. Cheques issued by the company carried the name O'Moore and Newman & Co. Ltd., prominently displayed.

The plaintiffs claimed that they, notwithstanding, were unaware of the change in the legal status and continued, as they thought, to supply goods to the partnership. The defendants believed that they were being supplied to the company. When they failed to obtain settlement of their account the plaintiffs issued proceedings against the former partners.

Held There was no binding contract. Judgment must be for the defendants. The parties were not *ad idem*.

Note: The judge did point out that the plaintiffs would have an arguable case that the defendants were estopped by their conduct from pleading or proving that they did not order goods from the plaintiffs and contract to pay for them. This, however had not been raised in the pleadings.

MISTAKE AS TO IDENTITY — FACE TO FACE
Phillips v. Brooks Ltd. [1919] 2 K.B. 243

The plaintiff, a jeweller in Oxford Street, London sued the defendants who were pawnbroker for the return of a ring or its value, and damages for its detention.

A man had entered the plaintiff's shop, selected pearls priced £2,550 and a ring priced £450. He wrote out a cheque for £3,000 and in signing it, said: "You see who I am, I am Sir George Bullough." and he gave an address in St. James Square. The plaintiff knew that there was such a person as Sir George Bullough and finding on reference to a directory that Sir George lived at the address mentioned, he said "Would you like to take the articles with you ?, to which the man replied: "You had better have the cheque cleared first, but I should like to take the ring as it is my wife's birthday to-morrow." Whereupon the plaintiff let him have the ring.

The cheque was dishonoured, the person who gave it was in fact a fraudulent person named North who was subsequently convicted of obtaining the ring by false pretences. He had pledged the ring with the defendants who, *bona fide* and without notice, advanced £350, upon it.

In evidence the plaintiff said that he thought he was contracting with Sir George Bullough, and if he had known who the man really was he would not have let him have the ring. In re-examination he said that he had no intention of making a contract with any person other than Sir George.

Held The plaintiffs action must fail. There was a passing of the property in the ring and the purchaser had a good title, there must be judgment for the defendants with costs.

> "The question, therefore, in this case is whether or not the property had passed to the swindler as to entitle him to give a good title to any person who gave value and acted *bona fide* without notice. This question seems to have been decided in an American case of *Edmunds v. Merchants Despatch Transportation Co.*
>
> I think the seller intended to contract with the person present, and there was no error as to the person with whom he contracted, although the plaintiff would not have made the contract if there had not been a fraudulent misrepresentation." Per Horridge J.

Edmunds v. Merchants Despatch Transportation Co. (1883) 135 Mass. 283 followed.

Note: In general shopkeepers intend to contract with the person actually present in their shop regardless of identity and the onus of displacing this assumption must be supported by hard evidence.

MUTUAL MISTAKE AS TO THE TRUE NATURE OF AN AGREEMENT
Mespil v. Capaldi (1986) I.L.R.M. 373

On the day before a hearing for possession of premises, for arrears of rent and mesne rates, counsel for the defendants approached counsel for the plaintiffs in the Law Library and there was a tentative and inconclusive discussion as to a settlement. On the morning of the hearing the discussion was resumed and, after negotiations a settlement was agreed between the two counsel.

The settlement was reduced to writing by counsel for the defendants and after three words were interpolated by him in his hand-written draft, at the request of counsel for the plaintiffs, the written settlement was authenticated by the signatures of both counsel. The actions were then adjourned for the implementation of the settlement.

In its final form the settlement read: "Full and final settlement of all matters and acts in dispute between the parties: in these proceedings." The three underlined words were those inserted at the request of counsel for the plaintiffs.

Counsel for the defendants considered that notwithstanding the addition of the three words "in these proceedings" the settlement covered all matters and acts in dispute between the parties and not simply the matters in issue in the proceedings in question.

Counsel for the plaintiffs had insisted on the inclusion of the three words because he knew that there was some dispute between the parties as to the defendants user of the premises, which did not arise in the proceedings, and he did not wish that matter to be covered by the settlement.

The defendants paid some of the money payable under the settlement but did not pay a further £21,000 because they considered that a notice served on them determining the lease on some of the premises on the ground of a breach of covenant as to user, constituted a breach of the settlement. In the High Court it was accepted that there was an element of mutual mistake involved in the transaction but that notwithstanding this the defendants were bound to pay the £21,000 outstanding.

Held Henchy J. (*nem diss.*):
Objectively viewed, the situation justified the misapprehension on each side. The result was that, for want of correspondence between offer and acceptance, no enforceable contract was made. The alleged settlement, whether in the interpretation of the plaintiffs or in that of the defendants, must be held to be nullity. There was in fact no agreement. The action should proceed to trial.

Henchy J.:

"Having regard to the evidence given in the High Court, I am satisfied that the finding of mutual mistake was fully justified.... Notwithstanding the finding of mutual mistake, the judge held the defendants were bound by the terms of the settlement to the extent of having to pay the £21,000 outstanding. This conclusion was reached on the basis of cases which have decided that **when a person enters into an agreement, giving the other person the impression that he understands the nature and effect of the agreement, the general rule is that he will not be allowed to say later that he should not be bound by the agreement because he did not at the time understand its import or effect That is undoubtedly correct law. . . . The position is essentially different when, as is the case here, there was mutual or bi-lateral mistake as to the true nature of the agreement. Different and more fundamental principles of the law of contract come to be applied in such circumstances.**

It is of the essence of an enforceable simple contract that there be a consensus ad idem, expressed in an offer and an acceptance. Such a consensus cannot be said to exist unless there is a correspondence between the offer and the acceptance. **If the offer made is accepted by the other person in a fundamentally different sense from that in which it was tendered by the offeror, and the circumstances are objectively such as to justify such an acceptance, there cannot be said to be the meeting of minds which is essential for an enforceable contract. In such circumstances the alleged contract is a nullity.**" (i. e. no contract)

Mistake had negatived consent and prevented agreement.

Note: See *O'Neill v. Ryan ante.*

NON EST FACTUM AND MISTAKE ABOUT A DOCUMENT SIGNED

DOCUMENT NOT FUNDAMENTALLY DIFFERENT

Saunders v. Anglia Building Society [1971] A.C. 1004 (H.L.(E)
(on appeal from **Gallie v. Lee**)

A 78-year-old widow, G, gave the title deeds of her leasehold interest in her home in Dagenham, to her nephew. She knew that he wished to raise money on the house and that his friend L was involved with him in this. L asked her to sign a document. She could not read it because she had broken her spectacles and she asked L what it was. He told her it was a deed of gift of the house to her nephew. She signed it, believing it to be such, and her nephew witnessed it. The document was in fact an assignment (with the nephew's knowledge) of the house to L.

L mortgaged the house for £2,000 to the Anglia Building Society, used the money to pay his debts and defaulted on the mortgage instalments. The building society sought possession of the house. G at her nephew's instigation began an action, pleading *non est factum* and sought a declaration that the assignment was void and that the title deeds should be handed back to her.

Held by House of Lords: The widow had signed a document of the same character as she intended to sign and she was bound by it.

The plea of *non est factum* which would make the assignment void against the innocent building society had not been established. G., had signed what was obviously a legal document on which money was advanced, on the faith of it being her document, could not now disavow her signature.

Decision of the Court of Appeal affirmed. *Howatson v. Webb* [1907] 1 Ch. 537 *considered. Carlisle and Cumberland Co. v. Bragg* [1911] 1 K.B. 489, C.A *overruled.*

Lord Reid:

"The plea of *non est factum* obviously applies when the person sought to be held liable did not in fact sign the document. But at least since the sixteenth century it has also been held to apply in certain cases so as to enable a person who in fact signed a document to say that it is not his deed.

Obviously any such extension must be kept within narrow limits if it is not to shake the confidence of those who habitually and rightly rely on signatures when there is no obvious reason to doubt their validity. Originally this extension appears to have been made in favour of those who were unable to read owing to blindness or illiteracy and who therefore had to trust someone to tell them what they were signing.

I think it must also apply in favour of those who are permanently or temporarily unable through no fault of their own, to have without explanation any real understanding of the purport of a particular document, whether that be from defective education, illness or innate incapacity. But that does not excuse them from taking such precautions as they reasonably can . . . there must be a heavy burden of proof on the person who seeks to invoke this remedy. . . . The plea cannot be available to anyone who was content to sign without taking the trouble to try to find out at least the general effect of the document.

Further, **the plea cannot be available to a person whose mistake was really a mistake as to the legal effect of the document, whether this was his own mistake or that of his adviser**. . . . I do not think that the modern division between the character and the contents of a document is at all satisfactory. . . . There must, I think, be a **radical difference between what he signed and what he thought he was signing** — or one could use the words "fundamental" or "serious" or "very substantial". But what amounts to a radical difference will depend on the circumstances."

DOCUMENT FUNDAMENTALLY DIFFERENT
Bank of Ireland v. McManamy [1916] 2 I.R. 161 (K.B.D.)

The plaintiff sued the defendants for a sum of £1034 odd and interest on foot of a letter of guarantee dated the 7th April, 1911, whereby the defendants jointly and severally guaranteed all debts, liabilities and engagements of the Boyle Co-Operative and Dairy Society Limited to the plaintiffs, to the extent of £1000 with interest at 5 per cent per annum from date of demand.

The defendants alleged that they signed the document on the false representation made by the plaintiff's agent, that it was inter alia "a book or other paper to enable them to receive manures or other goods from the said society at a special price and that the said document was so signed by them and each of them under a total mistake as to its nature and in the bona fide belief that they were executing an instrument of a wholly different kind from that which the plaintiffs now allege."

They claimed that they were induced to make and give the guarantee alleged by the fraud of the plaintiffs' agent. None of the defendants except one, knew, that the document was a guarantee and there had been no negligence of the part of the defendants in signing the document. At first instance a jury found for the defendants except one person and the bank brought a motion to have the judgment set aside.

Held The verdict and judgment should stand. The defence of non est factum applied to all the defendants except one.

Cherry L.C.J. with Boyd J. concurring:

> "It is true that in *Foster v. McKinnon* L.R. 4 C.P. 704, and I think also in nearly all the cases which have followed it, the cause of the error has been fraud on the part of some person, but this is due to the fact that such error as to the nature of the document can scarcely ever exist without fraud on somebody's part.
>
> The principle of the cases is not, however that fraud vitiates consent, but rather that there is an entire absence of consent. That **the mind of the party who signs under a fundamental error does not go with the act of signing, and that there is consequently no contract at all in fact**. The defendant if he succeeds, does so upon the issue non est factum, not upon the issue of fraud, though fraud, as I have said, is usually present, and is generally found by the jury to have existed."

Cherry L.C.J. also quoted the judgment of Kennedy L.J. in *Carlisle and Cumberland Co. v. Bragg* [1911] 1 K.B. 489:

> "The principle involved, as I understand it, is that a consenting mind is

essential to the making of a contract and that in such a case as this there was really no consensus, because there was no intention to make a contract of the kind in question."

Note: Carlisle and Cumberland Co. v. Bragg [1911] 1 K.B. 489, C.A was overruled by the House of Lords in *Saunders v. Anglia Building Society, supra*. In the Carlisle case the defendant denied that he signed a guarantee upon which the action was brought and alleged that, if he did, his signature was fraudulently obtained by the principal debtor (Rigg) who falsely represented to him that it was an insurance paper. It was held that the defendant was not estopped from denying that he had contracted to guarantee the debt, the proximate cause of the plaintiffs loss was the fraudulent action of R, and not the defendants supposed negligence. It was also held that the defendant was not negligent in the breach of any duty to the plaintiff as might have been the case if the document had been a negotiable instrument.

> "The plea of *non est factum* could not be available to anyone who signed without taking the trouble to find out at least the general effect of the document." — *per* Lord Reid.

CHAPTER 11

Misrepresentation

Misrepresentation is a false statement of past or existing fact, made before or at the time of contracting by one of the parties, which is intended and does induce the other party to enter into the contract. It is not a term of the contract itself.

It must be a statement. In general, silence does not amount to a misrepresentation. In *Power v. Barrett*, however, silence did amount to a misrepresentation. In the following instances a failure to communicate will amount to a misrepresentation, a) in contracts *uberrimae fidei* where there is a duty to make full disclosure of all material facts, (See Ch. 9 Insurance) b) where there has been a material change in circumstances between the time of negotiation and the time of contracting, (*With v. O'Flanagan* [1936] Ch. 575 C.A.): In *Sargent v. Irish Multiwheel* where the defendants did not point out an error in their advertisement, they were liable because the plaintiff contracted with them in reliance on the advert and c) in some fiduciary relationships. e. g. Contracts between the promoters of a company and the company, between an Agent and his Principal, or contracts between partners.

There is a positive duty to disclose material facts in contracts *uberrimae fidei* e.g. As already indicated contracts of insurance fall within this category.

In the 19th century, case of *Nottingham Patent Brick and Tile Co. v. Butler* (1886) C.A., the English Court of Appeal held that a half truth relating to knowledge of covenants is a contract for the sale of land amounted to a misrepresentation

The statement itself:

(1) must be a **statement of fact** (*Edgington v. Fitzmaurice*) not be a statement of law. A representation about the meaning of a Public Act of Parliament is a representation of law, whereas a representation as to private rights or of foreign law is treated as one of fact.

(2) must **not be a mere sales puff** i.e. statements couched in vague generalities which do not relate to a specific fact or attribute. "This is a great horse" is mere sales talk and has no effect in law. See judgment of Curran J. in *Smyth v. Lynn*.

(3) must **not be a statement of opinion**. An erroneous opinion even where relied on will not amount to a misrepresentation (*Bissett v. Wilkinson*) except where the opinion is based on facts particularly within the knowledge of the representor, in which case he is implying that these facts justify the opinion

which he has expressed. (*Esso Petroleum v. Mardon*).

(4) must **not be a statement as to the future**. The statement must be about an existing fact.

A statement of present intention about future conduct. A statement of intention may involve a statement of fact. (*Edgington v. Fitzmaurice*).

(5) It **must have been directed at the contracting party or to his agent**. *Securities Trust Ltd. v. Hugh Moore & Alexander Ltd.*

(6) The **representee must have acted in reliance on it**. The statement must be in the nature of an inducement which was relied on. If the true facts were already known to the representee and he did not rely on the statement *Grafton Court v. Wadson Sales*, or if he did not rely on the statement but called in his own experts, *Attwood v. Small* (1838) then misrepresentation cannot be claimed. Likewise reliance cannot be claimed where an obligation is imposed on the offeree to verify statements or particulars.

Finally the use of a disclaimer or a clause designed to protect from liability for statements, by disclaiming responsibility for their accuracy and placing an onus on the other party to establish the true position for himself, was fully discussed in *Pearson v. Dublin Corporation*. Reliance may be negatived where an obligation is imposed to verify statements or particulars. A representation may also be implied. (see *Loughnan v. Barry and Byrne*.)

TYPES OF MISREPRESENTATION

There are three types of misrepresentation — fraudulent, innocent, and negligent. A fraudulent misrepresentation is one made knowingly or without belief in its truth or reckless, careless whether it be true or false. In most cases it is extremely difficult to prove fraud as against negligence but in *Fenton and Anor v. Schofield & Ors.* (1965) 100 ILT 69 and in *Carbin v. Sommerville* Irish courts have held that there was fraudulent misrepresentation. Damages were awarded in the former case and rescission was granted in the latter.

Innocent misrepresentation is one which although false is not fraudulent or negligent and is made by a party who genuinely believes in its truth. The sole remedy is rescission. *Derry v. Peek* was a case of innocent misrepresentation wherein Lord Herschell established the criterion for fraudulent misrepresentation.

A negligent misrepresentation is a statement of material fact made negligently which is intended, and which does, induce a contract. A negligent misstatement may be a statement made negligently where there is no contract induced between the parties but where there is a "special relationship" as expounded in *Hedley Byrne & Co. Ltd. v. Heller* and is an extension of the duty of care owed in tort. Treitel in *The Law of Contract*, 7th ed. 1987 at page 267 states "The main importance of *Hedley Byrne's* case lies in its recognition of liability in damages for negligent misrepresentation. . . ." Guest in *Anson's Law of Contract* 26th ed. at page 218 correctly points out that ". . . the effect of this

decision on the law relating to misrepresentation was not directly considered."
He then however, cites *Esso Petroleum Ltd. v. Mardon* (1976) Q.B. 801 as
authority for stating "it has subsequently been held that a negligent misrepresentation made preparatory to entering a contract can give rise to an action for
damages in tort for negligent misstatement. . . ." The ambit of negligent
misstatement is therefore wider than negligent misrepresentation and so encom-
passes the latter that it is difficult to see negligent misrepresentation surviving
as a cause of action.

Although the Irish cases of *Brogan v. Bennett* and *Macken v. Munster &
Leinster Bank & Anor.*, both pre-dated the *Hedley Byrne case, neither were
adverted to in that decision or in Sisk & Son Ltd. v. Flinn & Ors.* In the latter
case the duty of care in relation to careless statements where there is a special
relationship between the parties as established in the Hedley Byrne case was
adopted by Finlay P. (as he then was) in addition to the general principles as to
the standard of care. The extension of the duty of care in negligence where there
is a special relationship between the parties and such relationship if not fiduciary, or arising out of a contract for consideration must be "equivalent to
contract" before any liability can arise, is reviewed in a separate extract from
Kenny J. in *Bank of Ireland v. Smith & Ors.*

Despite the provisions of section 46 of the Sale of Goods and Supply of
Services Act, 1980, the Irish equivalent of section 3 of the British Misrepresentation Act 1967 on the basis of the decision in Overbrook Properties Ltd., it
appears that a principal may exclude liability for misrepresentation by his agent.

SILENCE EQUIVALENT TO A REPRESENTATION

Power v. Barrett (1887) L.R. Ir. 450 (Ch.D.)

The plaintiff held certain premises under a lease, which contained a covenant
not to use them for certain purposes or to carry on certain businesses, or any
other dangerous, noxious, or offensive trade, business or profession.

He agreed to sell his interest in the lease to the defendant, an oil merchant,
and previous to the contract was aware that the defendant would require to store
large quantities of oil therein.

The defendant, on discovering the existence of the covenant, refused to
complete and the plaintiff denied that he was unaware of it and sought specific
performance. The plaintiff had asked the defendant if he intended to engage in
manufacturing.

Held: (*inter alia*) The plaintiff should have known of the existence of the
restrictive covenant, that he was bound to have informed the defendant of it,
that his silence on the subject was equivalent to a representation that there was
no such covenant. The plaintiff was not entitled to a decree of specific performance.

SILENCE WHERE THERE HAS BEEN A CHANGE BETWEEN NEGOTIATION AND CONTRACTING

With v. O'Flanagan [1936] Ch. 575 (C.A.)

The plaintiffs sought rescission of a contract dated 1 May, 1934 to purchase the defendants medical practice. In January, 1934, the parties entered into negotiations for the sale of a medical practice and a medical agent represented that it was "doing at the rate of £2,000 a year" and that Dr. O'Flanagan was asking £4,000 for it. The plaintiffs saw Dr. O'Flanagan who confirmed this statement.

In the interval between the 1 January and the 1 May when the contract was signed, Dr. O'Flanagan was away seriously ill from time to time with the result that the receipts fell off. From the evidence it appeared that during the three weeks preceding May 1, the practice was not producing more than an average of £5 a week. The change of circumstances was not disclosed to the purchasers and when they took possession on 1 May they found that the practice was almost nonexistent. They stayed two or three days, but found that no private patients came. They now claimed rescission and repayment of the purchase money.

It was admitted that the statement as to £2,000 a year was true at the time it was made, The defendant claimed that no representation was made about the present state of the practice that they only represented the taking to be £2,000 a year for the period of a little over two years ending at the end of the last year, during which Dr. O'Flanagan was in control of the practice.

Held: that the representation was made with a view to induce the purchasers to enter into the contract and must be treated as continuing until the contract was signed. It was the duty of the vendor to communicate the change of circumstances to the purchasers. *Traill v. Baring* (1864) 4 De G. J & S 318 and *Davies v. London and Provincial Marine Insurance Co.* (1878) 8 Ch.D. 469 *considered and applied.*

Lord Wright M.R. referred to the judgment of Lord Blackburn in *Brownlie v. Campbell* 5 App. Cas. 925,950 and to his statement that silence when a representation becomes untrue amounts to fraud, commented:

> "nowadays the Court is more reluctant to use the word 'fraud' and would not generally use the word 'fraud' in that connection because the failure to disclose, though wrong and a breach of duty, may be due to inadvertence or a failure to realise that the duty rests upon the party who has made the representation not to leave the other party under an error when the representation has become falsified by a change of circumstances. This question **only occurs when there is an interval between the time when the representation is made and when it is acted upon** by the party to whom it is made, who either concludes the contract or does some similar decisive act; but the representation remains in effect and it is because that

is so, and because the Court is satisfied in a proper case on the facts that it remained operative in the mind of the representee, that the Court holds that under such circumstances the representee should not be bound. . . . I think that **this doctrine is not limited to a case of contracts *uberrimae fidei* or to any cases in which owing to confidential relationship there is a peculiar duty of disclosure. . . .**"

A HALF-TRUTH CAN AMOUNT TO A MISREPRESENTATION
Nottingham Patent Brick and Tile Co. v. Butler (1886) Vol. XVI Q.B.D.

In 1882 the plaintiff company contracted to purchase land from the defendant under conditions of sale which stated that the property was sold subject to any matter or thing affecting the same, whether disclosed at the time of sale or not; and provided that any error or omission in the particulars should not annul the sale, nor entitle the purchaser to compensation.

The existence of restrictive covenants was not mentioned in the contract, but during negotiations the defendant stated that there were covenants restricting the use of the land as a brick-yard. The defendants solicitor, a Mr. Gilbert, who was present, and to whom the plaintiff's solicitor applied for information, stated that he was not aware of any such covenants. Gilbert did not say that (as the fact was) he had not read the earlier title deeds, and knew nothing about their contents. A director of the plaintiff company, thereupon signed a contract to purchase and paid a deposit of £610. The plaintiffs on discovering that there were restrictive covenants, brought an action claiming rescission and the return of their deposit. The defendant counter-claimed for specific performance.

Held: That the plaintiffs were not precluded by the terms of the conditions of sale, nor by the Conveyancing Act, 1881, from refusing to complete the purchase, and they were therefore entitled to recover the amount of the deposit.

Lords Esher M.R.:

"It is impossible for a vendor, knowing of a defect in his title, either by himself or his agent to put forward conditions of sale which are to force upon a purchaser a bad title of which he knew, but which he did not disclose. A court of Equity would not be of much use if it could not meet such a case as that, and it seems to me clear that a court of Equity would never have enforced a contract under such circumstances. Does the Conveyancing Act make any difference? I entirely agree that, whatever construction you put upon it, it cannot have that effect. It cannot cure that defect in the title of the defendant. . . . I am sorry to say that I have come to the conclusion that the defendant's solicitor allowed himself to be carried away by his zeal for his client, and that he did not act with that candour to the other side with which a solicitor is bound to act under such circumstances. He allowed himself, in his zeal for his client, to make **statements which were calculated to lead the other side to believe that he was stating facts within his own knowledge, and his statements in fact misled them, so that what he said amounts to a mis-statement of facts**."

Note: Parol evidence over-rode the written conditions.

MISSTATEMENT OF FACT

Edgington v. Fitzmaurice (1885) CH. D. Vol. XXIX 459 (C.A.)

Rev. Charles Edgington a shareholder in a company, the Army and Navy Provision Market (Limited) received a prospectus issued by order of the directors inviting subscriptions for debenture bonds at 6 per cent interest. A clause in the prospectus stated that the Society had purchased a valuable property and the objects for which the issue of debentures was made were "To enable the society to complete the alterations and additions to the buildings, to purchase horses and vans and to develop the trade of the company." The real object of the debenture loan was to enable the directors to pay off pressing liabilities.

The plaintiff took debenture bonds to the amount of £1,500 and some months later when the company was wound up the assets were not sufficient to pay the debenture holders more than a small dividend. The plaintiff claimed repayment of the sum he had advanced on the ground that it had been obtained from him by the fraudulent misstatements and omissions in the prospectus and the fraudulent misrepresentations of the Secretary and General Manager of the company.

Held: that the misstatement of the objects for which the debentures were issued was a material misstatement of fact, influencing the conduct of the plaintiff, and rendered the directors liable to an action for deceit, although the plaintiff was also influenced by his own mistake.

Bowen L.J.:

"There must be a misstatement of existing fact; but **the state of a man's mind is as much a fact as the state of his digestion**. It is true that it is very difficult to prove what the state of a man's mind at a particular time is, but if it can be ascertained it is as much a fact as anything else. A misrepresentation as to the state of a man's mind is therefore, a misstatement of fact."

Fry L.J.:

> "The prospectus was intended to influence the mind of the reader . . . the plaintiff admits that he was induced to make the advance not merely by this false statement, but by the belief that the debentures would give him a charge on the company's property, and it is admitted that this was a mistake of the plaintiff. Therefore it is said that the plaintiff was the author of his own injury . . . but in my opinion **if the false statement of fact actually influenced the plaintiff, the defendants are liable, even though the plaintiff may have been also influenced by other matters.**"

Cotton L.J.:

> "**It is not necessary to show that the misstatement was the sole cause of his acting** as he did. If he acted on that misstatement, though he was influenced by an erroneous supposition, the defendants will be still liable."

STATEMENT OF OPINION

Smyth v. Lynn [1951] 85 I.L.T.R. 57 (N.I.) (Ch.D.)

A firm of auctioneers in Belfast advertised a dwelling house and grounds for sale. The advertisement described the premises as follows: "The property is brick built, pebble dashed, and slated and of sound construction. It is in excellent structural and decorative repair, and ready for immediate owner occupation."

The defendant saw the advert and inspected the premises. At the auction the defendant was outbidden by the plaintiff. Later that same month the plaintiff instructed his solicitor to have the property re-sold by public auction. The same auctioneers were employed and a similar advertisement to that used in the first sale was used.

The defendant, enquired as to the reason for the re-sale so soon after the plaintiff's purchase and was told that the reason was merely a personal one and assured that the description of the property in the second advertisement was correct. He was the successful bidder at the auction but when he inspected the premises, later the same day, he found extensive woodworm infestation in and around the hall and stairs and refused to go ahead with the purchase.

He claimed that a latent defect in the premises of a serious nature was concealed from him, that there was a serious misrepresentation as to the quality of the premises and that the misrepresentation was contained in the advertisement where the property was described as being of "sound construction and in excellent structural and decorative repair and ready for immediate owner occupation."

Held: That on the evidence the statements complained of did not in any positive sense induce the defendant to purchase or contribute to the inducement of the defendant. The plaintiff and the defendant must both be treated as innocent parties in the transaction and in all the circumstances the plaintiff was entitled to specific performance of the contract.

Curran J.:

> "The principles . . . and what are the relevant enquiries in a case such as the present are discussed in the judgment of the Privy Council in the case of *Bissett v. Wilkinson and Another* [1927] A.C. 177. At page 181, Lord Merrivale says: "In an action for rescission, as in an action for specific performance of an executory contract, when misrepresentation repudiates the contract it is of course essential to ascertain whether that which is relied upon is a representation of fact or a representation of opinion, since an erroneous opinion stated by the party affirming the contract, though it may have been relied upon and induced the contract on the part of the party who seeks rescission, gives no title to relief unless fraud is established.
>
> The learned judge then cited *Karberg's* case [1892] 3 Ch. 1 and *Smith v. Land and House Property Corporation* (1884) 28 Ch.D. 7. In Karberg's case the test used to ascertain whether a representation was one of opinion or belief, was: "was the statement of expectation a statement of things not really expected?"

> "The advertisement," Curran J. continued, "contains statements which are undoubtedly statements of fact such as 'the property is brick built, pebble dashed and slated.' . . . When the advertisement goes on, however, to state that the property is 'in excellent structural and decorative repair and ready for immediate owner occupation' one is faced with the question — What standard has the person making these statements applied?
>
> It is my view that the statements referred to are expressions of opinion, and that the opinions expressed are erroneous. . . . Such advertisements, however, must be looked at in their true perspective. They do not purport to be detailed reports by experts as to the condition of the property to be sold. It is common knowledge, that the purpose of such advertisements is to draw attention to the good points of the property, and that one usually finds in such advertisements rather flourishing statements. In my opinion the defendant is not the type of person to rely on "Auctioneers encomiums." . . . I am inclined to the view that the statement in the advertisement assumed a more positive importance in the defendants mind after his discovery of the woodworm and when he came to consider with his advisers what grounds he had for getting out of his contract. . . ."

MISREPRESENTATION MUST BE DIRECTED TO THE CONTRACTING PARTY

Securities Trust Ltd. v. Hugh Moore & Alexander Ltd.
[1964] I.R. 417 (H.C.) Davitt P.

A Mr. Anderson, a registered shareholder of H applied for, and was sent a copy of the Memorandum and Articles of Association of H by the company. Mr. Anderson was Chairman and Managing Director of S for whom he held the shares in H as a trustee. H was unaware of this.

On the faith of an inaccurate copy of the Articles S purchased shares in the H company which was subsequently wound up. S sued H for negligent misrepresentation.

Held: The Memorandum and Articles were supplied to Mr. Anderson in his personal capacity and not as an agent for S. The duty to ensure that the copy supplied was accurate was only owed to Mr. Anderson and not to the community at large including the plaintiff company, S.

Note: The decision of the House of Lords in *Hedley Byrne & Co., Ltd. v. Heller & Co. Ltd.*, which enlarged the duty of care in tort to cover statements in circumstances where a special relationship exists between the parties was *approved* of in this case but there was no special relationship and therefore no duty of care was owed to S.

NON-RELIANCE ON A MISREPRESENTATION — REPRESENTEE COULD SEE FOR HIMSELF

Grafton Court v. Wadson Sales
High Court, unreported, 17 February, 1975 Finlay P.

The plaintiff claimed rent, a site fine and outlay charges alleged to be due to them by the defendant by virtue of the lease of a lock up shop (Unit 1) in a shopping complex known as Grafton Court in Grafton Street, Dublin, to the defendants.

It was conceded on behalf of the defendants that the lease was a valid lease validly executed. The defendant, however, counterclaimed that they had entered into the lease relying on certain representations and promises made on behalf of the plaintiffs and that there had been a breach or failure of these representations and promises.

The defendants claimed that it had been represented that the other tenants taking units in it would all be of a high class quality retail type and that the building would be completed in accordance with a high standard. The main representation relied upon was that the Grafton Court complex would receive extensive advertising promotion.

Held: (*inter alia*) the defendant had not relied on any misrepresentation that the other tenants would all be of a high class quality retail type and could not recover on this account. Đamages of £1270 were awarded in respect of failure to promote and breach of covenants for lighting and maintenance.

Finlay T. President of the High Court:

"I am satisfied that at a very early stage before the lease of the 14th April, 1972 was executed it was represented that the other tenants occupying stalls or units in Grafton Court would be of a high class quality retail type. The evidence before me, however, established that as of the 14th April, 1972 by far the great majority of all the stalls originally occupied by various leaseholders had already been taken up and that Mr. M's position at the time his company entered into the lease was that **he knew the identity, type of trade and quality of trade which was being carried on by almost all the other tenants** in Grafton Court.

If therefore, and I do not so decide, the quality and nature of those tenants and the type of trade they carried on fell short of the representations which were made . . . that failure must have been known to the defendant company (in the person of Mr.M) . . . before the lease was executed and he could not therefore, in my judgment, have still been relying on any representation that had been made to him. I accordingly do not consider that there was any breach or failure of this representation in respect of which any relief can be afforded to the defendant company."

NON-RELIANCE ON A MISREPRESENTATION — EXPERTS CALLED IN

Attwood v. Small (1838) 6 Cl & Fin 232

The appellant and the respondent entered into negotiations for the sale and purchase of an estate with an iron mine collieries and works, partly in Staffordshire and partly in Worcestershire.

The respondent Small, wrote to the appellant that they were willing to purchase the property for £600,000 on the understanding that a Mr. P. Taylor would be given every facility to ascertain the correctness of representations made to them respecting the property. A deputation from Small with the assistance of three scientists who had practical experience in mining operations devoted the greater part of two days to examining the property and the books of account. They concluded that Attwood's calculations and figures were correct and well founded. Mr. Taylor wrote to Small that the calculations appeared to prove that the statements made by Attwood were more favourable to the buyer (Small) than the seller (Attwood).

Later Small claimed that several statements and accounts were false, particularly as regards costs of manufacturing iron at the ironworks and that the works were less profitable than Attwood had claimed. It was claimed that wilful misrepresentations had been made by Attwood to induce Small to enter into the contract and that the contract should be rescinded.

Held: There was no misrepresentation. The purchaser did not rely on the representation. The contract must stand.

Lord Brougham:

> "We find there is no misrepresentation which gave rise to the contract, we find that the purchasers did not rely upon the representation, but said, we will enquire ourselves; . . . from 6th June, 1825, downwards they constantly proceeded upon the plan of satisfying themselves, then by enquiring themselves, then even afterwards by sending other agents to enquire, and those agents reporting that the representation was true. . . . The parties should not be released from their contract."

Lord Cottenham L.C.:

> ". . .the plaintiffs did not rely on any representation of Mr. Attwood, but had free access to all the books they required, and satisfied themselves of the accuracy of his representations, first, whether fraud was practiced, and secondly, whether that which is alleged, as fraud, or rather the facts from which fraud is inferred, were not known to the plaintiffs, or to those on whose conduct and by whose knowledge they must be affected from the very commencement of this transaction. I have satisfied myself that both these propositions are in favour of the defendants. Fraud is not established."

NOT AWARE OF REPRESENTATION
Horsfall v. Thomas (1862) 1 H & C 90

The defendant employed the Plaintiff iron-founders to make a cannon, for the purpose of testing experiments which he desired to submit to the War Office. He was to pay by two bills of exchange. The plaintiff delivered a gun with a defect in it which the defendant might have seen on examination, and which would have justified him in refusing to accept it. Thomas accepted the gun without examining it and gave the plaintiff the Bills of Exchange. A metal plug had been driven into the breech of the gun to plug a defect, but the plaintiff in a letter to the defendant, stated that "the gun is of the best metal all through, and has no weak points that we are aware of, and we hope it will turn out all that Mr. Thomas desires."

During trials the gun blew apart. The metal was unsound and strong flaws opened gradually behind the trunnions. Thomas called on the plaintiff to supply a perfectly sound facsimile of the gun at their own expense and refused to honour a Bill of Exchange. The plaintiff sued for payment on the Bill and the defendant claimed that he had been induced to accept the Bill by the fraud of the plaintiff. The defendants counsel argued that the plug could not have been inserted into the gun without the plaintiffs knowledge and that their statement that it "was of the best metal all through, and has no weak points that we are aware of." was false and fraudulent. That because the defendant having been induced by the false and fraudulent representation the plaintiff could not recover.

Held: There was no evidence to support the defendants plea that he had been induced by a fraudulent misrepresentation. The defendant had never examined the gun, and therefore it was impossible that an attempt to conceal the defect could have had any operation on his mind or conduct. If the plug, which it was said was put in to conceal the defect, had never been there, his position would have been the same; for, as he did not examine the gun or form an opinion as to whether it was sound, its condition did not affect him.

Bramwell B.:

"To constitute fraud, there must be an assertion of something false with the knowledge of the party asserting it, or the suppression of that which is true and which it was his duty to communicate. Here there was no assertion of an untruth, and the only question is whether there was a suppression of anything which the plaintiff was bound to make known to the defendant. Now, the manufacturer of an article is not always bound to point out its defects to the purchaser. If, indeed, there be a defect known to the manufacturer, and which cannot be discovered on inspection he is bound to point it out; but if there be a defect which is patent, and of which the purchaser is as capable of judging as the manufacturer, he is not bound to call the attention of the purchaser to it, . . . it cannot be said that there is any fraud in the manufacturer when the purchaser sees the defect and either accepts or rejects the article or does not see it because he has not used sufficient diligence to discover it."

DISCLAIMER AND MISREPRESENTATION
Pearson v. Dublin Corporation [1907] A.C. 351 (H. L.)

The plaintiff contracted with the defendant to build a sewer works at Ringsend. The contract provided that the contractor must verify all representations for himself and not rely on the accuracy of the Corporation's plans, specifications or drawings.

A clause in the specifications provided that the contractor was to satisfy himself as to dimensions, levels, character and nature of all existing works, to obtain his own information on all matters which could influence his tender and to verify the levels for himself. Another clause stated that no charges for extra work would be allowed in consequence of any incorrect information or inaccuracies which might appear in the drawings, specifications or estimates of quantities.

The plans supplied by the Corporation were inaccurate. The Plaintiff sued for the additional expense to which they had been put as damages for fraudulent misrepresentation.

Held: In the King's Bench Division — There was sufficient evidence to suggest to a jury that the representation was either wilfully false, or if not wilfully false, was made without any *bona fide* or real belief in its truth (*Derry v. Peek* 14 A.C. 337) and there was evidence that the plaintiff in making their tender and entering into the contract took into account and acted on this representation.

Held: In The House of Lords — No one can escape liability for his own fraudulent statements by inserting in the contract a clause that the other party shall not rely upon them . . . the clauses protect only against honest mistakes. — *per* Lord Loreburn L.C.

> "Such clauses may be appropriate and fairly apply to errors, inaccuracies and mistakes, but not to cases like the present." — *per* Lord Ashbourne.

QUALIFICATION/DISCLAIMER
John Sisk and Son Ltd. v. Flinn and Others
[1986] I.L.R.M. 128 (H.C.) Finlay P.

The plaintiff purchased 15,000 shares in a company on the basis of accounts audited and prepared by the defendants, partners in a firm of accountants. The Auditors report contained a qualification: "We have obtained all the information and explanations which to the best of our knowledge and belief were necessary for the purpose of our audit except that stock and work in progress at the beginning and end of the financial period are as certified by the management and have not been physically observed by us."

The company made heavy losses the following year and another firm of Auditors and Accountants who were called in, concluded that the work in progress figure in the accounts had been overstated by approximately £180,000.

The plaintiffs claimed that the defendants made representations and submitted accounts and financial statements which were untrue and that in doing so they were negligent.

Held: The defendants were not liable. The interpretation of the qualification contained in their report meant that they had no responsibility for the work in progress figures. No case had been made against them of negligence material to the losses other than in respect of the work in progress figures.

Finlay P. applied the three tests of Haldane L.J. in *Derry v. Peek* and found (1) that the plaintiff was trusting the defendants to exercise such a degree of care as the circumstances required, (2) that it was reasonable for them to do so, (3) that the defendants ought to have known that the plaintiff was relying on them.

A reasonable man knowing that he was being trusted or that his skill and judgment were being relied on would have three courses open to him:

1. To keep silent or decline to give the information or advice sought.

2. Give the answer with a clear qualification that he accepted no responsibility for it or that it was given without that reflection or enquiry which a careful answer would require;

3. Simply answer without such qualification.

The defendants had adopted the second course. *Hedley Byrne & Co. Ltd. v. Heller & Partners Ltd.* [1964] A.C. 465 *approved.*

FRAUDULENT MISREPRESENTATION

Sargeant v. Irish Multiwheel Ltd.
(Cir.Ct.) [1955- 56] Ir. Jur. Rep. 42 MacCarthy J.

The defendants advertised a 1947 Austin 10 cwt., English assembled van for sale. The plaintiff saw the advertisement and purchased the van in the belief that it was English assembled. The defendants knew that it was Irish- assembled and that the description in the advertisement was an error, but did not mention this to the plaintiff during negotiations.

The plaintiff subsequently sold the van as English-assembled and was sued for breach of warranty, suffering losses and expense as a result. He then instituted proceedings against Irish Multiwheel for damages.

Held: The plaintiff fully relied on the representation given in the advertisement. That representation was false to the knowledge of the defendants. There was a duty on the defendants to warn the plaintiff of the error. They failed in that duty, and were liable to the plaintiff for the loss he suffered.

Fenton & Anor. v. Schofield & Ors. [1965] 100 I.L.T.R. 69 (S.C.)

The plaintiff claimed damages for fraudulent misrepresentation and fraud in the sale to the plaintiff of a house and lands in Co. Kilkenny, together with a fishery on the River Nore.

The plaintiff claimed that Schofield had instructed a firm of estate agents that about 300 salmon each year, were caught with rod and line at the fishery, and authorised them so to inform intending purchasers.

He also claimed that Schofield represented verbally to him that an average of 250 salmon were caught each year in the fishery, in order to induce him to buy the said lands and fishery, and showed him a fishing register which he represented as a true record of the salmon caught with rod and line from 1956 to July 1960.

Held: (High Court) by Davitt P. There were no reliable records and no reliable evidence otherwise, of the number of fish caught. Schofield could not have got anything like an average of 250. The representation was both false and fraudulent. The plaintiffs were entitled to damages of £11,700 the difference between the actual value of the property and the price paid. The defendant was awarded £210 on a counterclaim.

Held: (Supreme Court) On the evidence the property was at the relevant time worth £22,000. The damages awarded to the plaintiff would accordingly be varied to the sum of £5,000. The order of the High Court must be affirmed as varied.

Carbin v. Sommerville [1933] I.R. 276. (S.C.)

The plaintiff sought rescission of a contract to purchase a house at Vernon Avenue, Clontarf, Dublin. The trial judge found that the defendant, when selling the property, was asked if the house was dry and free from damp and if the roof was alright, and that he had stated in reply to each question that it was.

The defendant had re-papered the house on three occasions during the previous three years because of dampness, and had also applied black pitch paint on the interior walls to prevent the damp from discolouring the new wallpaper.

Held: by the Supreme Court on appeal *per* Fitzgibbon J.:

> "it is perfectly clear that when the defendant answered the question in the affirmative, as the judge has found he did, he intended his answer to be taken in the sense in which the question was asked, and in the sense in which the judge has found the plaintiff did take it and act upon it, and so given, the misrepresentation was false and fraudulent."

The plaintiff was entitled to rescission of the contract and the return of her purchase money.

Note: Fitzgibbon J. did not accept the plaintiffs submission that she would still have been entitled to rescission on the ground of a failure of consideration had the representation been innocent or inadvertent because "There was only an inferiority in quality which would sound in damages only." Repudiation was only possible at common law if there was a total failure of consideration. Robert Clark, *Contract Law*, p. 237 points out that Fitzgibbon J. overlooked the fact that courts of equity permitted rescission if an innocent misrepresentation was made.

INNOCENT MISREPRESENTATION
Derry v. Peek (1889) 14 App. Cas 337 (H.L. (E)

In February, 1883 the appellants as directors of the Plymouth Devenport and District Tramways Company issued a prospectus which stated:

> ". . . one great feature of this undertaking . . . is that by the special Act of Parliament obtained, the company has the right to use steam or mechanical motive power, instead of horses, and it is fully expected that by means of this a considerable saving will result in the working expenses of the line compared with other tramways worked by horses."

The respondent claimed that in reliance on these representations he applied for and obtained shares in the company, that the statements in the prospectus were untrue, that the appellants well knew that they were false and that the representation was made fraudulently with a view to inducing the plaintiff to take shares in the company.

Held: the appellants honestly believed in the truth of the representation.

Lord Herschell:

> "A man who forms his belief carelessly, or is unreasonably credulous, may be blameworthy, when he makes a representation on which another is to act, but he is not, in my opinion, fraudulent in the sense in which the word was used in all the cases from Payley Fiteman (2 Smith's L.C. 74) down to that with which I am now dealing. . . . I think the authorities establish the following propositions:
> **First**, in order to sustain an action of deceit, there must **be proof of fraud, and nothing short of that will suffice**.
> **Secondly**, fraud is proved when it is shown that **a false representation has been made (1) knowingly, or (2) without belief in its truth, or (3) recklessly, careless whether it be true or false**. Although I have treated the second and third as distinct cases, I think the third is but an instance of the second, for one who makes a statement under such circumstances can have no real belief in its truth. And this probably covers the whole ground, for one who knowingly alleges that which is false, has obviously no such honest belief.
> **Thirdly**, if fraud be proved, **the motive of the person guilty of it is immaterial**. It matters not that there was no intention to cheat or injure the person to whom the statement was made."

NEGLIGENT MISREPRESENTATION
Esso Petroleum Co. Ltd. v. Mardon [1976] 11. Q.B. 801 (C.A.)

A servant of the plaintiff with 40 years experience of the trade, calculated that a site on a busy main street had a potential throughput likely to reach 200,000 gallons by the third year of operation. The plaintiffs built a filling station as a retail outlet for their petrol on the site, but because of planning restrictions the station had to be built back to front with the pumps away from the main street. Despite the alteration in siting, the same experienced servant and a colleague told the defendant, a prospective tenant, that the estimated throughput was 200,000 gallons. The defendant suggested that 100,000 to 150,000 was more likely but his doubts were quelled by his trust in the greater experience and expertise of the plaintiff's servants. He entered into a written tenancy with the plaintiff at a rent of £2,500 for the first two years and £3,000 for the third.

The throughput in the first 15 months was only 78,000 gallons mainly because the pumps were screened from passing public. He gave the plaintiffs notice and was offered a new tenancy at a rent of £1000 plus a surcharge on petrol sold and he entered into this new agreement. Losses continued and when he could not pay cash for petrol the plaintiffs cut off his supply, issued a writ claiming possession of the premises and money's owed.

Held:

(1) The statement as to potential throughput was a contractual warranty for it was a factual statement on a crucial matter made by a party who had, or professed to have, special knowledge and skill with the intention of inducing the other party to enter into the contract of tenancy; that it did induce the defendant to enter into the contract and therefore the plaintiffs were in breach of the warranty and liable in damages for the breach.

(2) The statement was a negligent representation made by a party holding himself out as having special expertise in circumstances which gave rise to the duty to take reasonable care to see that the representation was correct; that that duty of care existed during the pre-contractual negotiations and survived the making of the written contract which was the outcome of the negotiations; and that therefore the plaintiffs were also liable for damages for the tort of negligence.

That the measure of damages for breach of the warranty and for the negligent statement was the same whether the action was founded in contract or in tort; that the damages recoverable were what the defendant had lost by being induced to enter into the contract. *Hedley Byrne & Co. Ltd. v. Heller & Partners Ltd.* [1964] A.C. 465. H.L. (E) *applied. Bissett v. Wilkinson* [1927] A.C. 177 P.C. *distinguished.*

Denning M.R.:

> "... Esso made an error which the judge described as a "fatal error". They did not revise their original estimate. . . . They still assessed the e.a.c (estimated annual consumption) of petrol at 200,000 gallons. Whereas they should have made a reappraisal in the light of the building being now "back to front". This adversely affected the site's potential because passing traffic could not see the station. It would reduce the throughput greatly. The judge found that this "fatal error" was due to want of care on the part of Esso. There can be no doubt about it. . . ."

Denning M.R. then held that Esso were in breach of a collateral warranty for which they were liable in damages and then continued:

> "Assuming that there was no warranty, the question arises whether Esso are liable for negligent misstatement under the doctrine in *Hedley Byrne & Co. Ltd. v. Heller & Partners Ltd.* [1964] A.C. 465." Lord Denning then referred to cases cited by counsel and suggested that they were in conflict with other decisions. "These decisions show that, **in the case of a professional man, the duty to use reasonable care arises not only in contract, but is also imposed by the law apart from contract, and is therefore actionable in tort**. It is comparable to the duty of reasonable care which is owed by a master to his servant, or vice versa. It can be put either in contract or in tort; see *Lister v. Romford Ice and Cold Storage Co. Ltd.* [1957] A.C. 555, 587 by Lord Radcliffe and *Matthews v. Kuwait Beechel Corporation* [1959] 2. Q.B. 57.
>
> It seems to me that *Hedley Byrne & Co. Ltd. v. Heller & Partners Ltd.* [1964] A.C. 465, properly understood, covers this particular proposition: if a man, who has or professes to have special knowledge or skills, makes a representation by virtue thereof to another — be it advice, information or opinion — with the intention of inducting him to enter into a contract with him, he is under a duty to use reasonable care to see that the representation is correct, and that the advise, information or opinion is reliable. If he negligently gives unsound advise or misleading information or expresses an erroneous opinion, and thereby induces the other side to enter into a contract with him, he is liable in damages. . . . Applying this principle, it is plain that Esso professed to have — and did in fact have — special knowledge or skill in estimating the throughput of a filling station. They made the representation — they forecast a throughput of 200,000 gallons — intending to induce Mr. Mardon to enter into a tenancy on the faith of it. They made it negligently. It was a "fatal error." And thereby induced Mr. Mardon to enter into a contract of tenancy which was disastrous to him. For this misrepresentation they are liable in damages."

NEGLIGENT MISREPRESENTATION
Brogan v. Bennett [1955] I.R. 119 (S. C.)

A pamphlet published by the defendant claimed that he had cured persons suffering from tuberculosis. Christopher Brogan, undergoing treatment for this disease in both lungs, in reliance on the representations in the pamphlet, paid Bennett's fee and undertook his treatment. Brogan left hospital at Bennett's insistence (against the advice of his doctors), refused conventional medical assistance and followed the regime prescribed by Bennett.

On no occasion did the defendant visit the patient. He had diagnosed the patients illness by the use of a bullet on the end of a piece of string and he guaranteed to cure him and make him fit for work in three months. Brogan died some five weeks later.

Held: If a person professes to use skill for reward he is liable for negligence in not using that skill. The defendant failed to fulfil the representations which he had made and was therefore liable.

Note: Mr. Justice Niall McCarthy in the foreword to The Irish Legal System by Raymond Byrne and Paul McCutcheon refers to the enviable brevity of Murnaghan J's decision and asks "is this much different from what it took the House of Lords innumerable pages to express in *Hedley Byrne and Co. Ltd. v. Heller and Partners Ltd.?*"

NEGLIGENT MISSTATEMENT
Macken v. Munster and Leinster Bank
[1961] I.L.T.R. 17 (Cir. Ct.) Deale J.

The plaintiff, a grocer and merchant in Wexford town, acting upon a statement made by the Manager of the defendant bank that a Dutchman had 71,000 gulden in Holland and that there would not be the slightest risk, signed a promissory note for a loan which the Dutchman was given by the bank.

The bank manager had been shown a letter in Dutch which he could not read and did not have translated. The Dutchman did not have the money and defaulted on the loan. Macken was not a customer of the bank and there was therefore no contractual relationship between them when the bank manager made the statement to him.

Held: Where parties are about to contract with each other and one of them is in possession of material information upon which another party, was to his knowledge relying, that party is bound to take reasonable care in the statements he makes.

The manager did not take reasonable care, he was negligent in not having the letter translated. The plaintiff was not liable if called upon by the bank to honour the promissory note.

Note: This decision was prior to *Hedley Byrne & Co. Ltd. v. Heller & Partners Ltd.* [1964] A.C. 465.

NEGLIGENT MISSTATEMENT
Hedley Byrne & Co. Ltd. v. Heller & Partners Ltd.
[1964] A.C. 465 (H. L.)

Hedley Byrne & Co Ltd., a firm of advertising agents proposed to engage in a £100,000 advertising programme on behalf of a client, Easipower Ltd. They wanted a bank credit status report on Easipower and asked their own bank to obtain one for them. A representative of their bank telephoned Heller, asked about the respectability and standing of Easipower and whether they were good for £8,000 to £9,000. He was told by phone and by letter "believed to be respectably constituted, considered good for its normal business engagements". Later, on a further enquiry as to trustworthiness for £100,000 they received a reply:

> Confidential
> For your private use and without responsibility on the part of this bank or its officers

> Dear Sir,
> In reply to your inquiring latter of 7 th instant we beg to advise;

> RE. E..............Ltd.

> "Respectably constituted company, considered good for its ordinary business engagements, Your figures are larger than we are accustomed to see.

> Yours faithfully,
> Per Pro Heller & Partners Ltd.

This information was given by the respondent gratuitously.

Held: that a negligent, though honest misrepresentation, spoken or written, may give rise to an action for damages for financial loss caused thereby, apart from any contract or fiduciary relationship, since the law will imply a duty of care when a party seeking information from a party possessed of a special skill trusts him to exercise due care, and that party knew or ought to have known that reliance was being placed on his skill and judgment. However since there was an express disclaimer of responsibility, no such duty was, in any event, implied.

CARELESS STATEMENTS and SPECIAL RELATIONSHIPS

Kenny J. in *Bank of Ireland v. Smith* [1966] I.R. 660 interpreted the decision in the Hedley Byrne case as deciding "that if a person seeks information from another in circumstances in which a reasonable man would know that his judgment is being relied on, the person giving the information must use reasonable care to ensure that his answer is correct, and if he does not do so, he is liable in damages: but the relationship between the person seeking the information and the person giving it, if not fiduciary or arising out of a contract for consideration, must be, to use the words of Lord Devlin, "equivalent to contract", before any liability can arise. The basis of the decision in *Hedley Byrne & Co. Ltd. v. Heller & Partners Ltd.* is, I think, contained in the speech of Lord Devlin when he said (at p. 528):

> "I think, therefore, that there is ample authority to justify your Lordships in saying now that the categories of special relationships which may give rise to a duty to take care in word as well as in deed are not limited to contractual relationships or to relationships of fiduciary duty, but include also relationships which in the words of Lord Shaw in *Nocton v. Ashburton* are "equivalent to contract," that is, where there is an assumption of responsibility in circumstances in which, but for the absence of consideration, there would be a contract."

In *Finlay v. Murtagh* [1979] I.R. 249 Henchy J. stated:

> ". .. Since the decision of the House of Lords in *Hedley Byrne & Co. Ltd. v. Heller & Partners* [1964] A.C. 465 and the cases following in its wake, it is clear that, whether a contractual relationship exists or not, once the circumstances are such that a defendant undertakes to show professional care and skill towards a person who may be expected to rely on such care and skill and who does so rely, then if he has been damnified by such default that person may sue the defendant in the tort of negligence for failure to show such care and skill. For the purpose of such an action, the existence of a contract is merely an incident of the relationship. If, on the one side, there is a proximity of relationship creating a general duty and, on the other, a reliance on that duty, it matters not whether the parties are bound together in contract".

The following year Doyle J. in *Staford v. Mahony & Others* (High Court, unreported, 21 March, 1980) explained "There is no magic in the phrase 'special relationship'; it means no more than a relationship the nature of which is such that one party, for a variety of possible reasons, would be regarded by the law as under a duty of care to the other".

The absence of a contractual relationship between the parties also arose in *Junior Books v. Veitchi* [1982] 3 All E.R. 201 H.L. where it was held that where the proximity between a person who produced faulty work or a faulty article and the user was sufficiently close, the duty of care owed by the producer to the user extended beyond a duty merely to prevent harm being done by the faulty work or article and included a duty to avoid faults being present in the work or article itself, so that the producer was liable for the cost of remedying defects in the work or article or for replacing it and for any consequential economic or financial loss, notwithstanding that there was no contractual relationship between the parties.

INNOCENT MISREPRESENTATION TREATED AS BREACH OF WARRANTY

Bank of Ireland v. Smith and Others [1966] I.R. 646. (H.C.) Kenny J.

Smith created an equitable mortgage of his farm in favour of the bank by deposit of title deeds. Some years later, the bank took a mortgage suit against S and arranged for a court sale of the farm by auction.

An advertisement inserted in the press stated:

> "The lands are prime quality. At present they are all under grass with the exception of approximately 40 acres of barley which is undersown with permanent pasture."

This was in fact, inaccurate because the 40 acres were not undersown. The land was not sold by auction but was sold afterwards to a Mr. Cosgrave who read the advertisement and had inspected the land.

Undersowing is a process by which lands which have been sown with a crop e.g. barley are then sown with grass, so that there is a crop of grass when the barley is removed.

The statement in the advertisement about undersowing made by the auctioneers was honest but mistaken.

Mr. Cosgrave applied to the High Court to withdraw from the purchase for a refund of the purchase money and for compensation for the damage done to the land after the date of sale. It had been ploughed in the interim.

Held: The purchaser could not succeed. He had taken possession of the land when he knew that it had been ploughed and was not in permanent pasture. The statement in the advertisement was a representation which was incorrect but made innocently and honestly. The purchaser was entitled to recover damages for breach of warranty relating to the undersowing of 40 acres.

The modern cases in the opinion of Kenny J. showed a welcome tendency to treat a representation made in connection with a sale as being a warranty, unless the person who made it can show that he was innocent of fault in connection with it.

"The rule that an innocent misrepresentation causing loss does not entitle a person to recover damages for its falsity produces injustice in many cases.

In *Oscar Chess Ltd. v. Williams* [1957] 1 All E.R. 325, Denning L.J., having referred to the famous ruling of Holt C.J., said:

"The question whether a warranty was intended depends on the conduct of the parties, on their words and behaviour rather than on their thoughts. If an intelligent bystander would reasonably infer that a warranty was intended, that will suffice," and in *Dick Bently Productions v. Smith (Motors) Ltd.* [1965] 2 All E.R. 65 the same judge said: "It seems to me that if a representation is made in the course of dealings for a contract, for the very purpose of inducing the other party to act on it by entering into the contract, that is *prima facie* ground for inferring that the representation was intended to be acted upon and was in fact acted on. But the maker of the representation can rebut this inference if he can show that it really was an innocent misrepresentation, in that he was in fact innocent of fault in making it, and that it would not be reasonable in the circumstances for him to be bound by it."

I have not had the advantage of hearing counsel on these two cases but I believe that they express the true rule." — Kenny J.

Note: The author prefers the notion that when an innocent misrepresentation has become a term of the contract (i.e. a warranty) an aggrieved party may be entitled to either sue for damages or to the equitable remedy of rescission.

RESCISSION OF SALE BY AUCTION FOR MISREPRESENTATION

Airlie & Keenan v. Fallon
unreported, High Court, 27 January 1976, Hamilton J.

The plaintiffs decided to buy a public house in Roosky, Co. Roscommon, and authorised a solicitor to bid on their behalf at the auction. When asked about the turnover the auctioneer said that they had nothing. The first plaintiff, who was present at the auction alleged that the defendant (vendor) then stood up and stated that the turnover was between £60,000 and £65,000 and that this was his returns to the Revenue Commissioners. The plaintiff, having heard this statement was satisfied and he signalled his solicitor to proceed bidding on his behalf up to £95,000. Without figures as to turn-over he would not have authorised a bid of much more than £60,000.

An auditor and accountant testified that for the two years ended on the 30th September, 1973, the turn-over submitted to the Revenue Commissioners was £12,000 for the first year and £20,000 for the second year, a total of £32,000.

The defendant denied that he had intervened at the auction or said anything to the plaintiff's solicitor about the turn-over.

Held: The defendant had stated that the figures returned to the Revenue Commissioners for the previous year were in the region of £60,000 to £65,000. The statement was made with the intention of inducing people present at the auction, including the plaintiffs to bid for the premises, and the plaintiffs were so induced. The statement was untrue.

The plaintiff was entitled to rescind the contract, to the return of the deposit and auction fees and also to interest by way of damages in the sum of £9.00.

Hamilton P.:

> "I accept that having regard to the circumstances in which this statement was made, it was made with the intention of inducing the people present at the auction, including the plaintiffs, to bid for the said premises and that the plaintiffs were so induced. I also accept having regard to the evidence ... that the statement was untrue, that Mr. Fallon knew it was untrue and to say the least was made recklessly."

CHAPTER 12

Duress and Equitable Relief

DURESS

The voluntary consent of a party which is essential for a valid contract, may be negated by duress at common law or undue influence and equitable fraud at equity. The original and most blatant concept of duress is contained in the traditional definition that duress is the use or threat of force or imprisonment to compel a party to enter into a contract. In the *Pao On v. Lau Yiu Long* case duress was described as a coercion of the will so as to vitiate consent.

In Matrimonial cases duress is not confined by the Irish courts to the traditional concept of duress applicable to other contracts, but a broader view of the concept has been invoked. It is not confined to cases of immediate fear to life, limb or liberty.

The case of *Griffin v. Griffin* [1940] I.R. 35 (H.C.) is an illustration of the traditional concept of a threat of prosecution and imprisonment constituting duress leading to a decree of nullity. In more recent times there have been many cases of decrees of nullity of marriage contracts on the basis of lack of free consent because of duress. (*W. v. C.*, Irish Times Law Report, 10th April 1989.)

One would have expected that the fact that the lack of free consent was the result of social pressure would have inclined a court more toward holding that there was undue influence rather than duress but this is not what happened.

Duress, however, need not be the predominant reason that a party entered into a contract. The very presence of duress is sufficient to have the contract set aside. In *Barton v. Armstrong* the Privy Council held that the onus of disproving duress was on the respondent and the applicant was entitled to relief even though he might well have entered into the contract if the respondent had uttered no threats to induce him to do so. In this most extraordinary case the trail judge held that death threats were made to induce consent.

The principle that the doctrine of duress can be extended to include economic duress was accepted by the English Privy Council in *Pao On v. Lau Yiu Long* [1980] A.C. 614 P.C.

The equitable rule which enables a contract entered into as a result of fraudulent misrepresentation to be set aside also applied in the case of fraud or duress. *Barton v. Armstrong* [1976] A.C. 104.

DURESS — THREAT TO LIFE
Barton v. Armstrong [1976] A.C. 104

Barton and Armstrong executed a deed in 1967 which allowed Barton to buy out Armstrong's interest in an Australian public company in which they were both the major shareholders. Barton later alleged that Armstrong had coerced him into the agreement by threatening to have him murdered and by exerting other unlawful pressure on him. He sought to have the deed declared void because of duress. At first hearing the trial judge held that the following threats were made. "The city is not as safe as you may think between office and home. You will see what I can do against you and you will regret the day when you decided not to work with me." Phone calls between 4 and 5 a.m. in the morning, heavy breathing and on occasions a voice saying "You will be killed". "You stink, you stink. I will fix you. You had better sign this agreement — or else."

Held:
  (1) that the equitable rule, which enabled a contract entered into as a result of fraudulent misrepresentation to be set aside, applied in cases of duress so that if the respondents threats were a reason for the appellant executing the deed he was entitled to relief even though he might well have entered into the contract if the respondent had uttered no threats to induce him to do so.
  (2) The proper inference to be drawn from the facts found was that the threats and unlawful pressure did in fact contribute to the appellant's decision to sign the deeds, the deeds were executed under duress and were void.

DURESS — PERSONAL SUFFERING — THREAT OF LOSS OF LIBERTY
Cumming v. Ince and Hooper (1847) Q.B. 11

The defendants, daughters of the plaintiff, were prosecuting a commission of lunacy against her. During the proceedings when certain witnesses had been examined before the Commission and before any verdict was taken, a written agreement was entered into by the parties. This agreement provided that the plaintiff would be discharged and the Commission stopped, on condition that the plaintiff would hand over title deeds to property and vest the property in trustees. The plaintiff was to be entitled to rents and profits of the estate for life (but she could not alienate the property).

  The plaintiff had been confined in an asylum and on her release after the Commission hearing she contended that the written agreement was not binding on her because it had been obtained by duress. She claimed that her confinement was illegal and that her health and state of mind had been effected and endangered by the treatment she underwent in the asylum. She contended that even if her confinement was lawful, it was a restraint on her will which prevented any contract made under that duress from binding her and she sought to get the deeds back.

Held: The plaintiff had been induced to relinquish the deeds by fear of personal suffering brought upon her by confinement in a lunatic asylum by act of the defendants. She had not made the agreement of her own free will. She was entitled to recover the deeds.

MATRIMONIAL DURESS — THREAT TO LIBERTY
Griffith v. Griffith [1944] I.R. 35 (H.C.) Haugh J.

The plaintiff was accused of being the father of the respondents child and informed that he would be liable to criminal proceedings and possible imprisonment if he did not marry her. Believing both statements to be true he married her. Later she admitted that she had deceived him and that he was not the father. He sought a decree of nullity because of the want of real consent on his part and the fraud and intimidation of the respondent.

Held: An Order of nullity must be granted. The petitioner was not bound because his consent had been obtained by a combination of fraud and fear. There was no real consent in law, there was no valid marriage. (The respondent was under 17 at the time.)

Note: A similar type of pressure was held by O'Hanlon J. to have existed in *M.C. v. M.C.* (H.C) [1982] I.L.R.M. 277 where the parties married after the petitioner found that she was pregnant and both sets of parents subjected the parties to parental pressure to marry. "An unwilling bride and a resentful husband were dragged to the alter and went through a ceremony of marriage which neither of them wanted. . . ." The duress exercised by the petitioner's parents had been sufficiently compulsive to deprive the petitioner of exercising her free will in deciding to marry the respondent.

STRAIN — LACK OF ABILITY FOR NORMAL THOUGHT
W. v. C., Ir. Times LR, 10th April 1989 (H.C.) Barron J.

The petitioner sought a decree of nullity of marriage on the grounds that she had not given a valid consent to the marriage and that the respondent was incapable of a proper marital relationship because of a gross personality disorder, which made him unable to form a meaningful relationship.

The petitioner was a teacher who claimed that she could not have continued her career as an unmarried mother. Her sole reason for marrying was to be able to resume her teaching career and her place in society. There was no element in her decision of a wish or desire to set up a matrimonial home with the respondent. A psychiatrist who had treated the respondent gave evidence of his gross personality disorder.

Held: The petitioners decision to marry was brought about by the strain of her circumstances and her lack of ability for normal thought at the time. A consent given solely in order to resume her career and her place in society was not a true consent. The second submission about the respondent's personality disorder was also valid and a decree of nullity would be granted on both grounds.

Note: Whether external circumstances constitute duress is one of the headings to the case.

MATRIMONIAL DURESS — IRISH CONCEPT
N. v. K., Supreme Court, unreported, 15 November 1985

The petitioner went through a ceremony of marriage to the respondent when she was 19. They had gone out with each other on a casual basis and when she informed her parents that she was pregnant she was brought by her father to the home of the respondent. She was put into one room and her father interviewed the respondents parents, informing them that there were only two alternatives abortion or marriage. The respondent said to the petitioner "I suppose we will get married, it is all we can do." He then told the petitioners father that they would marry. Both sets of parents made the marriage arrangements without any intervention or interest by the parties, and the wedding took place six weeks later.

Held: The petitioners consent to the marriage was apparent rather than real. The necessary full and valid consent by the petitioner to the marriage never existed. No valid marriage, therefore, took place. Decree of nullity granted.

Finlay C.J. (Griffin J. and Hederman J. in agreement):

> "The fundamental *ratio decidendi* of the decision in *McC. v. McC.* appears to me, however, to be **a rejection of the earlier decisions which restricted the concept of duress in nullity to threats of physical harm or threats falsely based, of harmful consequences**. That decision I accept. . . . Whilst a court faced with a challenge to the validity of a marriage, based on the absence of real consent, should conduct its enquiry in accordance with defined legal concepts such as duress or, what has been described by O'Hanlon J., as "the related topic of undue influence", these concepts and the legal definition of them must remain subservient to the ultimate objective of ascertaining in accordance with the onus of proof whether the consent of the petitioning party was real or apparent."

Griffin J:

"In recent years, our Courts and the courts in England have differed on the nature of the duress or pressure that is necessary to overbear the mind of one of the parties to the marriage and thus invalidate the marriage. In *M.K. (McC. v. McC.)* [1982] I.L.R.M. 277 O'Hanlon J. made an examination of the Irish and English cases and contrasted the more rigid approach of the English Courts with that taken in the courts here. **The English Courts confined duress as vitiating marriage** to cases in which the will of one of the parties has been overborne by genuine and reasonably held **fear caused by threat of immediate danger, for which the party is not himself responsible, to life, limb or liberty** so that the constraint destroys the reality of consent to ordinary wedlock — see *Szechter (orse Karsov) v. Szechter* [1971] 2 W.L.R. 170 per Sir Jocelyn Simon P.; *Singh v. Singh* [1971] 2 W.L.R. 964.

In our courts a broader view is taken. In *B v. D.*, unreported, 20th June 1973, Murnaghan J. granted a decree of nullity on the ground of duress where the will of the wife was overborne by the domineering nature and conduct of the husband. In *S. v. O'S.*, unreported, 28th February 1979, Finlay P. (as he then was) held that as the wife was in the **emotional bondage** of the husband during the period leading up to the marriage she was not capable of having the freedom of will necessary to enter into a valid marriage. O'Hanlon J., in my view correctly, took the broader view of the concept of duress adopted by our Courts and granted a decree of nullity, holding that **the will of both the husband and wife was overborne by the compulsion of their respective parents**.

It is of interest to note that some months after that case was decided by O'Hanlon J., the Court of Appeal in England in *Hirami v. Hirami* [1983] 4 F.L.R. 232, held that to establish duress as vitiating consent to a marriage it was not necessary to find a threat to life, limb or liberty; that the crucial question was whether the threats or pressure were such as to overbear the will of the individual and destroy the reality of consent; and that duress, whatever form it took, was a coercion of the will so as to vitiate consent. In considering the effect of pressure on the will of a petitioner, and whether such pressure vitiates the necessary consent, a subjective test must be applied — the test is not whether a reasonable person would have succumbed to the pressure, but whether the pressure alleged was such as to overbear the will of the particular petitioner."

ECONOMIC DURESS

Pao On v. Lau Yiu Long [1980] A.C. 614 (Privy Council)

The Plaintiffs, having entered into a contract with a company refused to carry out their obligations unless the defendants, who were shareholders in the company, guaranteed them against loss which might occur. They gave the guarantee and the plaintiffs carried out their obligations under the contract. The defendants sought to repudiate the guarantee but were held to be bound by it on the basis that a promise to perform, or performance of a pre-existing contractual duty owed to a third party, may constitute valid consideration. See Consideration *ante*.

Held: That, although the defendants had been subjected to commercial pressure, the facts disclosed that they had not been coerced into the contract of guarantee and, therefore, the contract was not voidable on the ground of duress; that in the absence of duress, public policy does not require a contract negotiated at arm's length to be invalidated because a party had either threatened to repudiate an existing contractual obligation or had unfairly used his dominant bargaining position in negotiating the agreement.

Per curiam: There is nothing contrary to principle in recognising **economic duress as a factor which may render a contract voidable provided always that the basis of such recognition is that it must amount to a coercion of will which vitiates consent**. It must be shown that the payment made or the contract entered into was not a voluntary act.

Lord Scarman,

> "Duress, whatever form it takes, **is a coercion of the will so as to vitiate consent**. Their Lordships agree with the observation of Kerr J. in *Occidental World-wide Investments Corporation v. Skibs A/S Avanti* [1976] 1 Lloyd's Rep. 293, 336 that in a contractual situation commercial pressure is not enough. There must be present some factor 'which could in law be regarded as coercion of his will so as vitiate his consent.' This conception is in line with what was said in this Board's decision in *Barton v. Armstrong* [1976] A.C. 104, 121 by Lord Wilberforce and Lord Simon of Glaisdale — observations with which the majority judgment appears to be in agreement. **In determining whether there was a coercion of will such that there was no true consent, it is material to inquire**
>
> whether the person alleged to have been coerced did or did not protest;
>
> — whether, at the time he was allegedly coerced into making the contract, he did or did not have an alternative course open to him such as an adequate legal remedy;
>
> — whether he was independently advised; and
>
> — whether after entering the contract he took steps to avoid it.
>
> All these matters are, as was recognised in *Maskell v. Horner* [1915] 3

K.B. 106, relevant in determining whether he acted voluntarily or not. . .
. In the present case . . . there was commercial pressure but no coercion.
. . . It is, therefore, unnecessary for the Board to embark upon an inquiry
into the question whether English law recognises a category of duress
known as "economic duress." But, since the question has been fully
argued in this appeal their Lordships will indicate very briefly the view
which they have formed. At common law money paid under economic
compulsion could be recovered in an action for money had and received.
Astley v. Reynolds (1731) 2 Str. 915. The compulsion had to be such that
the party was deprived of "his freedom of exercising his will" (see p. 916).
It is doubtful, however, whether at common law any duress other than
duress to the person sufficed to render a contract voidable; see Blackstone's *Commentaries*, Book 1, 12th ed. pp 130-131 and *Skeate v. Beale*
(1841) 11 Ad. & E. 983. American law (*Williston on Contracts*, 3rd ed.)
now recognises that a contract may be avoided on the ground of economic
duress. The commercial pressure alleged to constitute such duress must,
however, be such that the victim must have entered the contract against
his will, must have had no alternative course open to him, and must have
been confronted with coercive acts by the party exerting the pressure:
Williston on Contracts, 3rd ed., vol. 13 [1970]. section 1603."

UNDUE INFLUENCE

Undue influence is said to exist where a contract has been brought into existence
and the will of one of the parties has been overborne or dominated by the will
of the other. It indicates that the consent of one party has been obtained by
mental pressure or influence.

Undue influence is presumed to exist in certain relationships and in these
cases the onus is on the dominant party to rebut this presumption. In *Slator v.
Nolan* the use of token independent legal advise was rejected in very emphatic
terms by the Master of the Rolls as a perfect sham. To allow the deed to stand
on such a plea would "be offering a tempting premium for chicanery and legal
cunning." Independent advice is not the sole requirement to rebut the presumption. In *Wright v. Carter* (1903) 1 Ch 27 at p.60) the law as to the duty of a
solicitor, called in to advise a donor intending to make a gift to a donee standing
in a fiduciary relationship, as stated by Farwell J. in *Powell v. Powell* was
approved of. It was stated that in a sale to his solicitor the client must also be
fully informed and the price fair.

The categories of parties between whom a special relationship can be
presumed to exist is not closed, but where there is no special relationship the
onus of proof is on the claimant. Andrews L.J. in the Northern Ireland case of
O'Neill v. Murphy and Ors., [1936] N.I.16 specifically referred to public policy
as the grounds on which a court acts where undue influence is suspected but

Lord Scarman in *National Westminster Bank Ltd. v. Morgan* rejected that view and stated "The principle justifying the court in setting aside a transaction for undue influence is not a vague 'public policy' but specifically the victimization of one party by another." The decision in Westminster Bank reflected this view.

It is suggested that this may be to unduly emphasize the end result whereas the means by which the consent to such an agreement has been procured is fundamental to the doctrine, and the main distinguishing factor from other types of equitable fraud. One of the parties must have been unduly influenced. Inadequacy of consideration might be a factor, but only one factor, and indeed, it might be possible to prove undue influence even where the consideration appears to be adequate. This of course, flies in the face of Lord Scarman's notion that the presumption of undue influence only arises if a transaction is "manifestly disadvantageous".

Professor Atiyah in the *Rise and Fall of Freedom of Contract*, Oxford University Press, 1979 at page 436 states "the idea that a man's will is 'overborne' by certain types of pressure and not by others is in logic indefensible and in practice impossible of application . . . the line can be only be drawn by distinguishing between different kinds of pressure, not by attempting to analyse the effect of the pressure on a man's mind." (See Modern Law Review, Vol. 47, No. 9, November 1984, page 747 and also Undue Influence by David Tiplady, Notes of Cases, Modern Law Review, Vol. 48, No. 5, September 1985, page 579.)

The cases cited postulate three grounds upon which the doctrine of undue influence is founded, (1) public policy, (2) inequality of bargaining power, and (3) fraud.

In *National Westminster Bank plc v. Morgan* [1985] 1 All E.R. 821 the House of Lords held that **a transaction could not be set aside on the grounds of undue influence unless it** was shown that **the transaction was to the manifest disadvantage** of the person subjected to the dominating influence. The basis of the principle was not public policy but the prevention of the victimization of one party by another, and therefore a presumption of undue influence would not necessarily arise merely from the fact that a confidential relationship existed between the parties, and although undue influence was not restricted to gifts but could extend to commercial transactions, it was not based simply on inequality of bargaining power.

Public policy is central to a court's attitude in contracts of restraint of trade and has been described as an unruly horse which first mounted cannot be dismounted with ease. In *O'Flanagan v. Ray-Ger Ltd. & Ors.* Costello J. reviewed the principles applicable to "undue influence" and "unconscionable bargains".

CHILD/PARENT
Gregg v. Kidd and Kidd [1956] I.R. 183 (H.C.) Budd J.

George Gregg (decd.) transferred all his estate and interest in lands in Co. Carlow to William Gregg Kidd in trust for life and after his death to the use of John George Kidd (nephew of the settlor) in purported consideration of the affection which the settlor had for his nephew. The executor sought to have the settlement set aside on the grounds that at the date of the settlement the settlor was reduced by mental ill-health and by physical and mental debility. That the settlement was an improvident one, obtained by undue influence and executed when the parties were not on equal terms.

Held: That the relations between the deceased and the defendant, the defendant's mother (his own sister) were such as to raise a presumption of undue influence.

The onus was on the donee to establish that the gift was the spontaneous act of the donor, acting in circumstances which enabled him to exercise a free and independent will. The defendant had not discharged this onus of rebutting the presumption of influence and the disposition must be set aside and cancelled.

Note: Finlay J. adopted and repeated this reasoning in *McCormack v. Bennett* [1973] 107 ILTR 127.

SPIRITUAL ADVISER
O'Neill v. Murphy and Others [1935] N.I. (C.A.)

The plaintiff, an architect, claimed a sum of £1,105.3s. in connection with the planning and erection of buildings at Ballycastle, Co. Antrim.

The defendant pleaded that the plaintiff had agreed to accept a sum of £200 and prayers of a religious order as full payment.

The plaintiff pleaded that if he made such an agreement he was induced to do so by undue influence of the first defendant, Canon Murphy, his spiritual adviser, and that there was no consideration for the agreement.

At first instance the jury found that there was undue influence but the Chief Justice reported to the Court of Appeal that in his opinion the finding was against the weight of the evidence.

Held: by the Court of Appeal: — undue influence is a form of fraud and fraud is essentially a question for a jury. The finding of the jury must stand.

"If a relation of confidence is shown to exist, or is presumed from the position of the parties, then, on the grounds of public policy, the law presumes that the gift was not a free one, but that it was the effect of influence induced by these relations and the burden of disproof of undue influence, i. e. the burden of supporting the gift is thrown upon the donee." *per* Andrews L.J.

SPIRITUAL TERROR OF VOWS

McCarthy v. McCarthy (1846) 9 Ir. Eq. R 620 (Ch.)

The father of two nuns in a convent in Blackrock, Co. Cork died intestate in 1843. Both nuns had taken vows of poverty, chastity and obedience.

Against their wishes but under compulsion of their vows of obedience both nuns executed deeds assigning their shares to the superioresses of the convent. The deeds also contained powers of attorney.

The superioresses then instituted proceedings in the name of one of the sisters to obtain their shares for the convent. It was claimed that the assignments were obtained by undue influence and compulsion "against their wills and without their free concurrence, under pressure of their belief and coercion of conscience induced by their vow of obedience."

Held: The nuns had executed the deeds, not as free agents, not of their own volition, but signed them merely as persons who knew how to write, and had a pen put into their hands and guided by another.

The fact that the proceedings were instituted in the name of one of the nuns, under a power given by deed was not an admission that she admitted the title of other co-plaintiffs and was not sufficient evidence of their title.

The Lord Chancellor (The Right Hon. M. Brady)

> "From first to last, up to this very moment, the same vow, the same profession, the same compulsion continues, and I must regard Maria and Catherine as no more parties to this record than the deed is theirs. . . . During the argument I put the case of a prisoner in a dungeon, and a jailor extorting a deed from him, and coming into Court and saying "I have that person still in the dungeon, but I want the property for him and myself." Am I bound to give it to him? I protest I will do no such thing. This Court cannot listen to such a claim."

RELIGIOUS

Allcard v. Skinner (1887) 36 Ch. D. 145 (C. A.)

In 1871 A, having passed through the grades of postulant and novice, was professed a member of a Protestant order of nuns "The Sisters of the Poor" and bound herself to observe (inter alia) the rules of poverty, chastity and obedience of the order. These rules had been made known to her before she became a postulant.

The rule of poverty required a member to give up all individual property, either to a relative, the poor, or to the sisterhood itself. Rule 30 provided "Let no sister speak or write to externs about what happens in the convent unless she have reason to think that it is the wish of the Superior. Rule 31 stated "Let no sister seek advice of any extern without the Superior's leave."

Between 1871 and 1876 the plaintiff made over cheques and various shares to the Mother Superior. She left the order in 1879 and in 1885 commenced an action claiming the return of her property on the ground that it was made over by her while under the paramount and undue influence of the Superior, Miss Skinner, and without any independent and separate advice.

Held: At the time the plaintiff made the gifts she was subject to the influence of Miss Skinner, and to the rules of the sisterhood. She would have been entitled to claim restitution of such part of he property as was still in the hands of Miss Skinner, but not of such part as had been expended on the purposes of the sisterhood while she remained in it. In the circumstances the plaintiff was barred by her laches and acquiescence since she left the sisterhood.

Referring to previous decisions of the Court of Chancery to set aside gifts Cotton L.J. stated:

> "These decisions may be divided into two classes- First, where the court has been satisfied that the gift was the result of influence expressly used by the donee for the purpose; second, where the relations between the donor and donee have at or shortly before the execution of the gift been such as to raise a presumption that the donee had influence over the donor. ... The first class of cases may be considered as depending on the principle that no one shall be allowed to retain any benefit arising from his own fraud or wrongful act. In the second class of cases the court interferes, not on the ground that any wrongful act has in fact been committed by the donee, but on the ground of public policy, and to prevent the relations which existed between the parties and the influence arising therefrom being abused."

Note: The McCarthy case *ante* was some years before *Allcard v. Skinner.*

FRIEND

O'Flanagan v. Ray-Ger Limited
High Court, Unreported, 28 April 83, Costello J.

The plaintiffs late husband and the second defendant entered into a business relationship which involved the formation of a company (the first named defendant) to buy a licensed premises at Walkinstown, Dublin. Both were to buy out their landlords interest in their shop premises and to raise money by selling the properties subject to their leases. Each was to contribute equally and to share profits equally being the only shareholders in the company. Sums of money were advanced by the O'Flanagans to the second defendant for the purpose of the agreement. When Mr O'Flanagan died it was discovered that instead of using the money to purchase the freehold the second defendant had used it to purchase the premises for the company and then used the premises as security for a loan. He never put a penny into the venture during Mr O'Flanagans lifetime.

A clause in an agreement which the deceased had signed, provided that a partners estate would have no claim on the company and that the surviving partner would be entitled to the entire share capital of the company. The second defendant claimed that as a result the deceased's estate had no interest in the company and no claim on its assets.

The defendant and O'Flanagan went out drinking together over many years, at least three or four nights every week.

Held: The agreement must be set aside being obtained by undue influence.

Costello J.:

"The defendant has a strong and forceful personality and had obviously exercised considerable influence amounting to domination of the deceased on previous occasions. The deceased was infirm and ill when he signed the agreement. The agreement was egregiously unfair to the deceased's wife and family. The mutual promises it contained were largely illusory in that both parties knew that it was highly probable that the deceased would predecease the defendant. (The deceased had suffered three heart attacks and undergone major surgery for cancer.) Further the lack of candour of the defendant raises very serious suspicions about the circumstances in which it came to be executed. . . . The evidence satisfies me that I should set the agreement aside."

SOLICITOR/CLIENT

In *Wright v. Carter* [1903] 1 Ch. 27 it was stated that a gift by a client to his solicitor raises *prima facie* the presumption that it was unduly influenced by the fiduciary relationship subsisting between them; and the onus is on the solicitor to prove that the gift was uninfluenced by that relation. There is no objection to a sale by a client to his solicitor provided that the solicitor can prove 1) that the client was fully informed; 2) that he had competent independent advice; and 3) that the price given was a fair one. The onus lies on the solicitor to prove these matters.

Stirling L.J.:

> "The duties of the advisor have been considered by Farwell J. in the recent case of *Powell v. Powell* [1900] 1 Ch. 243, and in the course of his judgment he says this 'The solicitor does **not** discharge his duty by satisfying himself simply that **the donor understands and wishes to carry out the particular transaction. He must also satisfy himself that the gift is one that it is right and proper for the donor to make under all the circumstances**, and if he is not so satisfied, **his duty is to advise his client not to go on with the transaction, and to refuse to act further for him if he persists**' with that view of a solicitor's duty I agree. I think that a solicitor would fail in his duty if he neglected to inform himself of the circumstances in which the transaction was taking place. It might turn out, for example, to be one in which a poor man was divesting himself of all his property in favour of the solicitor; in such a case it would be impossible, it seems to me, whatever the advice may have been to uphold the transaction."

"WITHOUT PREJUDICE"

In general a communication made "without prejudice" cannot be admitted in evidence against the party who made it. In *O'Flanagan v. Ray-Ger Limited* the second defendant, Pope, had written a letter headed "without prejudice" to the plaintiff which contained an acknowledgment that the premises had been purchased in trust by the company Ray-Ger for the benefit of the plaintiff and her deceased husband. The letter also acknowledged that the premises was not part of the company's share capital. Because of this, the letter was strongly supportive of the plaintiff's claim and strenuous objection was taken by the defence to its admissibility, on the grounds that it was written on a privileged occasion.

Costello J. admitting the letter in evidence, referred to the heading "without prejudice" and stated that **these words alone possess no magic properties** and that some more substantial ground had to be found to justify the defendants objection to the admissibility of the letter. He added: "The rule which excludes documents marked **"without prejudice" has no application unless some person is in dispute or negotiation with another and terms are offered for the settlement of a dispute or negotiation** (see *In Re Daintry* (1893) 2 Q.B. 116, 119). Mrs O'Flanagan did not threaten any legal proceedings, her main concern was to ascertain from the defendant's solicitor what the true position was about her property. Having admitted the document in evidence without having read it, my view as to its admissibility was confirmed when I did so, as it will be seen that **the defendant was not offering to settle a dispute but was making a statement as to the rights of the plaintiff and her husband in relation to the property."**

Note: This decision seems to be in line with the reasoning of Hanies J. in the Canadian case of *Kirschbaum v. 'Our Voices' Publishing Co.* [1972] 1 OR 737 where he held that the question to be considered was the view and intention of the party making the admission; whether it was to concede a fact hypothetically, in order to effect a settlement or to declare the existence of a fact. Discovery of correspondence between solicitors may be allowed where relevant, e.g. in a libel action.

EQUITY — IMPROVIDENT DISPOSITION

A deed which cannot be set aside by the courts on the grounds of undue influence may, nonetheless be set aside as an improvident disposition or as being brought about by inequality of bargaining power.

The doctrine of inequality of bargaining power adopted by Gavan Duffy J. in *Grealish v. Murphy* was examined some thirty years later in *Lloyd's Bank v. Bundy* by Denning M.R. who stated that undue influence was one category within the wider inequality of bargaining power. Although no Irish case was cited by Denning in a passage strikingly reminiscent of *Slator v. Nolan* he stated "one who is in extreme need may knowingly consent to a most improvident bargain, solely to relieve the straits in which he finds himself in. I do not mean to suggest that every transaction is saved by independent advice."

In *Schroeder Music Publishing Co. Ltd. v. Maculay* [1974] the House of Lords held assuming that such a one sided agreement could be justified, it had been for the publishers to justify it, especially since it had not been arrived at as the result of negotiation between the parties in an equal bargaining position.

The doctrine of inequality of bargaining power as expounded by Lord Denning has been rejected by Lord Scarman on a number of occasions. Firstly in *Pao On v. Lau Yiu Long* where he described it as being un-necessary and un-helpful. "Where businessmen are negotiating at arm's length it is un-necessary for the achievement of justice, and un-helpful in the development of the law, to invoke such a rule of public policy that in a case where duress is not established, public policy may nevertheless invalidate the consideration if there has been a threat to repudiate a pre-existing contractual obligation or an unfair use of a dominating bargaining position." His reference to businessmen negotiating at arm's length was totally at variance with the facts in the Bundy and Schroeder cases as well as the previous Irish cases. (See E.C Competition Law Article 86 Treaty of Rome regarding abuse of dominant position in the market-place.)

Lord Scarman's second rejection took place in *National Westminster Bank plc v. Morgan* where he delivered the unanimous decision of the House of Lords and pointed out that the majority of the court in the Bundy case did not follow Denning and that Denning's opinion was not the basis of the court's judgment but rather the traditional doctrine as expounded in *Allcard v. Skinner* (1887) 36

Ch.D 143. (Mr Cairns L.J. had agreed with Sir Eric Sachs not with Lord Denning) He also stated that the doctrine of undue influence did not need the support of a principle which was not appropriate to cover gifts where there was no bargain. Sachs had not expressed any opinion on the wider areas covered in the Denning judgment.

It must be pointed out that uncharacteristically, Denning himself, had some reservations when he stated ". . . But, in case the principle is wrong, I would also say that the case falls within the category of undue influence of the second class stated by Cotton L.J. in *Allcard v. Skinner.*"

INEQUALITY OF BARGAINING POWER
Slator v. Nolan (1877-78) Ir. R. Eq. Vol XI 367

The plaintiff, a reckless and improvident man, committed to the Marshalsea prison as an insolvent debtor, agreed to sell his interest in lands to his brother-in-law, Thomas Nolan, for an utterly inadequate consideration. He did not understand that he was actually the possessor of a large estate more than sufficient in the words of Sullivan M.R. "to extricate him from his hopeless state." He was tenant for life of the Rossduff estate, worth about £400 a year, had a life interest in £11,000 Government three per cent stock and a right to raise £729 cash out of the Crosskeys estate.

He was not incapable, but his utter recklessness prevented him from understanding anything about his affairs. When he was discharged from prison he sometimes slept on a bench in the Phoenix Park or in an armchair in the room of a broken down relative, without a shilling except what he got in charity from his former fellow prisoners.

The brother-in-law Nolan trained in a solicitors office, was protected in the transaction by a solicitor and counsel. After the terms of the contract had been fully arranged a solicitor and counsel acting on behalf of the plaintiff aided in the preparation and execution of the deed.

Held: The deed must be set aside. The principle adopted in *Basker v. Monk*, following the rules laid down in *Evans v. Lewellyn* was one to be extended and applied to every conceivable case where one man by fraud or chicanery gets advantage over another not standing in an equal position to negotiate with him. The defendant had grossly overreached the plaintiff in the transaction, had knowingly taken advantage of his recklessness and no adequate advice or protection had been afforded to the plaintiff by the counsel and solicitor.

Sullivan M.R.:

> ". . . changes in the law have in no degree whatever altered the onus probandi in those cases which, according to the language of Lord Hard- wick, 'raise from the circumstances or conditions of the parties contract-

ing-weakness on one side, usury on the other, or extortion.or advantage taken of that weakness, a presumption of fraud. **Fraud does not here mean deceit or circumvention; it means an unconscientious use of power arising out of these circumstances and conditions**; and when the relative position of the parties is such as prima facie to raise this presumption, the transaction cannot stand unless the person claiming the benefit of it is able to repel the presumption by contrary evidence, proving it to have been in point of fact, just, and reasonable'. . . . I regard the so called professional aid alleged to be given to Slator as a perfect sham, and a sham to the knowledge of Nolan himself. . . . To allow under the circumstances of this case Mr Nolan to keep the benefit of his unfair and unconscionable deed, obtained from this desperate, reckless and pennyless man, under the plea that he, Slator, had independent professional advice, would seem to me to be offering a tempting premium for chicanery and legal cunning."

IMPROVIDENT DISPOSITION
Grealish v. Murphy [1946] I.R. 35 (H.C.) Gavan Duffy J.

The plaintiff a mentally deficient farmer in his sixties, who lived at Oranmore, Co. Galway executed a deed assigning his farm after his death to the defendant. He also gave the defendant a right to reside in his house and to be supported out of the land during the plaintiff's life. The defendant on his part agreed to reside in the house, to work and manage the farm, without reward and to account for all moneys. The plaintiff's Solicitor did not know all the material facts and did not give the plaintiff a complete explanation of the nature and effect of the deed. He was also unaware of the full extent of the plaintiff's mental deficiency.

Held: The settlement was an improvident one. On the facts the deed could not be set aside on the ground of undue influence, but the plaintiff by reason of his weakness of mind coupled with the deficiencies in the legal advice under which he acted, was entitled to have the settlement set aside.

> "The transaction was shocking and the two men did not stand on equal terms, so that I think I might, following Lord Hatherley's principle, or perhaps the even more emphatic language of Sullivan M.R. in *Slator v. Nolan* (1877-78) Ir. R. Eq. Vol XI 367, against any party taking undue advantage of another, uphold the Plaintiff's claim, without any regard to the peculiar relations of the parties." *per* Gavan Duffy J.

Note: Grealish v. Murphy was considered by McLoughlin J. in *Haverty v. Brooks & Ors.* (1970) I.R. 214 which he held was not an improvident transaction. Although undue influence was pleaded no evidence was given to justify the plea nor was there any indication that the deceased, Haverty, was unequal to protecting his own interests at the time he entered into the disputed transaction. In *Noonan v. Murphy*, High Court, unreported, 10 April 1987 the court held that while there was no undue influence, the relationship between the parties was one of inequality and the transfer was improvident.

UNCONSCIONABLE BARGAIN
Lydon v. Coyne [1946] 12 Ir. Jur. Rep. 64. (H.C.) O'Byrne J.

Martin Lydon, an old man, assigned his farm to his nephew Martin Coyne by deed in consideration of natural love and affection, subject to a life estate for himself and his wife.

The nephew agreed to live in the house, work the land, support the old man and his wife and to pay £100 by instalments. Coyne brought a Solicitor to the house to draw up the deed and paid his fees.

Held: Martin Lydon did not understand the transaction, the deed contained no power of revocation, no independent advice was given, the assignment could not be allowed to stand.

INDEPENDENT ADVICE
Kelly v. Morrisroe [1919] 53 I.L.T.R. 145 (C.A.)

G., an old woman in humble circumstances and of eccentric habits, lived alone in a dilapidated cottage on a plot of land, at Chapel Street, in the town of Swinford. She had no near relatives or dependants. The plot was situated between the business premises of the defendant on one side and of C. on the other, both of whom stated that the plot would be of substantial value to them as a site.

The defendant offered to purchase the premises for £20, and to allow G., the use of the cottage, rent free, during her lifetime. G. thereupon consulted her former employer, a merchant in the town and he advised her to ask for £25. The defendant agreed to give her that amount and instructed his solicitor to prepare a conveyance. G. called to the solicitor's office, accompanied by her former employer, and executed the conveyance, the solicitor having first read it over and explained it to her.

After G.'s death, the plaintiff, who was her executor and universal legatee and divisee, sought to have the deed set aside, evidence being given by C. whose business premises adjoined the plot, that he would have given £100 for it.

Held: by the Court of Appeal that G. had all the advice and protection necessary, and that although her age and circumstances threw the onus on the defendant of showing that the transaction was a fair and honest one, that onus had been discharged. There was no evidence upon which the deed should be set aside.

"We have all experience of eccentric old ladies- eccentric in habits and eccentric in dress, but as cute as possible in money matters, and quite well able to understand the value of money and transact business, yet not mentally sane. Evidence was given by her former employer, a banker and merchant and magistrate that she came to him for advice. How is it possible to say that this old lady was without advice, or the best possible advice." — Sir James Campbell L.C.

IMPROVIDENT DISPOSITION
McCormack v. Bennett (1973) 107 I.L.T.R. 127 (H.C.)

The plaintiff brought an action as legal representative of her father James Seery to set aside and cancel a transfer of lands in Westmeath to the defendant, another daughter of James Seery and sister of the plaintiff, who had agreed to take care of himself and his wife as long as they lived.

The deed was challenged on the grounds that it was improvident, that at the time, the transferor had no independent advice, that he did not know or appreciate the consequences of the deed and that it was procured by undue influence.

When he executed the deed James Seery was aged 79 and his wife Mary was 80. The lands were let at £380 a year and the only other income the Seery's had was their social welfare benefits amounting to about £500. James Seery himself choose the Solicitor in Mullingar, gave all the instructions and did all the discussions with the Solicitor.

Finlay J. was satisfied that he did not suffer from mental abnormality at the time of the deed. The Solicitor urged him to make a will instead and of the possibility of inserting a revocation clause in the deed, but Seery refused.

Held:

(1) The Defendant did not exercise any influence over James Seery to induce him to enter into the transaction. On the evidence the execution of the deed was his own act and resulted from an exercise of his own free will therefore the deed must stand.

(2) The settlor did not suffer from any mental or relevant physical infirmity.

(3) That he had the benefit of independent legal advice from a solicitor of his choice.

(4) That he had wished to make a final disposition of his registered land and had deliberately excluded any power of revocation.

(5) That the deed of settlement was *prima facie* improvident in that it made no provision for the settlor and his wife other than the reserved life estate.

CHAPTER 13

Illegal Contracts

Some contracts are illegal by virtue of the common law, others are illegal by statute. Illegality may exist at the making of the contract or in its performance.

Contracts illegal at common law include certain contracts which although not obviously illegal have been deemed to be so on the grounds of public policy. Contracts to commit a crime or tort are obviously illegal, *Beresford v. Royal Insurance Co. Ltd.*, but contracts tending to sexual immorality, contracts affecting freedom of marriage, contracts of champerty and maintenance, contracts tending to injure the public service or defraud the revenue, and contracts in restraint of trade are also illegal on grounds of public policy. The courts interpretation of public policy as expressed in the Constitution is illustrated by *Dalton v. Dalton* and *Ormsby v. Ormsby*.

The burden of proving illegality is to establish as a matter of probability that the contract was, an illegal one at the time of its formation — *per* Finlay P. in *Whitecross Potatoes v. Coyle*. The legal principles applicable to such contracts are set out in this judgment. The probability test was applied by the E.A.T in *Lewis v. Squash Ireland*. The doctrine of severance may permit an illegal term in a contract to be severed or disgarded while leaving the remainder of the contract valid and enforceable. (*Skerry v. Moles*) It will only be permitted if it accords with public policy that it should operate in a particular case (*Lewis v. Squash Ireland*) and if it is possible to delete or sever the offending part while leaving the meaning of what remains intact.

In *Corporation of Dublin v. Hayes* the defendants agreement to pay over the fees he received in consideration of his being appointed Marshal of the City of Dublin was held to be contrary to public policy. Irish public policy relative to divorce as reflected in the Constitution, meant that the court in Dalton v. Dalton could not make the separation agreement a rule of court because it provided that the parties would obtain a divorce a vinculo. On the other hand a separation deed which provided for weekly payments was not contrary to public policy in *Orsmby v. Ormsby*.

ILLEGALITY

BURDEN OF PROOF

Whitecross Potatoes v. Coyle
High Court, unreported, 23 February 1978, Finlay P.

The Plaintiff, an English potato merchant, entered into a written contract to purchase 700 tonnes of ware potatoes from the defendant, a potato grower at a price of £58 per tonne. In the event of import, export controls by either Government the potatoes were to be supplied from Northern Ireland and a supplement of £5.50 per tonne was to be paid by Whitecross to Coyle.

The defendant claimed that he was not liable for damages for breach of the contract because it involved smuggling potatoes and was illegal and void.

Held: The contract was enforceable and the plaintiff was entitled to damages. 'If this was a contract which, on the apparent intention of the parties at the time of its formation, could be and would be carried out in a legal fashion, then, even though one of the parties . . . in reality intended to carry it out in an illegal fashion, it is enforceable. . . . The onus is on the defendant to establish . . . **as a matter of probability** that the contract was, at the time of its formation, an illegal contract....he has failed to discharge it.'

Per Finlay P.:

> If the acknowledged and accepted intention of both parties at the time of the formation of the contract, was, that in the event of this export or import control being imposed, the contract would be carried out by a smuggling operation, it is unenforceable and is contrary to public policy and cannot be upheld by the Court. . . . I have willingly come to the conclusion that the onus being on the defendant, he has failed to discharge it and to establish to my satisfaction **as a matter of probability** that the agreed understanding between him and the plaintiff was that the contract should, in the event of a restriction on export, be carried out by a smuggling operation. The contract was not an illegal contract.

Note: In *Lewis v. Squash Ireland Ltd.* (EAT UD 146/1982) the Tribunal applied the test of '**probability**' as set out in *Whitecross Potatoes v. Coyle* and found that the payment of a pay increase of £2,000 as 'salary expenses' not included in PAYE returns and treated by the company as expenses, tainted the contract with illegality and rendered it unenforceable.

CONTRACT TO DEFRAUD THE REVENUE

Lewis v. Squash Ireland Ltd. [1983] I.L.R.M. 363 (EAT UD146/1982)

The claimant was employed as Managing Director of the respondent company from 1975 until he was dismissed in November, 1981. During evidence at the hearing of a claim for compensation under the Unfair Dismissals Act it emerged that he was paid in two ways.

A salary of £14,000, and a further £2,000 as 'salary expenses'. When the respondent had requested a salary increase it was agreed that a separate monthly cheque would be paid in respect of 'expenses' which was not included in his PAYE returns and treated in the company accounts as an expense.

Held: The 'scheme' misdescribed the increase to avoid accountability/liability for tax and applying **the test of 'probability'** as set out in *Whitecross Potatoes v. Coyle*, the scheme adopted in relation to the pay increase was illegal. The contract was not void because it was perfectly valid until it became tainted with illegality. It was unenforceable and deprived the claimant of the basis on which to establish that he was an employee of the respondent as required by the Unfair Dismissals Act, 1977.

Note: Although severance was possible it was not allowed. The court felt that the parties knowingly incorporated the illegal agreement into the contract through a vital term viz. the claimant's consideration (his salary/remuneration) and the illegality infected the whole of the claimant's consideration and through it the whole contract.

An employees statutory rights under the Unfair dismissals Act, 1977 depended on his holding his employment under a legal and enforceable contract of employment.

ILLEGAL BY STATUTE

Conway v. Smith [1950] Ir. Jur. Rep. 33. (H.C.) Davitt J.

Section 83 of the Public Health (Ireland) Act, 1878 provided that it was unlawful to let a cellar unless the ceiling was at least seven feet high and at least three feet of its height from the surface of the street or ground adjoining it.

On being convicted under section 83 and fined under section 84 for letting a cellar unfit for human habitation, the defendant terminated the plaintiffs tenancy and ejected him. The plaintiff sued for breach of the implied condition of fitness for human habitation.

Held: The plaintiff could not succeed by proving an agreement to which the law could give no effect because it had expressly forbidden it. It was immaterial that the illegality was not pleaded in the defence. Once the fact of the illegality became clearly apparent on the hearing, the Court could give no effect to an agreement which was unlawful.

ILLEGAL BY STATUTE

O'Shaughnessy v. Lyons[1957] Ir. Jur. Rep. 90 (Cir. Ct.) O'Briain J.

The plaintiff sought payment for training the defendant's dog for 36 weeks and an extra £54 for transporting it to race meetings.

Section 36(1) of the Road Transport Act, 1933 provided that it was not lawful for a person to carry merchandise for reward unless he held a merchandise licence. The plaintiff did not hold such a licence.

Held: The carrying of the dog to meetings for reward was illegal and the plaintiff could not succeed in his claim.

PUFFER AT AN AUCTION

Airlie and Keenan v. Fallon, High Court, Unreported, 27 July 1976

See Chapter 11 Misrepresentation.

The defendant put a public house in Roosky, Co. Roscommon up for auction and the property was knocked down to the plaintiff at £95,000. The plaintiff sought and was granted rescission on the grounds of misrepresentation. Another factor in the case was the fact that the premises were sold without reaching the reserved price and that there was a puffer at the auction. Originally the reserve price was £120,000 but this was subsequently reduced to £100,000.

Hamilton J. found that it was clear from the evidence that at a certain stage the property was put on the market. At this stage it was to go to the highest bidder and there was no question of a reserve price. It was also clear from the evidence that a solicitor who had made bids at the auction was employed to do so on behalf of the vendor. This evidence was confirmed by this solicitor when he stated that he probably made a bid after the property was put on the market.

Held: A sale by auction in these circumstances was invalid by reason of the terms of the Sale of Land by Auction Act, 1867. For that reason also the plaintiffs were entitled to succeed. (In addition to having the contract rescinded on the grounds of misrepresentation.)

Note: Section 5 Sale of Land by Auction Act, 1867 provides:

> "The particulars or conditions of sale by auction of any land shall state whether such land be sold without reserve, . . . or subject to a reserved price, or whether a right to bid is reserved; if it is stated that such land will be sold without reserve, or to that effect, then it is not lawful for the seller

to employ any person to bid at such sale, or for the auctioneer to take knowingly any bidding from any such person.

MONEY LENT FOR GAMING
Anthony v. Shea [1951] 86 I.L.T.R. 229 (Cir. Ct.) McCarthy J.

The plaintiff claimed repayment of a sum of £43 which he had lent to Shea, for the purpose of gaming. Shea had called at his house and borrowed the money promising to re-pay it the following day when he had an opportunity of cashing a cheque. Shea was killed two days later in a motor accident and the plaintiff claimed payment from his executors.

Held: Money lent, which to the knowledge of the lender, was to be used by the borrower for the purposes of gaming cannot be recovered even if it is not proved that the money was used for that purpose.

The money was knowingly lent for the purpose of gaming, and the claim must be dismissed. Gaming Acts, 1710 and 1835.

AGREEMENT AGAINST PUBLIC POLICY
Corporation of Dublin v. Hayes
(1876) I.R. 10 C.L. 226 (Common Pleas) Morris C.J.

In consideration of being appointed to the office of Marshal of the City of Dublin, the defendant entered into an agreement with the plaintiff that he would relinquish the fees of the office for the plaintiff's use and accept a fixed salary in lieu. A term of the agreement provided that he would account for and pay over all fees and moneys, and deposit a statement in writing of such fees and moneys. The plaintiff alleged that he did not account, or pay over, or deposit a statement.

Held: It would be to the last degree against public policy to allow the plaintiffs to bargain for fees with which they had no connection and to which they had no shadow of claim.

PUBLIC POLICY AND THE CONSTITUION — ILLEGAL
Dalton v. Dalton [1982] I.L.R.M. 418 (H.C.) O'Hanlon J.

The plaintiff applied to have a separation agreement made a rule of court. The agreement contained a clause that the husband and wife agreed to obtain a divorce a vinculo and that the husband agreed not to contest any divorce proceedings. The parties were domiciled in Ireland.

Held: To ask the court to make the agreement a rule of court, was to ask the court to lend its support to a course of conduct which was contrary to public policy within this jurisdiction. For this reason the application must be refused.

Note: Kingsmill Moore J. in *Mayo-Perrott v. Mayo-Perrott* [1958] I.R. 336. was cited as stating 'It cannot be doubted that the public policy of this country as reflected in the Constitution does not favour divorce *a vinculo*'.

PUBLIC POLICY AND THE CONSTITUION — NOT ILLEGAL
Ormsby v. Ormsby [1945] I.L.T.R. 97 (S.C.)

A deed of separation was executed by both parties. In it the defendant agreed to make a weekly payment. When he ceased to make the payment the plaintiff sued. The defendant claimed that the deed was not binding and that it was invalid and contrary to public policy.

Held: The State does not regard, under Article 41 of the Constitution that separation deeds are an attack on the institution of marriage. The deed was not contrary to public policy.

CHAPTER 14

Contracts in Restraint of Trade

All contracts which interfere with and limit freedom to trade are regarded by the courts as *prima facie* void. A restraint may, however, be upheld if it is: (a) reasonable as between the parties and (b) reasonable in the public interest. See *Esso Petroleum Co. Ltd. v. Harpers Garage (Stourport) Ltd.* [1968] A.C. 269 It is in area of contracts in restraint of trade that the doctrine of public policy impinges on most individuals. These contracts fall into one of the following categories:

(a) Contracts between an employer and an employee or independent contractor.

(b) Contracts involving the sale of the goodwill of a business.

(c) Rules of associations or trading agreements, including solus agreements.

In the first category it was submitted in *Dosser v. Monaghan & Ors.*, that there is no reported decision in which the courts have precluded a person from earning a livelihood and the court refused to uphold the restraint because the contract was not reasonable. The restraint clauses went further than was reasonably necessary for the plaintiffs protection. In *Mulligan v. Corr*, Fitzgibbon J. stated that **if the restraint exceeded in area or duration the limits which the court considers reasonable it is void**. A restriction although without geographic limitation may be reasonable if confined to a period of reasonable duration. In *Skerry Wynn v. Moles* the doctrine of severance was applied and the reasonable part of the restraint up-held. The doctrine of restraint of trade was extended and applied to contracts for services in *Schroeder v. Maculey*.

The leading authority on exclusive trading agreements is the Irish case of *McEllistrim v. Ballymacelligott Co-Op.* Lord Birkenhead in the House of Lords stated that there was much to be said for the view that the restraint objected to, would be opposed to the public interest, but he did not think it necessary to decide this having formed the view that it was unreasonable as between the parties.

In more recent times the doctrine has been applied to rules of other types of associations and in *Macken v. O'Reilly & Ors.*, the rules of the Equestrian Federation of Ireland were examined by the Supreme Court. This decision clearly infers that the test of reasonableness as between the parties in such a case is subordinate to that of reasonableness in the public interest. Robert Clark (*Contract*, 3rd ed., p. 348) states that the rules on restraint as they stand do not require

> "such a balancing process: if the rule is unreasonable *inter partes* it is unnecessary to consider the public interest; indeed most cases are decided entirely on reasonableness *inter partes*. The view that individual interests which are unreasonably prejudiced must be sacrificed if they conflict with wider public interests is a novel doctrine".

While restraints reasonable as between the parties have been presumed to be reasonable in the public interest, there are many occasions when private and public interests do not coincide and an agreement reasonable as between the parties is not in the public interest. EEC competition cases seem to indicate that public policy is the predominant basis of the doctrine when trading agreements are concerned. Thesiger J. in *Bull v. Pitney-Bowes Ltd.* [1966] All E.R. 388 states

> "public policy has been described as an unruly horse which in the *Wyatt* case (*Wyatt v. Kreglinger and Fernau* [1933] All E.R. 349) has taken the Court of Appeal for quite a gallop".

He also cites Treitel, *Law of Contract*, 2nd ed., p. 322 that the principle of the public interest may not operate very often but it is in the last resort a useful one. The Supreme Court may have found it so in the *Macken* case.

It has to be recognized that reasonableness *inter partes* is not necessarily synonymous with the public interest. Thesiger J. instanced a take-over bid, where the bidder may not be interested in developing exports, whereas it may be very much in the public interest that the services of an experienced, skilled, salesman should be available to promote sales.

RESTRAINT OF TRADE

CONTRACT FOR THE SALE OF A BUSINESS

John Orr Ltd. and Vescom B.V. v. John Orr
[1987] I.L.R.M. 702 (H.C.) Costello J.

The second plaintiff purchased the first plaintiff from the defendant and another. The purchase agreement contained service agreements, restraint of trade clauses and restraint on soliciting customer clauses.

The business of John Orr Ltd., was manufacturing and selling upholstery and garment fabrics.

The restraint of trade clause provided that until the expiry of one year from the determination of his service agreement the defendant should:

"Not have any interest in any other firm or company nor be employed by, or as representative or agent for any other person firm or company which manufactures or trades or markets similar or competing goods to those manufactured or traded or marketed by the Company or by Vescom".

The defendant resigned in 1985 and the restraints began to run from 31 October when his resignation became effective. The plaintiffs ascertained that he had established a company in England which began trading on 1 November, 1985 in upholstery fabrics and that he had solicited business from some of their customers in the United States.

Costello J. noted the following points about the restraints on competition: (a) they were for a twelve month period; (b) they were world wide; (c) they applied to goods similar to and competing with goods manufactured by (1) John Orr Ltd., and (2) its parent company Vescom B.V.

Held: (*inter alia*) John Orr Ltd. manufactured and sold upholstery and garment fabrics and did not manufacture or trade in wall coverings, which were the goods manufactured by Vescom B.V. It had no intention of entering the market in these goods. **The range of goods subject to the restraint was therefore unreasonably wide** as it was not necessary for the protection of Vescom's interest in John Orr Ltd., that the defendant should be restrained from manufacturing or trading in wall coverings.

Costello J. held that the reasonableness of the restraints imposed on the defendant was to be tested by the commercial realities of the situation which existed when they were imposed, that was in the year 1977. So the question for determination was whether in that year it was reasonably necessary for the protection of John Orr Ltd's trade connections that it should impose the restraints contained in the service agreement. What was in the reasonable contemplation of the parties for the future development of the first plaintiff was also relevant.

He considered that it was also excessively restrictive because it prohibited the defendant from manufacturing or trading in upholstery fabrics **in any part of the world** during the limitation period. "It might even have been possible to justify a wider restriction if it could have been shown that in 1977 John Orr Ltd., had definite proposals for expanding into markets outside North America and Europe. But a blanket restraint based merely on the possibility that markets in other parts of the world might be entered by the company is to my mind an unreasonable one as it was not reasonably required for the protection of Vescom's investment in the company".

ASSOCIATIONS

McEllistrim v. Ballymacelligott Co-Op [1919] A.C. 548 (H.L.) (I.)

McEllistrim a farmer at Ballymacelligott, Co. Kerry was a member of the local Co-Op. The rules provided that no member could sell their milk to any other creamery or society and that a member was not entitled to leave the society without the consent of the management committee.

Held: The rules read in combination imposed upon members a greater restraint than was reasonably required for the protection of the society, and was illegal as in restraint of trade and *ultra vires* the society.

AREA OF RESTRAINT

Tipperary Co-Op v. Hanley [1912] 2. I.R. 586 (C.A.)

The plaintiffs claimed payment of £25 for the defendant's non compliance with rules of their society. The rules obliged the society to purchase all the milk provided by a member's cows and obliged a milk supplying member to deliver all the milk he produced to the society's creamery. For default in doing so a member became obliged to pay liquidated damages at the rate of one shilling per cow per day.

The defendant, although a member of the society, with 30 £1 shares never delivered any milk to the society.

The rules did not provide for the voluntary withdrawal of a member from the society except by transfer of his shares, to which the consent of the committee was necessary.

Held: The rule requiring delivery of milk was void as an illegal restraint of trade. The rule had a scope and operation altogether beyond what was reasonable for the protection of the society:

Barry L.C.:

> ". . . there was no limitation whatever as to the locality of the lands in which the cows might be found, whether in County Tipperary itself, or in any other county of Ireland. . . . The words themselves, *prima facie*, take effect over the whole country . . . it was not possible for us . . . to impose bounds upon the scope of the rule . . . the public inconvenience is plain".

Macken v. O'Reilly, Supreme Court, unreported, 31 May 1979

The plaintiff, a professional show jumper and horseman claimed that a decision of the Equestrian Federation of Ireland that they would not select any horse to represent Ireland at certain events unless the horse was Irish bred, interfered with his freedom to earn his living and was a restraint of trade which was not reasonable. He also contended that the decision incorporated in a resolution was ultra vires the powers of the defendants.

Held: The resolution and ruling of the Federation although in restraint of trade was, in the circumstances, reasonable and fair and was not *ultra vires*.

Chief Justice O'Higgins:

"All interference with an individuals freedom of action in trading is *per se*, contrary to public policy and, therefore void. This general prohibition is subject to the exception that certain restraints may be justified. Restraints, restrictions or interferences are permitted, if they are, in the circumstances obtaining, fair and reasonable.
    Whether what is complained of can be justified on this basis involves a careful examination of all the circumstances—

• the need for the restraint

• the object sought to be attained

• the interests sought to be protected and

• the general interests of the public

what is done or sought to be done must be established as being reasonable and necessary and on balance to serve the public interest. . . . A policy of restraint which is held to be reasonable, having regard to all effected, including the public, cannot, in my view properly be described as being unjust and unfair simply because in its particular application to one individual an inconvenience or loss is experienced".

DURATION

REASONABLENESS

Esso Petroleum v. Harpers Garage Ltd [1968] A.C. 269 (H.L.)

The plaintiffs, suppliers of motor fuels, entered into two solus agreements with the defendants in relation to two garages, one at Mustow Green, and the other called the Corner Garage.
    The agreement in respect of the Mustow Green garage was for a period of 4 years and 5 months and the agreement in relation to the Corner Garage was for 21 years. The Corner Garage agreement was coupled with a mortgage for a similar period which was not redeemable before 21 years except with the plaintiff's consent. The defendant agreed to purchase their total requirements

of motor fuels at the plaintiff's wholesale price and not to resell except in accordance with the plaintiff's retail schedule prices. They also agreed not to operate any discount, dividend or cash scheme in connection with sales.

Because of low price petrol competitors, the plaintiffs wrote to all their dealers (including the defendant) that they would not insist on the resale price maintenance clause being implemented. The defendants replied that they deemed the solus agreement null and void by reason of the removal of the resale price clause, and began to sell another brand of petrol. They also announced their intention of redeeming the mortgage. The appellants considered that the mortgage could not be redeemed without their consent, otherwise than in accordance with the covenant for repayment. The appellants sought injunctions (*inter alia*) restraining the respondents from buying or selling motor fuels other than those of the appellant at the garages.

Held: (*inter alia*): That a period of five years was not in the circumstances longer than was necessary to afford adequate protection to the legitimate interests of the appellants.

That a tie of 21 years went beyond any period for which developments were reasonably foreseeable and in the absence of evidence of some advantage to the appellants for which a shorter period would not be adequate, the agreement was void. That the existence of the mortgage did not exclude the doctrine of restraint of trade.

FIVE YEARS REASONABLE IN SOLUS AGREEMENT

Continental Oil Company of Ireland Ltd. v. Moynihan
[1977] 111 I.L.T.R. 5 (H.C.) Kenny J.

The plaintiff entered into a supply or solus agreement on the 19th August, 1970 to supply motor fuel to the defendant over a five year period. Under the solus system a dealer binds himself to sell the products of one company only.

The plaintiff agreed *inter alia*, to supply the defendant's total requirement of motor fuel for resale for five years and the defendant agreed *inter alia* to purchase his total requirement of motor fuel from them and not to purchase, receive, or sell any other motor fuels at the premises. The defendant also entered into an agreement for the acquisition of new petrol pumps on hire purchase from the plaintiff.

The defendant refused to pay an increase in the price of motor fuel and the plaintiff discontinued supplying him. The defendant then made an arrangement with an other supplier and the plaintiff applied for an injunction to restrain the interference with the solus agreement.

Held: (*inter alia*): The agreement in restraint of trade for five years, was reasonable between the parties when it was made. The agreement was reasonable from the defendant's stand-point as he got new pumps on hire-purchase terms without having to pay the heavy interest charges which are usually connected with these transactions. The period of five years was reasonable both as between the parties and in the public interest.

Nordenfelt v. Maxim Nordenfelt Guns & Ammunition Co. Ltd. (1894) A.C. 535 and *Esso Petroleum Company v. Harpers Garage* [1968] A.C. 269 *considered* and *applied.* See also *Dolan v. A.B. Ltd.*, 104 I.L.T.R. 101.

TWENTY YEARS EXCESSIVE
McMullan Bros. Ltd. v. Condell
unreported, High Court, 30 January 1970, Kenny J.

On 1st September, 1959 the plaintiff entered into two contracts with the defendant. The first contract was a loan agreement the second a 'solus' agreement.

Under the loan agreement the plaintiff advanced the sum of £4,400 to assist the defendant to improve his business and this sum was repayable by equal yearly instalments of £220. The last payment to be made on the 1st September, 1979.

Clause 3 of the loan agreement provided that during the continuance of the agreement, the defendant would purchase exclusively from the plaintiff, all supplies of motor spirits, oils, fuels and equipment.

The 'solus' agreement provided it was to come into force on 1st September, 1959 and remain in force for twenty years, and obliged the defendant to purchase a minimum quantity of 70,000 gallons of petrol each year. The defendant could not sell 70,000 gallons of petrol a year and the plaintiff terminated the 'solus' agreement. When Condell proposed to sell the business the plaintiff would not consent unless the purchaser took over the agreement.

Held: The loan agreement was intended to bolster up the the 'solus' agreement. There was no evidence to justify the length of the restriction and the clauses in the loan agreement and the 'solus' agreement were invalid and not justified either in the interest of the parties or in the public interest. The plaintiff was not entitled to restrain the defendant from selling the business.

Kenny J.:

> "It is not possible to treat the interests of the parties concerned and the interests of the public separately because the interests of the parties which justify or do not justify an agreement restrictive of trade, rest on considerations of public policy; if they did not, the courts could not release parties from obligations which they had voluntarily accepted".

RESTRAINTS IN CONTRACTS OF EMPLOYMENT

Dossor v. Monaghan and Others [1932] N.I. 209 (Ch. D.)

The defendants were musicians employed by the plaintiff under contracts of employment which contained a clause that they would not, within three years from termination of their employment enter into any future engagements within fifty miles of five cities including Belfast.

While the defendants were playing as members of his orchestra at the Carlton Restaurant Belfast, the plaintiff terminated their employment and the defendants entered into an engagement with the proprietor to play there on their own account.

Head: Having regard to all the circumstances the contracts were not reasonable. They went further than was reasonably necessary for the plaintiff's protection and an injunction was refused. (*Mason v. Provident Clothing & Supply Co. Ltd.* [1913] A.C. 733)

AREA OF RESTRAINT

Mulligan v. Corr [1925] I.R. 169 (S.C.)

A solicitor with offices at Ballina, Co. Mayo and Charlestown agreed to employ the defendant as a solicitors clerk and to give him articles of apprenticeship.

The defendant agreed that when he qualified as a Solicitor he would not practice within 30 miles of Ballina and Charlestown or within 20 miles of Ballaghadreen, Co. Roscommon.

When he qualified, the defendant entered into practice in the town of Ballina and the plaintiff sought an injunction to restrain him.

Held: The area which the plaintiff endeavoured to protect was too large. It covered practically the whole of Mayo, more than half of Sligo, a large part of Roscommon and portions of Galway and Leitrim. The agreement could not be upheld in its entirety. Questions arose whether it could be divided, if so, whether any fraction of it could be supported as reasonable. It was not.

SEVERANCE

Skerry v. Moles (1907) 42 I.L.T.R. 46 (H.C.) (Ch.) Barton J.

The defendant was employed as a teacher of shorthand etc., by the plaintiff in a business academy in Belfast. It was a term of the defendant's contract that he should not carry on or engage in the business of teacher of shorthand, typewriting and general business training or in any or either of the said businesses in Dublin, Belfast or Cork or within a seven mile radius from Skerry & Wynne's place of business in any of the said cities for a period of three years from leaving their employment.

M. left their employment and set up a school for shorthand, typewriting and general business training in Belfast and S. sought to enforce the restrictive clause in the contract.

Held: The plaintiffs were entitled to an injunction restraining the defendant from carrying on a business in Belfast. The covenant was reasonable qua Belfast, but unreasonable qua Dublin and Cork, the reasonable part thereof being separable from the unreasonable. See *Seymour Jones v. Seymour Jones.*

Note: In *Schroeder Music Publishing Co. Ltd. v. Macauley* [1974] 1 W.L.R. 1308 the House of Lords applied the doctrine of restraint of trade to a contract for services. It now applies to both contracts 'for services' and contracts 'of service'.

DURATION OF RESTRAINT
Arclex Optical Corp. Ltd. v. McMurray
[1958] Ir. Jur. Rep. 65 (H.C.) Dixon J.

The defendant, who was employed as a salesman by the plaintiffs entered into a written agreement, that for a period of five years after leaving their employment, he would not engage in any business carried on by the plaintiffs in any of the districts assigned to him by them.

He terminated his contract in June, 1957 but it appeared that from some time in May, 1957 he had been trading in optical goods for another firm and had got orders from some of the plaintiffs customers.

The plaintiff sought an interlocutory injunction pending the hearing of an action for an injunction and damages,

Held: There were good grounds for granting an injunction for the limited period pending the hearing. The form the injunction would take was one against the canvasing and soliciting of orders by the defendant or his being associated with or connected with the canvassing and soliciting of orders from existing customers of the plaintiff. (See also *Premier Dairies v. Jameson*, 1983).

Note: At Common Law an employee owes his employer a duty of faithful service and a duty of good faith and fidelity while in his employment. The duty of faithful service means that an employee must not make a list of his employers customers or use information obtained in confidence during the course of his employment. The duty of fidelity imposes an obligation on an employee to respect and not to abuse confidential information relating to his employers business.

After the termination of employment a person may canvass his previous employers customers unless he is bound by a restraint clause with his former employer.

See *Wessex Dairies Ltd. v. Smith* (19350 2 K.B. 80 and *Robb v. Green* [1895] 2 Q.B. 315

ACTIVITY COVERED BY RESTRAINT

Oates v. Romano [1950] 84 I.L.T.R. 166 (Cir. Ct.) Shannon J.

Oates, a high class ladies hairdresser engaged the defendant as an assistant. The contract of employment provided that the defendant would not carry on or take employment in a 'like business' to within a mile of the plaintiffs premises during the employment and for three years after it terminated.

On leaving the employment, the defendant entered the employment of a firm engaged in a 'like business' within a mile of the plaintiff's premises and the plaintiff sought an injunction to restrain the breach of covenant.

Held: The restriction was unnecessarily wide and accordingly void. In fact the covenant prohibited the defendant from carrying on the business of hairdresser at all, not merely ladies hairdressing, and that part of the covenant could not be severed. This was sufficient to decide the case.

Shannon J.:

"Furthermore, if the defendant merely had shares in such a business he would have an 'interest' therein, and thus contravene the clause, and on that ground, also, the covenant is too wide".

CHAPTER 15

Capacity

Legal capacity to enter into a binding contract is another essential required by law. Agreement, intention and consent are crucial in the formation of a contract, and it follows that a contracting party must have the use of reason and be able to freely give consent if a contract is to be a valid one.

Everyone does not have this capacity. It is recognized that persons who lack understanding or might be taken advantage of, like infants, drunkards, lunatics and wards of court need special consideration. It is also recognized that some legal persons, as distinct from human persons viz. corporations lack capacity to enter into certain contracts.

INFANTS

The Infants relief Act 1872 was specially enacted to protect infants. Infants are persons under eighteen years of age. This Act provides that certain contracts entered into by an infant are void viz. those for the repayment of money lent or to be lent, those for goods other than necessaries, and all accounts stated. An infant is bound by contracts for necessaries and by contracts which are for his benefit. Necessaries are goods appropriate to the persons station in life and need by him at the time of sale and delivery whereas contracts of education or training are considered to be contracts for an infants benefit. Contracts by which an infant acquires an interest in property of a permanent kind are voidable at the infants option but must be avoided before or within a reasonable time of reaching his majority. Money paid by an infant under a voidable contract cannot be recovered unless there has been a total failure of consideration.

NECESSARIES

Skrine v. Gordon (1875) 9 C.L. 479 (Com. Pleas.)

The defendant, an English youth on a visit to Ireland contracted to buy a hunter from the plaintiff who he met while hunting. The youth told him that he was a member of the Surrey Stag Hunt and that he rode his father's hunters.

The plaintiff accepted payment by a bill for £150 payable in six months.

The defendant hunted the horse until the end of the season, then went to London, leaving the horse in a livery stable to be returned to the plaintiff.

The plaintiff sued for the price of the horse and the defendant pleaded infancy. The plaintiff replied that the horse was a necessary.

Held: There was no evidence which could properly be left to the jury that the hunter was a necessary. The defendant was not obliged to pay.

Note: It was submitted for the plaintiff that 'Articles of mere luxury cannot be necessaries but articles of utility, although luxurious and expensive may be'; per Alderson B. in *Chapple v. Cooper*, 13 M & W 2252, 258. In *Peters v. Fleming* 6 M & W 47 a gold watch-chain and a pair of breast pins were held necessaries, though rings were not. In *Ryder v. Wombwell* L.R. 4 Ex. 32 a pair of crystal, ruby, and diamond solitaire studs were deemed necessaries while a gold goblet was not.

INFANT NOT LIABLE FOR NON-NECESSARIES
Griffith v. Delaney [1938] Ir. Jur. Rep. 1 (H.C.) O'Byrne J.

The plaintiff commenced an action against three brothers trading as Delaney Brothers, for payment of money due for goods sold and delivered. The goods could not be described as 'necessaries'.

One of the brothers claimed that at the time of the order and delivery of the goods, he was an infant, and not liable to pay the price by reason of his infancy because the goods were not necessaries).

Held: Judgment for the plaintiff could be entered against the two brothers of full age but the action against the infant must be dismissed. (Infants Relief Act, 1874.)

LIABILITY FOR OCCUPATION AND ENJOYMENT OF LAND
Blake v. Concannon (1870) I.R. 4 C.L. 323 Pigot C.B.

Certain lands were let to an infant. He possessed and enjoyed the lands for a year and an instalment of rent became due. Later he attained his majority, repudiated the contract and refused to pay the rent due.

Held: The infant was liable to pay the rent which accrued while he occupied the lands and before he repudiated. He was not liable on the contract of tenancy alone. His liability arose from his occupation and enjoyment of the land. An infant can repudiate a contract but he cannot repudiate an occupation and enjoyment which are past. He has had a *quid pro quo*.

Pigot C.B.:

> "He is not, in an action of debt for the rent, held liable upon the contract of tenancy alone. his liability arises from his occupation and enjoyment of the land, under the tenancy so created.
>
> If his liability arose from the contract alone, the repudiation of the contract by annulling it, would annul its obligations, which would then exist only by reason of the contract. But the infant, though he can repudiate the contract of demise, and the tenancy under it, and can so revest the land in the landlord, cannot repudiate an occupation and enjoyment which are past, or restore to the landlord what he has lost by that occupation and enjoyment of the infant. The reason given by Justice Newton, in 21 Hen. 6, 31b lies at the root of the infant's liability; 'he has had a *quid pro quo*".

See *Velentini v. Canali* [1886-90] All E.R. Rep. 883 and *Davies v. Benyon Harris* [1931] 47 T.L.R. 424.

Money paid by an infant under a voidable contract cannot be recovered unless there has been a complete failure of consideration.

REPUDIATION MUST TAKE PLACE WITHIN A REASONABLE TIME

Stapleton v Prudential Insurance Co. Ltd.
(1928) 62 I.L.T.R. 56.(H.C.) Sullivan P. & O'Byrne J.

The infant plaintiff took out an insurance policy with the defendant, having been canvassed by two of the defendant company's agents. She alleged that she understood she would be paid a lump sum after eleven years. The policy, in fact, was payable on death at any time within eleven years and convertible at the end of that period into a paid up policy.

She paid the premiums for eleven years and then sued the company for the return of the premiums.

Held: The court could not order the return of the premiums, as repudiation had not occurred within a reasonable time, and the company's liability in the event of death at any time after the making of the contract amounted to a consideration.

Sullivan P. stated that there was no misrepresentation by the defendant, but bona fide mistake on the part of the plaintiff. This was a continuing contract, and the plaintiff, if she wished to repudiate it on attaining full age, was bound to do so within a reasonable time.

Even if she could now repudiate, it did not follow that the premiums should be returned to her. If she had died between 1916 and 1927, the company would have been bound to pay, so it could not be held that no consideration had passed during those years.

REPUDIATION MUST BE IN A WAY THE OTHER PARTY CAN DISPUTE

Slator v. Brady (1863) 14 Ir. C.L.R. 61 (Ex.)

Slator brought an action of ejectment on title for 43 acres of land in County Longford. He claimed under a lease made to him by Alexander Slator on 29 April 1861 at a rent of £500 per annum, for the life of the grantor or twenty one years.

The defendant relied upon a lease made to him by Alexander Slator, when he was an infant, on the 19 June, the previous year, and claimed that a receipt from the defendant of the rent after Alexander Slator attained full age, amounted to confirmation of the defendants lease.

Held: A lease made by an infant is not void, but voidable only. A lease made by an infant, reserving a rent, is not avoided by a lease of the same lands to a third party on the infant coming of age.

To avoid such a lease made by an infant, when he came of age, some act of notoriety, viz. ejectment, entry or demand of possession is required. (The repudiation must be in a way the other party can dispute.)

CONTRACT FOR INFANTS BENEFIT

Keays v. Great Southern Railway Co. [1941] I.R. 534 (H.C.) Hanna J.

The plaintiff a child of twelve travelled daily to school in Limerick by rail from Killonan. She held a monthly season ticket issued by the defendant company at a reduced rate upon special conditions exempting the company from all liability for injuries that might be caused to the ticket holder through the negligence of the company its servants or agents.

While crossing the railway line near Killonan she was knocked down and injured by a goods train. The company relied on the exempting conditions. The plaintiff claimed that the contract was not for her benefit and was void. The company replied that it was for her benefit in that it helped her receive a higher standard of education in Limerick.

Held: The court must consider the contract as a whole. It is not sufficient that the infant gets some benefit from the contract, the court has to consider the obligations or limitations imposed by the company on the natural or legal rights of the infant.

The contract in this case was very unfair to the infant because it deprived her of practically every common law right she had against the railway in respect of the negligence of themselves or their servants. For that reason it was not for her benefit. See also *Harnedy v. National Greyhound Racing Co. Ltd.* [1944] I.R. 160.

Note: In England the Minors' Contracts Act, 1987 has effectively reversed the decision in *Coutts & Co. v. Browne-Lecky* [1974] K.B. 104 regarding contracts guaranteeing infants debts entered into after the 9th June, 1987. Section 2 provides that such a guarantee of an obligation incurred by a minor may be enforceable against the guarantor even though the obligation is unenforceable against (or the contract was repudiated by) the minor on the ground of his minority. See Infants Relief Act 1874, section 1.

CONTRACT FOR EDUCATION OR TRAINING
Butler, an Infant v. Dillon [1952] 87 I.L.T.R. 95 (H.C.)

The infant, plaintiff entered into an Indenture of Apprenticeship with the defendant in July, 1950. It provided that the plaintiff would serve the Master in his trade as a joiner for five years and that the Master was to instruct him in the trade and pay him a pound per week during the first year rising to five pounds per week in the fifth year. The apprentice was to regularly attend wood work and carpentry classes at Letterkenny Technical School.

Clause 3(f) permitted the Master to discharge the Apprentice from his service if he wilfully disobeyed the lawful orders or commands of the Master or was wilfully disobedient or negligent or otherwise grossly misbehaved himself towards the Master or his family.

The Apprentice only attended the technical school for a few weeks. Although his Master spoke to him about his non-attendance and told him what the consequences might be, he did not mend his ways and the Master discharged him for non-attendance at the Technical School. The infant Apprentice then instituted proceedings claiming breach of covenant on the Master's part.

Held: The conduct of the Apprentice did not warrant his dismissal. The master's conduct amounted to a repudiation of the agreement.

The father and the apprentice were entitled to accept such repudiation only if, it was for the infant's benefit. In all the circumstances the repudiation was for the infant's benefit.

Kingsmill Moore J.:

> "It is well settled that misconduct, falling short of the very grossest kind, does not entitle a master to repudiate a contract of apprenticeship: *Winstone v. Linn* 1 B. & C. 460; *Wise v. Wilson* 1 C. & K. 662 (where the apprentice got drunk on some occasions); *Phillips v. Clift* 4 H. & N. 168 (where there was some dishonesty on the apprentices part).
>
> On the other hand, habitual theft by the apprentice from his master as in *Learoyd v. Brook* (1891) 1 Q.B. 433, or his complete refusal to learn the trade, as in *Raymond v. Minton* (1866) L.R. 1 Exch. 244, or his

persistence in absenting himself from his master's service, as in *Hughes v. Humphreys* 6 B. & C. 680, have been held to justify the dismissal of an apprentice on the ground that the conduct of the apprentice rendered it impossible for the master to carry out his side of the bargain. The law on the matter was stated very fully as recently as 1921 in *Waterman v. Fryar* [1922] 1. K.B. 499. The present position can only be regarded as very unsatisfactory from the master's viewpoint".

LUNATICS AND DRUNKEN PERSONS

Contracts entered into by lunatics or drunken persons are voidable provided, (a) they were incapable of understanding the nature of the transaction at the time they entered into it and (b) that the party contracted with, knew this. Both things must be proved in order to avoid a contract on the ground of insanity. The rule that a person who was non compos mentis could not plead his own disability was amended by Pollock C.B. in *Molton v. Camroux* (1848) 2 Ex 493.

A defendant must in the words of Lopes L.J. in *Imperial Loan Company v. Stone* (1892) 1 Q.B. 599 prove 'not merely his incapacity, but also the plaintiffs knowledge of that fact, and unless he proves these two things he cannot succeed.'

Lunatics or drunken persons are, of course, liable if they affirm the contract later during a lucid or sober period. They are also liable to pay a reasonable price for necessaries. A ward of court is probably the only human person who permanently lacks contractual capacity.

LUNATIC

Hassard v. Smith (1872) I.R. 6 Eq. 429 (Eq.)

The plaintiff leased a house and lands in Co. Wicklow to the defendant for a period of five years, at a rent of £155 by a lease dated 25 January, 1871.

On 23 January, 1872, the plaintiff was found a lunatic, by inquisition and the jury found that his lunacy commenced on 29th October, 1870, before the execution of the lease.

His wife contended that he must be taken to have been insane when he executed the lease, that he was incompetent to contract, that the reserved rent was much less than the value of the premises, and that the lease should be set aside. It was also claimed that the onus was on the defendant to prove that he had the capacity to make the lease.

Held:

(1) The rule, both of law and equity, as to a contract entered into by a person apparently of unsound mind, and not known by the other contract-

ing party to be insane, is, that such a contract, if fair, *bona fide*, and completely executed, is valid: and, even though such a contract might be void at law, it will only be set aside in equity for fraud.

(2) The ordinary presumption of sanity is removed by an inquisition finding a person to be of unsound mind; and, in the case of a contract subsequently entered into by him, the burden of proof is shifted; but the finding, being usually *ex parte*, is not conclusive, and the court has jurisdiction (which, however, it will be slow in exercising) to arrive at a contrary conclusion without the aid of another jury.

(3) To vitiate a contract, the knowledge of the lunacy or incapacity must be, not merely actual, but presumably sufficient — from circumstances known to the other contracting party — to lead him to a reasonable conclusion that the person with whom he is dealing is of unsound mind.

Note: A.G. Guest, *Anson's Law of Contract*, Oxford, 1984, 26th. ed. at page 207 referring to the principle that the contract of a mentally disordered or drunken person is not binding upon him if it can be shown that at the time of making the contract he was incapable of understanding what he was doing, and that the other party knew of his condition states 'This principle was established by Lord Esher M.R. in *Imperial Loan Co. v. Stone*;' The Imperial Loan case was in 1892 some 20 years after *Hassard v. Smith*. It had been the case that a person who was *non compos mentis* could not set up his own disability but this rule was mitigated in 1848 by Pollock C.B in *Molton v. Camroux* (1848) 2 Exch. 487 where he held that unsoundness of mind would now be a good defence to an action on a contract, if it could be shown that the defendant was not of capacity to contract, 'and the plaintiff knew it.' Lord Esher, M.R. in the *Imperial Loan* case stated 'The burden of proof in such a case, must lie on the defendant.'

LUNATIC OBLIGED TO PAY FOR NECESSARIES
In re Byrne [1941] I.R. 378 (H.C.) Maguire J.

H.B, a person of unsound mind, was admitted to an asylum. He was taken into wardship and a guardian appointed. His estate consisted of a farm encumbered by debts.

From time to time asylum authorities applied to the courts for the cost of his maintenance and various sums were paid out to them by order of the court.

When he died, a number of mental hospitals claimed payments for maintenance and were awarded lesser amounts than they claimed by the Circuit court. The hospitals appealed.

Held: (*inter alia*): That the estate of a person of unsound mind is liable for his maintenance and that sums due for maintenance constitute valid debts against his estate. There is an implied obligation upon the part of a person of unsound mind who is maintained in an institution or mental home to pay or contribute towards the cost of his maintenance, and if his estate be sufficient, to pay the charges for maintenance in full.

DRUNKNESS

White v. McCooey, High Court, unreported, 26, April, 1976.

The plaintiff claimed specific performance of a contract of sale of a licensed premises in the town of Monaghan. The defendant claimed that there was no agreement and that at the time of making the contract he was so drunk that he was incapable of contracting. He claimed that he had no recollection of the plaintiff's coming into the dining room of Hayden's Hotel, Ballinasloe, on 3 August, 1972, during the Galway races. He recalled being told when he awoke in the Imperial Hotel in Galway on the 4 May, that 'he had sold a pub the night before.'

The plaintiff further claimed that the agreed price was so much below the fair price for the property as to be unfair and unconscionable and but for his intoxicated state he would not have agreed to so low a price.

Held:

(1) That the defendant was not incapable through drunkness of entering into a binding agreement such as was proved.

(2) The plaintiff did not know and had no reason to suppose that the defendant was incapable through drunkness of entering into a binding agreement. The defendant had not discharged the onus of proof which lay on him in respect of his defence as alleged of incapacity to contract by reason of drunkness or of his counterclaim to have the contract avoided.

(3) The proper relief in this case, was to award the plaintiff a sum for damages in lieu of specific performance. This sum was estimated at £4,500 and accordingly judgment given for that amount.

Per Gannon J.:

"The defendant seeking on equitable grounds to avoid the contract undertakes the onus of proving all the circumstances on which he relies for that purpose including the drunkness alleged and the knowledge thereof of the plaintiff. . . . I do not believe the evidence that he had as many drinks as 18 brandies and 22 Harps on the 3 August, 1972 or that he showed the signs of intoxification suggested by the evidence (of two witnesses) before he went to the dining table. . . . The defendant's evidence is so heavily burdened with improbability I have no alternative but to reject it.

I am satisfied that the plaintiff, so far as the onus lies on him, has proved the consensus of the parties to the contract and its terms with that degree of certainty the law requires and the existence of a note or memorandum thereof in writing signed by the defendant which complies with the requirements of the Statute of Frauds".

RATIFICATION
Matthews v. Baxter (1873) L.R. 8 Ex. 132

The defendant bid for and bought houses and land at an auction. When sued for breach of contract he pleaded that at the time he was so drunk as to be incapable of transacting business or knowing what he was about, and that the plaintiff knew this. The plaintiff replied that after the defendant became sober, and able to transact business, he ratified and confirmed the contract and now sought to change his mind.

Held: The contract of a man, too drunk to know what he is about, is voidable only, and not void, and therefore capable of ratification by him when he becomes sober. Baxter had ratified the contract and he was bound by it. Judgment must be for the plaintiff.

Note: In *Matthews v. Baxter* it was argued that the contract of a totally drunk and incapable man could not be ratified because it was void and not merely voidable and the case of *Gore v. Gibson* (1843) 13 M&W 623 was cited in support of this submission. Martin B stated "the judges in *Gore v. Gibson* use the word 'void', it is true, but I cannot think they meant absolutely void. They simply meant to say that a drunken man's contract could not be enforced against his will. But it by no means follows that it is incapable of ratificatio".

WARD OF COURT NOT COMPETENT TO CONTRACT
In re R. [1941] Ir. Jur. 67 (H.C.) Maguire P.

R., an inmate in a mental asylum, was declared to be a person of unsound mind and a ward of court. His estate was placed under the care of the court and a committee appointed to look after it.

Shortly afterwards, he was discharged from the asylum and he leased a house in County Limerick for 3 years at a rent of £100 a year. He became a troublesome and violent tenant, and on March 19, 1941, the premises were destroyed by fire.

The landlord applied to have the lease declared void.

Held: The contract, having been entered into by a ward of court, without the concurrence of the committee of his estate, was void *ab initio* and was not binding on the landlord.

CORPORATIONS AND ASSOCIATIONS

The contractual capacity of corporations or associations is governed by the instrument under which they were established. i. e. by the Charter, by the Statute or more commonly by the objects clause of the Memorandum of Association. These set out the objects of the corporation and any contract which is not within the ambit of these objects is **ultra vires** and void. This meant that third parties involved in such a transaction could not seek to enforce it against the corporation. Third parties contracting with a company were deemed to have constructive knowledge of the objects clause. This situation was modified first by section 8 of the Companies Act, 1963 which provided that a third party could enforce an *ultra vires* contract against a company unless he was **actually aware** that it was *ultra vires*. This was further modified by regulation 6 of the European Community Company Law Regulations, SI No. 163 of 1973 which permit a third party, dealing in good faith, to enforce a contract approved of by the board of a company or entered into by a person authorized to contract on its behalf.

ULTRA VIRES

Ashbury Railway Carriage Co. Ltd. v. Riche (1875) L.R. 7 H.L. 653

The objects of the company were, *inter alia*, 'to make and sell, or lend or hire, railway carriages and wagons and railway plant, fittings, machines and rolling stock.' The directors agreed to purchase a concession to build a railway from Antwerp to Tournay, in Belgium and contracted the construction work to Messrs Riche.

Difficulties about payment arose as the work went on. The company repudiated the contract for constructing the line as being *ultra vires* and Messrs Riche brought an action for damages for breach of contract. On appeal to the House of Lords:

Held: The objects of a company incorporated under the Companies Act, 1862 cannot be departed from. The Memorandum is the Charter of the company. Consequently a contract made by the directors of such a company upon a matter not included in the memorandum is *ultra vires* and not binding on the company nor can such a contract be rendered binding by the subsequent ratification of the shareholders at a general meeting.

See also *Securities Trust Ltd. v. Associated Properties Ltd.*, High Court, unreported, 19 November, 1980

CORPORATIONS AND ASSOCIATIONS

Martin v. Irish Industrial Building Society
[1960] Ir. Jur. 42 (Cir. Ct.) Barra O'Briain J.

The plaintiff had money on deposit with the defendant building society, but was not a member of it.

She withdrew money to purchase a house and she asked the society to survey it, with a view to purchase. The society furnished a report upon the condition of the house for a fee, and on the strength of the report she purchased the house.

The wood joists were rotten and she sued the society for damages for negligence in the performance of the contract.

The defence claimed that the society never had any power to enter into such a contract that it was *ultra vires*.

Held: The contract was not one expressly prohibited. It was reasonably incidental to the objects of the society and as the objects clause permitted the doing of acts reasonably incidental to the main object.

This contract was within the powers of the society and was not *ultra vires*. The plaintiff was entitled to succeed. Estoppel cannot be pleaded against a corporation in respect of its *ultra vires* acts.

KNOWLEDGE THAT ACT ULTRA VIRES

In re Cummins, Barton v. Bank of Ireland
[1939] I.R. 60 (H.C.) Johnston J.

The objects clause of M.J. Cummins Ltd., a small firm in Mullingar included 'To acquire as a going concern the business of a hardware and leather merchant. The business was offered to Mr. Cummins for a sum of £3,000. He did not have sufficient cash. A scheme was devised whereby the company exercised its borrowing powers to raise cash to enable him to become a director and owner of most of the capital.

The company got into difficulties and Mr. Barton was appointed liquidator in a voluntary winding up. He contended that there was no valid debt due and owing to the bank because they were aware that the company was exceeding its powers when they advanced the loan.

Held: On the evidence the bank had full knowledge, and had lent money to a company for a purpose *ultra vires* the powers of the company and was not entitled on the liquidation to be admitted as a creditor of the company in respect of the money lent.

ACTUAL NOTICE WITHIN SECTION 8(1) OF THE COMPANIES
ACT, 1963

Northern Bank Finacne Corporation Ltd. v. Quinn and Achates Investment Co. [1979] I.L.R.M. 221 (H.C.) Keane J.

The plaintiff bank lent money to the first defendant on the security of a mortgage of certain property by the second defendant.

The company's solicitor sent a copy of the company's memorandum and articles of association to the bank's solicitor who was unable to recall having read them, although it was his practice to do so. At the time he did not consider that the transaction was *ultra vires* the company.

When the first defendant defaulted on the loan, the bank began proceedings against the second defendant. The company argued that the memorandum did not authorise the execution of a guarantee and mortgage in connection with the debts of a third party. That the transaction was ultra vires.

The bank submitted that the mortgage was not ultra vires, but that if it was, they were protected by the provisions of s.8(1) of the Companies Act, 1963, which had modified the *ultra vires* rule.

Held:

(1) The transaction was *ultra vires*. The objects specified in the memorandum could not be interpreted as applying to the mortgage and guarantee in question since only the bank and the first plaintiff could possibly derive any benefit from the transaction, and so it could not be deemed conducive to the attainment of any of the company's objects.

(2) The evidence indicated that the bank's solicitor read the company's memorandum and came to the conclusion that the guarantee and mortgage was *intra vires*, mistakenly believing that the transaction was authorized. Since the bank had possession of the memorandum and articles there were no further facts which they could have been made aware of. What they failed to do was draw the correct inference from the facts and in these circumstances the bank had 'actual notice' within the meaning of s. 8(1) of the Companies Act, 1963 and therefore could not rely on its provisions.

Note: Actual notice of something is different from knowing. Section 8 requires that a person should be '*actually aware*' that the act was not within the powers of the company. Patrick Ussher, *Company Law in Ireland* (Sweet and Maxwell, 1986, pp. 125-128) has commented: 'It does not seem permissible on these words to hold, as Keane J. did, that once there are no further facts of which an outsider could be put upon notice he is deemed to have drawn the correct inference from them on the principle *ignorantia juris haud neminem excusat*. This is a form of constructive knowledge, and confuses notice with knowledge.' He points out that Keane J. has drawn a distinction between cases where the outsider has read the memorandum and those where he has not. In the former he will be deemed to have understood it, and in the latter he will remain fully protected by section 8. This case has imposed only a duty to comprehend: there still remains no duty to investigate. Mr. Ussher also points out that a solicitor might be under a duty not to investigate the company's capacity to enter into a transaction since his consequent awareness of lack of capacity might put in jeopardy, what would otherwise have been an advantageous transaction.

IMMUNITY

In general courts cannot entertain an action against a foreign sovereign or state. In addition accredited diplomatic representatives are among the class of persons whose liability to be sued is restricted by diplomatic privilege and immunity. Article 31 of the Vienna Convention on Diplomatic Relations, enacted into Irish law by The Diplomatic Relations and Immunities Act, 1967 gives a diplomatic agent immunity from criminal, civil (with three exceptions) and administrative jurisdiction. A list of persons claiming diplomatic privilege is furnished to the Department of Foreign Affairs by the head of mission. Such a list is not conclusive and the head of mission may waive any immunity conferred on himself or any person in the service of his country's government.

FOREIGN STATE NOT IMPLEADED MERELY BECAUSE ITS AGENT IS SUED

Saorstat and Continental Steamship Co. Ltd. v. De Las Morenas
[1945] I.R. 291 (S.C.)

The defendant a Colonel in the Spanish Army, came to Ireland on an official mission to purchase horses for the Spanish Army. The expenses incurred in connection with the mission were to be paid from Spanish government funds.

He entered into a contract to reserve space for 52 horses on the plaintiffs ship from Dublin to Lisbon at £50 per head. The contract contained a clause that if he failed to tender the horses for shipment he would be liable for dead freight. He failed to deliver the horses for shipment and the plaintiff claimed £2,600 damages. The defendant did not claim diplomatic immunity but applied to have the proceedings set aside as being in effect an impleading of the sovereign State of Spain or its Government in the courts of this country.

Held: The proceedings would not be set aside there being no grounds for the suggestion that the Government of Spain was being impleaded, either directly or indirectly.

Per O'Byrne J.:

"It is contended that the true rule of international law, as recognised in the

Courts of this country, is that a foreign Sovereign cannot be impleaded directly or indirectly in these Courts. . . . There is only one way in which a Sovereign or State may be directly impleaded, viz., by his being named as defendant in the proceedings, and it is conceded that this has not been done in this case It is however, argued that there are many ways in which a Sovereign or State may be indirectly impleaded, and it is contended that the Spanish State is impleaded here, because the defendant is an official agent of the State and would be entitled to be indemnified out of State funds in respect of any expenses incurred by him in carrying out his mission, including any damages awarded against, and any costs incurred by him in these proceedings.

It may well be that, by virtue of the terms of his appointment, the appellant is, as between himself and his Government, entitled to be so indemnified; but it seems to me that this is far short of saying that the Government is being impleaded. There is one matter which is quite clear, and it seems wholly inconsistent with the appellant's contention, and that is, that no property belonging to Spain or its Government could be made available to satisfy any judgment which may be obtained against the appellant in this action.

The proceedings are brought against a person who is, *ex concessis*, an agent of the Spanish Government; but counsel have been unable to refer us to a single case in which a Government was held to be impleaded merely because its agent was sued".

APPLICATION OF RESTRICTIVE IMMUNITY

Government of Canada v. The Employment Appeals Tribunal
[1992] I.L.R.M. 325 (S.C.)

B. brought proceedings before the Employment Appeals Tribunal claiming unfair dismissal from his employment as a driver with the Canadian Embassy in Dublin. He was not a member of the Canadian foreign service and enjoyed no diplomatic privileges. The Government of Canada claimed that the EAT had no jurisdiction to entertain the claim on the grounds that it was entitled to sovereign immunity. The Tribunal rejected this submission and awarded B. £10,000 for unfair dismissal and £200 in respect of a claim under the Minimum Notice and Terms of Employment Act, 1973. The Government of Canada appealed.

Held: by the Supreme Court in quoshing the determination of the Tribunal:

(1) The doctrine of sovereign immunity is one of the generally recognised principles of international law which, by Article 29.3 of the Constitution of 1937, Ireland has accepted as its rules of conduct in relations with other States.

(2) These general principles of international law have so developed as to depart radically from the absolute State immunity doctrine to a much more restrictive view of sovereign immunity. (Hederman J. *dubitante*)

(3) The Court must decide whether the relevant act upon which the claim is based should be considered as fairly within an area of activity, trading or commercial or otherwise of a private law character or whether it should be considered as having been done outside that area and within the sphere of governmental or sovereign activity. Dicta of Lord Wilberforce in *I Congreso del Partido* (1983) AC 244 *adopted.*

(4) The employment of an embassy chauffeur was within the sphere of governmental or sovereign activity and accordingly, the doctrine of restrictive immunity applied.

Mr. Justice O'Flaherty (Finlay C.J. and Egan J. concurring) referred to *Saorstat and Continental Steamship Company v. de las Morenas* (*supra*) and to the fact that anything that court had to say about sovereign immunity was *obiter* since the case was decided on the grounds (*inter alia*) that there was no ground for the suggestion that the Government of Spain was being impleded, and therefore, there was no basis for the claim that the proceedings should be set aside. He also referred to the judgment of Hanna J. in *Zarene v. Owners of S.S. 'Ramava'* (1942) I.R. 148 and stated '. . . it would seem to be clear that at that time Hanna J. was recognising a form of restricted sovereign immunity rather than the absolute immunity that appeared to have been established in the leading United States and House of Lords cases. . . . I am prepared to rest my judgment, therefore, on the proposition that Hanna J. was right all those years ago and before the tide came to obliterate, to the point of extinction, the doctrine of sovereign state immunity in most countries of the world. But, as an alternative, and to put the matter beyond doubt, I am prepared to say that our law should be shown to be in alignment with modern legal developments. . . . ' O'Flaherty J. then reviewed the developments and concluded:

(1) I doubt if the doctrine of absolute sovereign immunity was ever conclusively established in our jurisdiction.

(2) Assuming that it was, I believe that it is a doctrine which has expired.

(3) The doctrine flourished at a time when a sovereign State were concerned only with the conduct of of its armed forces, foreign affairs and the operation of its currency. Now with so many States engaged in the business of trade, direct or indirect, the rule of absolute immunity is not appropriate to such conditions.

(4) However, If the activity called in question truly touches the actual business or policy of the foreign government then immunity should still be accorded to such activity.

CHAPTER 16

Privity of Contract

The common law notion that the relationship between the parties to a contract is a private one is illustrated by the fact that at common law a stranger to a contract is not allowed to enforce it.

Murphy v. Bower (1866) and *Clitheroe v. Simpson* are Irish illustrations of the concept of privity which predate Dunlop v. Selfridge (1915) the leading English authority normally cited but came after *Tweedle v. Atkinson* in 1861. The principle enunciated by Viscount Haldane L.C. in the *Dunlop* case was followed and restated in *Scruttons Ltd., v. Midland Silicones Ltd.* [1962] 1 All E.R. 1 thus 'It is a principle of English law that, apart from special considerations of agency, trust, assignment or statute, a person who is not a party to a contract, cannot enforce or rely for protection on its provisions.' *Mackey v. Jones* (see Intention to create legal relations) is also an unfortunate example of the notion of privity.

The rule has been modified, by agency, by assignment, by operation of law (e.g. Bankruptcy) but most importantly by equity and by statute. Equity has used the doctrine of the constructive trust, see *Kelly v. Larkin* and *Drimmie v. Davies* while various statutes like the Road Traffic Acts, the Married Women's Status Act, 1957 and the Companies Act, 1963 have created statutory exceptions. An exception under the Road Traffic Acts is illustrated by the case of *Bellew v. Zurich G.A.*

It should be noted that while *Drimmie v. Davies* and *Kelly v. Larkin* still constitute a line of authority, the use of the constructive 'trust' as method of evading the doctrine of privacy is currently out of favour with the U.K. and Irish courts. Since the finding by the Privy Council in *Vandepitte v. Preferred Accident Insurance Corp.* (1933) A.C. 70 that there cannot be a trust without an intention to create one the English courts have not upheld the existence of a trust in any similar case. In Ireland, Barrington J. in the *Cadbury* case clearly echoed the reasoning of Du Park in *In re Schebsman* [1944] Ch. 83 C.A. where he stated 'unless an intention to create a trust is clearly to be collected from the language used' there cannot be one.

Since the emergence of the remedy of damages for economic loss in tort (See *Junior Books Ltd. v. Veitch Co. Ltd.* [1983] H.L.) the privity rule is only important where an action in contract is the sole possibility.

PRIVITY OF CONTRACT

Murphy v. Bower (1868) I.R. 2 C.L. 506 (Com. Pleas.)

The plaintiffs were the assignees of the estate and effects of three brothers who were bankrupt railway contractors.

The defendant was an engineer of the Finn Valley Railway Company for the planning and supervising the construction of a railway from Stranorlar, Co. Donegal to the Derry and Eniskillen railway, near Strabane which the brothers agreed to construct by July, 1862. The terms of the contract provided that payments during the progress of the works would be made after the (Company Engineer) defendant had certified that the work had been executed to his satisfaction.

The brothers completed work to the value of £6,659 but the defendant refused and neglected to issue a certificate, and the brothers were unable to obtain payment.

Held: The engineer was not a party to the original agreement and his duty to give a certificate arose from the fact that he was employed by the company to superintend their works. When the foundation of the right of action rested upon contract, no one can maintain an action who is not a party to the contract.

Monahan C.J.:

"If collusion did exist between the engineer and the company . . . the proper course, for the plaintiff was to proceed not against the engineer alone, but against both the engineer and the railway company, if he go into a court of Equity, or if he elected to sue at law, he must proceed against the company who contracted with him".

Clitheroe v. Simpson (1879) 4 L.R.Ir. 59 (Com. Pleas.)

In May 1874 the defendant agreed by deed with his father, that he would pay £100 plus interest to his sister Alice, six months after the date of the deed, in consideration of his father assigning premises at Kilmainham, Dublin to him.

The defendant did not make the payment to his sister as agreed. She died in 1876 and her husband, having obtained letters of administration instituted proceedings claiming payment of the £100 plus £21 interest.

Held: The statement of claim did not purport to be founded upon any equitable rights or liabilities between the parties. It was founded on contract upon the deed. But the deed was not one between the defendant and the plaintiff, or Alice Clitheroe. It was a deed between John Simpson (the father) and the defendant. The defendants demurrer was allowed and the plaintiff lost the action — *per* Morris C.J.

See *Tweedle v. Atkinson* (1861) 1 B&S. 393. A demurrer is a plea that the facts, even if true, do not amount to a good cause of action.

Mackey v. Jones [1958] 93 I.L.T.R. 177 (Cir. Ct.) Deale J.

The plaintiffs uncle verbally promised his mother that he would leave his farm to him and the plaintiff laboured on the farm without remuneration for fourteen years in expectation of inheriting it. (See Intention to create legal relations.)

The uncle left the farm to a cousin and when the plaintiff sought specific performance it was:

Held:
(1) that the statement made by the uncle was only a statement of intention.
(2) Even if the words did amount to a promise and if the whole conversation could bind the deceased in a contractual manner, there was a further difficulty in that the plaintiff was not a party to the proposal. He was not consulted about it, and in no way considered the matter; he was simply told by his mother to go to his uncle's farm and he obeyed . . . he did not accept the offer, if offer it was; he obeyed his mother's orders and that was not enough to create the relationship of contracting parties between the deceased and himself.

Note: In *Cadbury (Ireland) Ltd. v. Kerry Co-Op. Ltd.* [1981] unreported, 17th July, 1981 Barrington J. held it to be well established that the parties to a contract can create a trust of contractual rights for the benefit of a third party and that third party can himself enforce those rights, if his trustee does not enforce them for him, by suing a person placed under a duty to him by the contract and by joining his trustee as co-defendant. The principle had been laid down in *Lloyd's v. Harper* (1880-81) 16 Ch. D. 290.

However, he did not believe that the concept of a trust of contractual rights for the benefit of a third party could be extended to cover a case as complex and unusual as the present one in Cadbury (Ireland) Ltd.

STATUTORY EXCEPTION

Bellew v. Zurich General Accident and Liability Insurance Co. Ltd.
[1937] Ir. Jur. Rep. 69 (H.C.) Hanna J.

The plaintiff stated that he suffered personal injuries as a result of being struck and knocked down by a motor car while cycling in the town of Dundalk.

His solicitor was unable to trace the address of the owner of the car because he had left the Dundalk area and was generally believed to have left the State. It was not possible to effect service of proceedings on him, and the plaintiff asked for leave to proceed directly against the vehicle insurers under s. 78(1)(d) of the Road Traffic Act, 1933 in lieu of the owner.

Held: Leave to institute and prosecute proceedings granted.

CONSTRUCTIVE TRUST EXCEPTION

Kelly v. Larkin and Carter (No. 1) (1) [1910] 2 I.R. 550 (K.B.D.)

The plaintiff's brother leased lands at Dunmore to his sister and her heirs. A covenant provided that the sister would pay one half of the annual rent to the plaintiff during his life.

The sister died having by will devised the lands to the defendants who discontinued the payment.

The plaintiff sued for payment of one half of the net rent for two years.

Held: The plaintiff was in the position of a cestui que trust (beneficiary of a trust) under the covenant, entitled to claim payment and therefore entitled to maintain the action. *Gandy v. Gandy* (30 Ch. D. 57) *followed.*

Andrews J.:

> "... we were referred to the well recognized common law rule on the point laid down in *Tweeedle v. Atkinson* (1. B& S. 393) ... in *Gandy v. Gandy* the principle involved in the case is correctly stated in the headnote which is as follows 'to entitle a third person, not named as a party to a contract to sue either of the contracting parties, that third person must possess an actual beneficial right which places him in the position of cestui que trust under the contract' ... we are therefore of opinion that the plaintiff comes within the purview of the equitable exception to which I have referred".

Drimmie v. Davies [1899] 1 I.R. 176 (Ch. D.)

Frederick Davies, a dental surgeon, agreed by deed to admit his son as a partner in a dental practice in Westmoreland Street, Dublin for a five year period from 1st April, 1895.

A valuation of the furniture, instruments etc., which were owned by Frederick in the Westmoreland Street premises was to be carried out and the son given a right to buy a one half share for half the amount of the valuation. In the event of a dissolution of the partnership the son was to have a right to purchase the whole at the valuation price.

A clause in the agreement provided that in the event of the death of the father while the partnership continued, the son would pay each of his sisters a yearly sum of £40 for seven years and each of his brothers a sum of £15 a year for a maximum of seven years. The father Frederick died within the five year period and the son bought the practice.

The deceased father's executor, Drimmie, and the brothers and sisters, brought an action to enforce the payment of the annuities. The defendant pleaded that he had received no consideration — that the brothers and sisters were not parties to the deed.

Held: The plaintiffs were entitled to payment of the annuities.

Note: The common law rule is that in the case of contracts under seal no one can sue who is not a party to the deed. That rule is fully stated in the case of *Tweedle v. Atkinson* (1 B&S.393). But this rule did not prevail in equity, and since the Judicature Act, the rules in equity are to prevail where such a conflict exists. The equitable rule was that the party to whose use or for whose benefit the contract had been entered into, has a remedy in equity against the person with whom it was expressed to be made.

INTENTION TO CREATE TRUST MUST BE PROVED
Vandepitte v. Preferrred Accident Insurance Corp.
[1933] A.C. 70 (Privy Council)

The appellant, Alice Vandepitte obtained a judgment in British Columbia against the daughter of a Mr. R.E. Berry, for damages for personal injuries due to the negligent driving of a car belonging to him, with his permission. The appellant contended that the daughter was insured by the policy because the respondents agreed to indemnify the insured (R.E. Berry) against third party risks and such indemnity should be available to any person operating the car with the permission of the insured.

Section 24 of the British Columbia Insurance Act, 1925 provided: "where a person incurs liability for injury or damage to the person or property of another, and is insured against such liability, and fails to satisfy a judgment awarding damages against him in respect of such liability . . . the person entitled to the damages may recover by action against the insurer. . . ."

Held: Section 24 applies only where the person liable under the judgment is insured by an actual contract in law. The action failed as there was no evidence that R.E. Berry had contracted on behalf of anybody but himself.

Even if the section had a wider application the action failed, because there was no evidence that R.E. Berry intended to create a beneficial interest for his daughter, nor did the fact that the respondents conducted the defence of the action raise an estoppel available to the appellant.

Lord Wright:

> "No doubt at common law no one can sue on a contract except those who are contracting parties from and between whom consideration proceeds. . . . But though the general rule is clear, the present question is whether R.E. Berry can be held in this case to have constituted such a trust. But here again the intention to constitute the trust must be affirmatively proved; the general intention cannot necessarily be inferred from the mere general words of the policy".

Note: See the Equivalent Irish Provision in *Bellew v. Zurich General Accident and Liability Insurance Co. Ltd.* ante.

ASSIGNMENT EXCEPTION
Price v. Easton (1833) 4 B & Ad. 433

William Price owed the plaintiff John Price a sum of £13 for timber supplied to him. In consideration that William Price agreed to work for him, Easton (the defendant) undertook and promised William that he would pay off his debt owed to John Price. William did the work for the defendant who did not pay off the debt owed to John Price. The plaintiff John Price obtained a verdict against Easton but the judgment was stayed because it was alleged that he was a stranger to the consideration.

Held: An act from which the defendant receives a benefit, and from which inconvenience arises to the plaintiff, is a sufficient consideration to support an assumpsit. Here there was an advantage to the defendant, for he had the benefit of the labour of William Price, and was not bound to pay for it until 31st of March. *Starkey v. Myle, Disborne v. Denabie and Wilson v. Coupland*, 5 B&A 228, show, that where there is a privity between the three parties, assumpsit is maintainable without an immediate consideration from the plaintiff to the defendant.

IMPLIED CONTRACT EXCEPTION
Maunsell v. Minister for Education and Breen
[1940] I.R. 213. (H.C.) Gavan Duffy J.

The plaintiff was employed by Canon Breen (the Manager) as an assistant teacher in Ballyduff National School, Co. Kerry, under an agreement prescribed under a code of Rules and Regulations of the Commissioners of National Education for Ireland, issued in May 1914.

As a result of a fall in the average attendance of pupils below the prescribed minimum number of 95 for the two preceding quarters, his salary was withdrawn after 30th September, 1934.

He claimed a declaration that he was a duly appointed assistant teacher and entitled to be paid.

Held: The periodical salary payable under the Rules and Regulations to the plaintiff, as a duly appointed assistant teacher at the Ballyduff National School, had not been lawfully withdrawn. The payment of salary was discontinued without lawful authority.

Gavan Duffy J.:

"Though there is in terms no express contract between Board and teacher, I have no doubt that the Board obtained public money in trust to pay (*inter alia*) teachers' salaries and that the Board by prescribing the agreement which would admit him to its recognized service, committed itself to him to pay him the sum due under its code, upon receiving it. There was at least an implied contract to pay and, had there been none, the Board would have been bound by estoppel. In my opinion, the implied contract would have precluded the Board from sheltering behind an agreement ostensibly made with the manager only, as a defence to a claim by the teacher in respect of salary in the hands of the Board and due to him under the code".

CHAPTER 17

Collateral Warranties and Contracts

The terms 'collateral contract' and 'collateral warranty' are used to denote an additional contract or an additional term which is collateral or alongside an original contract. This is so even where the additional term or contract preceded the main contract rather than took place alongside it.

A collateral contract is a stratagem by which the entry or agreement of a party to enter into one contract, is treated as sufficient consideration for another promise or contract. *Webster v. Higgin* [1948] 2 All E.R. 127. Both contracts are related the collateral one being additional.

The word 'warranty' is used in this context in the old sense to denote a term of a contract and not in the contra distinction sense to a 'condition', as an indicator of the relative importance of a contractual term. "A warranty is an express or implied statement of something which the party undertakes shall be part of a contract; and though part of the contract, yet collateral to the express object of it" — *per* Lord Abinger, C.B. in *Chanter v. Hopkins* (1838) 4 M&W 399. See Chapter 5.

In the building and development sphere of activities warranties are commonplace between an employer and a sub-contractor who has contracted with the main contractor and between the purchaser of the building and an architect who has contracted with the developer. These 'warranties' create contractual liability between persons who acquire an interest in the property and whoever has designed and constructed it.

The 'collateral warranty' devise has gained increased prominence since the loss of a remedy in negligence as a result of the decision in *Sunderland v. Louth County Council* [1990] ILRM 658 (S.C.) where the purchaser of a house contended that the county council was negligent and in breach of its statutory duty under the Planning Act, 1963 in granting permission to build and/or to retain a house on a site liable to flooding. The Supreme Court held that a planning authority in the exercise of its powers under the Local Government (Planning and Development) Act, 1963 owes no duty of care at common law towards the occupiers of buildings erected in its functional area to avoid damage due to defective sites and construction. As to liability in contract see *Siney v. Dublin Corporation* [1980] I.R. 400.

Another significant case in the development of the collateral warranty devise is *Murphy v. Brentwood District Council* [1990] 2 All E.R. 908 where the House of Lords reversed its own earlier decision in *Anns v. Merton London Borough Council* [1978] A.C. 728 and overruled the decision of the Court of Appeal in *Dutton v. Bognor Regis UDC* [1972] 1 Q.B. 373. **The *Donoghue v. Stevenson* principle now, only applies where there is actual physical injury to persons or damage to property other than the property or thing which is the product of the negligence**.

A preliminary statement or assurance given by a party during negotiations for a contract may be construed by the courts as an additional warranty or an additional contract and this devise of collateral warranty or contract may be used effectively by the courts in a number of ways including the following:

- (1) **To circumvent the parol evidence rule** and enforce an oral warranty where the terms of the principal contract have been reduced to writing. In order to do so the court must conclude that contractual intent existed in relation to the accuracy of the statement or assurance. If the statement takes the form of an assurance a court will have a greater inducement to hold that it is collateral. (Printed standard form contract) *Evans v. Marzario* (1976), *Clayton Love v. B & I* (1966). (An employee has the power to give a warranty *Rooney v. Fielden* (1899) and it has become the practice in Travel Brochures to insert a clause that no employee or agent has the authority to vary the written terms by giving a warranty.)

- (2) As **a way of bringing** a term which would otherwise be **a representation within the ambit of an action for breach of contract**. Statements made during negotiations may be representations which are not part of the contract at all. *Schawel v. Reade* [1913], *McGuinness v. Hunter* (1853), *Bank of Ireland v. Smith* [1966], *Carlill v. The Carbolic Smoke Ball Co.*

- (3) As **a way of circumventing an exemption clause**. A parol collateral warranty may not be covered by a written exclusion clause. *Couchman v. Hill* [1947] K.B. 554, *Webster v. Higgin* [1948] 2 All E.R. 127, *Clayton Love v. B & I* [1970] I.L.T.R.

- (4) Where the **main contract was illegal and void**. *Strongman (1945) Ltd. v. Sincock* [1955] 2 Q.B. 525.

- (5) To overcome **difficulty in proving a contractual relationship**. *Clarke v. Dunraven* [1897] A.C. 59.

- (6) To **circumvent a defective memorandum** in a contract for the sale of land. *Godley v. Power*, 95 I.L.T.R. 135.

- (7) To avoid **privity of contract and difficulty in proving consideration**. *Shanklin Pier v. Detel Products*. See page 238.

CONSIDERATION — THE MAKING OF THE MAIN CONTRACT
Webster v. Higgin [1948] 2 All E.R. 127 (C.A.)

The plaintiff a garage owner advertised a second hand car as a 1933 Hillman 10 horse power car. During negotiations the foreman of the garage told the defendant 'If you buy the Hillman 10 we will guarantee that it is in good condition and that you will have no trouble with it.' The defendant signed a hire purchase agreement which contained the following clause; 'The hirer is deemed to have examined (or caused to be examined) the vehicle prior to this agreement and satisfied himself as to its condition, and no warranty, condition, description or representation on the part of the owner as to the state or quality of the vehicle is given or implied . . . any statutory or other warranty, condition, description or representation whether express or implied as to the state, quality, fitness or road-worthiness being hereby expressly excluded.'

Held: The foreman's words were in the context, an offer of a separate collateral guarantee. The wording of the exemption clause in the hire purchase agreement was not sufficiently clear to abrogate that separate collateral agreement constituted by the offer of the guarantee and its acceptance by the signing of the hire purchase agreement by the purchaser.

Lord Greene M. R.:

> "To succeed the plaintiff must satisfy us that these words not merely exclude the giving of any warranty in the contract of sale itself, but that they are sufficient to exclude the operation of a warranty which was given in consideration of the purchaser entering into the contract. . . . If the words had been, not merely 'no warranty is given or implied,' but 'any warranty given collateral to this agreement is hereby extinguished' the position, no doubt, would have been different. If words to that effect had been given, the result would, as I have said, been farcical because the guarantee would then be offered in consideration of the purchaser signing a document by which he agreed that the guarantee should be of no value whatsoever. It seems to me that to produce such a result very clear words are wanted, and I do not find them in what I have read".

PAROL EVIDENCE — ADDITIONAL ORAL TERMS
J. Evans & Son (Portsmouth) Ltd. v. Andrea Merzario
[1976] 1 W.L.R. 1078 (C.A.)

The plaintiffs, importers of Italian machinery, employed the defendant forwarding agent to arrange the carriage of the machines to England. In the autumn of 1967 a manager of the defendant company told the plaintiff's traffic agent that they proposed to use containers for the transportation. The plaintiff's traffic agent said 'I have heard about these containers. I am afraid that our machines may get rusty if they are carried on deck.' The manager of the defendant company gave an oral assurance that in the future machines would be in containers shipped below deck stating 'If we do use containers, they will not be carried on deck.' The parties entered into a contract but nothing was put in writing about the machinery not being carried on deck.

In October 1968 (nearly a year later) machines were shipped on deck and the defendants accepted a bill of lading which contained an exempting clause 'Shipped on deck at shipper's risk' therefore no claim could lie against the shipowners. A container with one of the plaintiffs machines valued at nearly £3,000 fell overboard and was lost. The plaintiff claimed on their insurance and the underwriter sought by right of subrogation to recover what he had paid out in an action against the defendant. The defendant company which denied liability relied on the exemption clauses in their printed conditions of carriage and claimed that there was no contractual promise that the goods would be carried under deck.

Held: The defendants had given the plaintiff an enforceable contractual promise that in future their goods shipped in containers would be shipped under and not on deck. They were in breach of that promise and were liable in damages.

They could not rely on the printed conditions to exempt them from liability for breach of the oral promise that the container would be carried under deck. The printed conditions were repugnant to the oral promise, which therefore, overrode them. *Mendelssohn v. Normand Ltd.* [1970] 1 Q.B. 177 C.A. *applied.*

Per Lord Denning M.R. It was a binding collateral warranty.

Denning L.J.:

"The judge held that there was no contractual promise that these containers should be carried under deck. He thought that, in order to be binding the initial conversation ought to be contemporaneous; and that, here, it was too remote in point of time from the actual transport. . . . Where a person gives a promise or an assurance to another, intending that he should act on it by entering into a contract, and he does act on it by entering into the contract, we hold that it is binding. See *Dick Bentley Productions Ltd. v. Harold Smith (Motors) Ltd.* [1965] 1 WLR 623. This case was concerned with a representation of fact, but it applies also to promises as to the future".

Geoffrey Lane L.J.:

"This was not a collateral contract in the sense of an oral agreement varying the terms of a written contract. It was a new express term which was to be included thereafter in the contracts between the plaintiffs and the defendants".

REPRESENTATION A WARRANTY
Schawel v. Reade [1913] Ir. Rep. 81 (H.L.)

The plaintiff was a buyer of horses for the Austrian Government, which required a stallion for stud purposes. While inspecting horses at the defendant's stables at Carnew, Co. Wexford a horse 'Mallow Man' was shown to him. The defendant said 'You need not look for anything; the horse is perfectly sound. If there was anything the matter with the horse, I would tell you.' The plaintiff terminated his examination and a few days later a price was agreed upon.

When the horse arrived at Vienna, a veterinary inspector disclosed that it had an incurable and hereditary disease of the eyes which rendered it totally unfit for stud purposes.

The plaintiff sought damages alleging false representation and breach of an express warranty. The question left to the jury was 'Did the defendant at the time of the sale represent to the plaintiff in order that the plaintiff might purchase the horse, that the horse was fit for stud purposes and did the plaintiff act upon that representation in the purchase of the horse.

Held: The words used by the defendant constituted an express warranty of the soundness of the horse and that although the word 'warrant' or 'warranty' did not appear in the question submitted to the jury it contained all the elements of a warranty.

Note: The judgment in this case was three weeks before Heilbut Symons but Denning *M.R. in Evans v. Merzario* said that much of what was said in *Heilbut Symons* was entirely out of date in England.

INNOCENT MISREPRESENTATION NOT A WARRANTY — NO RIGHT TO DAMAGES
Heilbut, Symons & Co. v. Buckleton [1913] A.C. 30 (H.L.)

B. telephoned H. and inquired if they were promoting a rubber company. When told that they were, he asked if there was a prospectus and was told that there was none. B. then asked if the company was all right and was told 'We are bringing it out,' to which he replied 'That is good enough for me.' B. contracted to take 5,000 shares at a premium.

Later the shares fell in value and B. brought an action for fraudulent misrepresentation, and alternatively for damages for breach of warranty that the company was a rubber company.

At the trial of the action the jury found that the representation was not fraudulent but that the company could not properly be described as a rubber company and that it had been warranted that it was.

Held: that there was no evidence proper to be submitted to the jury upon the question of warranty.

Lord Moulton (Viscount Haldane L.C. concurring):

> "The question whether an affirmation made by the vendor at the time of sale constitutes a warranty depends on the intention of the parties to be deduced from the whole of the evidence, and the circumstances that the vendor assumes to assert a fact of which the purchaser is ignorant, though valuable as evidence of intention, is not conclusive of the question. . . . He must show a warranty, i.e. a contract collateral to the main contract to take the shares, whereby the defendants in consideration of the plaintiff taking the shares promised that the company itself was a rubber company.
>
> . . . It is evident, both on principle, and on authority, that there may be a contract the consideration for which is the making of some other contract. . . . Such collateral contracts, the sole effect of which is to vary or add to the terms of the principle contract, are therefore viewed with suspicion by the law. They must be proved strictly. Not only the terms of such contracts but the existence of an animus contrahendi on the part of all the parties to them must be clearly shewn....There is in the present case an entire absence of any evidence to support the existence of such a collateral contract.
>
> . . . The whole case for the existence of a collateral contract therefore rests on the mere fact that the statement was made as to the character of the company, and if this is to be treated as evidence sufficient to establish the existence of a collateral contract of the kind alleged the same result must follow with regard to any other statement relating to the subject matter of a contract made by a contracting party prior to its execution. This would negative entirely the firmly established rule that an innocent representation gives no right to damages".

Note: In the *Merzario* case Denning L.J. stated that much of what was said in Heilbut, Symons was entirely out of date. 'We now have the Misrepresentation Act 1967 under which damages can be obtained for innocent misrepresentation of fact. This Act does not apply here because we are concerned with an assurance as to the future.'

WARRANTY AND EXEMPTION CLAUSE
Couchman v. Hill (1947) K.B. 554

The plaintiff, a farmer, purchased a heifer at an auction. The heifer was described in the sale catalogue as 'unserved' and a note in the same document stated:

"The sale will be subject to the auctioneers usual conditions, copies of which will be exhibited. The auctioneers will not be responsible for any error or misstatement in this catalogue, or in the dates of calving of any cattle. The information contained herein is supplied by the vendor and is believed to be correct, but its accuracy is not guaranteed, and all lots must be taken subject to all faults or errors of description (if any), and no compensation will be paid for the same".

The conditions of sale exhibited at the auction stated:

"The lots are sold with all faults, imperfections and errors of description, the auctioneers not being responsible for the correct description, genuiness, or authenticity of, or any fault or defect in any lot, and giving no warranty whatever".

When the heifers was in the sales ring before the auction the plaintiff asked both the defendant and the auctioneer; 'Can you confirm heifers unserved?' and received from both the answer 'Yes.' He thereupon bid for the heifer and it was knocked down to him. Later the heifer was found to be in calf and died as a result of carrying a calf at too young an age.

Held: In the circumstances, the answers of the defendant and the auctioneer to the plaintiff's question amounted to an offer of a warranty overriding the conditions of sale, that such offer was accepted by the plaintiffs bid for the heifer; and that the description amounted to a condition on the breach of which the plaintiff was entitled to treat it as a warranty and recover damages.

Note: The warranty must be part of the contract. In *Hopkins v. Tanqueray* (1854) 15 C.B. 130 the statement alleged to constitute a warranty, was made the previous day to the auctioneer and was held not to be part of the contract, which resulted from the sale at the auction. But see Denning L.J. re remoteness of the oral promise in *Evans v. Merzario ante.*

MAIN CONTRACT ILLEGAL AND VOID

Strongman (1945) Ltd. v. Sincock [1955] 2 Q.B. 525 (C.A.)

The Defendant an Architect employed the Plaintiff, a firm of builders in Cornwall to carry out work on two premises owned by him. At the date in question a licence was required to permit the work to be done on the premises. The architect promised orally that he would obtain all the necessary licences. He did obtain two licences authorising costs of £2,150 and actually paid over £2,900 odd.

The value of the work carried out by the builder amounted to £6,905 but the architect refused to pay the balance claiming that since it was not licensed, it would be illegal.

The plaintiff claimed payment for work done and materials supplied and in the alternative (should the absence of a licence render the contract illegal) they claimed entitlement to a similar sum in damages for breach of warranty.

Held:

(1) Since the contract was illegal the builder could not recover the price under the contract.

(2) That the assurance given by the architect amounted to a warranty or collateral contract that he would obtain the supplementary licences or stop the work if he could not obtain them.

(3) That unless the plaintiff had been morally to blame or culpably negligent they might recover damages in a civil action for breach of warranty (and similarly for fraud), since they had been led to commit the criminal offence which was absolutely prohibited by the promise or representation of the defendant. The plaintiff had not been culpably negligent and were entitled to damages. *Gregory v. Ford* [1951] 1 All E.R. 121 *approved*.

DIFFICULTY OF PROVING A CONTRACTUAL RELATIONSHIP

Clarke v. Dunraven [1897] A.C. 59 (H.L.)

A yacht club advertised a regatta to be held on the Clyde in July 1894 and Clarke entered his yacht the 'Satanita' while the Earl of Dunraven entered his yacht the 'Valkyrie'. Each owner signed a letter to the secretary of the club undertaking that while sailing under the entry he would obey and be bound by the sailing rules of the Yacht Club Association. These rules contained a number of regulations to be observed in races including one, Rule 32 which provided —

> Any yacht disobeying or infringing any of these rules, which shall apply to all yachts whether sailing in the same or different races, shall be disqualified from receiving any prize she would otherwise have won, and her owner shall be liable for all damages arising therefrom.

While sailing under the entry the 'Satanita' broke the 18th Rule and ran into and sank the 'Valkyrie'. The Earl of Dunraven and the master and crew of the sunken vessel claimed damages against Clarke.

Held: affirming the decision in the Court of Appeal, there was a contract between the owners upon which the owner of the damaged yacht could sue the owner of the other.

In the Court of Appeal the plaintiff claimed that by the terms of entry and in consideration that the owner of the Valkyrie would race with the defendant under the rules, the defendant agreed that if the Satanita fouled the Valkyrie in consequence of her neglect of any of the rules, the Satanita would pay all damages, The defendant denied that he had entered into any such agreement as alleged.

Note: The three judges in the Court of Appeal were unanimous that there was a contract between the competitors although they appear to have disagreed as to when it came into existence.

Lord Esher M.R.:

> "Here the defendant; the owner of the Satanita, entered into a relation with the plaintiff Lord Dunraven, **when he sailed his yacht** against Lord Dunraven's yacht".

Lopes L.J.:

> "In my opinion, **directly any owner entered his yacht to sail**, this contract arose".

Rigby L.J.:

> "The contract did not arise with any one, other than the managing committee, at the moment that the yacht owner signed the document, which it was necessary to sign in order to be a competitor. But when the owner of the Satanita on the one hand, and the owner of the Valkyrie on the other, **actually came forward and became competitors** upon those terms, I think it would be idle to say that there was not then, and thereby, a contract between them, provided always that there is something in the rule which points to a bargain between the owners of the yachts. . . . To whom is the owner of that yacht to pay those damages? He cannot pay them to the club, nor do I think the club could recover them. The true and sensible construction is that he must pay the owner of the yacht fouled".

DEFECTIVE MEMORANDUM
Godley v. Power (1961) 95 I.L.T.R. 135 (S.C.)

The defendant called upon auctioneers and subsequently went to see a licensed premises known as the Toby Jug in Cappoquin, Co. Waterford.

His solicitor in his presence telephoned the plaintiffs solicitor to confirm that Power had agreed with Godley to purchase the premises at a price of £2,250 for premises and contents as set out in an inventory. The vendor to be liable for half the auctioneer's fee. The defendants solicitor wrote a letter to the same effect, that same day.

A few days after the date of the oral contract, the defendant attempted to withdraw from the sale on the grounds that certain articles in the inventory had been removed, that audited figures had not been furnished and that the plaintiff had neglected to give possession within five days as agreed.

The plaintiff sued for specific performance or in the alternative for damages for breach of the oral agreement for sale.

Held: There was evidence of a concluded contract. The defendants solicitor's letter was a sufficient memorandum in writing to satisfy the Statute of Frauds.

Kingsmill Moore J.:

"A memorandum under the Statute of Frauds is only required of a contract or sale of lands. If it could be shown clearly that the agreement for the taking over of the stock was part of the consideration for the sale of the lands then the memorandum would be defective, because it did not fully set out the consideration. But it seems more likely that any such agreement was a collateral and subsidiary contract. Its execution, indeed, depended on the completion of the contract for the sale of the lands, for it was only on completion that the stock could be ascertained and its value discovered".

ENFORCEABLE WARRANTY WITH THIRD PARTY —
DIFFICULTY PROVING CONSIDERATION

Shanklin Pier Ltd. v. Detel Products Ltd. [1951] 2 All E.R. 471 (K.B.D.)

The plaintiffs who owned a pier at Shanklin, in the Isle of Wight entered into a contract with Carter(Erectors) Ltd., to have the pier repaired and repainted. A director of the defendant company approached the plaintiff to secure the contract to supply the paint and he assured them that their paint would have a life of at least seven years, would give a surface impervious to dampness and would prevent corrosion and creeping rust.

In reliance on this statement the plaintiff specified that such paint should be used by the contractor Carter (Erectors) Ltd. The contractor bought quantities of the paint from Detel Products Ltd., and used it on the pier as instructed. The paint did not protect the pier from damage, corrosion or rust and contrary to the warranty proved unsuitable within a short time.

Held: On the facts the representation was a warranty; the consideration for the warranty was that the plaintiffs should cause the contractor to enter into a contract with Detel Products Ltd., for the supply of the paint; and therefore, the warranty was enforceable and Detel Products Ltd., were liable in damages for its breach.

There can be an enforceable warranty between parties, other than those to the main contract for the sale of the article in respect of which the warranty is given.

McNair J.:

"Counsel for the defendants submitted that in law a warranty can give rise to no enforceable cause of action except between the same parties to the main contract in relation to which the warranty is given. In principle, this submission seems to me to be unsound. If, as is elementary, the consideration for the warranty in the usual case is the entering into of the main contract in relation to which the warranty is given, I see no reason why there may not be an enforceable warranty between A and B supported by the consideration that B should cause C to enter into a contract with A or that B should do some other act for the benefit of A".

CHAPTER 18

Discharge

A contract may be discharged by Performance, Agreement, Breach, Frustration, or Operation of law.

Performance: The general rule is that if a contract is entire, (*Cutter v. Powell*) a party who does not perform the entire cannot recover. The Irish case of *Coughlan v. Moloney* was such a contract. A building contract with no provision for payment by instalments, Palles L.C.B. held that the legal result was that the money was not to become due until complete performance had taken place.

The exceptions to this rule are:

- (a) severable contracts i.e. contracts in which the parties do not intend that complete performance is a prerequisite for payment. Building contracts generally provide for staged payments to be made as different stages of the building are completed.

- (b) substantial performance; Where a party has substantially performed his obligations under a contract a court may hold that he is entitled to enforce the contract and deduct the cost of remedying the uncompleted part from his claim. In *Hoenig v. Issacs* [1952] the Court of Appeal applied the doctrine and deducted the cost of remedying defects from the contract price.

The extent of the defective performance is crucial because substantial performance is only possible if the defect in the performance tendered amounts to a breach of warranty. It is not possible if the defect amounts to a breach of condition.

Notwithstanding substantial performance a party can be sued for breach of contract by the other party. In *Kincora Builders Ltd. v. Cronin* (High Court, unreported, 1973) Pringle J. suggested that if a party knowingly refuses to carry out his contractual duty this may constitute abandonment of the contract, in which case substantial performance will not apply to enable a party in default to recover.

- (c) if one party prevents the other from fully performing his obligations, the party prevented can sue for payment for the work he has already done on a quantum meruit basis or seek damages for the breach of contract. *Planche v. Colburn* (1831).

- (d) partial performance of a contract may be accepted by the other party, in which case, it is implied that reasonable payment for what has been performed will be forthcoming. In *Sumpter v. Hedges* where the plaintiff abandoned work under a contract to build two houses for £565 and claimed £333 for the work he had done, no promise by the defendant to pay for the part performance could be implied because as owner of the land on which the houses were being built he had no alternative. *Coughlan v. Moloney* illustrates the same principle.

Agreement: Parties who have agreed to enter into a contract may likewise subsequently agree to end it and to release each other from their liabilities under it. The initial agreement may itself contain a term providing for its discharge. Like the original agreement a subsequent one to discharge it must be supported by consideration to be legally effective. If one party has completely performed (promissory estoppel) his contractual obligations the other party must provide some new consideration to support the agreement to discharge. This is known as accord and satisfaction.

Variation: The parties to a contract may agree to vary or delete a term and change the contractual obligations imposed by the original contract. A variation can benefit both parties or be capable of benefiting both parties and in such cases the requirement of consideration is satisfied. If, in fact a variation is made wholly for the benefit of one party or to confer a legal benefit on one party, such variations do not provide their own consideration. A variation which is not supported by consideration is not enforceable. In the case of a sale of goods in excess of £10 (Section 4 SGA 1893) or of matters covered by Section 2 of the Statute of Frauds (Ireland) 1695 a note or memorandum in writing is also necessary.

Waiver: If a contracting party requests and is granted the concession of a degree of indulgence or forbearance in relation to the performance of the contract, he has been given a waiver. The concession or indulgence does not change the contractual obligations of the parties but makes the aspect of performance varied, unenforceable by virtue of the concession. A waiver is generally not supported by consideration and need not be evidenced in writing. A court of equity will apply the doctrine of promissory estoppel to a waiver.

Robert Clarke cites Denning L.J. in *Charles Richards Ltd. v. Oppenheim* [1950] 1. K.B. 616 as describing forbearance, waiver and variation as 'a kind of estoppel.' Cheshire Fifoot and Furmston, *Law of Contract*, 12th ed., London, 1991, commenting on the supposed distinction between variation and waiver claim 'the dichotomy is visionary and one from which reason recoils.'

Breach: 'Breach of contract occurs where that which is complained of is a breach of duty arising out of the obligations undertaken by the contract' *per* Greer L.J. in *Jarvis v. Moy, Davies, Smith Vandervell & Co.* [1936] 1 K.B. 399 at p. 405. A breach may occur because of non-performance, defective performance or a repudiation by one party of his obligations under the contract.

While an innocent party may always claim damages for breach of contract, he cannot elect to treat the contract as discharged unless (a) the other party has repudiated the contract, (b) the term which has been broken is a condition, or (c) the breach which has occurred is a 'fundamental breach.'

(a) *Repudiation:* Repudiation of his obligations by a party may be explicit, *Hochester v. De La Tour* or implicit Frost v. Knight (1870), *House of Spring Gardens Ltd. v. Point Blank Ltd.* [1985]. Repudiation may also be anticipatory, The Michalis Angelos (1970). Anticipatory breach occurs when one party indicates before the time for performance that he does not intend to fulfil his contractual obligation as in *Hochester v. De La Tour* (1853), applied in *Leeson v. North British Oil and Candle Co.* (1874) 8 I.R.C.L. 309 Q.B.D.

(b) *Breach of condition:* A term of a contract may be a condition, by statute, (e.g. The Sale of Goods Act, 1893) by previous judicial decision, or by express or implied intention of the parties in the contract. A breach of condition entitles an innocent party to reject goods, to repudiate the contract and to treat himself as discharged from performance. (See Chapter 6 Terms) Needless to say, an innocent party who elects to treat a breach of condition as a breach of warranty (*ex post facto*) is not entitled to treat the contract as repudiated but only to claim damages.

(c) *Fundamental Breach:* Where a term broken is not a condition, but an intermediate term, the innocent party is not automatically entitled to treat the contract as discharged. An entitlement to treat the contract as discharged only exists where the nature and consequence of the breach is fundamental. A fundamental breach means a breach which takes effect to deprive the innocent contractual party of substantially all of the benefit it was intended he would obtain from the contract. F.R. Davies, *Contract*, 5th. ed. London, 1986, p. 68 states 'In other words, 'fundamental breach' is the equivalent for breach of an intermediate term, of 'breach of condition.' For a definition of the expressions 'fundamental term' and 'fundamental breach' see *Suisse Atlantique* [1967] H.L, Chapter 8 *ante*.

Some breaches are so important in their consequences that they entitle an injured party to treat the contract as discharged. (*Dundalk Shopping Centre v. Roof Spray*, High Court, unreported, 21 March 1979).

Frustration: 'The expression 'the contract is frustrated' so commonly used to-day is misleading: the doctrine relates, not to the contract but to the events or transactions which are the basis of the contract. It is these which make performance of the contract impossible' *per* Kenny J. in the Supreme Court in *Brown v. Mulligan & Ors.* (Supreme Court, unreported, 23 March 1977). His Lordship explored three possible basis for the foundation of the doctrine but did not adopt any of them. The doctrine did not apply because the parties had contemplated the circumstances which had arisen. The fact that a contract became more onerous than contemplated did not amount to frustration in *Davis Contractors Ltd. v. Fareham U.D.C.*

Some seven principles to be applied when considering a claim of frustration were listed by McWilliam J. in *McGuill v. Aer Lingus Teo and United Airlines Incorporated.*

In the war time case of *Hermann v. Owners of SS Vicia* [1942] I.R. 305 Hanna J. adopted the view of Lord Wright in *Constantine v. Imperial Smelter Corporation Ltd.* [1942] A.C. 154, that 'self-induced' frustration provides no defence and declined to hold that it would be just and reasonable under the circumstances that the contracts had been frustrated.

The effects of frustration according to Viscount Simon L.C. in the Constantine case are that '. . . when frustration in the legal sense occurs, it does not merely provide one party with a defence in an action brought by the other. It kills the contract itself and discharges both parties automatically. The rule established in the *Fibrosa* case [1967] 1 Q.B. 534 is that frustration does not permit recovery of a payment if some benefit, however slight, has been received in return. A payee may suffer injustice where the payor has received no benefit and recovers his payment leaving the payee at the loss of expenses incurred in partial performance. There is no Irish equivalent to the English Law Reform (Frustrated Contracts) Act 1943 which permits the recovery of money paid even though there has been no failure of consideration and permits payment to be obtained for benefit conferred on the other party.

The unusual spectacle of a contract being discharged because legislation made further performance impossible is illustrated by *O'Crowley v. Minister For Finance and Minister for Justice.*

DISCHARGE BY PERFORMANCE

ENTIRE CONTRACT
Creagh v. Sheedy [1955-56] Ir. Jur. Rep. 85 (Cir. Ct.) O'Briain J.

The plaintiff made an oral contract to work for the defendant for a period of a year. During the year odd sums of money were paid to him on demand. Before the year expired the plaintiff left the employment of the defendant and claimed payment of £45 due for wages or alternatively due as a *quantum meruit.*

Held: Since the plaintiff had left the employment of his own volition he was not entitled to succeed on either claim, the Agricultural Wages Act, 1936 had not altered the common law position.

O Briain J.:

> "In the 10th edition of *Mayne on Damages* at p. 247 there is a statement which is in point: 'When the contract is to serve for a specified time for a specified sum, the plaintiff cannot recover that sum upon the contract unless he has performed it: nor upon a *quantum meruit*, unless the non-performance arises from the defendant's act; therefore where a seaman was hired for a certain sum, 'provided he proceeds, continues, and does his duty in the ship for the voyage' and he died before its arrival, it was held that no wages could be claimed either on the contract, or upon a quantum meruit: *Cutter v. Powell.*' The contract in this case was one of service for a year . . . the workman was to be paid at the end of the year".

COMPLETE PERFORMANCE
Coughlan v. Moloney [1905] 39 I.L.T.R. 153 (C.A.)

The plaintiff contracted to build a house for the defendant at Martinstown, Co. Limerick for £200. The work was to be completed before Christmas 1902. The work was not completed in time. In November 1903, the defendant took possession of the un-finished house and prevented the plaintiff having further access. The plaintiff sued.

Held: There was no provision for payment by instalments in the contract therefore the legal result was that the money was not to become due until complete performance.

It was claimed that the plaintiff was entitled to recover on a quantum meruit based upon the fact that possession was taken by the defendant of the work and that he had retained the benefit of it. Palles L.C.J. decided:

> "The decision in *Munro v. Butt* is that this principle does not apply to a house on a man's land, because there is no possibility of rejecting the benefit of what has been done, unless he destroys the house built on it".

Note: In relation to the sale of goods s.30(1) of the Sale of Goods Act, 1893 provides that where the seller delivers a quantity of goods either larger or less than he contracted to sell, the buyer may reject them. He can, of course, if he wishes, accept and pay at the contract rate. Section 31 provides that unless otherwise agreed, the buyer of goods is not bound to accept delivery of them by instalments.

SUBSTANTIAL PERFORMANCE

Kincora Builders v. Cronin
High Court, Unreported, 5 March 1979 Pringle J.

The plaintiff sued the defendant for a balance of £6,000 due on foot of a contract to build a house at Sutton, Co. Dublin. A clause in the specification provided that internal walls should be insulated with insulation board and ceilings insulated between the joists. This work had not been done but the builders claimed that the defendant had accepted £350 compensation for this deviation. They also claimed that as the contract had been substantially completed they were entitled to payment, subject to deductions for defective work (if any) and to interest on the unpaid balance of the purchase price.

Held: The payment of £350 was only in settlement of the omission to insulate the walls, it did not include the failure to insulate the ceiling. The plaintiff refused to insulate the ceiling i.e. to carry out part of their contract and this amounted to an abandonment of the contract and disentitled them to payment of the balance of the price until they did this work.

They were therefore not entitled to interest on the balance. Judgment for the plaintiff in the sum of £6,000 and judgment for the defendant in his counterclaim for £863. £25 of the counterclaim was to insulate the ceilings.

In the course of his judgment Pringle J. referred to Lord Justice Sach's judgment in *Bolton v. Mahadava* [1972] 1 WLR 1009 and his citation of *Cheshire and Fifoot's Law of Contract* 7th ed. (1969) statement that

> ". . . the present rule is that, so long as there is a substantial performance, the contractor is entitled to the stipulated priced, subject only to a cross-action or counterclaim for the omissions or defects in execution. The converse however is equally correct, if there is not a substantial compliance the contractor cannot recover".

Note: The omission to do every item perfectly is not an abandonment of the contract. ". . . to say that a builder cannot recover from a building owner merely because some item of the work has been done negligently, or ineffectively, or improperly, is a proposition which I should not listen to, unless compelled by a decision of the House of Lords." — Lord Cozens Hardy, M.R. in *H. Dakin & Co. v. Lee* [1916] 1 KB. 566.

In *Coughlan v. Moloney* the builder could be said to have abandoned the contract whereas the existence of defects may be indicative of negligence in the performance of the work.

DISCHARGE BY BREACH

EXPLICITY REPUDIATION
Hochester v De Le Tour (1853) 2 E& B. 678.

On the 12th April, 1852 the plaintiff at the request of the defendant agreed to enter his employment in the capacity of a courier, from the 1st June, 1852, to serve the defendant in that capacity and to travel with him on the continent for a period of three months, at a wage of £10 per month.

On the 11th May, 1852, the defendant wrote to the plaintiff that he had changed his mind and would not want his services. He refused to pay him any compensation and the plaintiff commenced an action on the 22nd May.

Held: that a party to an executory agreement may, before the time for executing it, break the agreement either by disabling himself from fulfilling it, or by renouncing the contract; and that an action will lie for such a breach before the time for the fulfilment of the agreement.

There was on the part of the defendant, not merely an intention to break the contract, . . . but a renunciation communicated to the plaintiff, on which the plaintiff was entitled to judgment.

Note: This case illustrates explicit repudiation because it was clearly communicated to the offeror and anticipatory breach because it took place before the time for performance. Approved in *Frost v. Knight post.*

ANTICIPATORY BREACH
Frost v. Knight (1872) L.R. 7 Ex 111.

The defendant promised to marry the plaintiff so soon as his father should die. During the father's lifetime he announced his intention of not fulfilling his promise when his father died and he broke off the engagement. The plaintiff without waiting for the defendant's father to die brought an action for breach of promise of marriage.

Held: that the principle of *Hochester v. De La Tour* was applicable. A breach of contract had been committed on which the plaintiff could sue.

Cockburn C.J.:

> "The law with reference to a contract to be performed at a future time, where the party bound to performance announces prior to the time his intention not to perform it, as established by the case of *Hochester v. De La Tour* and the *Danube and Black Sea Co. v. Xenos* (134 C.B. (n.s.) 825) on the one hand, and *Avery v. Bowden* (5 E&B 714), *Reid v. Hoskins* (6

E&B 953) and *Barwick v. Buha* (2 C.B. (n.s.) 563) on the other, may be thus stated. **The promisee, if he pleases, may treat the notice of intention (by the promisor not to perform his contractual obligation) as inoperative, and await the time when the contract is to be executed, and then hold the other party responsible for all the consequences of non-performance; but in that case he keeps the contract alive for the benefit of the other party as well as his own; he remains subject to all his own obligations and liabilities under it, and enables the other party not only to complete the contract if so advised, notwithstanding his previous repudiation of it, but also to take advantage of any supervening circumstances which would justify him in declining to complete it.**

The considerations on which the decision in *Hochester v. De La Tour* is founded are that the announcement of the contracting party of his intention not to fulfil the contract amounts to a breach, and that it is for the common benefit of both parties that the contract shall be taken to be broken as to all its incidents, including non-performance to appointed time; as by an action being brought at once, and the damages consequent on non-performance being assessed at the earliest moment, many of the injurious effects of such non-performance may possibly be averted or mitigated . . . the eventual non-performance may therefore, by anticipation, be treated as a cause of action, and damages be assessed and recovered in respect of it, though the time for performance may yet be remote".

ANTICIPATORY BREACH
Leeson v. North British Oil & Gas Co. (1874) I.R. 8 C.L. 309 (Q.B.)

Leeson contracted with the company to buy 300 casks of paraffin oil, to be supplied as required. The company failed to deliver one order and their Dublin agent stated that they did not have the oil. On the basis of this statement Leeson refused orders from his customers and suffered loss of profits. He sued for breach of contract.

Held: Damages of £6 were awarded for non delivery of oil ordered and damages of £50 for oil not yet ordered. See *Hochester v. De La Tour* (1853) 2 E.& B. 678.

REPUDIATION AND BREACH OF AN INTERMEDIATE TERM
Hong Kong Fir Shipping Co. Ltd. v. Kawasaki Kisen Kaisha Ltd.
[1962] 2. Q.B. 26 (C.A.)

By a time charter dated the 26th December, 1956 the plaintiffs chartered the m.v. Hongkong Fir to the defendants for a period of 24 calendar months '. . . she being in every way fitted for ordinary cargo service . . . the owners to maintain her in a thoroughly efficient state in hull and machinery during service. . . .' Another clause provided that in the event of dry-docking, breakdown of machinery, damage to hull, or other accident either hindering or preventing the working of the vessel for more than 24 consecutive hours, no hire was to be paid in respect of the time lost.

The vessel was delivered at Liverpool and sailed for Newport Virginia to pick up a cargo of coal and carry it to Osaka, Japan. At Newport she was off hire for nearly 2 days and between Liverpool and Osaka was at sea for about eight and a half weeks, and off hire for about five weeks. While at Osaka a further period of about 15 weeks was required to make her seaworthy.

When she sailed from Liverpool the chief engineer was inefficient and addicted to drink, the engine room was undermanned and chiefly for that reason the breakdowns occurred.

In June, 1957 the charterers wrote repudiating the charter and claiming damages for breach of contract. On September 11 the charterers wrote again repudiating the charter and the owners formally accepted the repudiation on September 13. On November 8 the owners issued a writ claiming damages for wrongful repudiation of the charter and the charterers claimed breach of the clauses in the contract, that the charter was frustrated by the breakdowns and repairs, and counterclaimed for damages.

Held:

(1) That although the shipowners were in breach of clause 1 of the charter, the vessel being unseaworthy on delivery. Sea-worthiness was not a condition of the charter a breach of which entitled the charterer at once to repudiate.

Per Lord Diplock:

> "**The obligation of sea-worthiness was** neither a condition or a warranty but **one of the large class of contractual undertakings one breach of which might have the effect ascribed to a breach of 'condition'** under the Sale of Goods Act 1893, **and a different breach of which might have only the same effect as that ascribed to a breach of 'warranty'**."

(2) That the delays caused by the breakdowns and repairs were not so great as to frustrate the commercial purpose of the charter.

Per Upjohn L.J.:

> "It is open to the parties to a contract to make a particular stipulation a condition, but where, upon the true construction of the contract they have not done so, it would be unsound and misleading to conclude that, being a warranty, damages is necessarily a sufficient remedy. **The remedies**

**open to an innocent party for breach of a stipulation which is not a
condition strictly so called, depend entirely upon the nature of the
breach and its foreseeable consequences**. As the stipulation as to sea-
worthiness is not a condition in the strict sense, the question is whether
the unsea-worthiness found by the judge went so much to the root of the
contract that the charterers were entitled then and there to treat the
charterparty as at an end. It could not be so treated and, accordingly, on
that part of the case the charterer failed".

DISCHARGE BY FRUSTRATION

CONTRACT FRUSTRATED BY DESTRUCTION OF ESSENTIAL OBJECT

Kearney v. Saorstat and Continental Shipping Co. Ltd.
[1943] Ir. Jur. Rep. 8 (Cir. Ct.) Davitt J.

The Applicant sought workmen's compensation on behalf of the dependents of
his son Edward, who had been a seaman on board the Respondent's merchant
ship the 'City of Waterford' which sailed under the Irish flag. The ship sank as
a result of a collision and Edward Kearney and others were rescued by another
merchant ship the 'Walmer Castle' which sailed under the British flag. Two
days later the 'Walmer Castle' was bombed and sunk in the course of the war
and Edward Kearney was killed.

Held: The employment of Edward Kearney terminated with the sinking of the
'City of Waterford' on which he was employed and accordingly his death did
not arise 'out of, and in the course of his employment' with the Respondents.

Davitt J.:

"When two parties contract on the basis that a certain object will be in
existence, and that object comes to an end, then the contract must come
to an end".

CONTRACT NOT DISCHARGED BY FRUSTRATION

Herman and Ors. v. The Owners and Masters of S.S. Vicia
[1942] I.R. 305 (H.C.) Hanna J.

During World War 2 the plaintiffs contracted to serve on the 'Vicia' on a voyage
to a port (*inter alia*) in England and back to the U.S.A. At that time it was
necessary to obtain a British ship's warrant to prevent the ship being seized by
the British. The ship had a warrant but it had expired when the plaintiffs signed
on, and it had never been renewed.

While the ship was docked in Dublin in 1941, the Master paid off the crew claiming that their contracts were discharged by frustration and impossibility of performance because they were unable to obtain a new warrant.

Held: The voyage was not frustrated by impossibility of performance, but partly by the negligence of the Master in not renewing the warrant and partly by the desire of the agents to save expense. The plaintiffs were entitled to the expenses of repatriation to a port in the U.S.A. or other suitable port.

The evidence was not sufficient to justify a finding that the seamen's contracts were frustrated. There was no ground for concluding that there was an impossibility of performance. The ship was detained in Dublin and the seamen dismissed by the orders of the agent's not on account of impossibility of performance or frustration, but to save expense.

CONTRACT NOT FRUSTRATED WHERE EVENT CONTEMPLATED

Brown v. Mulligan and Others (S.C.) Unreported, 23 November 1977.

The plaintiff was appointed Physician to the Shiel Hospital Ballyshannon, under an agreement which provided that the appointment was terminable by the Governors if (inter alia) there were insufficient funds to enable the hospital to continue or it should have to close down for any other reason.

In 1974 a High Court Order, made on the application of the trustees, stated that it appeared that funds were insufficient and the Governors and Trustees granted a lease of the hospital to the North Western Health Board. The plaintiff was notified that his employment was terminated and offered three months salary in lieu of notice. He refused to accept this and instituted proceedings.

The defendants argued that the contract had been frustrated by the Court and that nothing was payable to the plaintiff.

Held: The doctrine of frustration did not apply. The event which terminated the contract was within the contemplation of the parties viz. insufficient funds to allow it to continue. There were insufficient funds and circumstances had arisen which justified the Governors action in terminating the plaintiffs contract.

FRUSTRATION — SUBJECT MATTER CEASING TO EXIST

Cummings v. Stewart (No. 2) [1913] 1 I.R. 95 (Ch.D.)

The plaintiff instituted proceedings against the defendant for the payment of royalties allegedly due in respect of a licence granted by the plaintiff to exploit and use a certain system of reinforced concrete construction, for which the plaintiff had taken out patents in the U.K., France, and Austria.

The defendant did not make a success of the Cummings System. It was a failure in the U.K, where he tried to work it. He had agreed to pay a royalty of 2.5% on the total amount include in every contract, the royalty not to be less than 5,000 dollars in any year, except during the first three years when 1,000 dollars was to be paid, 1,500 dollars was payable in year 2 and 2,5000 dollars in year three.

On the work done by the defendant in the first year the royalty payable at 2.5% was $31 odd, but he was liable under the agreement to the minimum of 1,000 dollars. The defendant submitted to a decree for the royalties for year one and paid a sum of 902 which discharged his liability for that year.

Renewal fees were payable to the patent authorities in the U.K. France and Austria by the plaintiff in order to maintain the patents, but without informing the defendant he stopped paying the renewal fees from July, 1909.

When sued for payment under the licensing agreement the defendant claimed that the patents had lapsed in consequence of the plaintiffs failure to pay the fees and that this lapse of patents relieved him from all further liability to pay royalties.

Held: (*inter alia*) That, owing to the lapse of the foreign patents, a substantial part of the subject-matter of the agreement was destroyed, and the agreement in a substantial part became impossible of performance and ceased to be binding; and that as the royalty was a fixed sum, the consideration was indivisible, and the failure of part was equivalent to failure of the entire. See. *Taylor v. Caldwell* (1863) 3 B. & S. 826.

CONTRACT NOT FRUSTRATED BY BECOMING MORE ONEROUS

Davis Contractors Ltd. v. Fareham U.D.C. [1956] A.C. 696 (H.L.) (E.)

The plaintiff company entered into a contract with the defendant U.D.C., to build 78 houses at Fareham at a price of £92,425.00 within a period of eight months. The plaintiff's tender was accompanied by a letter which contained a clause 'Our tender is subject to adequate supplies of material and labour being available as and when required to carry out the work within the time specified.'For various reasons, the chief of them being the lack of skilled labour, the work took, not eight but 22 months. The plaintiffs were paid the contract price but they contended that owing to the long delay the contract price had ceased to be applicable, that the original contract was frustrated, and that they were entitled to payment on a *quantum meruit* basis of a sum in excess of the contract price. Additional cost and expense of £17,651 was claimed for wastage due to unbalanced labour force, stoppage due to shortage of materials, a long period of frost, and excessive muddy conditions on the site.

Held:

(1) The letter was not incorporated in the contract.

(2) That the contract had not been frustrated. The fact that without the fault of either party there had been an unexpected turn of events, which rendered the contract more onerous than had been contemplated, was not a ground for releasing the contractor of the obligation which they had undertaken and allowing them to recover on the basis of a *quantum meruit.*

IMPOSSIBILITY OF PERFORMACE BY ACT OF GOD

The Earl of Leitrim v. Stewart (1870) I.R. 5 C.L. 27 (Q.B.)

The plaintiff sued a man named Maddison for trespass and wrongs committed by him against his property and obtained judgment against Maddison for two shillings and six pence damages and costs.

Maddison served notice of appeal and the Earl applied for security for costs. Maddison entered into a recognizance fixed at £1,000 and Stewart, the defendant, went surety for him in the recognizance. Maddison died while the appeal was pending and the Earl sought to make the defendant pay the £1,000 security for costs to cover his legal expenses.

Held: The death of the appellant was an answer to the action on the recognizance.

LIABILITY OF PARTY IN DEFAULT

M'Connell v. Kilgallen (1878) 2 L.R. Ir. 119 (Q.B.D.)

The defendant, a builder, contracted with the plaintiff, a building surveyor, that if the plaintiff would supply the quantities for building a Catholic Church at Castlebar, the defendant would, if accepted as contractor, pay the plaintiff out of the first instalment.

The plaintiff furnished the quantities, but the defendant subsequently abandoned the building contract.

Held:

(1) That it was implied that the defendant should duly proceed with the building contract.

(2) That performance of his contract with the plaintiff having been rendered impossible by his own act, the defendant was bound to pay the plaintiff for the quantities furnished.

FRUSTRATION — PRINCIPLES TO BE APPLIED

McGuill v. Aer Lingus Teo and United Airlines
High Court, Unreported, 3 October 1983, McWilliam J.

The plaintiff a tour promoter, sued for damages for breach of a contract to carry 234 vintners in the U.S.A. A strike at United Airlines commenced on 31 March, 1979 and United managers were directed to notify all airlines not to issue tickets until notified of resumption of service. Despite the fact that they became aware of the strike within a couple of days, Aer Lingus issued tickets to the group on 6th April. United argued that the contract was frustrated by the outbreak of the strike.

Held: Aer Lingus was acting as an agent for United and as agent for a disclosed principal could not be held liable in contract.

McWilliam J. concluded that the following principles apply where frustration is claimed.

1. A party may bind himself by an absolute contract to perform something which subsequently becomes impossible.

2. Frustration occurs when, without default of either party, a contractual obligation has become incapable of being performed.

3. The circumstances alleged to occasion frustration should be strictly scrutinized and the doctrine is not to be lightly applied.

4. Where the circumstances alleged to cause the frustration have arisen from the act or default of one of the parties, that party cannot rely on the doctrine.

5. All the circumstances of the contract should be strictly scrutinised.

6. The event must be an unexpected event.

7. If one party anticipated or should have anticipated the possibility of the event which is alleged to cause the frustration and did not incorporate a clause in the contract to deal with it, he should not be permitted to rely on the happening of the event as causing frustration.

United being anxious to obtain the business, took the risk of entering into the contract without including a provision to safeguard its position in the event of a strike taking place.

Held: Under these circumstances United was not entitled to succeed in its defence that the contract was frustrated.

DISCHARGED BY LEGISLATION

O'Crowley v. Minister for Finance and Minister for Justice
(1934) 68. I.L.T.R. 174 (H.C.) Johnston J.

The plaintiff was appointed a Judge of the Supreme Court in 1920 by Dáil Éireann. The authority of the court was deemed to have been withdrawn by the

Dáil Éireann Courts (Winding Up) Act, 1923 and the court became extinct on July 25, 1922. The plaintiff later accepted a yearly pension granted under the Dáil Éireann Supreme Court (Pensions) Act, 1925.

He now claimed that his appointment was for life, that his office had not been abolished and that he was entitled to his salary and arrears thereof.

Held: The plaintiffs appointment as a judge was terminated by the 1923 Act and, further, that he was estopped by his acceptance of a pension under the 1925 Act. His claim was unsustainable by virtue of the extinction of the office by statute law.

Johnston J. cited and adopted the judgment of the Privy Council in the Canadian case of *Reilly v. The King* [1934] A.C. 176 'But the present case appears to their Lordships to be determined by the elementary proposition that if further performance of a contract becomes impossible by legislation having that effect, the contract is discharged.'

CHAPTER 19

Remedies for breach of Contract

DAMAGES

In tort damages are awarded to compensate the injured party for the loss suffered and to restore him (in so far as money can) to his position prior to the commission of the tort against him. Damages in contract, are awarded to put the injured party in the position he would have been in, had the contract not been broken. Punishing the contract breaker is not the objective. There is an equitable rule that a clause in a contract cannot validly impose an obligation or liability in excess of an amount which would compensate for the loss suffered by the breach. It is therefore important to distinguish whether a provision in a contract is a penalty or a genuine pre-estimate of loss. A penalty will fail under the equitable rule whereas a court will uphold a genuine pre-estimate of loss or damage.

A plaintiff in an action for breach of contract may claim damages (a) for his loss of profit or (b) for his wasted expenditure.

(a) Damages for loss of profit are awarded to put the injured party in the position he would have been in, had the contract not been broken. i.e. the loss suffered by the injured party is the quantum. The injured party receives damages which cover his expectations from the contract. In this type of claim the plaintiff must prove the value of his expectations.

(b) Damages for wasted expenditure or reliance loss damages, provide compensation for loss suffered or expenses incurred in reliance on the contract and may cover pre-contractual or post contractual expenditure. If a plaintiff cannot prove the value of his expectations (See *Anglia T.V. v. Reed* or where it was not possible to prove the profit which would have resulted) reliance loss may be claimed.

Restitution damages deprive the defendant of a benefit (see *Hickey v. Roches Stores Ltd.*) and is thus a better choice of remedy for a plaintiff who has made a bad bargain.

In the *Roches Stores* case Finlay P. (as he then was) held that where a contracting party intends by his wrongdoing to achieve a gain or profit he could not otherwise obtain acts mala fide, the court should, in assessing damages look not only at the loss to the injured party but also to the unjust profit of the wrongdoer, and damages should be assessed so as to deprive the wrongdoer of that profit. (This judgment has been criticized by Robert Clark 29 NILQ 128-130)

Some twenty years earlier Dixon J. who concluded that the defendant in *Hawkins v. Rogers* [1951] I.R. 48 was actuated by ill will toward the plaintiff encountered difficulty in assessing damages because it was a matter of probability, consisting of the loss of prize money in three races in which 'Lonely Maid' had been entered to run, and the future loss of its enhanced value if the animal had done well. Such loss, he declared, clearly depended on a contingency, the second branch of it on a double contingency, but this only made the assessment of damages more difficult.

In *Lee and Donoghue v. Rowan*, Costello J. found that the plaintiffs could not have contemplated that all the defendant's sowing and cultivation costs would be lost when the breach of contract to build a store to dry vegetables resulted in the loss of 20 acres of onions and 46 acres of seed potatoes, and he dismissed the plaintiff's claim, having applied the two branches of the rule in *Hadley v. Baxendale* (9 Exch. 354).

The plaintiff in *Johnson v. Longleath Properties (Dublin) Ltd.*, claimed damages for inconvenience and loss of enjoyment and McMahon J. referring to *Jarvis v. Swan Tours Ltd.* [1973] 1 All E.R. 71 accepted in principle, that damages for inconvenience or loss of enjoyment may be awarded when these are within the presumed contemplation of the parties. This was normally the case in contracts to provide entertainment or enjoyment but he saw no reason why it should not also be the case in other types of contract where the parties can foresee that enjoyment or convenience was likely to be an important benefit to be obtained by one party from the due performance of the contract. The present contract fell within that class and he held for the plaintiff.

The previous year Lawson J. in *Cox v. Phillips Industries Ltd.* [1975] I.R.L.R. 344 considered that damages for distress, vexation and frustration, including consequent ill-health, could be recovered for breach of a contract of employment if the parties had contemplated that such distress would be caused by the breach. (See note on damages below).

The Court of Appeal in *Bliss v. S.E. Thames Regional Health Authority* [1985] ruled out the approach in *Cox v. Phillips* until the House of Lords has reconsidered its decision in *Addis v. Gramophone Co. Ltd.* [1909] A.C. 488, and held that general damages should not be awarded for frustration and mental distress.

O'Higgins C.J. in *Siney v. Dublin Corporation* [1980] I.R. 401 five years before the *Bliss* case distinguished (physical aspects) viz. physical inconvenience and discomfort from (mental aspects) annoyance, loss of temper, vexation or disappointment and held that the trial judge had been correct in including damages for physical inconvenience and discomfort in his award.

Siney v. Dublin Corporation is compatible with both Addis and the more recent *Bliss* cases and to-date has not been the Pandora's Box that some commentators had expected.

If a plaintiff claims for his wasted expenditure, damages may be awarded to restore him to the position he would have been in if the contract had not been made. This course is usually adopted by a plaintiff who has not suffered any loss of profit or who cannot prove what his loss of profit would have been.

In *Anglia Television Ltd. v. Reed* [1971] 3 All E.R. the Court of Appeal held that a claim for wasted expenditure was not limited to the expenditure incurred after the contract had been concluded but could encompass expenditure incurred before the contract was made, provided such expenditure would reasonably be in the contemplation of the parties as likely to be wasted if the contract was broken. *Anglia Television Ltd. v. Reed* has been criticised by academic writers on the grounds (*inter alia*) that the award of pre-contractual expenditure is not compatible with protection of a reliance interest, because such expenditure would have been incurred whether the defendant contracted or not. Even if it were reasonable foreseeable the loss was not caused by the breach.

Professor D. W. McLauchlan (Damages for-Pre Contractual Expenditure, New Zealand University Law Review, December, 1985, Vol. 11, No. 4, p. 354.) argues that pre-contractual expenditure only becomes a loss when the contract does not materialize and the expenditure cannot be salvaged, i.e. after the breach has occurred.

DAMAGES — THE RULE
Hadley v. Baxendale (1854) 9 Exch. Rep. 341

The plaintiffs who owned a flour mill in Gloucester were forced to cease production when the crank shaft of a steam engine broke.

In order that a replacement shaft be made to measure, with the broken shaft as a pattern, the broken shaft was given to the defendants a firm of carriers to deliver it to a firm of engineers in Greenwich. They claimed that parcels received before a certain time were delivered within two days. They were told that the mill was stopped and that the shaft must be delivered immediately but despite this they took seven days to deliver it, with the result that the mill was closed down for five extra days.

The plaintiff sued for the loss of profits caused by the extra five days delay. The defendant replied that such damages were too remote to warrant payment of damages.

Held: The defendants were not liable. The loss of profits could not reasonably be considered as a consequence of the breach of contract or could have been fairly and reasonably contemplated by both parties when they made the contract. (The plaintiff could have had another shaft in their possession being installed at the time.). Such loss would neither have flowed naturally from the breach of this contract in the great multitude of such cases occurring under ordinary circumstances, nor were the special circumstances, which perhaps would have made it a reasonable and natural consequence of such breach of contract; communicated to or known by the defendants.

Anderton B.:

> "Now we think the proper rule in such a case as the present is this: Where two parties have made a contract which one of them has broken, the damages which the other party ought to receive in respect of such breach of contract should be either **such as may fairly and reasonably be considered arising naturally, i.e., according to the usual course of things, from such breach of contract itself, or such as may reasonably be supposed to have been in the contemplation of both parties, at the time they made the contract, as the probable result of the breach of it**".

Note: Sir Frederick Pollock states that it was distinctly intended to lay down a rule for future guidance in the assessment of damages and has always been so understood. Doubts about the second part of the rule were resolved by the Court of Appeal decision in *Agius v. G.W. Colliery Co.* [1899] 1 Q.B. 413 when it adopted *Hadley v. Baxendale* unreservedly and affirmed liability under the second branch of the rule.

MEASURE OF DAMAGES

Parker v. Dickie, Common Pleas (1879) 4 L.R. Ir. 244 (C.P. Div.)

A solicitor, employed to raise a sum of money upon a mortgage for a client who was emigrating to New Zealand, kept portion of the loan for a year without paying it to the client.

The client sought damages. A sum of money was paid into court, which was sufficient (with the payments made before the action) to cover the amount and in addition interest at 10 per cent, per annum. This was the rate of interest during the time the solicitor had the money. The client did not accept the amount lodged as satisfaction but continued the action for damages in excess of that amount.

Held: The client was not entitled to damages in excess of the sum lodged in court. No special damage was alleged or proved.

Lawson J.:

> "It is quite settled that where the action is brought to recover a money demand, the proper measure of damages is the interest of the money during the period it has remained in the hands of the debtor".

LIQUIDATED DAMAGES

Toomey v. Murphy [1897] 2 I.R. 601 Q.B.

The defendant by an agreement dated the 10th June, 1896 agreed to carry out certain work and alterations in the plaintiff's dwelling house and premises, in accordance with plans and specifications, by the 1st of October, 1896.

The work was to be carried out to the satisfaction of the plaintiff's engineer and if not completed in time the defendant was to be liable to pay the plaintiff 'a penalty as liquidated damages' of £5 a week until completion. The plaintiff claimed £160, being £5 a week for thirty two weeks as liquidated damages because the defendant did not complete the work.

It was submitted that although the statement of claim and the agreement described the amount payable as a penalty, it was really not a penalty, but in the nature of liquidated damages: *Elphinstone v. Iron and Coal Company*, 11 App. Cas. 332; *Wright v. Tracey*, I.R. 7 C.L. 134.

Held: The claim was a liquidated demand for which in default of appearance the plaintiff was entitled to judgment.

PENALTY OR DAMAGES

Schiesser International (Ireland) Ltd. v. Gallagher
[1972] 106 I.L.T.R. 22 (Cir. Ct.)

The plaintiff contracted to employ the defendant and to train him as a textile cutter. This training included a period in Germany. The written contract of employment contained a clause that in the event of the defendant leaving the plaintiff's employment within three years of his return from Germany he would repay the travelling expenses and the cost of training him incurred by the plaintiff.

The defendant left the employment of the plaintiff within two years of returning from Germany and the plaintiff claimed a sum of £225 as money due under the contract, or alternatively as damages for breach of contract.

Held: (*inter alia*)

(1) The clause in the contract providing for repayment was a penalty clause, in that the sum to be repaid was the same whether the defendant left the employment of the plaintiff one day after his return from Germany, or if he had left just one day short of the three years.

(2) Exercising the equitable jurisdiction of the court, the plaintiff would only be awarded the loss proved.

The President:

"The law relating to the distinction between a penalty and liquidated damages is stated in the *Law of Contracts* by Cheshire and Fifoot, 7th ed. (1969) at p. 561 as follows: 'The parties to a contract may agree beforehand what sum shall be payable by way of damages in the event of breach. . . . A sum fixed in this manner falls into one of two classes.

First, it may be a genuine pre-estimate of the loss that will be caused to one party if the contract is broken by the other. In this case it is called liquidated damages, and it constitutes the amount, no more no less, that the plaintiff is entitled to recover in the event of a breach without being required to prove actual damage. . . .

Secondly, it may be in the nature of a threat held over the other party in terrorem — a security to the promisee that the contract will be performed. A sum of this nature is called a penalty, and it has long been subject to equitable jurisdiction. Courts of Equity have taken the view that, since a penalty is designed as mere security for the performance of the contract, the promisee is sufficiently compensated by being indemnified for his actual loss, and that he acts unconscionably if he demands a sum which, although fixed by agreement, may well be disproportionate to the injury'. I accept this as a correct statement of the law."

PENALTY

Lombank Ltd. v. Kennedy and Whitelaw [1961] NILR 192 (C.A.)
Lombank Ltd. v. Crossan

In two actions a hire-purchase company claimed a sum for 'agreed depreciation' of a motor car which was the subject of a hire-purchase agreement.

The agreements contained identical clauses for the calculation of the 'agreed depreciation' viz. 45 per cent of the total hire purchase price plus a further 5 per cent per month between the date of the agreement and receipt of the goods by the owners, up to 75 per cent of the total price less the total of the sum already paid.

In the first case the company terminated the agreement because of the hirers failure to pay the rental. In the second case the hirer voluntarily terminated the agreement.

In each case the company applied for judgment in default of appearance on the basis that the sums claimed were a liquidated demand. Judgment was refused and the company appealed to the Court of Appeal.

Held:

(1) That in each case the amount calculated under the 'agreed depreciation' clause was a penal sum, rather than a genuine pre-estimate of damage.

(2) Black and Curran L.JJ., Lord MacDermott L.C.J. dissenting) that the penalty rule can only come into operation where there has been an actionable breach of contract, and that it did not, therefore, apply to the case where the contract was voluntarily terminated by the hirer.

Black L.J.:

"As stated in the third of Lord Dunedin's propositions in *Dunlop Pneumatic Tyre Co. Ltd. v. New Garage and Motor Co. Ltd.* [1915] A.C. 79 the question whether a sum stipulated is a penalty or liquidated damages is a question of construction to be decided upon the terms and inherent circumstances of each particular contract, judged of as at the time of the making of the contract , not as at the time of the breach. . . . There is high authority for the proposition that the only cases in which the doctrine that Equity relieves against penalties, applies, are cases where the penalty is imposed for breach of a contractual obligation.

. . . it may appear to the ordinary layman not only anomalous but unjust if, while on the one hand the law will relieve a defaulting hirer against the payment of the penal sum stipulated for by clause 6(c) when the finance company retake the car, yet on the other hand it will not give any such relief to a hirer who, without being guilty of any breach of his agreement, decides to determine the hiring and return the car under the provisions of clause 3(a) but will in this case leave the finance company to extract from such a man the full amount of the sum fixed by clause 6(c). This however is the legal position as I understand it. And if this view is correct, the anomaly and any injustice which it may involve can, I fear, only be corrected- if it is thought that it ought to be corrected — by the Legislature. Lord MacDermott L.C.J. cited Cheshire and Fifoot, *Law on Contracts*, 5th ed. (1960) and stated 'Courts of Equity have taken the view that, since a penalty is designed as mere security for the performance of the contract, the promisee is sufficiently compensated by being indemnified for his actual loss, and that he acts unconscionably if he demands a sum which, though certainly fixed by agreement, may well be disproportionate to the injury".

Note: It is difficult to reconcile this judgment with equitable principles of doing what is right and just and in accordance with the principles of good conscience and the author would prefer the minority view of Lord MacDermott L.C.J.

REMOTENESS OF DAMAGE
Lee & Donoghue v. Rowan
(H.C.) Unreported, 17 November 1981, Costello J.

The plaintiffs were partners in a firm which contracted to do some of the building work on a vegetable drying store for the defendant. The work was to be completed about the end of May 1977 to be ready for the vegetable harvest of that year. A dispute about the work arose and the plaintiff stopped work in early April and were excluded from the site in May. There was no provision in the contract for payment by instalments. The plaintiffs claimed payment of

£6,443.35 for materials and labour on a *quantum meruit*.

The defendant counterclaimed for the loss of 20 acres of onions and 46 acres of seed potatoes which he had nowhere to store when harvested. He was unsuccessful in finding other drying or storage facilities.

Held: The plaintiffs were entitled to £1,291.63 on their quantum meruit claim against which the defendant was entitled to set off his damages for breach of contract.

Costello J.:

> "The rule relating to damages for breach of contract had been stated in Hadley v. Baxendale (9 Exch at p.354). Under the first branch of this rule the defendants extra building costs of £2,000 could fairly and reasonably be considered as arising according to the usual course of things from the plaintiff's breach of contract. The remainder of the defendant's loss was sustainable, if at all, under the second branch of the rule i.e damages reasonably supposed to have been in the contemplation of the parties at the time they made the contract as the probable result of its breach.
>
> The plaintiffs could not have contemplated that all the defendant's sowing and cultivation costs would be lost but they could have contemplated that he would be put to the expense of hiring alternative storage and extra transport. The claim for loss of profits was limited to £9,240 being the extra transport and storage costs. The defendants total damages were £11,240 and he was entitled to set this sum against the plaintiff's claim of £31,291 and recover the balance of £9,949 on the counterclaim."
> See *Hadley v. Baxendale*, 9 Exch. 354. *ante.*

CONTINGENCY NOT TOO REMOTE
Hawkins v. Rogers [1951] I.R. 48 (H.C.)

H. and R. were partners owning and racing racehorses. They dissolved the partnership and agreed to sell the assets which included a filly 'Lonely Maid' registered in the sole name of R. The filly had been entered for three important races.

H. purchased the filly at public auction understanding that he was purchasing with the three engagements but R. withdrew the filly from all engagements in his name, in effect all her engagements. H. sued.

Held: There was a sale of the horse with her engagements to H. In acting as he did R. was actuated by some ill will i.e. malice towards H. The matter came within the established principle 'a violation of a legal right committed knowingly is a cause of action.'

Dixon J.:

> "The plaintiffs status as a partner prevents him suing the partnership and neither can he sue the defendant, who is only partner in respect of partnership liability . . . the gist of the plaintiff's complaint is an interference by the defendant, in his personal capacity and not as a partner, with property of the plaintiff . . . the matter comes within what I regard as an established principle, which may be stated in the words of Lord Macnaghten, at p. 510, in *Quinn v. Leatham* [1901] A.C. 495, viz,: . . . a violation of a legal right committed knowingly is a cause of action, and . . . it is a violation of legal right to interfere with contractual relations recognized by law if there be no sufficient justification for the interference."

DUTY TO MITIGATE DAMAGES
Malone v. Malone (H.C.), unreported, 9 March 1982, Costello J.

In July 1978 the defendant agreed to sell a guest house known as 'Lacken House' Dublin Road, Kilkenny to the plaintiff for £35,000. Shortly after the contract was signed and the purchase price paid over, she repudiated the agreement.

The plaintiff had borrowed £25,000 on an eight year term loan to buy the premises. The vendor's solicitor returned the purchase price early in November, 1979 but the plaintiff did not repay the bank loan. The plaintiff sought an order for specific performance and damages, which included a claim for additional interest payable to the bank.

Held (*inter alia*): Specific performance would be granted but in relation to the claim for additional interest. The plaintiff could have repaid the bank in full and this would have stopped the interest running on, the loss now claimed could therefore have been mitigated by the plaintiff.

His failure to mitigate his loss meant that if any sum was payable under the heading of additional interest, it could only arise for the fifteen month period from 2 August, 1978 during which the defendant kept the purchase price but repudiated the contract.

QUANTUM OF DAMAGES
Johnson v. Longleat Properties (Dublin) Ltd.
(H.C.), unreported, 19 May 1976, McMahon J.

The plaintiff claimed damages for the defendants breach of an agreement to build a house in Castleknock, Co. Dublin. The plaintiffs claim was presented under three main headings:

(1) The cost of remedying the defects in the dwelling.

(2) Damages for diminution in value by the defendant, in breach of an implied warranty, failing to construct adjoining houses to a high standard and quality.

(3) Damages for inconvenience, anxiety and disappointment caused to the plaintiff by the defects in the house.

Held: The proper cost of the necessary remedial work was their cost in November, 1973 (the earliest reasonable opportunity rule). No such warranty about adjoining houses could be inferred from the dealings between the plaintiff and the defendants.

In relation to the claim for damages for inconvenience, anxiety and disappointment. Damages for inconvenience and loss of enjoyment had received recognition in *Jarvis v. Swan Tours Ltd.* (1973 1 All E.R. 71).

McMahon J.:

"It appears to me that in principle damages may be awarded for inconvenience or loss of enjoyment when these are within the presumed contemplation of the parties as likely to result from the breach of contract. That would usually be in contacts to provide entertainment or enjoyment but there was no reason why it should not also be the case in other types of contract. In my view, the present contract fell within the class for breach of which damages may be awarded for inconvenience and loss of enjoyment but there is no evidence that apart from the period when the plaintiff and his family removed to the Four Courts Hotel, his enjoyment or convenience in living in the house was affected by structural defects. The repairs necessary to make the central heating installation work properly will obviously lead to substantial inconvenience . . . because these will involve having workmen in the house and taking up carpets and tiles and excavating the concrete sub floor in order to expose heating ducts. In my view damages should be recovered for this inconvenience and I measure the damages at £200 on this head."

DAMAGES FOR PHYSICAL INCONVENIENCE AND
DISCOMFORT

Siney v. Corporation of Dublin [1980] I.R. 40 (S.C.)

The plaintiff leased a flat from the defendant in Tallaght, Co. Dublin. Water appeared under the floor covering in the bedroom and putty like fungus appeared on the bedroom wall and under a window.

A Circuit Court found that the problem was insufficient ventilation, that the flat was unsuitable for habitation by the plaintiff and awarded damages of £150 for interference with the ordinary comfort and convenience of the plaintiff and his family. The defendants contended that damages should be confined to physical or material damage and that the sum in respect of inconvenience was not recoverable.

Held: O'Higgins C.J.

> "It is true that damages arising from breach of contract may not be recovered for annoyance, or loss of temper or vexation or disappointment. However, damages may be recovered for physical inconvenience and discomfort."

This was the kind of discomfort and inconvenience which the Circuit Court Judge had in mind.

Note: In *Jarvis v. Swan Tours Ltd.* [1973] Q.B. 233 it was held by the English Court of Appeal that damages could include not only the difference in value between what was promised and what was obtained but also damages for mental distress, inconvenience, upset, disappointment and frustration caused.

In *Jackson v. Horizon Holidays* [1975] 3 All E.R. 92 the judge at first hearing held that he could only consider the mental distress to Mr. Jackson himself, and that he could not consider the distress to his wife and children.

Lord Denning M.R. in the Court of Appeal said 'The case comes within the principle stated by Lush L.J. in *Lloyd's v. Harper* (1880) 16 Ch.D. 290, 321: 'I consider it to be an established rule of law that where a contract is made with A., for the benefit of B., A. can sue on the contract for the benefit of B., and recover all that B. could have recovered if the contract had been made with B. himself . . . it is the only way in which a just result can be achieved.' Lord Denning applied the principle to *Jackson's* case and awarded £1,000 to Mr. Jackson, his wife and children. See 'Contracts for the Benefit of Third Persons', 46 L Q Rev. 120

INFLATION AND TAX

Hickey & Co. v. Roches Stores (Dublin) (No. 2)
(H.C.) Unreported, 8 April 1980, Finlay P.

Subsequent to the judgment in *Hickey & Co. v. Roches Stores (Dublin) (No. 1)* the parties failed to reach agreement on the amount of damages and the matter was re-entered for hearing by the President of the High Court.

The plaintiff claimed that the proper measure of damages should include a factor for inflation to bring the figure under each heading up to the appropriate buying power of money at the date of the judgment. The defendants contested this and contended that a figure equivalent to the Corporation Profits Tax and Income Tax which the plaintiff would have paid should be deducted.

Held: Any person engaged in trade as the defendants had been in the decade before 1969 would have been able to foresee that inflation and a consequential decrease in the purchasing power of money would probably continue. The defendants could not have reasonably foreseen that in the event of a breach of contract by them in 1971 the damages would not be assessed until 1980. Therefore the increase in the losses to compensate for inflation could not be allowed in this case.

With regard to Reduction of damages for liability to Corporation Profit Tax and Income Tax. The defendants relied in the main upon the decision of Mr. Justice Kenny in *Glover v. BLN (No. 2)* [1973] I.R. 432 where he held that damages for loss of future earnings were not chargable to income tax and that the gross amount of damages should be reduced by the equivalent tax that the plaintiff would have paid.

Finlay P. accepted and followed this decision and held that if the damages recoverable by the plaintiffs were not chargeable to tax when recovered, that it was appropriate that a deduction in respect of the Corporations Profit Tax and Income Tax which they would have paid should be deducted from the gross amount assessed. Loss of net trading profits are chargeable to tax and therefore it was not appropriate to make a deduction for CPT Or Income Tax:

Finlay P.:

> "The legal position is that the rule or principle followed by Mr. Justice Kenny in *Glover v. BLN (No. 2)* applies only to damages for wrongful dismissal and breach of contract of service and is so expressly to be confined and that damages as occur in this case for loss of profits are prima facie chargeable to tax. I therefore reject the defendants submission on this aspect of the case".

Note: Should damages awarded contain a factor to allow for inflation? Finlay P. in *Hickey and Company v. Roches Stores Ltd.*, accepted the principles stated in *Victoria Laundry Windsor Ltd. v. Newman Industries Ltd.* [1949] 2 K.B. subject to the comments made on that decision by the House of Lords in *Czarnikow v. Koufos* [1969] 1 Appeal Cases, and applied two tests.

(1) was the addition of an inflationary factor necessary to put the plaintiffs in the same position as if their rights under the contract had been observed? and

(2) whether the defendants at the time of contracting could reasonably foresee this loss as liable to result from the breach.

With regard to the counterclaim that damages should be reduced in respect of what would have been due in corporation profit tax and income tax by the plaintiff the President concluded that damages assessed as loss of net trading profits are chargeable to tax and therefore it was not appropriate to make any deduction in respect of liability for tax.

DAMAGES IN CONTRACTS FOR THE SALE OF REAL ESTATE
The rule in Bain v. Fothergill (1874) L.R. 7 158 (H.L.)

The rule has been stated by Lord Chelmsford as follows:

"I think the rule as to the limits within which damages may be recovered upon breach of a contract for the sale of real estate must be taken to be without exception. If a person enters into a contract for the sale of a real estate knowing that he has no title to it, nor any means of acquiring it, the purchaser cannot recover damages beyond the expenses he has incurred by an action for the breach of contract; he can only obtain other damages by an action for deceit."

Note: See also *McQuaid v. Lynam and Another* [1965] I.R. 564. Section 45(1) of The Sale of Goods and Supply of Services Act, 1980 does not apply to contracts for the sale of land because the definition of contract in section 43 does not include contracts for the sale of land. Innocent misrepresentation in the sale of land does not therefore have a statutory right to damages.

In *Sharneyford Supplies Ltd. v. Edge* [1987] 2 W.L.R. 363 the Court of Appeal decided that full damages were payable where a vendor failed to give a purchaser vacant possession of a maggot farm. The three Lord Justices condemned the rule in *Bain v. Fothergill* to the effect that damages were limited. This event was very aptly described in the Autumn 1987 Students' Law Reporter as 'The worm has turned in Bain v. Fothergill.'

DAMAGES PLUS SPECIFIC PERFORMANCE
Murphy v. Quality Homes (H.C.) Unreported, 22 June 1976, McWilliam J.

The plaintiff sought specific performance of an earlier agreement to settle proceedings for breach of contract. The agreement provided that the plaintiff would sell a house to the defendant for £16,000 and for the payment of £4,000 by the defendant as a deposit on the exchange of contracts before the 20th October 1975. It also provided for the payment of £1,600 costs by the defendant and that a sum of £2,005 lodged in Court should be paid out to the plaintiff. The defendant released the £2,005 lodged in Court but did not perform the rest of the settlement agreement.

The plaintiff sought damages: (1) for loss of the bargain to purchase another house and (2) for discomfort, inconvenience and distress by having to remain in the old uninhabitable house.

Held: The plaintiff was entitled to £750 for loss due to increase in prices before the decree and to £51,250 for loss due to increase in prices after the decree. The plaintiff was also allowed a sum of £7,000 for discomfort, inconvenience and distress.

McWilliam J. was referred to *Capital and Suburban Properties v. Swycher* [1976] 2 W.L.R. 822 wherein it was held that the vendor was not entitled to damages in addition to rescission. He distinguished that judgment on the ground that it did not decide that a vendor was not entitled to damages in addition to a decree for specific performance in a proper case and that this is expressly allowed under Lord Cairns' Act.

McWilliam J.:

> "In so far as the decision in the Capital Properties case was based on the statement at p.828 that 'if the sale is eventually carried through under a decree of specific performance, he (the vendor) suffers no damage except to any extent to which he is unable to recover from the purchaser additional expense to which he has been put.' It had no application to the present case, in which it had been clearly established that the vendor had suffered very considerable damage which ought to have been within the contemplation of the purchaser."

DAMAGES FOR PRE-CONTRACTUAL EXPENDITURE
Anglia Television v. Reed [1971] 3 All E.R. 690.

The plaintiff decided to make a television film 'The Man in the Wood' and they found a location for filming and engaged a Director and other persons at a cost of £2,750. They then sought an actor to play the leading role. The defendants agent contracted on his behalf to make the film. Later it was found that he was already booked for the same period and he repudiated the contract with Anglia.

Anglia were unable to find another actor to play the part and had to abandon the project. They then sued Reed for damages of £2,750, being the expenditure incurred before the contract with Reed was made. They could not say what their profit would have been had the contract been performed.

Held: Anglia were entitled to recover the pre-contractual expenditure from the defendant as damages.

Lord Denning M.R.:

> "It seems to me that a plaintiff in such a case as this had an election: he can either claim for his loss of profits; or for his wasted expenditure. But he must elect between them... he is not limited to the expenditure incurred after the contract was concluded. He can claim also the expenditure incurred before the contract, provided that it was such as would reasonably be in the contemplation of the parties as likely to be wasted if the contract was broken. . . ."

Note: Because of the inadequacy of the common law remedy of damages in certain cases equity intervened and granted a range of equitable remedies, mainly where damages were insufficient. These remedies include Quantum Meruit, Restitution and Quasi Contract, Specific Performance and Injunctions.

QUANTUM MERUIT

O'Connell v. Listowel U.D.C. [1957] Ir. Jur. Rep. 43 (Cir. Ct.).

The plaintiff was appointed as an engineer and town surveyor by the U.D.C. Appointments made by the council were required to be approved by the Minister for Local Government. The Minister refused his approval some five months after the appointment, and a month later the plaintiff was dismissed from his post.

During the previous six months, the plaintiff, purporting to act under the appointment, rendered services for the U.D.C., and he sued for payment.

Held: The appointment being void, the plaintiff was entitled to receive a reasonable remuneration, on a quantum meruit, for the services which he had rendered. *Craven-Ellis v. Canons Ltd.* [1936] 2 K.B. 403 *approved and followed.*

Note: Where the parties think that they are acting under a valid contract which subsequently turns out to be void, liability to pay on a quantum meruit arises. This is only one of the grounds.

RESTITUTION AND QUASI CONTRACT

If one party to a contract has performed his obligation or paid money under a purported contract he may be entitled to recover under the doctrine of restitution or quasi contract. If work has been done in such circumstances at the request of the other party the doctrine of quantum meruit may apply to recover an appropriate payment. (See *O'Connell v. Listowel U.D.C.* ante) But if money has been paid or a benefit conferred it may amount to an unjust enrichment or an unjust benefit which it would be unconscionable to allow the recipient to keep. (See the adoption of this concept in paragraph 3 of the judgment in *Hickey & Co. v. Roches Stores (Dublin) Ltd.: post*).

Lord Mansfield in *Moses v. MacFerlan* (1760) 2 Burr 1005:

> "If the defendant be under an obligation from the ties of natural justice, to refund; the law implies a debt and gives this action founded on the equity of the plaintiffs case, as it were upon a contract (quasi ex contractu') as the Roman Law expressed it . . ."

According to Lord Wright: 'Such remedies in English Law are generically different from remedies in contract or in tort, and are now recognised to fall within a third category of the common law which has been called quasi contract or restitution.' Chitty points out that a claim in quasi contract is an alternative to an action for damages for breach of contract. It is usually invoked where none or only limited damages are in prospect, or where the payer has made a bad bargain. 'Restitution therefore, has a clear advantage over a claim for reliance losses since such a claim will not succeed if the defendant shows the reliance loss is greater that the expected profit. Apart from this the quasi contractual claim has procedural and evidential advantages in that it is a liquidated claim.'

Chitty on Contracts, 26th ed. at p. 1315 suggests that the implied contract theory should be rejected as the basis of restitution by the House of Lords in the same way as it rejected the 'implied term' theory of frustration. Many academic commentators suggest that the doctrine of restitution does not need the support of the quasi contract theory.

UNJUST ENRICHMENT

Hickey & Co. v. Roches Stores (Dublin) Ltd.
H.C., unreported, 14 July 1976.

The plaintiff contracted to open a retail fashion fabric outlet in the defendants shop as a joint venture until the 17th of June, 1972. The defendant terminated the agreement on 2 February, 1972.

It was a term of the agreement that the plaintiff would be given six months notice of termination and that the defendant would not compete in a similar business for a further period of twelve months following the expiration of the notice.

Hickeys claimed that they were entitled, *inter alia*, to the value of the goodwill of the trade in fashion fabrics on the 17 June 1973 calculated on the basis of three years profits, that it would be unjust to permit Roches Stores to retain without payment, this valuable asset which they acquired by a wrongful act. The court in this case should look beyond the loss to the injured party and take into account the profit obtained by the wrongdoer.

Held:
(1) The general rule is that damages in tort and breach of contract is to put the injured party into the position he would have been, had the wrong not been committed, and should be referable to the loss suffered by the injured party.

(2) There are exceptions to this rule.

(3) Where the wrongdoer has calculated and intended by his wrongdoing the court should also look, to the profit or gain unjustly or wrongly obtained by the wrongdoer.

If the assessment of damages confined to the loss of the injured party should still leave the wrongdoer profiting from his calculated breach of the law, damages should be assessed so as to deprive him of that profit.

(4) In breach of contract cases, (but not in tort) where *mala fides* has not occurred, the necessity to create certainty as to the obligations which may arise from the contract and from a breach and the necessity for permitting the parties to provide for such obligations make it necessary to confine damages to the loss suffered by the injured party even though such a restriction may result in a profit to the wrongdoer.

(5) In assessing damages for loss incurred either in tort or breach of contract, the court, if satisfied that a loss has occurred, under a particular heading, should not by reason of difficulty in proof of the amount of that loss, as distinct from failure to adduce available evidence of it, be deterred from assessing compensation for it and should, in this context be both alert and ingenious in assessing a general sum for damages even though it may involve some element of speculation.

Since it was neither alleged or established that Roches Stores designed and calculated the breach to enable them to acquire the goodwill, damages should not be assessed on the basis of the profit derived by them in so far as it exceeded the loss suffered by Hickeys.

Finlay P. stated:

"In extending the measure of damages, which heretofore has been confined to tort, to cases of breach of contract I have acted upon a conclusion that the protection of a party to a contract from uncertain or extensive damages, against which he had no opportunity to provide by the terms of the contract, should not apply where he has acted *mala fide*".

He further added that difficulty in proof of the amount of loss under a particular heading should not deter a court from assessing compensation for it and the court should be both alert and ingenious in doing so even though it may involve some element of speculation. See ante.

Note: Under the doctrine of restitution it may be possible to recover money paid in the following circumstances:

(1) Money paid under a mistake of fact.

(2) Money paid for a consideration which has failed.

(3) Money paid under a conditional contract.

(4) Money obtained wrongfully i.e. through oppression, extortion, or imposition.

(5) Money paid under an illegal contract.

(6) Money paid under a void contract.

MONEY PAID UNDER A MISTAKE OF FACT
Kelly v. Solari (1881) M&W 54

In 1836 the husband of the defendant effected a life assurance policy with the Argus Life Assurance Company for £200. He died on the 18th of October, 1840, leaving the defendant his executrix, and not having (by mistake) paid the quarterly premium on the policy, which became due on the preceding 3rd September.

In November an actuary in the assurance company informed the directors that the policy had lapsed by reason of non payment of the premium and the word 'lapsed' was written on the policy in pencil. On the 13th of February, 1841, the defendant (executrix) applied for payment of the sum secured on the policy, and was paid £197, the directors having forgotten that the policy in question had lapsed. Mr. Kelly, a director of the assurance company took an action to recover the sum of money paid to the defendant.

Held: that the company were entitled to recover the money which had been paid under a mistake of fact. It is not sufficient to preclude a party from recovering money paid by him under a mistake of fact, that he had the means of knowledge of the fact, unless he paid it intentionally not choosing to investigate the fact.

Parke B.:

> "... If it (money) is paid under the impression of the truth of a fact which is untrue, it may, generally speaking, be recovered back, however careless the party paying may have been, in omitting to use due diligence to enquire into the fact. In such a case the receiver is not entitled to it, nor intended to have it. If money is paid to another under the influence of a mistake, that is, upon the supposition that a specific fact is true, which would entitle the other to the money, but which fact is untrue, . . . an action will lie to recover it back, and it is against conscience to retain it . . ."

Lord Abinger C.B.:

> "I think the knowledge of the facts which disentitles the party from recovering must mean knowledge existing in the mind at the time of payment."

MONEY PAID UNDER MISTAKE OF LAW — NOT IN PARI DELICTO
Kiriri Cotton Co. Ltd. v. Dewani [1960] A.C. 192.

The respondent Dewani, an Indian merchant living at Kampala in Uganda paid a premium of Shillings 10,000 to the appellant company for a sub-lease of a flat in Kampala. Section 3(2) of the Uganda Rent Restriction Ordinance, 1949 made such payments illegal but made no provision for the recovery of such illegal premiums. The respondent having gone into occupation of the flat under the sublease claimed the return of the 10,000 shillings as money had and received by the appellant company for the use of the respondent.

Held: that the duty of observing the law was firmly placed by the Ordinance on the shoulders of the landlord for the protection of the tenant, and the appellant company and the respondent were not therefore *in pari delicto* in receiving and paying respectively the illegal premium, which, therefore, in accordance with established common law principles, the respondent was entitled to recover from the landlord. The omission of a statutory remedy did not in cases of this kind, exclude the remedy by money had and received.

    Dicta of Lord Mansfield in *Lowry v. Bourdieu* (1780) 2 Doug. K.B. 468 at 472, and in *Browning v. Morris* (1778) 2 Cowp. 790 at 792 *applied. Rex v. Godinho* [1950] 17 E.A.C.A. 132 at 134 *disapproved.*

Held also, it is not correct to say that everyone is presumed to know the law. The true proposition is that no man can excuse himself from doing his duty by saying that he did not know the law on the matter. *Ignorantia juris neminem excusat.*

Denning L.J.:

> "Nor is it correct to say that money paid under a mistake of law can never be recovered back. James L.J., pointed that out in *Rogers v. Ingham* (1876). If there is something more in addition to a mistake of law — if there is something in the defendants conduct which shows, that of the two of them, he is the one primarily responsible for the mistake — then it may be recovered back. . . . All the particular heads of money had and received, such as money paid under a mistake of fact, paid under a consideration that has wholly failed, money paid by one who is not *in pari delicto* with the defendant, are only instances where the law says the money ought to be returned."

MONEY PAID FOR A CONSIDERATION WHICH HAS TOTALLY FAILED

Fibrosa v. Fairbairn Ltd. [1943] A.C. 332 (H.L.).

The appellants, a Polish Company by a contract in writing of 12 July, 1939 with the respondent English company agreed to purchase machinery for £4,800 of which one-third was to be paid with the order. The goods were to be packed and delivered C.i.f. Gdynia, Poland. Clause seven of the contract stated 'Should dispatch be hindered or delayed . . . by any cause whatsoever beyond our reasonable control, including . . . war . . . a reasonable extension of time shall be granted.' Only a sum of £1,000 instead of £1,600 was paid with the order and on September 1, 1939 war broke out between Germany and Poland and on September 3 Great Britain declared war on Germany. On and after September 23 Gdynia was occupied by the Germans;

Held:

(1) Clause seven being limited in its ambit to a delay in respect of which 'a reasonable extension of time' might be granted, did not prevent frustration of the contract by reason of the war on the ground that it made express provision for that contingency, since the war involved prolonged and indefinite interruption of prompt contractual performance.

(2) that, there having been a total failure of consideration and the payment of £1,000 being, under the terms of the contract, a conditional payment on account of the purchase price and not an absolute final or 'out and out' payment, the appellants could recover that sum from the respondents.

The claim of a party who has paid money under a contract, to recover it on the ground that the consideration for which he paid it has wholly failed is not based on any provision in the contract, but **arises because in the circumstances the law gives a remedy in quasi contract to the party who has not got what he bargained for**. Although, in the formation of a contract, a promise to do a thing may be the consideration, in dealing with the law of failure of consideration and the right to recover money on that ground, it is, generally speaking, not the promise which is referred to as the consideration, but its performance. *Chandler v. Webster* [1904] 1 K.B. 493, *overruled*.

Lord Russell of Killowen:

> "But I am of opinion that this appeal should succeed because. . . . There was a total failure of consideration for which the money was paid. In those circumstances why should the appellants not be entitled to recover back the money, as money had and received to their use, on the ground that it was paid for a consideration which has wholly failed?
>
> . . . This is **a right which in no way depends upon the continued existence of the frustrated contract. It arises from the fact that the impossibility of performance has caused a total failure of the consideration for which the money was paid.** In his judgment in *Chandler v. Webster* the Master of the Rolls states that the right to recover moneys paid for a consideration which has failed only arises where the contract is 'wiped out' altogether, by which expression I understand him to mean is void *ab initio*. This is clearly a misapprehension on the part of the learned judge. The money was recoverable under the common indebitatus count, as money received for the use of the plaintiff. The right to recover money paid for a consideration that has failed did not depend on the contract being void *ab initio*."

Lord Macmillan:

> "So *Chandler v. Webster* and its congeners must be consigned to the limbo of cases *disapproved* and *overruled*."

MONEY PAID WHERE NO TOTAL FAILURE OF CONSIDERATION

Stapleton v. Prudential Assurance [1928] 62 I.L.T.R. 56. (See Chapter 15).

MONEY PAID UNDER A CONDITIONAL CONTRACT

Lowis v. Wilson [1949] I.R. 347. (See Chapter 1).

RESTITUTION OF MONEY OBTAINED WRONGFULLY

Great Southern & Western Railway v. Robertson (1878) 2 L.R. (Ir.) 548

The appellant was a carrier, who in pursuance of a contract with the British War Office consigned stores and ammunition by the plaintiff's railway and required that they be carried at a special low rate not exceeding two pence per ton per mile as prescribed by the Statute 7 & 8 Vict. c.85, s.12

The Railway company insisted upon charging their ordinary (higher) rate, in total a sum of £601 more and the carrier was obliged to pay it. Later he instituted proceedings to recover this excess and on being unsuccessful in the Court of Exchequer appealed.

Held: (reversing the Court of Exchequer), that the carrier was entitled to have the baggage carried at the statutory rate, and to recover back the excess as **money had and received to his use**.

Ball C. adopted and approved the dictum of Willes J. in *GWR Co. v. Sutton* (1869) L.R. 4 H.L:

> "When a man pays more that he is bound to do for the performance of a duty which the law says is owed to him for nothing, or for less than he has paid, there is a compulsion in respect of which he is entitled to recover the excess by action for money had and received. Mr. Robertson . . . is entitled to demand back the amount by which he overpaid".

Note: See also *Irish National Insurance Co. Ltd., v. Scannell* [1959] Ir. Jur. R. 41 (H.C.) where in consequence of judgments obtained by former clients of the defendant auctioneer, the plaintiff company were obliged to pay a sum of £987 under a guarantee bond and were held entitled to recover that sum from the defendant as money paid for and on his behalf.

MONEY PAID UNDER AN ILLEGAL CONTRACT
Parkinson v. College of Ambulance Ltd. [1925] 2 K.B. 1.

The secretary of a charity, the College of Ambulance, formed to establish a college to teach first aid and ambulance work, fraudulently represented to Colonel Parkinson, that he or the college would arrange for the grant to the plaintiff of a knighthood in return for a substantial donation to the college. Relying on that representation Parkinson paid £3,000 to the college but did not receive a knighthood. When he enquired at the Unionist offices he was told that he had been fooled.

Parkinson then brought an action to recover the £3,000 as damages for deceit, or alternatively as money had and received by the defendants to the use of the plaintiff.

Held: that the contract for the purchase of a title, was an improper and illegal contract, as being against public policy and that as Parkinson knew that he was entering into an improper and illegal contract he could not recover back the money he had paid or recover damages.

Lush J.:

> "It is not correct to say, . . . that it is only if the contract is of a criminal nature that the plaintiff is precluded from recovery. The case of *Taylor v. Chester* (L.R. 4 Q.B. 309) is an authority against this proposition. No criminal offence was committed there. . . . In the present case the plaintiff knew that he was entering into and illegal and improper contract. He was not deceived as to the legality of the contract he was making. How then can he say that he is excused? . . . It is no excuse to say that (the secretary of the college) was more blameworthy than he, which is all that he really can say."

Note: In this case the illegal contract was relied upon to seek recovery. See *Scott v. Brown* [1892] 2. Q.B. 724.

RECOVERY — NON-RELIANCE ON ILLEGAL CONTRACT
Singh v. Kulubya [1964] A.C. 142 (Privy Council).

The respondent was the registered proprietor of certain land in Africa classified as 'Mailo land'. Section 2 of the Bugunda Possession of Land Law, c.25 of 1957 and s.2 of the Uganda Land Transfer Ordinance of 1951 prohibited the sale or lease of 'Mailo land' by an African to a non-African without the approval and consent in writing of the Governor.

Without obtaining the necessary approval or consent the respondent purported to lease the land in November 1946 to the appellant an Indian, in contravention of the law and thus committing an offence punishable by fine or imprisonment. When he wished to regain possession the respondent sought the eviction of the appellant, acknowledging that the transaction was illegal.

Held: that the appellant was not, and never had been, in lawful occupation of the lands and could not rely on the illegal agreement as justifying any right or claim to remain in possession, and without doing so he could not defeat the respondent's claim.

The respondent required no aid from the illegal transaction to establish his case; it was sufficient for him to show that he was the registered proprietor of the lands and that the appellant, a non-African, was in occupation without the consent of the Governor, and accordingly had no right to occupy. Since the respondent was neither obliged to found his claim on the illegal agreements nor, in order to support his claim to plead or depend on them, he was not in pari delicto with the appellant. Further, this conclusion was reinforced by the relevant legislation which was intended to be for the benefit of Africans as a class — the respondent was a member of a protected class. He was therefore entitled to possession. *Bowmakers Ltd v. Barnet Instruments Ltd.* [1945] K.B. 65; *Taylor v. Chester* (1869) L.R. 4 Q.B. and *Kearney v. Thomson* (1890) Q.B.D. 742 C.A., *considered.*

MONEY PAID UNDER A VOID CONTRACT
Strictland v. Turner (1852) 7 EX. 208.

Edward Lane of Sydney, New South Wales being entitled to an annuity for life, assigned it by deed to trustees in England to sell it for him. The plaintiff Strictland entered into correspondence with the trustees to purchase the annuity, agreed terms on the 28th of February and paid the trustees a sum of £973 It was subsequently ascertained that Edward Lane had died at Sydney on the 6th of February having appointed the defendant sole executrix of his will. Strictland sought to recover the money paid.

Held: that, as at the time of the purchase the annuity had ceased to exist, the plaintiff was entitled to recover back the whole of the purchase money, on the ground that the money had been paid without consideration. Mistake as to the existence of the subject matter had rendered the contract void. (See *Couturier v. Hastie*, Chapter 10 *ante.*)

QUASI CONTRACT

Folens & Co. Ltd. v. The Minister for Education,
unreported, High Court, 4 October 1982.

The Managing Director of the plaintiff, conceived the idea of producing a childrens encyclopedia in Irish. He approached an official of the Department of Education who asked him to submit a proposition. A statement of the plaintiff's proposals for the production of the encyclopedia was submitted and these proposals were discussed at a meeting in the Department. No decisions were reached but it was recorded that the Department was in favour of the project. It was also stated that the Department of Finance would have to be consulted.

At a meeting in March, 1972, representatives of the Department of Education present appear to have agreed in principle both to the project and to an increased cost of £425,512, but no agreement was reached and it was emphasized that there could be no prospect of authority to go ahead unless the Department guaranteed the purchase of 6,000 copies of each volume.

In August 1971 the plaintiff had appointed an editor for the project and informed the Department of this fact. In May, 1973 a supervisory committee was appointed by and on behalf of the Department to supervise the work and to appoint an editorial advisory committee. Meetings of both committees continued to be held and the plaintiff continued the work of the preparation of the encyclopedia. On the 17th January, 1975, the Department wrote to say that no further commitments should be made in relation to the project as there were no funds available for it.

Held: by McWilliam J. Both parties had proceeded on the basis that a contract would be made between them. The plaintiff would not have done the work at its own risk as to cost, and on this basis was entitled to be paid for all the work which had been done with the approval or at the direction of the Department.

McWilliam J. was satisfied that there was no concluded contract. In each of the cases to which he was referred by counsel, there was a definite commitment or representation which was not present in this case. He agreed with Lord Denning M.R. who said, in *Brewer Street Investments Ltd. v. Barclay's Wooden Co. Ltd.* [1953] 3 U.L.R 869 that it was not easy to state the legal basis of the plaintiff's claim. He concluded that the case should be considered by reference to the principles adopted in *William Lacey Ltd. v. Davis* [1957] 2 AU. E.R. 712 where Barry J. was of the opinion that an action could be founded on 'quasi- contract' so that a court may look at the true facts and ascertain from them whether or not a promise to pay should be implied, irrespective of the actual views or intentions of the parties at the time when the work was done or the service rendered. *William Lacey Ltd. v. Davis* [1957] 2 AU. E.R. 712 *approved.*

Note: 'In principle'. See *Central Meat Products v. Carney* [1944] Ir. Jur. Rep. 34 and *Irish Mainport Holdings v. Crosshaven Sailing Centre*, unreported, High Court, 14 October 1980.

SPECIFIC PERFORMANCE

Specific Performance is an order of the court directing a party to specifically carry out his obligations under a contract. As stated by Black L.J. in Conlon v. Murray cited by McVeigh J. in *Buckley v. Irwin* it still retains the character of an equitable remedy which is not granted as of right but is discretionary. O'Higgins C.J. in *Smelter Corporation of Ireland v. O'Driscoll* [1977] I.R. 305 refused to grant the remedy and outlined how the discretion to grant or refuse it must be exercised. viz. in a manner "which is neither arbitrary nor capricious but which has regard to the essential fairness of the transaction involved".

It is not granted if other legal remedies are adequate. In *Roberts v. O'Neill* [1983] I.R. 47 the defendants contention that damages were an appropriate remedy and that specific performance should not be granted was rejected in the High Court by McWilliam J. who refused to apply the rule in *Bain v. Fothergill*.

TIME OF HARDSHIP
Roberts v. O'Neill [1983] I.R. 47 (S.C.).

Following the Supreme Court judgment in the case of *Carthy v. O'Neill*, unreported, 30 January, 1981 (see 'subject to contract', Chapter 5) the plaintiff proceeded with a claim for specific performance He had issued a Plenary Summons on the 7th March, 1978 and the defendant had pleaded, that because of the Carthy action, they were unable to complete the sale.

On 6th May, 1981, an amended defence and counterclaim on behalf of the first defendant, stated that in the period between the making of the contract for sale to the plaintiff in these proceedings and the delivery of the judgment of the Supreme Court in *Carthy v. O'Neill* the value of the premises had greatly increased, as had the value of licensed premises generally and that it would be grossly unjust if the defendants were obliged to sell the premises to the plaintiff at the contract price, which was now a gross undervalue.

The plaintiff would be unjustly enriched. The defendants would suffer hardship in acquiring a substitute public house because of the inflation in the prices and that accordingly the court should refuse to grant an order for specific performance.

In the High Court McWilliam J. rejected the defendants contention that specific performance should not be granted and that damages in lieu was the appropriate remedy. He rejected the proposition that the rule in *Bain v. Fothergill* applied, and he granted a decree for specific performance.

Held: by McWilliam J in granting the plaintiff a decree of specific performance and affirmed by the Supreme Court (O'Higgins C.J., Hederman and McCarthy JJ.)

(1) That in deciding the issue of hardship in relation to the grant of a decree of specific performance of a contract for the sale of land, as a general rule, the relevant point of time for ascertaining the existence the alleged hardship was the date of the contract of sale, and that hardship arising thereafter was not relevant to that issue.

(2) That the circumstances upon which the defendants relied did not constitute an exception to that rule.

(3) That the plaintiff was entitled to interest, at the current bank rate, on the amount of his deposit from the date fixed for completion by the contract until the date of judgment of the High Court.

Note: An examination of the evidence threw doubt upon the reality of the alleged claim of hardship. At all material times the defendants knew that they would have to complete a sale of the premises either to Mr.Carthy or to the plaintiff.

HARDSHIP AS A GROUND FOR REFUSING — SPECIFIC PERFORMANCE

McCarthy J. (O'Higgins C.J. and Hederman J. concurring):

> "The Court, it is well established, will not enforce the specific performance of a contract, the result of which would be to impose great hardship on either of the parties to it. It is conceded, however, that the question of hardship of a contract is generally to be judged at the time it is entered into. Change of circumstances taking place later, making the contract less beneficial to one party, are immaterial as a rule unless brought about by the action of the other party."

It is stated, however, in *Fry on Specific Performance* (6th ed. at p. 200):

> "It cannot, however be denied that there are cases in which the Court has refused its interference by reason of events subsequent to the contract.' From an examination of the cases of *The City of London v. Nash* and *Costigan v. Hastler* it appears that this is so, but exceptions to the general rule are very rare. . . . I must however, approach the consideration of these matters dispassionately and exercise what I conceive to be the proper judicial discretion. In the first place, as I have pointed out, it is undoubtedly the position in law that save in exceptional; cases only a matter of hardship existing at the time of the contract can be taken into consideration.
>
> Hardship existing at the time of the contract is out of the case. It thus

requires a strong case to be made out before one can accede to a plea for the exercise of judicial discretion in a quite unusual way, that is, by reason of hardship arising subsequently to the contract, and the onus being on the defendant to satisfy me of the existence and genuineness of the alleged hardship on her, the proof of it should be strong and above suspicion."

Note: The Supreme Court outlined the relationship between hardship and the granting of specific performance.

". . . Hardship is permitted to defeat specific performance where an existing hardship was not known at the relevant time, being the date of the contract. While recognizing that there may be cases in which hardship arising after the date of the contract is such, that to decree specific performance would result in great injury, there must be few such cases and, in my view they should not include ordinary cases of hardship resulting from inflation alone. To permit, as an ordinary rule, a defence of subsequent hardship, would be to add further hazard to the already trouble-strewn area of the law of contracts for the sale of land" — *per* McCarthy J. (O'Higgins C.J. and Hederman J. in agreement).

SPECIFIC PERFORMANCE — GROUNDS FOR REFUSAL
Buckley v. Irwin [1960] N.I. 98.

The defendant whom the trial judge found to be 'a person who would require protection and guidance in carrying out business affairs, even of a comparatively simple nature', agreed to sell his dwelling house, his farm and tractor to the plaintiff for £2,700, a price which the judge regarded as a substantial under-value, but not so gross an undervalue as of itself to be evidence of fraud.

Immediately after the agreement was reached, the plaintiff paid a cash deposit of £100 to the defendant and a companion who accompanied the plaintiff drew up a memorandum which was signed by both parties and the companion.

A few days later, in a solicitors office the defendant said that the deal was off and tried to return the £100 deposit.

The plaintiff sought specific performance of the agreement or alternatively damages for breach of contract.

Held: Specific performance and damages refused. The contract must be set aside.

McVeigh J.:

"I am satisfied that this was an unethical bargain, and infringed the principles of fairness, which a court of equity requires to be observed, in such a way and to such an extent that substantial justice would not be done unless the order for specific performance was refused. . . . Equitable relief may be refused even though there has been no improper conduct on the part of the plaintiff — it is enough, if the facts as a whole make it inequitable to grant the relief sought."

Twining v. Morrice (1788) 2 Bro. C.C. 326. and Black L.J. in *Conlon v. Murray* [1958] N.I. 17, 25 says:

"The remedy of specific performance still retains the character of an equitable remedy. It is not granted as of right but is a discretionary remedy which may be withheld in cases of a type where the court, having regard to the conduct of the parties and all the circumstances of the case, considers in its discretion that the remedy ought not to be granted."

SPECIFIC PERFORMANCE AND MISTAKE

Smelter Corporation of Ireland v. O'Driscoll [1977] I.R. 305 (S.C.).

An auctioneer, acting under a *bona fide* but mistaken belief, informed the defendant that if she did not sell her land at Carrigrenen, Co. Cork, to the plaintiff, as a site for a metal plant, it would be compulsorily acquired by the County Council. The defendant believing this to be true entered into an agreement giving the plaintiff an option to purchase the land. The plaintiff later purported to exercise their option and when the defendant refused to complete, instituted proceedings seeking specific performance of the agreement. The plaintiffs' action was tried in the High Court by Butler J. and the plaintiffs appealed to the Supreme Court from that judgment.

Held:

(1) Specific performance is a discretionary remedy which should not be exercised if the contract is not equal and fair.

(2) That, by reason of the plaintiffs misrepresentation, the defendant had been under a fundamental misapprehension about the true facts, and that it would be unjust to grant a decree of specific performance in the circumstances.

O'Higgins C.J. (Kenny J. and Parke J. in agreement):

"It is well established that the discretion to grant specific performance should not be exercised if the contract is not equal and fair. In this instance the defendant was under a fundamental misapprehension as to the true facts. This misapprehension was brought about by the plaintiffs' agent. It appears clear also that the plaintiffs' managing director was aware of the true position (and) should have been aware of the incorrect picture which (the agent) had painted. Nevertheless the plaintiffs' managing director allowed the negotiations to proceed.

In these circumstances it appears to me that there was a fundamental unfairness in the transaction. **The defendant agreed to sell believing that she had no real option, and the plaintiffs accepted her agreement to sell knowing that this was not so**. In my view it would create a hardship and be unjust to decree specific performance in this case."

SPECIFIC PERFORMANCE AND DECEIT

Bascomb v. Beckwith (1869) L.R. 8 Eq. 100.

Bascomb, the owner of an estate in Kent, put the whole estate (excluding one small plot) for sale in building lots, subject to a restrictive covenant that no public house should be built and no trade carried on in any of the properties built on the lots. The defendant agreed to purchase the Manor House. His solicitor noticed the reserved plot and the defendant refused to complete the purchase unless the plaintiff's conveyance contained the same restrictive covenant as to the reserved plot. The plaintiff refused and sought specific performance.

The defendant stated that he had no idea from inspection of the particulars and plan that the reserved plot belonged to the plaintiff, that during the negotiations the plaintiff and his solicitor or agents never disclosed that he intended to exempt any land from the restrictive covenants, that he had bought the Manor House for the purpose of a residence, and that he would not have bought it had he known that there was a possibility of a public house being erected on the reserved plot, 100 yards from the entrance to the Manor House.

Held: Specific performance would not be granted where the defendant has contracted under a mistake to which the plaintiff has by his acts, even unintentionally, contributed.

Lord Romilly M.R.:

"It is of the greatest importance that it should be understood that the most perfect truth and fullest disclosure should take place in all cases where the specific performance of a contract is required and that if this fails, even without any intentional expression, the court will grant relief to the man who has been thereby deceived, provided he has acted reasonably and openly."

INJUNCTION

An injunction is another court order commanding a person to do something or to refrain from doing something. It is not granted if an award of damages or another legal remedy would be adequate.

A contract itself may determine whether the remedy of injunction is available, as in *French v. McHale* (1842) 4 Ir. Eq. R. 568. (See Clark, p. 309-310).

The correct criteria to be applied in granting an interlocutory injunction was considered by the Supreme Court in *Campus Oil Ltd. and Others v. Minister for Industry and Energy and Others (No. 2)* [1983] I.R. 88 where it upheld a High Court decision of Keane J. to grant an interlocutory injunction. Keane J. had refused to follow the House of Lords decision in *American Cyanamid Co. v. Ethicon Ltd.* in deciding *T.M.G Group Ltd. v. Al Babtain Trading and Contracting Co. and Anor.* [1982] I.L.R.M. 349 holding that it did not represent the law in this country in so far as it suggested that different principles applied in relation to applications for interlocutory injunctions.

The Supreme Court decided that the test to be applied is whether there is **a fair question** to be determined at the trial **and** that **the balance of convenience** lies in favour of granting the injunction.

Meadox Medicals Inc. v. V.P.I. Ltd. & Ors., illustrates an injunction granted to restrain the use or dealing in confidential information which Hamilton J. considered constituted a trade secret. In *McGrattan v. Gold*, unreported, but see (Irish Times, 26 March, 1991) The President of the High Court, Mr. Justice Hamilton refused to grant an injunction because the proper purchase price of a site had not been disclosed. He stated that persons seeking equity must come with clean hands.

INJUNCTION AND PENALTY OR LIQUIDATED DAMAGES
French v. Macale (1842) 4 Ir. Eq. R. 568

The defendant covenanted with the plaintiff, his landlord, not to burn-bate lands of Pullevellane and two other places in County Galway 'under a penalty of £10 for every acre so burned to be recovered as additional rent.'

In March 1842 the plaintiff sought an injunction to stop the defendant from burning any part of the lands. The defendant admitted that he did intend to burn the lands and that the burning would deteriorate its value but submitted that he was entitled to do so, and that the £10 per acre was to be considered as liquidated damages for burning it.

Held: The Lord Chancellor Sir Edward Burtenshaw Sugden: that the defendant was not entitled to burn the land upon payment of the specified sum as liquidated damages for doing the act, and that the court would restrain him from doing it.

The Lord Chancellor:

"The question in every case is, whether the effect of the contract is that he should be at liberty to do the act upon payment of the stipulated price, or whether he is to be prohibited from doing the act, and the penalty is provided as a means of enforcing that agreement. . . .

I consider it entirely a question of construction . . . if the construction be that the tenant is to be at liberty to do the act upon payment of the penalty, the Court cannot interfere, because the court cannot act against the contract of the parties. But where it appears by the terms of the instrument that the tenant was not to be at liberty to do the act, but that if he did he would pay a penalty, the Court has perfect power to, prevent him from doing the act which he has undertaken not to do. I have no difficulty, therefore, in continuing the injunction until the hearing."

INTERLOCUTORY INJUNCTION/CRITERIA FOR GRANTING

Campus Oil Ltd. v. Minister for Industry & Ors. (No. 2)
[1983] I.R. 88 (S.C.)

The Minister made an Order, The Fuels (Control of Supplies) Order, 1982 requiring all importers of petroleum oils (including the plaintiffs) to purchase 35 per cent of their requirement from the State Oil Refinery at Whitegate, Co. Cork at prices and terms fixed by the Irish National Petroleum Corporation. In the High Court, the plaintiffs claimed that the Order contravened the provisions of Articles 30 and 31 of the Treaty of Rome, which prohibits quantative restrictions on imports between member states of the E.E.C.

The High Court sought a preliminary ruling from the Court of Justice of the European Communities on this matter and the Minister sought an interlocutory injunction to compel the plaintiffs to comply with the Order pending the outcome of the action.

Mr. Justice Keane granted the interlocutory injunction holding *inter alia* that probability of success at the trial was not the proper test to be applied. An application for an interlocutory injunction to be successful, must establish; **first that there is a fair question to be determined at the trail of the action** concerning the existence of the right which he seeks to protect or enforce by the injunction and **secondly, that the circumstances are such that the balance of convenience lies on the side of the granting of the injunction**. The plaintiffs appealed to the Supreme Court.

Held: O'Higgins C.J. (Griffin and Hederman JJ. in agreement) **The test to be applied is whether a fair bona fide question has been raised by the person seeking the relief**. The trial judge had applied the correct test. The appeal should be dismissed.

Griffin J.:
"In a number of cases in recent years this court has applied as the true test, the test of determining whether a fair or serious question has been raised for decision at the trial and if so, whether the balance of convenience was in favour of granting or refusing the interlocutory injunction sought."

Mr. Justice Keane had held that there was a fair question to be tried at the hearing of the action, and this was undoubtedly so. The appeal must be dismissed.

INJUNCTION — TRADE SECRETS
Meadox Medicals Inc. v. V.P.I. Ltd & Ors.
(H.C.) unreported, 27 April 1982, Hamilton J.

The plaintiff company sought an injunction restraining two former employees and V.P.I Ltd. a company formed by them from manufacturing, selling, advertising for sale or dealing in knitted or woven vascular replacements of a textile construction. They also sought an injunction to restrain the defendants from using, publishing, disclosing or in any other way dealing in confidential information or know how of the plaintiff. They also claimed damages for breach of contract and for wrongful use of their confidential information.

The two former employees had signed agreements to observe secrecy and disclose all inventions to the company while employed by it and for a year afterwards. The agreement to hold confidentiality was not to end unless Meadox gave a written release.

Held: The two former employees were in breach of their express agreement. The plaintiffs were entitled to the relief they sought.

Hamilton J. considered that knowledge and confidential date acquired by the defendants in the course of their employment enabled them, at the very least, to accelerate the development of a prosthesis. He added:

> "In the use of such knowledge and confidential date, the aggregation of which I am satisfied constituted a trade secret of Meadox, (the defendants) were in breach of their express agreement with Meadox."

THE MAREVA INJUNCTION AND ANTON PILLER ORDER

Both Mareva Injunction and Anton Piller Order are interlocutory court orders usually obtained ex parte and usually before the commencement of proceedings. Mareva is a temporary freezing of assets which the applicant claims may be needed to satisfy a court judgment or anticipated court judgment. Its purpose is to prevent a defendant removing or dissipating assets to outside the jurisdiction in anticipation and frustration of an adverse court judgment.

An Anton Piller Order is a court order which permits a plaintiffs solicitor to search a defendants premises and to seize items or documents which might constitute evidence, for a limited period. There must be a real fear that the defendant may remove or destroy documents or evidence which would incriminate him. The court, however, must be satisfied that the applicant is not trawling for evidence. See Richard N. Ough & William Flenley, *The Mareva Injunction and Anton Piller Order* (Butterworths, London, 1993).

MAREVA INJUNCTION

Mareva Compania Naviera SA v. International Bulk Carriers SA
[1980] 1 All E.R. 213.

The plaintiffs owned the vessel Mareva which they hired to the defendants on a time charter. The hire price was payable half monthly in advance. The defendants paid the first two instalments of the half monthly hire but failed to pay the third although a sum of £174,000 had been paid into a London bank to their credit.

The plaintiffs issued proceedings claiming the unpaid hire charges and damages for repudiation. Believing that there was a danger that the money in the London bank would disappear the plaintiffs applied for an injunction to restrain the disposal of the money.

They relied on the case of *Nippon Yusen Kaisha v. Karageorgis* [1975] 3 All E.R. 282 decided a month previously, in which the Court of Appeal (Lord Denning, Mr. Browne and Geoffrey Lane) held that the court had jurisdiction under s. 45(1) of the Supreme Court of Judicature (Consolidation) Act 1925 to grant an interlocutory injunction *ex parte*, pending trial of the plaintiff's action, restraining the defendant from disposing of assets within the jurisdiction where there was a strong prima facie case that a plaintiff is entitled to money from a defendant who has such assets within the jurisdiction. Section 45 of the Supreme Court of Judicature (Consolidation) Act 1925 provides:

> "A mandamus or an injunction may be granted or a receiver appointed by an interlocutory Order of the Court in all cases in which it shall appear to the Court to be just or convenient."

Lord Denning M.R.

> ". . . The court will not grant an injunction to protect a person who has no legal or equitable right whatever. That appears from *North London Railway Co. v. Great Northern Railway Co.* (1883) 11 QBD 30. But subject to that qualification, the statute gives a wide general power to the courts. It is well summarized in Halsbury's Laws of England' . . . now, therefore, whenever a right, which can be asserted either at law or in equity, does exist, then, whatever the previous practice may have been, the Court is enabled by virtue of this provision, in a proper case, to grant an injunction to protect that right.
>
> In my opinion that principle applies to a creditor who has a right to be paid the debt owing to him, even before he has established his right by

getting judgment for it. If it appears that the debt is due and owing, and there is a danger that the debtor may dispose of his assets so as to defeat it before judgment, the court has jurisdiction in a proper case to grant an interlocutory judgment so as to prevent him disposing of those assets. It seems to me that this is a proper case for the exercise of this jurisdiction. . . . I would therefore continue the injunction".

Note: Both Roskill LJ and Ormrod LJ agreed that the injunction should be extended in this particular case but expressed reservations having regard to the fact that it was an *ex parte* application and they had only heard argument from one side.

The Irish equivalent of s. 45 Supreme Court of Judicature (Consolidation) Act 1925 which repeats s. 25(8) of the Judicature Act 1873 is s. 28(8) Supreme Court of Judicature (Ireland) Act 1877. See *Halsbury's Laws* (4th edn.) para. 918.

A Mareva injunction is a judgment within Article 25 of the European Communities Convention on Jurisdiction and the Enforcement of Judgments in Civil and Commercial matter and **must** be recognised in the other contracting States without any special procedure by virtue of Article 26. Article 25 states that a judgment means any judgment given by a court or tribunal of a contracting state, whatever the judgment may be called, including a decree, order, decision or writ of execution.

Mareva injunctions have taken on an international character since the English courts asserted the right to extend their operation to foreign assets of defendants, who had none within the jurisdiction even though the defendant did not reside in England or Wales. The extra territorial enforceability of Mareva Orders by virtue of the European Judgments Convention was an important factor in this development. In *Babanaft International Co. S.A. v. Bassatne* (1989) 2 WLR 232 (C.A.) the court held that under s. 37 of the Supreme Court Act, 1981, the power to order Mareva injunctions extended to foreign assets and in *Republic of Haiti v. Duvalier* (1989) 2 WLR 261 (C.A.) the same court held that an extraterritorial Mareva would be granted even where the defendant did not reside within the jurisdiction.

A Mareva injunction was granted *ex parte* in the *Kelly's Carpetdrome* case 9th May, 1983.

ANTON PILLER ORDER

EX PARTE — ORDER TO PERMIT ENTRY, SEARCH AND
SEIZURE

Anton Piller KG v. Manurfacturing Procesess Ltd. and Others
[1976] 1 All E.R. 779

The plaintiff, a German manufacturing firm, owned the copyright in the design of a high frequency converter for supplying computers. They learned that the defendant, their English agent, intended to give confidential information about their machines (a manual and drawings) to rival companies so that they could manufacture a similar power unit to compete with the plaintiff.

Fearing that the English company might destroy documents relating to the machines, or send them out of the country, so that they would not be in existence at the discovery of documents stage, if they were given notice of the application, the German company applied *ex parte* for an interim injunction to restrain infringement of their copyright. They also applied for an order that the defendant permit two of their employees and two of their solicitors to enter the defendants premises (a) to inspect documents relating to copies of the plaintiff's equipment, (b) to remove all original documents supplied by the plaintiff to the defendant and (c) all documents or things relating to the plaintiff's equipment.

Brightman J. granted the interim injunction but refused to grant an order permitting entry, inspection, or removal of documents from the defendant's premises. The plaintiff then appealed to the Court of Appeal.

Held: Lord Denning M.R. (Ormrod LJ. and Shaw LJ. in agreement):

". . . it seems to me that such an order can be made by a judge *ex parte*, but it should only be made where it is essential that the plaintiff should have inspection so that justice can be done between the parties; and when, if the defendant were forewarned, there is a grave danger that vital evidence will be destroyed, that papers will be burnt or lost or hidden, or taken beyond the jurisdiction, and so the ends of justice be defeated; and when the inspection would do no real harm to the defendant or his case.

Nevertheless, in the enforcement of this order, the plaintiffs must act with due circumspection. On the service of it, **the plaintiffs should be attended by their solicitor**, who is an officer of the court. **They should give the defendants an opportunity of considering it and consulting their own solicitor**. If the defendants wish to apply to discharge the order as having been improperly obtained, they must be allowed to do so. If the defendants refuse permission to enter or to inspect, **the plaintiffs must not force their way in. They must accept that refusal, and bring it to the notice of the court afterwards**, if need be on application to commit . . . it serves to tell the defendant that, on the evidence put before it, the court is of opinion that he ought to permit inspection — nay, it orders him to permit — and that he refuses at his peril. It puts him in peril not only of proceedings for contempt, but also of adverse inferences being drawn against him; so much so that his own solicitor may often advise him to comply.

. . . the order sought in this case is not a search warrant. It does not authorize the plaintiffs' solicitor or anyone else to enter the defendants' premises against their will . . . it only authorizes entry and inspection by the permission of the defendants . . . it brings pressure on the defendants to give permission. It does more. It actually orders them to give permission — with I suppose, the result that if they do not give permission, they are guilty of contempt of court."

RESCISSION

Rescission can be the act of a party in cancelling a contract to which he is a party or an order of a court cancelling a contract.

A misled party wishing to rescind, may have no alternative but to go to court for such an order where the other party refuses to give back consideration transferred by him. Rescission normally involves both parties returning benefits obtained under the contract or making restituion. This is called *restituto in integrum* i.e. restoring the parties to their original positions.

It is available for Mistake and Misrepresentation, as well as for Duress and Undue Influence.

The right to rescind may be lost for a number of reasons including:

(a) If the misled party affirms the contract after the right to rescind has arisen.

(b) If it is impossible to restore the parties to their original positions. (Although rescission on terms may be granted where substantial restoration is possible.)

(c) Where a third party has acquired right under the contract in good faith.

Rescission releases a victim of a breach, from performing his obligations under a contract and may entitle him to recover performance which he has already made.

The party in breach is released from future obligation to perform his part of a contact but he remains liable for the failure to perform his primary obligation before the rescission and for losses suffered by reason of his repudiation of future obligations. The act of rescission turns the primary obligation to carry out duties under a contract into one to pay damages.

There is a distinction between rescission for Mistake, Misrepresentation, Duress or Undue Influence sometimes termed rescission *ab initio* and rescission by an innocent party after acceptance of a repudiary breach of contract.

Impossibility of *restituto in integrum* need not disentitle an injured party to rescission in the latter case.

RESCISSION AND MISTAKE
Gunn v. M'Carthy [1884] 13 L. R. Ir. 304 (Ch.) (See Ch. 10)

RESCISSION ON TERMS
Solle v. Butcher [1950] 1 K.B. 671 (C.A.) (See Ch. 10)

REMEDIES FOR BREACH OF CONTRACT
Grist v. Bailey [1967] Ch. 532 (See Ch. 10)

RESCISSION AND MISREPRESENTATION
Carbin v. Sommerville [1933] I.R. 276 (See Ch. 11)

RESCISSION AND DURESS
Barton v. Armstrong [1976] A.C. 104 (See Ch. 12)

RESCISSION REFUSED
Stapleton v. Prudential Ins. Co. [1928] 62 I.L.T.R. 56 (See Ch. 15)

Index

ACCEPTANCE, 16
    communication of, 18
    conduct by, 5
    post by, 20
    silence by, 19
    conduct and, 18
    unqualified must be, 16, 17
ADVERTISEMENT, 5, 12, 18
    offer and, 5
AGREEMENT, 1
Anticipatory breach, 246
Apprenticeship, 211
Auction sales, 2, 7, 8

BREACH, 242
    anticipatory breach, 246
    repudiation, 247

CAPACITY, 207
    corporations, 216, 217
    drunkards, 212, 214
    infants, 207, 208, 210
    lunatics, 212, 213
    mental patients, 213
    necessaries, 207
    ward of court, 215
COLLATERAL AGREEMENTS, 229
    consideration for, 231
    contracts, 229
    parol evidence and, 231
    Collateral waranties, 229
COLLECTIVE AGREEMENTS, 30, 31
COMPANIES, 214
CONDITIONAL AGREEMENTS, 23
CONDITION, 78
CONSENT, 207
    mistake nullifying, 104, 105

CONSIDERATION, 32
    adequacy of, 44
    contractual duty, 36
    detriment, 32
    existing duty, 39
    forbearance, 46
    law, 34
    past, 47
    sufficient, 46
CONTRA PROFERENTEM, 80, 81
    exemption clauses and, 107
CORPORATIONS, 216
    statutory, 216
    ultra vires and, 217
CUSTOM, 76
    implied terms and, 76
    parol evidence rule and, 77

DAMAGES, 255, 257
    adequacy of, 258
    compensation and, 255
    title to land, 267
    general principles, 255
    inflation and, 265
    loss of profits, 257
    misrepresentation for, 165
    mitigation of, 263
    reliance loss, 255
    remoteness of damage, 261
    rescission, 137
    restitution, 269
    specific performance and, 267
    tax and, 265
    frustration and, 253
DEED, 56
DISCHARGE, 240
    performance by, 240, 243
    agreement by, 241

breach by, 242, 246
frustration by, 242, 249, 253
DISPLAY OF GOODS, 8
in shop window, 8
on supermarket shelves, 9
DOCUMENTS, 56
joinder of, 60, 61
non est factum, 145
DRUNKARDS, 212
DURESS, 173
economic, 177
Irish concept, 176
loss of liberty, 174
matrimonial, 175
parents and, 181
pregnancy and, 175
strain and, 175
threat to life, 174

EJUSDEM GENERIS, 82, 83
EMPLOYMENT, 3, 6
restraint of trade, 197, 198
EQUITY, 134
mistake in , 135
ESTOPPEL, 48
common law, 49
contract by, 50
expectation and, 53
quasi estoppel, 52
shield as a, 52
EXEMPTION CLAUSE, 88
clear words and, 102
construction test, 89
contra preferentem, 107
course of dealing, 97
degree of notice, 96
fundamental breach, 100, 109
fundamental term, 108
incorporation test, 88
interpretation, 101
knowledge of, 94
main object, 104
misrepresentation and, 106
nature of document, 100
negligence and, 90, 103
own fraud, 105
previous knowledge, 98
signed agreement, 91, 93

strict liability, 103
third parties and, 112
ticket cases, 94, 96, 98
time of notice, 99
unreasonableness, 90
unsigned documents, 88, 94
EXPRESS TERMS, 72, 80
contra proferentem, 80, 81
ejusdem generis, 80, 82
expressio unius, 80, 83
interpretation of, 80
parol evidence and, 86
parol evidence rule, 80, 84

FORBEARANCE, 48
FORM, 55
contracts of guarantee, 56
evidenced in writing, 67, 55
in writing, 55
indemnity, 57
parties, 59
sale of land, 58
under seal, 56
FRUSTRATION, 242
destruction of object, 250
doctrine of, 242, 243
foreseeable event, 250
principles, 253
FUNDAMENTAL BREACH, 109
FUNDAMENTAL TERM, 108, 110

GUARANTEE CONTRACTS OF, 56
indemnity and, 57

HIRE PURCHASE, 9, 55

ILLEGALITY, 191
auction puffer and, 194
burden of proof, 192
by statute, 193
Constitution and, 195, 196
gaming and, 195
probability test, 192
public policy and, 195, 196
Revenue and, 193
severance and, 193
IMPLIED TERMS, 74, 75
custom and, 76

IMMUNITY, 219
   restrictive, 220
INDEMNITY, 57
   contract of, 49, 97
INFANTS, 207
   benefit, 210
   education, 211
   land and, 208
   repudiation and, 209
   training, 211
INFLATION, 265
   damages and, 265, 266
   Innocent misrepresentation, 150, 164
INJUNCTION, 283
   Anton Piller, 289
   criteria for, 286
   Mareva, 287
   trade secrets and, 286
INNOMINATE TERM, 72
INSANITY, 212
INSURANCE, 114
   agent, 124
   basis of contract, 115
   contribution and, 122
   indemnity and, 121
   insurable interest, 120
   non-disclosure and, 113, 118
   over the counter, 120
   subrogation and, 123
   uberrimae fidei, 114
INTENTION, 25
INVITATION TO TREAT, 9

LAND, 55
   contracts for sale of, 55
   failure to make title, 267
LEGITIMATE EXPECTATION, 46
LIMITATION CLAUSE, 113
LUNATICS, 212
   necessaries and, 213

MARRIAGE, 176,
   Memorandum defective, 136
   sufficiency, 59
MENTAL PATIENTS, 215
   disability, knowledge of, 212, 213
   necessaries and, 213

MINORS, see infants, 207
MISREPRESENTATION, 149
   acted on, 150
   change and, 152
   directed to, 157
   disclaimer and, 160
   fraudulent, 162
   future and, 126
   half truth and, 153
   innocent, 164, 170
   material fact, 150
   negligent, 165, 167
   opinions as, 155
   parol evidence and, 154
   prospectus and, 155, 164
   reliance and, 157
   rescission and, 171
   sales puff, 155
   silence and, 151
   state of mind, 154
   statement of fact, 154
   types of, 150
   uberrimae fidei, 149
MISTAKE, 125
   agreement about, 144
   appearances and, 134
   as to private rights, 129
   as to terms, 139
   at equity, 134
   common, 137
   document signed, 145, 146
   equity and, 134
   existence of person, 130
   existence of subject, 132
   fundamental, 127
   identity as to, 141, 142
   marriage and, 131
   money paid under, 272
   mutual, 144
   negativing consent, 126
   Non est factum, 145
   nullifying consent, 130
   of fact, 125
   of law, 128, 129
   operative, 127
   person as to, 143
   preventing agreement, 126
   private law and, 129

public law and, 128
rectification and, 136
specific performance and, 137
subject matter, 132, 140
terms construction of, 132
unilateral, 138
MITIGATION OF DAMAGE, 263

necessaries, 207, 208
NEGLIGENCE, 90
exemption clauses and, 90, 103
NON-DISCLOSURE, 152, 153
contracts uberrimae fidei, 114,
116
insurance contreacts, 114
NON EST FACTUM, 145
document and, 147

OFFER, 1, 3, 9
acceptance and, 15, 16
advertisement, 5, 12
auction, 7
conduct by, 1
counter offer. 15
definition of, 3
invitation to treat, 9
revocation of, 13
rejection of, 15

PAROL EVIDENCE RULE, 84
and oral terms, 85
exceptions to, 85, 86, 154
PENALTY, 260
PART PERFORMANCE, 58
Performance, 240
complete, 244
substantial, 245
POST, 16
acceptance by, 20
PRIVITY OF CONTRACT, 222, 223
constructive trust and, 225
statutory exception to, 224
PUBLIC POLICY, 195-196
assignment and, 192
implied contract and, 278
terms contrary to, 79

QUANTUM MERUIT, 269

quasi contract, 269, 278
void contract, 277

RECTIFICATION, 136
intention and, 136
REMEDIES, 255
REMOTENESS OF DAMAGE, 261
REPRESENTATION, 151
a warranty, 233
RESCISSION, 171
RESTRAINT OF TRADE, 197
activity and, 199, 206
area of, 195, 200
associations, 200
duration of, 201, 205
employment and, 204
excessive term, 197, 203
sale of business, 198
severance and, 204
solus agreement, 202, 203
REPUDIATION, 209
REVOCATION, 13
communication of, 14
RESTITUTION, 269
Quasi contract, 269
Unjust enrichment, 270

SALE OF GOODS, 75, 90, 98, 102,
159, 192, 200, 202, 203
SALE OF LAND, 58, 94, 145, 155,
158, 163, 195, 198, 267
Signature, 63, 64
Sovereign Immunity, 219
SPECIFIC PERFORMANCE, 279
deceit and, 283
hardship and, 279
mistake and, 282
refusal, grounds of, 281
STATUTE OF FRAUDS, 55
SUBJECT TO CONTRACT, 65, 66

TENDER, 18
TERMS, 72
certainty of, 73
condition, 77, 78
custom, 76
implied, 74, 76
knowledge of, 74

public policy and, 74
warrantee, 77, 79
intermediate term, 247

UBERRIMAE FIDEI, 114
UNCONSCIONABLE BARGAIN,
  189
UNDUE INFLUENCE, 179
child-parent, 181
Equitable remedies, 186
friend, 183
improvidence and, 188
Improvident disposition, 186, 188
independent advice, 189
Inequality and, 187
religious and, 182
Solicitor-Client and, 184
spiritual adviser, 181

Unconscionable and, 189
Without Prejudice, 185
UNENFORCEABLE CONTRACT,
  55
ULTRA VIRES, 216, 217
actual notice, 218
corporations and, 216
knowledge of, 217

VENDOR, 10, 69, 71

Ward of Court, 215
WARRANTY, 79
collateral, 229
ex post facto, 78
exemption clause and, 234
representation and, 233
WITHOUT PREJUDICE, 185